SMARTBOOK

TLS6: The Leader's SMARTbook, 6th Ed.

Military

LEADERSHIP
&TRAINING

in a Complex World

The Lightning Press
Norman M Wade

The Lightning Press

2227 Arrowhead Blvd.
Lakeland, FL 33813
24-hour Voicemail/Fax/Order: 1-800-997-8827
E-mail: SMARTbooks@TheLightningPress.com

www.TheLightningPress.com

(TLS6) The Leader's SMARTbook, 6th Ed.
Military Leadership & Training in a Complex World

TLS6 is the sixth edition of The Leader's SMARTbook, completely updated for 2020. TLS6 incorporates the full scope of new material from ADP 6-22 Army Leadership and the Profession (with Change 1), ADP 7-0 Training, and FM 7-0 Train to Win in a Complex World. Jam-packed at 392 pages, topics and chapters include military leadership (ADP 6-22); leader development (FM 6-22); coach, counsel, and mentor (ATP 6-22.1), team building; (ATP 6-22.6), military training (ADP 7-0), train to win in a complex world (FM 7-0); unit training plans, meetings, schedules, briefs; conducting training events and exercises; training assessments, evaluations and after action reviews.

Printed and bound in the United States of America.

(TLS6)
Notes to Reader

Among professions, the **Army Profession** has unique characteristics because of the lethality of our operations. The Nation tasks the Army to do many things besides combat operations, but ultimately the primary reason the Army exists is to fight and win the Nation's wars through prompt and sustained land combat, as part of the joint force. The Army must always be prepared to accomplish this mission through the application of **lethal force**.

Leadership is the process of influencing people by providing purpose, direction, and motivation to accomplish the mission and improve the organization. As an **element of combat power**, leadership unifies the other elements of combat power (information, mission command, movement and maneuver, intelligence, fires, sustainment and protection). Confident, competent, and informed leadership intensifies the effectiveness of the other elements of combat power.

The Army depends upon itself to develop adaptable leaders able to achieve mission accomplishment in dynamic, unstable, and complex environments. A robust, holistic **leader development** program is essential. Through a mix of education, training, and experience, Army leader development processes produce and sustain agile, adaptive, and innovative leaders who act with boldness and initiative in dynamic, complex situations to execute missions according to doctrine, orders, and training.

Leaders have three principal ways of developing others. They can provide knowledge and feedback through **counseling, coaching, and mentoring**. The military is a team of teams composed of numerous organizations with one overarching common mission: win the nation's wars. The ability to **build teams** through mutual trust and maintain effective, cohesive teams throughout military operations is an essential skill for all commanders, staffs, and leaders.

The Army trains to win in a complex world. To fight and win in a chaotic, ambiguous, and complex environment, the Army trains to provide forces ready to conduct unified land operations. The Army does this by conducting tough, realistic, and challenging training. Training is the most important thing the Army does to prepare for operations. **Training is the cornerstone of readiness.** Readiness determines our Nation's ability to fight and win in a complex global environment.

SMARTbooks - DIME is our DOMAIN!

SMARTbooks: Reference Essentials for the Instruments of National Power (D-I-M-E: Diplomatic, Informational, Military, Economic)! Recognized as a "whole of government" doctrinal reference standard by military, national security and government professionals around the world, SMARTbooks comprise a comprehensive professional library designed with all levels of Soldiers, Sailors, Airmen, Marines and Civilians in mind.

SMARTbooks can be used as quick reference guides during actual operations, as study guides at education and professional development courses, and as lesson plans and checklists in support of training. Visit **www.TheLightningPress.com**!

TLS6: The Leaders' SMARTbook, 6th Ed.
(Military Leadership & Training in a Complex World)

TLS6 is the sixth edition of The Leader's SMARTbook, completely updated for 2020. TLS6 incorporates the full scope of new material from ADP 6-22 Army Leadership and the Profession (with Change 1), ADP 7-0 Training, and FM 7-0 Train to Win in a Complex World. Jam-packed at 392 pages, topics and chapters include military leadership (ADP 6-22); leader development (FM 6-22); coach, counsel, and mentor (ATP 6-22.1); team building; (ATP 6-22.6), military training (ADP 7-0), train to win in a complex world (FM 7-0); unit training plans, meetings, schedules, briefs; conducting training events and exercises; training assessments, evaluations and after action reviews.

Military Leadership

ADP 6-22
(w/Chg 1)

FM 6-22

ATP 6-22.1

ATP 6-22.6

Chap 1: Army Leadership & Profession (ADP 6-22 w/Chg 1)

War is a lethal clash of wills and an inherently human endeavor that requires perseverance, sacrifice, and tenacity. Enduring the physical hardship, danger, and uncertainty of combat requires an **Army that is professionally committed and guided by an ethic** that motivates and guides its forces in the conduct of missions, performance of duty, and all aspects of life.

Leadership is the activity of influencing people by providing purpose, direction, and motivation to accomplish the mission and improve the organization. Leadership as an element of combat power, coupled with information, unifies the warfighting functions.

Chap 2: Leader Development (FM 6-22)

The Army depends upon itself to develop adaptable leaders able to achieve mission accomplishment in dynamic, unstable, and complex environments. A robust, holistic leader development program is essential. Through a mix of education, training, and experience, **Army leader development** processes produce and sustain agile, adaptive, and innovative leaders who act with boldness and initiative in dynamic, complex situations to execute missions according to doctrine, orders, and training. Furthermore, it also produces leaders that possess the integrity and willingness to act in the absence of orders, when existing orders, doctrine or their own experience no longer fit the situation, or when unforeseen opportunities or threats arise.

Chap 3: Counseling, Coaching, Mentoring (ATP 6-22.1)

Leaders have three principal ways of developing others. They can provide knowledge and feedback through counseling, coaching, and mentoring.

Counseling is central to leader development. Good counseling focuses on the subordinate's performance and issues with an eye toward tomorrow's plans and solutions. Leaders expect subordinates to be active participants seeking constructive feedback. Counseling cannot be an occasional event but should be part of a comprehensive program to develop subordinates.

While a mentor or counselor generally has more experience than the person being supported does, **coaching** relies primarily on teaching and guiding to bring out and enhance the capabilities already present.

To help leaders acquire the necessary abilities, the Army relies on a leader development system that compresses and accelerates development of professional expertise, maturity, and conceptual and team-building skills. **Mentoring** is a developmental tool that can effectively support many of these learning objectives.

Chap 4: Army Team Building (ATP 6-22.6)

Army organizations rely on effective **teams** to complete tasks, achieve objectives, and accomplish missions. The ability to build teams through mutual trust and maintain effective, cohesive teams throughout military operations is an essential skill for all Army commanders, staffs, and leaders.

Military Training

ADP 7-0   FM 7-0   Unit Training Mgmt Guide

Chap 5: Army Training (ADP 7-0 and FM 7-0)

The Army **trains** to fight and win. To do this, the Army trains by developing proficiencies in mission-essential tasks, weapon systems, and the effective integration and employment of both. These components of training readiness provide the backbone to the development of unit readiness—the Army's first priority.

Chap 6: Planning Training

Training readiness stems from attaining proficiency in individual and collective tasks. To do that, unit commanders develop their **unit training plan (UTP)**, focusing on the tasks to train, based on the higher commander's guidance. This is battle-focused training. Following the general framework of the military decisionmaking process (MDMP) (or troop leading procedures [TLP] for company and below), unit commanders begin the process to determine the METs—what to train. Training readiness is at the core of this determination—whether it is training to maintain and sustain certain capabilities or training to meet the requirements of an assigned mission.

Chap 7: Conducting Training Events & Exercises

Units **execute training** when they put a plan into action to meet the training proficiencies and training objectives specified by the commander. Commanders establish measurable and attainable training objectives that develop and demonstrate collective task proficiencies. Well planned and communicated training guidance, well-developed plans, and maximized opportunities and resources enable units to execute quality training.

Chap 8: Assessing Training

Assessing unit training is a two-step process of objectively evaluating performance and assessing the results of evaluations. Following observed and evaluated training, commanders assess the unit's ability to execute tasks to standard. In addition to evaluations, commanders consider after action reviews, the commander's own personal observations, and other sources of feedback before making objective, holistic assessments of tasks, weapons, and overall unit training proficiency.

(TLS6) References

The following primary references were used to compile *TLS6: The Leader's SMARTbook*. All references are open-source, public domain, available to the general public, and/or designated as "approved for public release; distribution is unlimited." *TLS6: The Leader's SMARTbook* does not contain classified or sensitive material restricted from public release

TLS6 is the sixth edition of The Leader's SMARTbook, completely updated for 2020. TLS6 incorporates the full scope of new material from ADP 6-22 Army Leadership and the Profession (with Change 1), ADP 7-0 Training, and FM 7-0 Train to Win in a Complex World. Jam-packed at 392 pages, topics and chapters include military leadership (ADP 6-22); leader development (FM 6-22); coach, counsel, and mentor (ATP 6-22.1), team building; (ATP 6-22.6), military training (ADP 7-0), train to win in a complex world (FM 7-0); unit training plans, meetings, schedules, briefs; conducting training events and exercises; training assessments, evaluations and after action reviews.

Army Doctrinal Publications (ADPs)

ADP 3-0*	Jul 2019	Operations
ADP 5-0*	Jul 2019	The Operations Process
ADP 6-0*	Jul 2019	Mission Command
ADP 6-22*	Nov 2019	Army Leadership and the Profession (INCL C1)
ADP 7-0*	Jul 2019	Training

Army Techniques Publications (ATPs)

ATP 6-22.1	Jul 2014	The Counseling Process
ATP 6-22.6	Oct 2015	Army Team Building

Field Manuals (FMs)

FM 6-0	Apr 2016	Commander and Staff Organization and Operations (w/change 2)
FM 6-22	Jun 2015	Leader Development
FM 7-0	Oct 2016	Train to Win in a Complex World

Other Publications

UTM Guide	Aug 2012	Unit Training Management (Guide), Combined Arms Center - Training

* New or updated reference publication since last edition.

(TLS6)
Table of Contents

Chap 1 | Army Leadership & the Profession

Chap 2
Leader Development

Chap 3

Counseling, Coaching, Mentoring

Army Team Building

Army Training (Train to Win a Complex World)

Planning Training (Unit Training Mgmt)

Chap 7

Conducting Training Events & Exercises

Chap 8
Assessing Training

Army Leadership & the Profession

Ref: ADP 6-22 (w/C1), Army Leadership and the Profession (Nov '19), chap. 1.

For more than 240 years, the United States Army has protected the people and interests of the Nation. The Army is not alone. The Marines Corps, Navy, Air Force, Coast Guard, government agencies, and local law enforcement and firefighters all perform similar services to the Nation and its communities. All volunteered. In many cases, they choose to place themselves in harm's way based on a conviction that personal service makes a difference. Leading Soldiers requires an understanding of the Army profession and ethic that are the basis for a shared professional identity and underpin all leader decisions and actions. To inspire Soldiers to risk their lives requires professional leaders capable of providing purpose, direction, and motivation.

The Army Profession and Ethic

War is a lethal clash of wills and an inherently human endeavor that requires perseverance, sacrifice, and tenacity. The United States Army's primary reason for existence is to deploy, fight,and win the Nation's wars by providing ready, prompt, and sustained land dominance by Army forces across the range of military operations as part of the joint force. Enduring the physical hardship, danger, and uncertainty of combat requires an Army that is professionally committed and guided by an ethic that motivates and guides its forces in the conduct of missions, performance of duty, and all aspects of life.

Providing the purpose, direction, and motivation required to inspire others to risk their lives to accomplish missions requires leaders committed to their profession and ethic. To prepare Army leaders to fulfill their responsibilities, the Army profession develops Soldiers and Army civilians who demonstrate character, competence, and commitment through career-long training, education, and experience.

See pp. 1-6 to 1-7 for an overview and further discussion of the Army profession.
See pp. 1-8 to 1-9 for an overview and further discussion of the Army ethic.

I. Army Leadership

The Army experience over more than two centuries is that most people have leadership potential and can learn to be effective leaders. The ability to influence others is a central component of leadership. As a result, leader development has long been an Army priority. This development begins with education, training, and experience, and requires understanding about what Army leaders do and why

See chap. 2, Leader Development, for further discussion from FM 6-22

Leadership is the activity of influencing people by providing purpose, direction, and motivation to accomplish the mission and improve the organization. Leadership as an element of combat power, coupled with information, unifies the warfighting functions (movement and maneuver, intelligence, fires, sustainment, protection and command and control). Leadership focuses and synchronizes organizations. Leaders inspire people to become energized and motivated to achieve desired outcomes. An Army leader is anyone who by virtue of assumed role or assigned responsibility inspires and influences people by providing purpose, direction, and motivation to accomplish the mission and improve the organization.

Influencing

Influencing is persuading people do what is necessary. Influencing entails more than simply passing along orders. Through words and personal example, leaders inspire purpose, provide direction, and when required motivation.

Purpose

Leaders provide clear purpose for their subordinates. Purpose gives subordinates a reason to achieve a desired outcome. Leaders convey purpose through direct means such as requests, directives, or orders. Leaders inspire subordinates to do their best by instilling a higher purpose that rises above self-interest. They explain why something should or must be done and provide context whenever possible. Subordinates who understand why they are doing something difficult and discern the higher purpose are more likely to do the right thing when leaders are not present to direct their every action.

Direction

Direction is telling others what to do. Providing effective direction requires that leaders communicate the desired end state for the direction they provide. To accomplish a mission, leaders prioritize tasks, assign responsibility, supervise, and ensure subordinates perform to standard. They ensure subordinates clearly understand their guidance, while allowing subordinates the opportunity to demonstrate initiative within the overall commander's intent. Providing clear direction allows subordinate initiative to adapt their tasks within the commander's intent when circumstances change.

The Army requires leaders who provide direction and subordinates who can execute without the need for continuous guidance. The Army needs leaders who understand, train, and employ mission command during the course of their duties. Mission command is the Army's approach to command and control that empowers subordinate decision making and decentralized execution appropriate to the situation (ADP 6-0). Mission command recognizes that no single person in an organization or unit can make every important decision at every critical moment, nor can a single person keep up with the number of simultaneous decisions organizations require during combat or other time-constrained environments.

Motivation

Motivation is the will and initiative to do what is necessary to accomplish a mission. While motivation comes from within, others' actions and words affect it. A leader's role in motivation is at times to understand others' needs and desires, to align and elevate individual desires into team goals, and to inspire others to accomplish those larger goals, even if it means risking their lives. At other times, such as time constrained or dangerous situations, the leader gets subordinates to do things quickly and explain the reasons why later.

Indirect approaches to motivation can be as successful as direct approaches. Setting a personal example can sustain the drive in others. This becomes apparent when leaders share hardship and risk with subordinates. Leaders who personally share hardship and risk demonstrate to subordinates that they are invested in the outcome and willing and able to do what they ask subordinates to do. Indirect approaches such as these build confidence about the judgment, commitment, and attitude of the leader.

How leaders motivate others matters. There are practices that are always positive, while others are good or bad depending on the context of the situation. There are those who can inspire others to act because they respect the leader's judgment, respect that the leader earned. Earning this type of personal respect takes time, so leaders may need to motivate others initially based upon the authorities and respect inherent in their duty position. In either case, leaders should be judicious about using pressure or threat of punishment when motivating others, because doing so too often or when unnecessary breeds resentment and low morale. Aspiring leaders observe many different methods others use to motivate subordinates, and should remember and practice those that were most effective while avoiding those that negatively affected an organization.

Army Profession, Ethic, and Leadership Overview (Logic Map)

Ref: ADP 6-22 (w/C1), Army Leadership and the Profession (Nov '19), intro fig. 1.

Enduring the physical hardship, danger, and uncertainty of combat requires an Army that is professionally committed, and guided by an ethic that motivates and guides its forces in the conduct of missions, duty performance, and all aspects of life.

The Army profession
A trusted vocation of Soldiers and Army civilians whose collective expertise is the ethical design, generation, support, and application of landpower; serving under civilian authority; and entrusted to defend the Constitution and the rights and interests of the American people.

Consists of...

Profession of Arms	**Army Civilian Corps**
Soldiers of the Regular Army, Army National Guard, and the Army Reserve	Army civilians serving in the Department of the Army

With a shared identity of...

Trusted Army professional
Honorable servants in defense of the nation—Experts in the performance of duty
Responsible stewards of the Army profession.

All decisions and actions are guided by...

The Army ethic
The set of enduring moral principles, values, beliefs, and laws that guide the Army profession and create the culture of trust essential to Army professionals in the conduct of missions, performance of duty, and all aspects of life.

The Army profession and ethic guide trusted Army professionals as they exercise...

Leadership
The activity of influencing people by providing purpose, direction, and motivation to accomplish the mission and improve the organization.

The leadership requirements model establishes a core set of requirements that inform leaders of the expectations for what they need to be, know, and do.

Combat power unifier and multiplier

Enables exercise of command; supports control through guidance

Establishes framework for leader development

The Army leadership requirements model

Outcomes

Highly trained Soldiers	Skilled, empowered leaders	Committed DA civilians
Mission accomplishment	Improved readiness	Organizational cohesion
Subordinate development	Mission command culture	Stewardship of resources
	Healthy organization climates	

ADP 6-22 establishes and describes the Army profession and the associated ethic that serve as the basis for a shared professional identity. It establishes and describes what leaders should be and do. Having a standard set of leader attributes and core leader competencies facilitates focused feedback, education, training, and development across all leadership levels.

Leadership (as an Element of Combat Power)

Ref: ADP 3-0, Operations (Jul '19), chap. 5 (and figure 5-1).

Combat power is the total means of destructive, constructive, and information capabilities that a military unit or formation can apply at a given time. Operations executed through simultaneous offensive, defensive, stability, or DSCA operations require the continuous generation and application of combat power. To an Army commander, Army forces generate combat power by converting potential into effective action. Combat power includes all capabilities provided by unified action partners that are integrated and synchronized with the commander's objectives to achieve unity of effort in sustained operations.

Elements of Combat Power

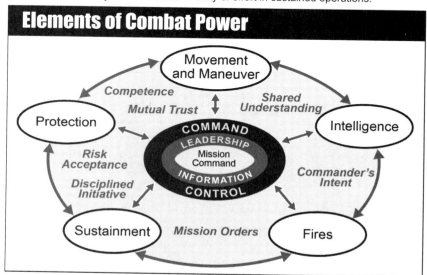

To execute combined arms operations, commanders conceptualize capabilities in terms of combat power. Combat power has eight elements: leadership, information, command and control, movement and maneuver, intelligence, fires, sustainment, and protection. The elements facilitate Army forces accessing joint and multinational fires and assets. The Army collectively describes the last six elements as **warfighting functions.** Commanders apply combat power through the warfighting functions using **leadership and information**.

Generating and maintaining combat power throughout an operation is essential. Factors that contribute to generating and maintaining combat power include reserves, force rotation, network viability, access to cyberspace and space enablers, and joint support. Commanders balance the ability to mass lethal and nonlethal effects with the need to deploy and sustain the units that produce those effects.

Leadership & Information

Commanders apply leadership through mission command. **Leadership** is the multiplying and unifying element of combat power. The Army defines leadership as the process of influencing people by providing purpose, direction, and motivation to accomplish the mission and improve the organization (ADP 6-22). An Army commander, by virtue of assumed role or assigned responsibility, inspires and influences people to accomplish organizational goals. **Information** enables commanders at all levels to make informed decisions on how best to apply combat power.

The Six Warfighting Functions

1. Command and Control

The command and control warfighting function is the related tasks and a system that enable commanders to synchronize and converge all elements of combat power. The primary purpose of the command and control warfighting function is to assist commanders in integrating the other elements of combat power (leadership, information, movement and maneuver, intelligence, fires, sustainment, and protection) to achieve objectives and accomplish missions.

2. Movement and Maneuver

The movement and maneuver warfighting function is the related tasks and systems that move and employ forces to achieve a position of relative advantage over the enemy and other threats. Direct fire and close combat are inherent in maneuver. The movement and maneuver warfighting function includes tasks associated with force projection. Movement is necessary to disperse and displace the force as a whole or in part when maneuvering. Maneuver directly gains or exploits positions of relative advantage. Commanders use maneuver for massing effects to achieve surprise, shock, and momentum

3. Intelligence

The intelligence warfighting function is the related tasks and systems that facilitate understanding the enemy, terrain, weather, civil considerations, and other significant aspects of the operational environment. Other significant aspects of an operational environment include threats, adversaries, and operational variables, which vary with the nature of operations. The intelligence warfighting function synchronizes information collection with primary tactical tasks of reconnaissance, surveillance, security, and intelligence operations. Intelligence is driven by commanders, and it involves analyzing information from all sources and conducting operations to develop the situation.

4. Fires

The fires warfighting function is the related tasks and systems that create and converge effects in all domains against the adversary or enemy to enable operations across the range of military operations (ADP 3-0). These tasks and systems create lethal and nonlethal effects delivered from both Army and joint forces, as well as other unified action partners.

5. Sustainment

The sustainment warfighting function is the related tasks and systems that provide support and services to ensure freedom of action, extended operational reach, and prolong endurance. Sustainment determines the depth and duration of Army operations. Successful sustainment enables freedom of action by increasing the number of options available to the commander. Sustainment is essential for retaining and exploiting the initiative.

6. Protection

The protection warfighting function is the related tasks and systems that preserve the force so the commander can apply maximum combat power to accomplish the mission. Commanders incorporate protection when they understand and visualize threats and hazards in an operational environment. This allows them to synchronize and integrate all protection capabilities to safeguard bases, secure routes, and protect forces. Preserving the force includes protecting personnel (combatants and noncombatants) and physical assets of the United States, unified action partners, and host nations.

Refer to AODS6-1 (w/SMARTupdate 1): The Army Operations & Doctrine SMARTbook (Guide to FM/ADP 3-0 Operations & the Elements of Combat Power). Completely updated with the Jul 2019 ADPs, Chg 1 to the 400-pg AODS6 includes operations (ADP 3-0), large-scale combat operations (FM 3-0 w/Chg 1), and refocused chapters on the elements of combat power: command & control (ADP 6-0), movement and maneuver (ADPs 3-90, 3-07, 3-28, 3-05), intelligence (ADP 2-0), fires (ADP 3-19), sustainment (ADP 4-0), & protection (ADP 3-37).

The Army Profession

Ref: ADP 6-22 (w/C1), Army Leadership and the Profession (Nov '19), pp. 1-1 to 1-6.

The Army has a dual nature as both a military department of government and a trusted military profession. The character of the Army as an institution and a profession are both essential to accomplishing the Army's mission. However, it is the American people's trust and confidence in the Army as an ethical profession that grants it the autonomy to exercise the disciplined initiative critical to accomplishing missions under diverse conditions around the world.

Traditional professions share essential characteristics. They provide a vital service to society, requiring expertise and skill developed through years of training, education, and experience. Professions establish standards of practice and certify that their members are qualified to serve the needs of society.

Professionals accept the responsibility to be stewards of the people and resources entrusted to them by society and to advance the state of their profession in anticipation of changes to the world around them. Professions motivate their members to answer a "calling to honorable service," to pursue lifelong learning, and to cooperate as members with a common purpose higher than individual gratification. A calling or vocation means that the mission is more important than the individual is, which is the basis of sacrifice.

Professions self-police and must live by an ethic with both legal and moral foundations. A professional ethic provides the set of moral principles that guide decisions and actions in professional practice. Traditional professions include medicine and law, science and engineering, architecture, higher education, ordained religious practice, and the military.

Ultimately, society trusts professions and grants them autonomy and discretion with prudent, balanced oversight or external controls. If a profession violates its ethic and loses the trust of society, it becomes subject to increased societal regulation and governance.

The Army profession is a trusted vocation of Soldiers and Army civilians whose collective expertise is the ethical design, generation, support, and application of landpower; serving under civilian authority; and entrusted to defend the Constitution and the rights and interests of the American people. The Army profession includes two complementary communities of practice—the Profession of Arms and the Army Civilian Corps.

- The Profession of Arms comprises the Soldiers of the Regular Army, Army National Guard, and the Army Reserve.
- The Army Civilian Corps is composed of Army civilians serving in the Department of the Army.

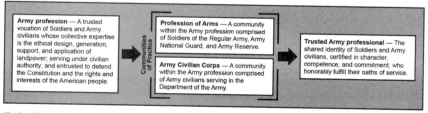

Ref: ADP 6-22 (w/C1), Figure 1-1. The Army profession.

These communities of practice are trusted Army professionals—honorable servants in defense of the Nation, experts in the performance of their duties, and responsible stewards of the Army profession. The Army ethic underpins the decision and actions of all Army professionals.

A profession is a trusted self-policing and relatively autonomous vocation whose members develop and apply expert knowledge as human expertise to render an essential service to society in a particular field:

- Professions provide a unique and vital service to the society served, one it cannot provide itself
- Professions provide this service by applying expert knowledge and practice
- Professions earn the trust of the society because of effective and ethical application of their expertise
- Professions self-regulate; they police the practice of their members to ensure it is effective and ethical (includes the educating and certifying professionals)
- Professions are therefore granted significant autonomy and discretion in their practice of expertise on behalf of the society

Five characteristics identify and establish the Army as a profession. These characteristics reflect American values, the Army ethic, and the Army's approach to conducting operations. Demonstrated consistently, these characteristics reinforce trust between the Army profession and the American people. The five characteristics of the Army profession are—

Trust
Trust is the foundation of the Army's relationship with the American people, who rely on the Army to ethically, effectively, and efficiently serve the Nation. Within the Army profession, trust is shared confidence among commanders, subordinates, and partners in that all can be relied on and all are competent in performing their assigned tasks.

Honorable Service
Honorable service is support and defense of the Constitution, the American people, and the national interest in a manner consistent with the Army ethic. Army professionals serve honorably by obeying the laws of the Nation and all legal orders. Army forces reject and report illegal, unethical, or immoral orders or actions.

Military Expertise
Military expertise is the ethical design, generation, support, and application of landpower, and the associated capabilities essential to accomplishing missions in defense of the American people. The Army profession demonstrates military expertise while conducting operations assigned by civilian authority. The Army is trusted to accomplish missions ethically, effectively, and efficiently. The Army profession develops and demonstrates military expertise in four broad fields of knowledge: leader and human development, moral-ethical, geo-cultural and political, and military-technical.

Stewardship
Stewardship is the responsibility of Soldiers and Army civilians to strengthen the Army as a profession. It includes caring for the people and resources entrusted to them by the American people, ensuring Army forces are ready, now and in the future, to accomplish the Army's missions.

Esprit de Corps
Esprit de corps denotes the Army's winning spirit—a collective ethos of camaraderie, mutual trust, and cohesive teamwork. Successfully accomplishing missions requires spirited and dedicated Soldiers and Army civilians who strive for standards of excellence. . Army forces embrace shared intent and situational understanding, accept prudent risk, and exercise disciplined initiative. These guiding principles, in harmony with the Army ethic,strengthen the Army's identity,resilience,and courage—a never-quit resolve—enabling Army forces to persevere and accomplish the mission in the presence of risk, uncertainty, and fear.

The Army Ethic

Ref: ADP 6-22 (w/C1), Army Leadership and the Profession (Nov '19), pp. 1-6 to 1-12.

True professions are guided by an ethic that establishes the personal and institutional standards expected of its members. A professional ethic creates a shared professional identity, and provides an enduring set of moral principles, values and beliefs that guide that profession as it provides its specialized service to society. The Army ethic is the set of enduring moral principles, values, beliefs, and laws that guide the Army profession and create the culture of trust essential to Army professionals in the conduct of missions, performance of duty, and all aspects of life.

The Army ethic is the basis of the Army's shared professional identity of trusted Army professionals. This identity expresses how Army professionals view their profession and why they serve. Love of country and family, preservation of the peace, and defense of the American people and the Army Values are inherent to the Army ethic. The ethical, effective, and efficient accomplishment of the mission is the core of this ethic. Soldiers and Army civilians are bound in common moral purpose to support and defend the Constitution and the American people.

The Army ethic has its origins in the philosophical heritage, theological and cultural traditions, and the historical legacy that frame our Nation. Army professionals swear to uphold the principles codified in the Constitution, which include establishing justice, ensuring domestic tranquility, providing for the common defense, promoting the general welfare, and securing the blessings of liberty to ourselves and our posterity. These principles are affirmed in oaths of service, and reflected in the Army motto—This We'll Defend.

Foundations of the Army Ethic		
Applicable to:	Legal Motivation of Compliance	Moral Motivation of Aspiration
Army profession Trust Honorable service Military expertise Stewardship Esprit de corps	United States Constitution United States Code Uniform Code of Military Justice Executive Orders Treaties, Law of Land Warfare	Declaration of Independence Universal Declaration of Human Rights Just War Tradition (Jus ad Bellum) Army culture of trust Professional organizational climate
Trusted Army professionals Honorable servants Army experts Stewards	Oaths of Service Standards of conduct Directives and policies The Soldier's Rules Rules of engagement	Natural moral reason – Golden Rule Army Values Soldier's and Army Civilian Corps creeds Justice in War (Jus in Bello)
The *Army ethic*, our professional ethic, is the set of enduring moral principles, values, beliefs, and applicable laws embedded within the Army *culture of trust* that motivates and guides the Army profession and *trusted Army professionals* in conduct of the mission, performance of duty, and all aspects of life.		

Ref: ADP 6-22 (w/C1), Table 1-1. The framework for the Army ethic.

Soldiers and Army civilians join the Army profession with personal values developed in childhood and nurtured through years of experience. Diverse backgrounds and perspectives reflect American society and are a great strength of the Army. The oath to support and defend the Constitution unites all Army professionals. In so doing, they agree to live by and uphold the Army ethic. The framework for the Army ethic (see table 1-1) illustrates the historic sources that inform its content.

In situations of uncertainty, where the rules do not provide clear, courses of action, Army professionals base their decisions and actions on the moral principles of the Army ethic.

The Army Ethic

The Heart of the Army

The Army ethic includes the moral principles that guide our decisions and actions as we fulfill our purpose: to support and defend the Constitution and our way of life. Living the Army ethic is the basis for our mutual trust with each other and the American people. Today our ethic is expressed in laws, values, and shared beliefs within American and Army cultures. The Army ethic motivates our commitment as Soldiers and Army civilians who are bound together to accomplish the Army mission as expressed in our historic and prophetic motto:

This We'll Defend

Living the Army ethic inspires our shared identity as trusted Army professionals with distinctive roles as honorable servants, Army experts, and stewards of the profession. To honor these obligations we adopt, live by, and uphold the moral principles of the Army ethic. Beginning with our solemn oath of service as defenders of the Nation, we voluntarily incur the extraordinary moral obligation to be:

Trusted Army Professionals

Honorable Servants of the Nation—Professionals of Character:

We serve honorably—according to the Army ethic—under civilian authority while obeying the laws of the Nation and all legal orders; further, we reject and report illegal, unethical, or immoral orders or actions.

We take pride in honorably serving the Nation with integrity, demonstrating character in all aspects of our lives. In war and peace, we recognize the intrinsic dignity and worth of all people, treating them with respect.

We lead by example and demonstrate courage by doing what is right despite risk, uncertainty, and fear; we candidly express our professional judgment to subordinates, peers, and superiors.

Army Experts—Competent Professionals:

We do our duty leading and following with discipline, striving for excellence, putting the needs of others above our own, and accomplishing the mission as a team. We accomplish the mission and understand it may demand risking our lives and justly taking the lives of others.

We continuously advance the expertise of our chosen profession through lifelong learning, professional development, and certifications.

Stewards of the Army Profession—Committed Professionals:

We embrace and uphold the Army Values and standards of the profession, always accountable to each other and the American people for our decisions and actions. We wisely use the resources entrusted to us, ensuring our Army is well-led and well-prepared, while caring for Soldiers, Army civilians, and families.

We continuously strengthen the essential characteristics of the Army profession, reinforcing our bond of trust with each other and the American people.

Army Values (See pp. 1-24 to 1-25.)

Loyalty–Duty–Respect–Service–Honor–Integrity–Courage. The Army Values set expectations for conduct and are fundamental to making the right decision in any situation.

Ref: Figure 1-2. The Army ethic, including Army Values.

II. Leadership Requirements Model

Ref: ADP 6-22 (w/C1), Army Leadership and the Profession (Nov '19), pp. 1-15 to 1-16.

The leadership requirements model is grounded in historical experience and determinations of what works best for the Army. Army research supports the model's completeness and validity. The model identifies core competencies and attributes applicable to all types and echelons of Army organizations. The model conveys expectations and establishes the capabilities needed of all Army leaders regardless of rank, grade, uniform, or attire. Collectively, the leadership requirements model is a significant contributor to individual and unit readiness and effectiveness.

As a common leadership model for the Army, the leadership requirements model aligns expectations with leader development activities and personnel management practices and systems. Understanding the expectations and applying the attributes and competencies prepares leaders for the situations they are most likely to encounter. The model informs leaders of the enduring capabilities needed regardless of echelon, mission, or assignment. All model components are interrelated and relate to the Department of Defense (DOD) civilian leader development framework found in DODI 1430.16.

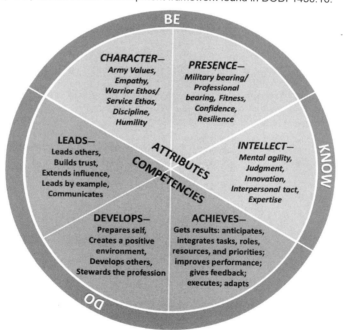

Ref: ADP 6-22 (w/C1), Figure 1-3. The Army leadership requirements model.

The model's components center on what a leader is (attributes—BE and KNOW) and what a leader does (competencies—DO). A leader's character, presence, and intellect enable them to apply the core leader competencies and enhance their proficiency. Leaders who gain expertise through operational assignments, institutional learning, and self-development will be versatile enough to adapt to most situations and grow into greater responsibilities. Figure 1-3 illustrates the framework.

A major distinction between the attributes and competencies of the leadership requirements model is that competencies are skills that can be trained and developed while attributes encompass enduring personal characteristics, which are molded through experience over time. A Soldier can be trained to be an effective machine gunner, but may not necessarily be a brave machine gunner without additional experience. Every educational, operational, and self-development event is an opportunity for observation, feedback, and reflection.

Core Leader Attributes

Attributes are characteristics internal to a leader. These affect how an individual behaves, thinks, and learns within certain conditions. Strong character, solid presence, and keen intellect enable individuals to perform the core leader competencies with greater effect. The three categories of core attributes are—

- **Character**: the moral and ethical qualities of the leader.
- **Presence**: characteristics open to display by the leader and open to viewing by others.
- **Intellect**: the mental and social abilities the leader applies while leading.

See pp. 1-19 to 1-32 for further discussion of core leader attributes.

Core Leader Competencies

The core leader competencies are actions that the Army expects leaders to do: lead, develop, and achieve. Competencies provide an enduring, clear, and consistent way of conveying expectations for Army leaders. The core competencies are universal for all Army leaders. The core competency categories are—

- **Leads**: provides purpose, direction, and motivation; builds trust; provides an example; communicates.
- **Develops**: develops themselves, creates a positive climate, develops subordinates, and stewards the profession.
- **Achieves**: executes, adjusts, and gets results to accomplish tasks and missions on time and to standard.

Core leader competencies are covered in further detail on the following pages: leads (pp. 1-35 to 1-52), develops (pp. 1-53 to 1-68), and achieves (pp. 1-69 to 1-72).

Core Leader Attributes

A. Character	B. Presence	C. Intellect
• Army values • Empathy • Warrior ethos and Service ethos • Discipline • Humility	• Military and professional bearing • Fitness • Confidence • Resilience	• Mental agility • Sound judgement • Innovation • Interpersonal tact • Expertise
A. Leads	B. Develops	C. Achieves
• Leads others • Builds trust • Extends influence beyond the chain of command • Leads by example • Communicates	• Prepares self • Creates a positive environment • Develops others • Stewards the profession	• Gets results

Core Leader Competencies

III. Dynamics of Leadership

The most effective leaders adapt their approach to the mission, the organization, and the situation. A division commander addressing brigade commanders before conducting large-scale combat operations leads and communicates differently than a drill sergeant training new recruits in basic training. Constant change affects peacetime and combat operations. Personnel change out. Timelines move. Anticipated resources do not materialize. Adversaries do what was least expected. Weather keeps CAS assets grounded. Commanders, leaders, and staffs plan for possible changes and continually monitor progress to engage as needed. Leaders account for the important factors affecting the dynamics of leadership. Three consistent factors are—

- The leader.
- The led.
- The situation.

A. The Leader

An Army leader influences others to accomplish missions. A leader has the opportunity to lead when assigned responsibility, assuming a role, or being an informal leader within a team. Leaders motivate people both inside and outside the chain of command toward action or to change their thinking when appropriate. Formally or informally, regardless of position or rank, all Army members can find themselves in situations to lead and influence others. Leaders who adapt their actions based on the dynamics of a situation achieve the best possible outcomes. Leaders take into account the level of their experience or skill, and their authority.

Everyone has an identity or a way they see themselves. Leaders internalize the roles, responsibilities, and actions that they understand of a leader to be, know, and do. Leaders who are unsure of themselves filling the role of a leader will be limited until they have confidence. Without a clear leader identity, others will question the type of leader they are, what they stand for, and the way they conduct themselves. What a leader believes about their role as a leader serves as a constant guide to behave as a leader of good character. Practice identifying as a leader—doing the right things in the right way—becomes habitual and helps junior personnel along the path to becoming seasoned, effective leaders.

Self-awareness is fundamental to understanding one's abilities. Leaders should know their strengths and weaknesses: what they do or do not know, what they are or are not skilled at, and what is in their span of control. Even though they should be self-aware, not all leaders are. Leaders vary in their proficiency levels in attributes and competencies and their preparation for each situation. Leaders require self-awareness if they are to accurately assess their own experience and competence as well as earn the trust of those they influence. Being self-aware means seeing one's self as viewed by others and understanding the levels of influence one is likely to have with followers. For instance, a newly assigned company commander understands that participating with Soldiers on a 12-mile ruck-march builds subordinates' respect for the leader and builds the leader's credibility with them. Awareness allows one to adjust one's leadership actions in the moment and know what areas to improve for the future.

Leaders have different responsibilities and authorities that can vary with duty positions and missions. Authority to lead is either formally derived from rank or position or is informal, such as when influencing peers or coalition partners. Formal authority allows use of commitment and compliance through the methods of influence. Informal authority primarily relies on obtaining commitment from others.

Formal Leadership

Formal leadership authority is granted to individuals by virtue of assignment to positions of responsibility, according to their rank and experience. The Uniform

Code of Military Justice supports military leaders in positions of legitimate authority. Formal leaders exercise their authority over subordinates through lawful orders and directives. An Army leader operates with clear expectations regarding conduct so that indiscipline does not jeopardize mission success. Leaders, through formally assigned authorities and clearly communicated standards, are responsible for ensuring adherence to standards, policies, and codes. Team leaders, squad leaders, platoon leaders, staff officers, commanders, and civilian supervisors are all examples of leaders in positions with formal designations of authority.

Command is the authority that a commander in the armed forces lawfully exercises over subordinates by virtue of rank or assignment (JP 1). Command includes the authority and responsibility for effectively using available resources and for planning the employment of, organizing, directing, coordinating, and controlling military forces for the accomplishment of assigned missions. Command also includes responsibility for health, welfare, morale, and discipline of assigned personnel.

In Army organizations, commanders establish standards and policies for achieving and rewarding exemplary performance, as well as for punishing misconduct. Military commanders enforce lawful orders under the Uniform Code of Military Justice. Consequently, commanders' personalities profoundly affect organizations. The Army expects leaders selected for command to lead beyond mere exercise of formal authority. They lead by example and serve as role models. Their personal example and actions carry tremendous weight.

Command is personal. In Army regulations and doctrine, an individual, not an institution or group, is given the authority to command. The legal and ethical responsibilities of a commander exceed those of any other leader of similar rank serving in a staff position or as a civilian manager. The relationships among commanders and subordinate officers, noncommissioned officers, enlisted Soldiers, and DA Civilians is distinct. Those not in command must understand that the commander alone is responsible for what their command does or fails to do. Subordinates have the responsibility to support the commander's intent for their command, unit, or organization.

Informal Leadership

Informal leadership exists throughout organizations and plays an important role in mission accomplishment. Informal leadership is not exercised based on rank or position in the organization. It stems from personal initiative, special knowledge, unique experiences, or technical expertise specific to an individual or team. Informal leadership occurs when someone takes the initiative to assume responsibility for action in a situation, takes charge when no formal leader is present, or to make formal leaders aware of something they need to know. Informal leaders contribute to team success.

Informal networks arise both inside and outside organizations. These informal networks include the noncommissioned officer (NCO) support channel. To build cohesive teams, leaders interact with both formal and informal teams, including the traditional chain of command and technical channels combining commanders and staff officers. The collaboration of first sergeants within a battalion is also an example of an informal network. Informal networks that operate in support of organizational goals are a force multiplier. Conversely, informal networks that operate at cross-purposes to the chain of command are destructive to an organization and intolerable.

B. The Led

The led are an important factor in leadership. Leaders, who consider their strengths along with subordinates' capabilities and the situational demands of missions, create the best chance at accomplishing tasks and missions. Inexperienced subordinates and those with limited competence require greater oversight and control. Seasoned, competent subordinates require less oversight and control.

Experience, competence, and commitment of those led vary with the mission and situation. For example, people with significant combat experience may be overly capable to perform a mission, but their commitment may lag if they do not consider the mission worth risking life or limb. Commitment varies with trust in the leader directing the mission. Trust between the leader and the led can vary across situations. A leader applies greater control over some subordinates than others. Generally, when subordinates have greater levels of expertise and commitment, leaders trust and empower them.

Every Army leader is a subordinate to someone, so all leaders are also followers. Each Soldier and DA Civilian begins service by swearing an oath of service that subordinates him or her to the Nation's civilian leadership. This obligation remains throughout a career regardless of position or rank attained. Effective Army organizations depend on the willingness of their leaders and their subordinates to serve faithfully and competently in both leadership and followership roles.

Followers respond to the authority of a leader and specific direction. Following is more than just doing what one is told to do. Motivation is an aspect of following. Effective followership requires an ability to take the initiative to get things done when necessary. Effective leaders learn to be trusted followers. Teaching weapons maintenance provides an example. New Soldiers clean their rifles how and when instructed to do so. Experienced Soldiers routinely clean their weapon without being told so that it will function when needed. This simple discipline of doing the right thing when no one is looking is fundamental to following.

There is a tendency to think of people as either a leader or subordinate, but leading and following are simultaneous responsibilities. This is particularly true in a hierarchical organization like the Army. Everyone charged with leading others has a responsibility to follow their superior in the chain of command. Being an effective follower requires the same attributes and competencies required to be an effective leader, although application is different. When following, Army leaders respond to their superiors' authority and guidance. The principles of mission command capture this: leaders empower followers, by fostering mutual trust and creating shared understanding, to take initiative based on the commander's intent. The subordinate leader transitions from follower to leader as they take action and direct their followers.

C. The Situation

The situation affects which actions leaders take. Leaders consider the unique characteristics of the task or mission at hand, the abilities of their subordinates, their familiarity with similar situations, and amount of time available. High-risk or urgent situations often require immediate and decisive actions, particularly in combat. Low-risk or slowly developing situations allow leaders to spend more time with deliberate and collaborative approaches, coaching, and teaching subordinates as they go along. This fosters a higher level of commitment, develops subordinates, and creates the organizational cohesion essential for leading successfully in challenging situations.

Leaders learn to adapt to the situation by disciplining themselves to practice different approaches. This prepares leaders to adapt to new, urgent, stressful, or high-risk situations. In general, leaders should strive to improve all of the leader attributes and core leadership competencies, adapt their leadership techniques to each situation, and become lifelong learners. This requires leaders to—

- Know how to assess tasks and conditions.
- Know how to assess their own capabilities and those of their followers.
- Know how to adjust their leadership techniques.
- Know those they lead.
- Understand how to employ the mission command approach to the situation.
- Develop themselves and the competence of subordinates.
- Establish and maintain positive leadership climates.

IV. Roles of Leadership

Every individual in the Army is a member of a team, as a leader or a follower. Each leadership role and responsibility is unique, yet leaders interact in common ways. The Army is comprised of Soldiers and DA Civilians. Soldiers are officers, NCOs, and enlisted. The Department of the Army employs DA Civilians and, like Soldiers, are members of the executive branch of the federal government. The Army charges all members to support and defend the Constitution against all enemies, foreign and domestic. They all take oaths to the Constitution that commit them to follow the laws of the Nation and orders of those appointed over them. Army professionals who embrace and live the Army Values are role models and standard-bearers for the organization. Army leaders come from three different categories—

- Officers.
- Noncommissioned officers.
- DA Civilians.

A. Officers

Officers command units, establish policy, and manage resources while balancing risks and caring for their people and families. They integrate collective, leader, and Soldier training to accomplish the Army's missions. They serve at all levels, from leading tactical unit operations to leading change at strategic levels. Command makes officers responsible and accountable for everything their command does or fails to do.

The technical characteristic that distinguishes officers (including warrant officers) the most is that they hold their grade and office under a commission or appointment issued by the authority of the President of the United States or the Secretary of the Army. They receive commissions based upon the basis of special trust and confidence placed in the officer's patriotism, valor, fidelity, and abilities. An officer's commission grants authority to direct subordinates and subsequently, an obligation to obey superiors.

Serving as an officer differs from other forms of Army leadership by the measure of responsibility attached, and in the magnitude of the consequences of inaction or ineffectiveness. An enlisted leader swears an oath of obedience to lawful orders, while an officer promises to, "well and faithfully discharge the duties of the office". Officers maintain the momentum of operations. While officers depend on the counsel, technical skill, maturity, and experience of subordinates to translate their orders into action, they are ultimately responsible for mission success.

Warrant officers possess a high degree of specialization in a particular field in contrast to the more general assignment pattern of other officers. Warrant officers may command aircraft, maritime vessels, and special units. Warrant officers provide expert tactical and technical advice, knowledge, counsel, and solutions to support their unit or organization. They maintain, administer, and manage the Army's equipment, support activities, and technical systems. Their extensive professional experience and technical knowledge qualifies warrant officers as invaluable role models and mentors for officers and NCOs.

While warrant officer positions are usually functionally oriented, warrant officers may lead and direct Soldiers. Senior warrant officers provide the commander with the benefit of years of tactical and technical experience. Warrant officers functioning at senior levels become systems experts rather than equipment experts. They must understand the conditions and know how to integrate the systems they manage into complex operational environments.

V. Levels of Leadership

Ref: ADP 6-22 (w/C1), Army Leadership and the Profession (Nov '19), pp. 1-22 to 1-23.

The Army acknowledges three levels of leadership—

- Direct.
- Organizational.
- Strategic.

The leader attributes and competencies apply across all leadership levels. The concept of subordination helps members understand the expectations the Army has for them across a career. Foundations include understanding oaths, dignity and respect for all people, the Army Values, leadership, command, authority, Army operations, military discipline, and similar basics (see figure 1-5). Leaders gain a firmer understanding of the enduring requirements and add specialized knowledge as they move through the levels.

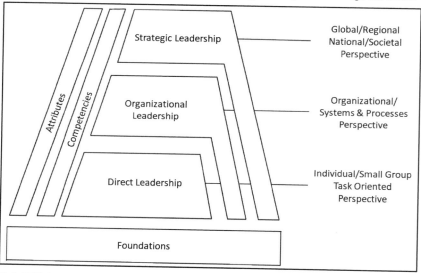

Ref: ADP 6-22 (w/C1), Figure 1-5. Army leadership levels.

Factors determining a leadership level include the leader's relationship to a subordinate, number of subordinates, scope of responsibility, and time horizons of missions. Regardless of which level they serve in, a leader is always a direct leader. Direct leaders are task oriented. Organizational leaders are both task and mission oriented and lead through subordinate leaders. Army organizations execute missions and tasks. Strategic leaders apply a global, regional, national, and societal perspective to the organizations they lead. Organizational and strategic leaders lead through others. Rank does not generally determine the difference between organizational and strategic leaders, positions do. The Sergeant Major of the Army is a sergeant major. A battalion sergeant major is also a sergeant major. While there are significant differences in seniority and responsibilities, they are both sergeants major. Junior leaders and some DA Civilians serve at the direct leadership level. NCOs and officers that direct other leaders to accomplish tasks are organizational leaders. Generally, senior grade and general officers and equivalent senior executive service DA Civilians and their sergeants major serve at the organizational or strategic leadership levels.

A. Direct Leadership

Direct leadership is face-to-face or first-line leadership that generally occurs in organizations where subordinates see their leaders all the time such as teams, squads, sections, platoons, departments, companies, batteries, and troops. The direct leader's span of influence may range from a few to dozens of people. The leader's day-to-day involvement is important for successful unit performance. Direct level leadership covers the same type of functions, such as those performed by an infantry squad or a graves registration unit.

Direct leaders develop others through coaching, counseling, mentoring, and setting the example. For instance, company grade officers and NCOs are close enough to Soldiers to exert direct influence when observing training or interacting with subordinates during other functions.

Direct leaders generally experience more certainty and less complexity than organizational and strategic leaders because of their close physical proximity to their subordinates. They direct actions, assign tasks, teach, coach, encourage, give guidance, and ensure successful completion of tasks or missions. They must be close enough to the action to determine or address problems. Examples of direct leadership tasks are vehicle maintenance, supervision of creating of fighting positions, and performance counseling.

Direct leaders understand the mission of their higher headquarters two levels up and when applicable the tasks assigned one level down. This provides them with the context in which they perform their duties.

B. Organizational Leadership *(See pp. 1-77 to 1-80.)*

Organizational leaders exercise leadership through subordinate leaders responsible for leading the various organizations that make up the larger organization. Organizational leaders establish a climate that supports their subordinate leaders. Subordinate units and organizations do not depend on daily guidance from their higher-level leaders to be successful. Organizational leaders, particularly commanders, are responsible for communicating intent two echelons down and understanding intent two echelons up. Organizational leaders operate within commanders' intent and communicate that intent to subordinates as a means of providing room for subordinate initiative and decreasing the number of decisions they must personally make to keep the organization operating effectively. Organizational leadership includes responsibility over multiple functions, such as leading and synchronizing combined arms operations.

Organizational leaders regularly and personally interact with their subordinates. They make time to verify that reports and briefings match their own perceptions of the organization's progress toward mission accomplishment. Organizational leaders use personal observation and visits by designated personnel to assess how well subordinates understand the commander's intent and to determine if they need to reinforce or reassess the organization's priorities.

C. Strategic Leadership *(See pp. 1-81 to 1-84.)*

Strategic leaders include military and civilian leaders at the major command through DOD levels. Strategic leadership guides and integrates multiple organizational level units that perform a wide range of functions. It influences several thousand to hundreds of thousands of people. These leaders allocate resources, communicate strategic vision, and prepare their commands and the Army itself for future missions. Strategic leaders shape Army culture by ensuring their directives, policies, programs, and systems are ethical, effective, and efficient.

Strategic leaders apply all core leader competencies they acquired as direct and organizational leaders, while further adapting them to the complex realities of their strategic conditions. Strategic leader decisions must consider congressional hearings, Army budgetary constraints, new systems acquisition, civilian programs, research, development, and inter-service cooperation. Every strategic leader decision has the potential of affecting the entire Army.

B. Noncommissioned Officers

Noncommissioned officers are the backbone of the Army and are responsible for maintaining Army standards and discipline. NCOs are critical to training, educating, and developing individuals, crews, and small teams. NCOs are accountable for the care of their Soldiers and setting examples for them.

The Army relies on NCOs capable of conducting daily operations, executing small unit tactical operations, and making commander's intent-driven decisions. Subordinates look to NCOs for solutions, guidance, and inspiration. Soldiers count on NCOs they trust and admire. They expect them to convey information and provide day-to-day guidance to accomplish tactical and technical tasks. All Soldiers look to NCOs to train them to cope, prepare, and perform courageously regardless of the situation.

While preparing Soldiers for missions, NCOs stress fieldcraft and physical and mental rigor. NCOs understand that improved warfighting technology will not reduce the need for mentally and physically fit Soldiers. Soldiers will continue to carry heavy loads, and engage enemy forces in close combat. Tactical success relates directly to the Soldiers' level of tactical and technical training, as well as their fitness and resiliency. Soldier care includes preparing them for future challenges and adversity.

NCOs are trainers, mentors, communicators, and advisors. NCOs advise and assist in the development of officers by sharing their experience and professional judgment. They form professional and personal bonds with officers based on mutual trust and common goals. Commanders at all levels have senior enlisted advisors who provide advice and serve as an important source of knowledge about enlisted matters, as well as experts about tactical and technical questions. At the highest level, the Sergeant Major of the Army is the Army Chief of Staff's personal advisor who recommends policy to support Soldiers throughout the Army.

C. Department of the Army Civilians

Department of the Army Civilians are professionals committed to serving the Nation as an integral part of the Army team. They provide mission-essential capability, stability, and continuity to support Soldiers. DA Civilians are committed to honorable service in the performance of their duties. The Army Civilian Corps Creed affirms their role as members of the Army team and their special contribution to organizational stability and continuity. Major roles and responsibilities of DA Civilians include—

- Establishing and executing policy.
- Leading Army organizations and managing programs, projects, and systems.
- Operating activities and facilities for Army equipment, support, research, and technical work supporting the Army around the world.

Selection of DA Civilians to a government position depends on their eligibility based on their credentials and expertise. Proficiency derives from previous education and training, prior experiences, and ties to career programs. DA Civilians hold the grade of the position in which they serve and primarily exercise authority based on the position held, not their grade. DA Civilians do not exercise military command, however when designated they may exercise general supervision over an Army installation or activity under the command of a military superior.

Civilian personnel have functional proponents for career fields that ensure provisions exist for career growth and are free to pursue positions and promotions as desired. Personnel policies generally state that DA Civilians should be in positions that do not require military personnel for reasons of law, training, security, discipline, rotation, or combat readiness.

While most DA Civilians historically support military forces at home stations, they also deploy with military forces to provide expertise and support. DA Civilians often remain for long periods within the same organization, providing continuity and stability that the dynamic personnel management system used for the military rarely allows.

I. Leader Attributes
(Character, Presence, Intellect)

Ref: ADP 6-22 (w/C1), Army Leadership and the Profession (Nov '19), part 1.

The Army Leader -
A Person of Character, Presence, and Intellect

Part One of ADP 6-22 highlights the critical attribute categories of character, presence, and intellect. All Army leaders use them to reach their full potential from direct leader to strategic leader. The attributes support leadership actions valuable for continued development and effective performance.

Core Leader Attributes

Attributes are characteristics internal to a leader. These affect how an individual behaves, thinks, and learns within certain conditions. Strong character, solid presence, and keen intellect enable individuals to perform the core leader competencies with greater effect.

Leader Attributes

The Army Leader - A Person of Character, Presence, and Intellect:

Attributes

A. Character	B. Presence	C. Intellect
• Army values	• Military and professional bearing	• Mental agility
• Empathy	• Fitness	• Sound judgement
• Warrior ethos and Service ethos	• Confidence	• Innovation
• Discipline	• Resilience	• Interpersonal tact
• Humility		• Expertise

The three categories of core attributes are—

Character *(See p. 1-22.)*
Character: the moral and ethical qualities of the leader.

Presence *(See p. 1-28.)*
Presence: characteristics open to display by the leader and open to viewing by others.

Intellect *(See p. 1-30.)*
Intellect: the mental and social abilities the leader applies while leading.

Leader Attributes (Overview)

Ref: ADP 6-22 (w/C1), Army Leadership and the Profession (Nov '19), pp. 6 to 7.

Attributes are characteristics internal to a leader. These affect how an individual behaves, thinks, and learns within certain conditions. Strong character, solid presence, and keen intellect enable individuals to perform the core leader competencies with greater effect. The three categories of core attributes are—

Leader Attributes

Core Leader Attributes

A. Character	B. Presence	C. Intellect
• Army values	• Military and professional bearing	• Mental agility
• Empathy	• Fitness	• Sound judgement
• Warrior ethos and Service ethos	• Confidence	• Innovation
• Discipline	• Resilience	• Interpersonal tact
• Humility		• Expertise

I. Character

A person's character affects how they lead. A leader's character consists of their true nature guided by their conscience, which affects their moral attitudes and actions. A leader's personal reputation is what others view as character. Leaders who firmly adhere to applicable laws, regulations, and unit standards build credibility with their subordinates and enhance trust of the Nation they serve.

Influences such as background, beliefs, education, and experiences affect all Soldiers and DA Civilians. An Army leader's role in developing others' character would be simple if it merely required checking and aligning personal values with the Army Values. Reality is much different. Becoming and remaining a leader of character is a process involving day-to-day experiences and internal fortitude. While education, self-development, counseling, coaching, and mentoring can refine the outward signs of character, modifying deeply held values is the only way to change character. Leaders are responsible for their own character and for encouraging, supporting, and assessing their subordinates' efforts to embody character.

Factors internal and central to a leader serving in either leader or follower roles that constitute an individual's character.	
Army Values	• Values are principles, standards, or qualities considered essential for successful leaders. • Guide leaders' decisions and actions in accomplishing missions, performing duty, and all aspects of life. • The Army has seven values applicable to all Army individuals: loyalty, duty, respect, selfless service, honor, integrity, and personal courage.
Empathy	• Propensity to experience something from another person's point of view. • Ability to identify with and enter into another person's feelings and emotions, enabling clearer communications and better guidance. • Desire to care for and take care of Soldiers and others.
Warrior Ethos/ Service Ethos	• Internal shared attitudes and beliefs that embody the spirit of the Army profession.
Discipline	• Decisions and actions consistent with the Army Values; willing obedience to lawful orders
Humility	• Inherently motivated to support mission goals ahead of actions that are self-serving. • Possesses honest and accurate self-understanding. • Eager for input and feedback from others.

Ref: ADP 6-22 (w/C1), Table 2-1. Attributes associated with CHARACTER.

II. Presence

The impression a leader makes on others contributes to success in getting people to follow. This impression is the sum of a leader's outward appearance, demeanor, actions and words and the inward character and intellect of the leader. Presence entails the projection of military and professional bearing, holistic fitness, confidence and resilience. Strong presence is important as a touchstone for subordinates, especially under duress. A leader who does not share the same risks could easily make a decision that could prove unworkable given the psychological state of Soldiers and Civilians affected by stress.

How others perceive a leader based on the leader's outward appearance, demeanor, actions, and words.	
Military and professional bearing	• Demonstrating character, competence, and commitment. • Setting the example and upholding standards. • Projecting a professional image of authority.
Fitness	• Having sound health, strength, and endurance that support one's emotional health and conceptual abilities under prolonged stress.
Confidence	• Sense of ability to make right decisions and take right action, tempered with humility and sense of human limitations. • Projecting self-confidence and certainty in the unit's ability to succeed. • Demonstrating composure and outward calm through control over one's emotions.
Resilience	• Tendency to recover quickly from setbacks, shock, injuries, adversity, and stress while maintaining a mission and organizational focus.

Ref: ADP 6-22 (w/C1), Table 3-1. Attributes associated with PRESENCE

III. Intellect

The leader's intellect affects how well a leader thinks about problems, creates solutions, makes decisions and leads others. People differ in intellectual strengths and ways of thinking. There is no one right way to think. Each leader needs to be self aware of strengths and limitations and apply them accordingly. Being mentally agile helps leaders address changes and adapt to the situation and the dynamics of operations. Critical and innovative thought are abilities that enable the leader to be adaptive. Sound judgment enables the best decision for the situation at hand. It is a key attribute of the transformation of knowledge into understanding and quality execution.

Mental resources or tendencies that influence a leader's conceptual abilities and effectiveness.	
Mental agility	• Flexibility of mind; the ability to break habitual thought patterns. • Anticipating or adapting to uncertain or changing situations; thinking through outcomes when current decisions or actions are not producing desired effects. • Ability to apply multiple perspectives and approaches.
Sound judgment	• Capacity to assess situations and draw sound, ethical conclusions. • Tendency to form sound opinions, make sensible decisions, and reliable guesses. • Ability to assess strengths and weaknesses of subordinates, peers, and enemies to create appropriate solutions and actions.
Innovation	• Ability to introduce new ideas based on opportunities or challenging circumstances. • Creativity in producing ideas and objects that are both novel and appropriate.
Interpersonal tact	• Being aware of others' perceptions and capacity to understand interactions with others. • Aware of the character, motives, and reactions of self and others and their effect on interpersonal interactions. • Recognizing diversity and displaying self-control, balance, and stability.
Expertise	• Possessing a high level of domain knowledge and competence in an area, and the ability to draw and apply accurate, logical conclusions.

Ref: ADP 6-22 (w/C1), Table 4-1. Attributes associated with INTELLECT.

I. Leader Character

Character consists of the moral and ethical qualities of an individual revealed through their decisions and actions. Leaders must consistently demonstrate good character and inspire others to do the same. The close teamwork demanded to execute military missions at all levels requires that everyone in the Army share certain desirable character attributes. Character attributes that are of special interest to the Army and its leaders are—

See table 2-1 on p. 1-20 for a summary of the character attributes.

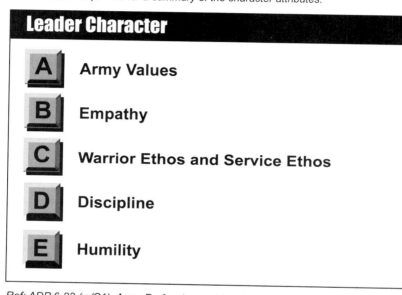

Leader Character

A Army Values

B Empathy

C Warrior Ethos and Service Ethos

D Discipline

E Humility

Ref: ADP 6-22 (w/C1), Army Profession and Leadership (Nov '19), chap. 2.

A. Army Values

Personal values develop over the years from childhood to adulthood. People are free to choose and hold their own values, but upon taking the oath of service, Soldiers and DA Civilians agree to live and act by the Army Values. Army Values consist of the principles, standards, and qualities considered essential for service. The Army Values set expectations for conduct and are fundamental to making the right decision in any situation. Living, teaching, and reinforcing Army Values is an important leader responsibility.

The Army recognizes seven values that all Soldiers and DA Civilians must internalize. Embracing the Army Values is the hallmark of being an Army professional. Doing so represents a pact with teammates and the American people to be trustworthy and accountable. When read in sequence, the first letters of the Army Values form the acronym LDRSHIP.

See following pages (pp. 1-24 to 1-25) for further discussion and overview of Army Values: LDRSHIP.

Values And Beliefs

Values and beliefs affect how people think and act. People join the Army from a society with diverse personal values and beliefs respected within the standards of legal and ethical behavior. Variation in upbringing, culture, religious belief, and tradition is reflected among those who choose to serve in the Army. Such diversity provides many benefits for a force globally engaged around the world. Good leaders value this diversity of outlook and experience and must treat all individuals with the inherent dignity and respect due every person. All leaders have the critical responsibility to ensure that subordinates adhere to the Army Values as well as standards consistent with the United States Constitution, the Uniform Code of Military Justice, and Army rules and regulations.

Values and beliefs create a foundation for ethical conduct. Adhering to the Army Values is essential to upholding high ethical standards of behavior. Unethical behavior quickly destroys organizational morale and cohesion—it undermines the trust and confidence essential to teamwork and mission accomplishment. Consistently doing the right thing for the right reasons forges strong character in individuals and expands to create a culture of trust throughout the organization.

Ethical Reasoning

To be an ethical leader requires more than merely knowing the Army Values. Leaders must be able to live by them to find moral solutions to diverse problems. Ethical reasoning must occur in everything leaders do—in planning, preparing, executing, and assessing operations.

Ethical choices may not always be obvious decisions between right and wrong. Leaders use multiple perspectives to think about ethical concerns, applying them to determine the most ethical choice. One perspective comes from a view that desirable virtues such as courage, justice, and benevolence define ethical outcomes. A second perspective comes from a set of agreed-upon values or rules, such as the Army Values or Constitutional rights. A third perspective bases the consequences of the decision on whatever produces the greatest good for the greatest number as most favorable. Leaders able to consider all perspectives applicable to a particular situation are more likely to be ethically astute. When time is available, consulting peers and seniors is often helpful. Chaplains can provide confidential advice to leaders about difficult personal and professional ethical issues to encourage moral decisions in accord with personal conscience and the Army Values.

Ethical Orders

Making the right choice and acting when faced with an ethical question can be difficult. Sometimes the situation requires a leader to stand firm and disagree with a supervisor on ethical grounds. These occasions test one's character and moral courage. Situations in which any Army member thinks an order is unlawful can be the most difficult.

Under typical circumstances, a leader executes a superior leader's decision with enthusiasm. Unlawful orders are the exception: a leader has a duty to question such orders and refuse to obey them if clarification of the order's intent fails to resolve objections. If a Soldier perceives an order is unlawful, the Soldier should fully understand the order's details and original intent. The Soldier should seek immediate clarification from the person who issued the order before proceeding.

If the question is more complex, seek legal counsel. If an issue requires an immediate decision, as may happen in the heat of combat, make the best judgment possible based on the Army Values, personal experience, critical thinking, previous study, and prior reflection. Chances are, when a Soldier disobeys what may be an unlawful order, it may be the most courageous decision they make. The Soldier's Rules codify the law of war and outline ethical and lawful conduct in operations (see AR 350-1). They distill the essence of the law of war, the Army Values, and inform ethical conduct.

Army Values

Ref: ADP 6-22 (w/C1), Army Leadership and the Profession (Nov '19), pp. 2-1 to 2-5.

Personal values develop over the years from childhood to adulthood. People are free to choose and hold their own values, but upon taking the oath of service, Soldiers and DA Civilians agree to live and act by the Army Values. Army Values consist of the principles, standards, and qualities considered essential for service. The Army Values set expectations for conduct and are fundamental to making the right decision in any situation. Living, teaching, and reinforcing Army Values is an important leader responsibility.

The Army recognizes seven values that all Soldiers and DA Civilians must internalize. Embracing the Army Values is the hallmark of being an Army professional. Doing so represents a pact with teammates and the American people to be trustworthy and accountable. When read in sequence, the first letters of the Army Values form the acronym LDRSHIP:

Army Values - "LDRSHIP"

L	**Loyalty**
D	**Duty**
R	**Respect**
S	**Selfless service**
H	**Honor**
I	**Integrity**
P	**Personal courage**

Ref: ADP 6-22 (w/C1), Army Profession and Leadership (Nov '19), pp. 2-1 to 2-5.

L - Loyalty: Bear True Faith And Allegiance To The U.S. Constitution, The Army, Your Unit And Other Soldiers

The first order of loyalty is to the Constitution and the ideals upon which it is based. One cannot remain loyal to the Constitution by being loyal to those who violate it. To create strong organizations, superiors, subordinates, and peers must embrace loyalty. One way that individuals demonstrate loyalty is by upholding all of the Army values. With those values as a foundation, loyalty is a two-way exchange: leaders earn loyalty and subordinates expect loyalty in return. Leaders earn subordinates' loyalty by training them well, treating them fairly, and living the Army Values. Subordinates demonstrate loyalty by working hard for their leaders and being as good as they can be at their jobs. Loyalty and trust enable the successful day-to-day operations of all organizations.

D - Duty: Fulfill Your Obligations -- Always Do Your Best

All Soldiers and DA Civilians strive to do their best. Duty extends beyond law, regulation, and orders. Army professionals exercise initiative when they fulfill the purpose, not merely the letter, of received orders. Leaders take responsibility for their actions and those of their subordinates; it is inherent in their duty to the larger organization, the Army, and the Nation. Conscientious leaders and subordinates possess a sense of responsibility to apply their best efforts to accomplish the mission. This guides Soldiers and DA Civilians to do what is right to the best of their ability.

R - Respect: Treat People as They Should Be Treated

The Army Values reinforce that all people have dignity and worth and must be treated with respect. The Nation was founded on the ideal that all are created equal. In the Army, each is judged by the content of their character. Army leaders should consistently foster a climate that treats everyone with dignity and respect, regardless of ethnicity, gender identity, sexual orientation, creed, or religious belief. Fostering a positive climate begins with a leader's personal example. Leaders treat others, including adversaries, with respect.

S - Selfless Service: Put the Welfare of the Nation, the Army and Your Subordinates Before Your Own

Selfless service means doing what is right for the Nation, the Army, the organization, and subordinates. While the needs of the Army and the Nation should come first, selfless service does not imply leaders should neglect their families or themselves. Unselfish, humble leaders set themselves apart as teammates who are approachable, trustworthy, and open to follower input and advice. Selfless leaders aspire to attain goals for the greater good, beyond their own interests and benefits.

H - Honor: Live Up to Army Values

Living honorably, in line with the Army Values, sets an example for every member of the organization and contributes to an organization's positive climate and morale. How leaders conduct themselves and meet their obligations to the mission, other people, and the organization defines them as people and leaders.

I - Integrity: Do What is Right, Legally and Morally

Leaders of integrity consistently follow honorable principles. The Army relies on leaders who are honest in word and deed. Leaders of integrity do the right thing because their character permits nothing less. To instill the Army Values in others, leaders must demonstrate them. As an Army leader and a person of integrity, personal values should reinforce the Army Values.

P - Personal Courage: Face Fear, Danger, or Adversity (Physical and Moral)

Personal courage is not the absence of fear; it is the ability to put fear aside and do what is necessary or right. Personal courage takes two forms: physical and moral. Effective leaders demonstrate both.

Physical courage requires overcoming fears of bodily harm and doing one's duty. It triggers bravery that allows a Soldier to take risks in combat in spite of the fear of injury or death. For leaders, mission accomplishment may demand risking their own lives or those of Soldiers and justly taking the lives of enemies.

Moral courage is the willingness to stand firm on values, principles, and convictions. It enables all leaders to stand up for what they believe is right, regardless of the consequences. Leaders, who take full responsibility for their decisions and actions, even when things go wrong, display moral courage. Moral courage also expresses itself as candor— being frank, honest, and sincere with others. Carefully considered professional judgment offered to subordinates, peers, and superiors is an expression of personal courage

B. Empathy

Army leaders show empathy when they genuinely relate to another person's situation, motives, or feelings. Empathy does not mean sympathy for another, but a realization that leads to a deeper understanding. Empathy allows the leader to anticipate what others are experiencing and feeling and gives insight to how decisions or actions affect them. Leaders extend empathy to others in both their leader and follower roles. Leaders with a strong tendency for empathy can apply it to understand people at a deeper level. This applies to DA Civilians, Soldiers and their Families, local populations, victims of natural disasters, and enemy combatants. Empathy enhances cultural understanding and enables an Army leader to better interact with others.

Empathetic leaders are better communicators, help others to understand what is occurring, and inspire others to meet mission objectives. During operations, Army leaders gain empathy when they share hardships to gauge Soldier morale and combat readiness. They recognize the need to provide reasonable comforts and rest periods to maintain morale and accomplish the mission.

C. Warrior Ethos and Service Ethos

The Warrior Ethos, contained within the Soldier's Creed, represents the professional attitudes and beliefs that characterize the American Soldier. It reflects a Soldier's selfless commitment to the Nation, mission, unit, and fellow Soldiers. DA Civilians, while not Soldiers, embody the principles of the Warrior Ethos through a service ethos embedded within the Army Civilian Corps Creed that shapes their conduct with the same commitment.

See facing page for the Soldier's Creed and the Army Civilian Corps Creed.

D. Discipline

Discipline is essential to character, just as it is to an organization. All leaders must demonstrate self-discipline—the ability to control one's own behavior—to do the harder right over the easier wrong. Doing tasks to the established Army standard without deviation reflects discipline.

Individual discipline supports the unit or an organization. At the unit level, leaders maintain discipline by enforcing standards impartially and consistently. Often this involves attending to mundane details, which may seem less urgent than an organization's key tasks, but are necessary to ensure success. Examples include preventive maintenance checks and services, pre-combat checks and inspections, effective Command Supply Discipline Programs, Organizational Inspection Programs, and training management. When enforcing standards, Soldiers expect their leaders to do so in an impartial, transparent, just, and consistent manner.

E. Humility

Humility in its simplest form is the absence of arrogance. It is a sign of a leader being unselfish, working toward something more important than themselves. A person of high integrity, honesty, and character embodies the qualities of humility. For humility to apply, a leader must first have competence and confidence. A leader with the right level of humility is a willing learner, maintains accurate self-awareness, and seeks out others' input and feedback. Leaders are seen as humble when they are aware of their limitations and abilities and apply that understanding in their leadership.

Humility exists on a continuum. Too little humility represents arrogance or hubris, which may lead to over confidence. Excess humility is problematic because it is interpreted as shyness, meekness, passivity, blind obedience, or timidity. Either extreme signals a lack of self-awareness that undermines followers' trust and confidence in the leader's ability to make good decisions, look out for the unit's welfare, and to achieve success.

Warrior Ethos and Service Ethos

Ref: ADP 6-22 (w/C1), Army Leadership and the Profession (Nov '19), p. 2-9.

The Warrior Ethos requires unrelenting resolve to do what is right regardless of the mission. Understanding what is right requires respect for everyone involved in complex missions, such as stability or defense support of civil authorities operations. Ambiguous situations, such as when to use lethal or nonlethal force, are a test of the leader's judgment and discipline. The Warrior Ethos creates a collective commitment to succeed with honor.

The Warrior Ethos connects Soldiers of today with those whose sacrifices have sustained America's existence. The Warrior Ethos is crucial but Soldier commitment may be perishable. Consequently, the Army must continually affirm, develop, and sustain its Warrior Ethos. The key to the Warrior Ethos is a mindset developed through purposeful mental preparation. Growth in character, confidence, composure, mental agility, and resilience are outcomes of internalizing the Warrior Ethos, as well as the service ethos of DA Civilians.

The Soldier's Creed

The Soldier's Creed captures the spirit of dedication Soldiers feel to be part of something greater than themselves. It outlines the fundamental obligations of Soldiers to their fellow Soldiers, their unit, and the Army itself. The Soldier's Creed extends beyond service as a Soldier; it includes commitment to family and society.

I am an American Soldier.

I am a Warrior and a member of a team.

I serve the people of the United States and live the Army Values.

I will always place the mission first.

I will never accept defeat.

I will never quit.

I will never leave a fallen comrade.

I am disciplined, physically and mentally tough, trained and proficient in my warrior tasks and drills. I always maintain my arms, my equipment, and myself.

I am an expert and I am a professional.

I stand ready to deploy, engage, and destroy the enemies of the United States of America in close combat.

I am a guardian of freedom and the American way of life.

I am an American Soldier.

The Army Civilian Corps Creed

The Army Civilian Creed reads—

I am an Army civilian—a member of the Army team.

I am dedicated to our Army, our Soldiers and civilians.

I will always support the mission.

I provide stability and continuity during war and peace.

I support and defend the Constitution of the United States and consider it an honor to serve our nation and our Army.

I live the Army values of loyalty, duty, respect, selfless service, honor, integrity, and personal courage.

I am an Army civilian.

It is difficult to judge our own humility. One's humility is largely determined by other people. It is a subjective perception of the leader. Humility is interpreted differently by different genders and cultures. Individuals need to guard against their biases and assess character based on the whole set of Army Values and attributes.

II. Leader Presence

Demonstrating presence is more than just showing up and being seen, although both are important. The actions, words, and the manner in which leaders carry themselves should convey confidence, competence, and a positive example for others to emulate. Presence represents who leaders are and what they stand for. Every leader has presence. Unfortunately, some lose the respect and confidence of their subordinates because their presence provides little or no positive effect on others. Part of projecting a positive leadership presence is being comfortable in one's own skin. While leaders should understand that their subordinates are always observing how leaders carry themselves, they should also understand that subordinates can quickly tell the difference between leaders who are trying to portray themselves as something they are not. This often happens when a leader is new to a duty position or lacks experience. Remembering that most subordinates want their leaders to be successful is important. When they sense that their leaders are genuine, honest, and willing to learn by putting themselves into positions where they might risk a little embarrassment learning a new skill, their level of respect for a leader increases. Leaders able to do what they ask others to do, who can 'walk the talk,' generate a positive reputation that contributes to their effective presence around Soldiers.

See table 3-1 on p. 1-21 for a summary of the presence attributes.

Leader Presence

A leader's effectiveness is dramatically enhanced by understanding and developing the following areas:

 A   **Military and Professional Bearing**

 B   **Fitness**

 C   **Confidence**

 D   **Resilience**

Ref: ADP 6-22 (w/C1), Army Profession and Leadership (Nov '19), chap. 3.

Through their presence, leaders show what they stand for and how they expect others to carry themselves. Leaders who routinely share in hardships and dangers have firsthand knowledge of what they are asking subordinates to do, and show their subordinates that they are not above putting themselves at the same level of risk or discomfort. It assures Soldiers that what they are doing is important. A leader's effectiveness is dramatically enhanced by understanding and developing the following areas:

- **Military and professional bearing**: projecting a commanding presence, a professional image of authority, calmness under pressure, and control over emotions.

- **Fitness**: looking like a fit, professional Soldier, having the strength, and endurance to lead others from the front, and being physically able to do what subordinates are expected to do.

- **Confidence**: projecting self-confidence and certainty in the unit's ability to accomplish the mission, able to retain composure and demonstrate calm through steady control over emotion.

- **Resilience**: demonstrating the psychological and physical capacity to overcome failures, setbacks, and hardship.

A. Military and Professional Bearing

The Army expects all Army members to look and act as professionals. Skillful use of professional bearing—fitness, courtesy, proper military appearance, appropriate civilian attire, and professionally correct behavior in accordance with established Army standards sets the professional tone with which a unit functions. A professional military demeanor establishes credibility, sets expectations, and reduces organizational ambiguity. Consistent professionalism strengthens mutual respect among members of the team.

B. Fitness

The Army's approach to holistic fitness reduces the risk of unnecessary harm during operations, while training, in garrison, and off duty. Holistic fitness recognizes that individual well-being depends on interdependent areas including physical fitness, resilience, training, individual spirituality (self-identity, beliefs, and life purpose beyond self), social interaction (positive connection with others), and physical, psychological, and behavioral health. Leaders promote policies and practices to maintain total fitness for themselves and their subordinates.

Unit readiness begins with physically fit Soldiers. Operations place physical, mental, and emotional demands upon the individuals conducting them. Physical fitness, while crucial for success in battle, is important for all members of the Army team in all environments. Physically fit people feel more competent and confident, handle stress better, can work longer more effectively, and recover faster from hardship. Physical fitness is the cornerstone of combat readiness.

The physical demands of leadership during repeated deployments or continuous operations can erode how well one thinks and emotional stability, both of which are essential to the effective decision making required for sound leadership. Poor physical fitness multiples the effects of stress, eventually compromising mental and emotional fitness. Operations in difficult terrain, extreme climates, or high altitudes require extensive physical conditioning. Once in the area of operations, leaders must continue efforts to sustain their own fitness and that of their subordinates.

Preparedness for operational missions should be the primary focus of the unit's fitness program. The forward-looking leader develops a balanced fitness program that enables Soldiers to execute the unit's most challenging missions.

It is a leader's duty to stay healthy and fit since the leader's decisions affect the welfare of the entire organization. Fit and healthy leaders motivate and challenge subordinates to become like them. Staying healthy and physically fit enables Soldiers to cope with the psychological effects of extended operations. To maintain peak performance, leaders and Soldiers need exercise, sufficient sleep, nutritional food, and adequate hydration.

Health fitness includes having routine physical exams and keeping immunizations current, as well as practicing dental hygiene, personal grooming, and cleanliness when in the field during training and operations. Health fitness includes avoiding things that can degrade personal health, such as, substance abuse, tobacco use, over-eating, as well as overuse of caffeine, energy drinks, and other stimulants (for

C. Confidence

Confidence is the faith leaders place in their abilities to make decisions and take appropriate action in any situation, no matter how stressful or ambiguous. Confidence grows from professional competence and a realistic appraisal of one's abilities. A leader's confidence is contagious and permeates the entire organization. Confident leaders who help Soldiers control doubt reduce anxiety in a unit. Effective leaders temper confidence with humility—the understanding that no one is perfect, all knowing, or always correct. Humility prevents overconfidence and arrogance.

D. Resilience

Resilience enables leaders and their organizations to endure and ultimately prevail over hardship. Resilience and commitment to accomplish the mission is critical to overcoming adversity. Resilient Soldiers can recover quickly from setbacks, shock, and injuries while maintaining focus on their jobs and the mission. Resilient leaders learn and grow from experiencing difficult situations. Leaders instill resilience and a winning spirit in subordinates through personal example and tough, realistic training.

III. Leader Intellect

Intellect is fundamental to successful leadership. Intellect consists of one's brainpower and knowledge. Intellect enables leaders to think creatively and critically to gain situational understanding, make sound judgments, solve problems, and take action. Intellect allows leaders to reason analytically, critically, ethically, and with cultural sensitivity. Intellect is involved in considering the intended and unintended consequences of the decisions a leader makes. Effective leaders must anticipate the second-and third-order effects of their decisions.

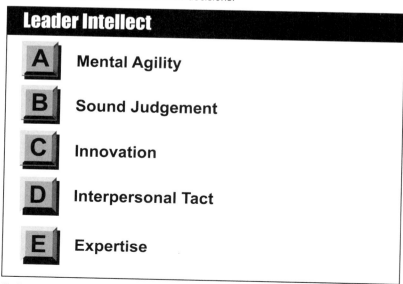

Leader Intellect

A **Mental Agility**

B **Sound Judgement**

C **Innovation**

D **Interpersonal Tact**

E **Expertise**

Ref: ADP 6-22 (w/C1), Army Profession and Leadership (Nov '19), chap. 4.

A leader's mental abilities affect how well they think and lead others. People differ in intellectual strengths and ways of thinking—there is no one right way to think. Each leader needs to be self-aware of their strengths and limitations and apply them accordingly. Experience informs intellect.

See table 4-1 on p. 1-21 for a summary of the intellect attributes.

A. Mental Agility

Mental agility is the ability to think flexibly. Mental agility helps leaders effectively react to change and adapt to the dynamic situations inherent to military operations. Mental agility keeps leaders from fixating on the wrong problems or getting stuck on poor solutions. Agility enables thinking when current decisions or actions are not producing the desired results and a new approach is necessary. Mental agility in leaders and followers provides organizations with the adaptability necessary for the disciplined initiative essential to mission command.

Mental agility relies upon curiosity and the ability to reason critically. Inquisitive or intellectually curious leaders are eager to understand a broad range of topics and keep an open mind to multiple possibilities before reaching decisions. Critical thinking is purposeful and helps find facts, challenge assumptions, solve problems, and make decisions. Critical thinking enables understanding of changing situations, arriving at justifiable conclusions, making judgments, and learning from experience. Critical and creative thinking provide the basis for understanding, visualizing, and describing complex, ill-structured problems and developing approaches to solve them. Critical thinking provides a basis for reflection and continual learning. Creative thinking involves thinking in innovative ways using imagination, insight, and novel ideas. Critical and innovative thought are abilities that enable adaptability.

Critical thinking examines a problem in depth from multiple points of view. The first and most important step in finding an appropriate solution is to isolate the main problem. A leader's mental agility to quickly isolate a problem and identify solutions facilitates seizing initiative and adapting effectively during operations when many things occur simultaneously and in close succession. Leaders must instill agility and initiative within subordinates by creating a climate that encourages risk taking within the commander's intent. Underwriting risk and accepting honest mistakes in training makes subordinates more likely to develop and take initiative.

B. Sound Judgment

Judgment requires the capacity to assess situations accurately, draw rational conclusions, and make decisions. Sound judgment enables leaders to make sensible decisions in a timely manner, a quality critical to building trust with subordinates and earning their confidence. Experience contributes to the development of sound judgment when it contributes to learning. Leaders acquire experience through trial and error and by observing others. Learning from others can occur through mentoring and coaching.

See chap. 4, Army Team Building, for further discussion of mentoring and coaching.

Often, leaders must balance facts, question assumptions, and sense intangible factors like morale or the enemy's intent. Judgment contributes to the ability to compare possible courses of action and decide what one to take. There are times, particularly in combat, where there are no good decisions, only the least bad decision possible in the moment. Sound judgment requires consideration of consequences. It also includes the ability to assess strengths and weaknesses of subordinates, peers, and the enemy. Like mental agility, sound judgment is a critical part of problem solving and decision making

C. Innovation

Innovation describes the ability to introduce or implement something new. Innovative problem solvers tend to be inquisitive, looking to understand why something is the way it is or questioning how something could work better. Being innovative requires creative thinking that uses both adaptive (drawing from expertise and prior knowledge) and innovative approaches (developing completely new ideas).

Innovative leaders prevent complacency by finding new ways to challenge subordinates with alternative approaches and ideas. They recognize that other people have good ideas and they recognize those who do. To be innovators, leaders rely on intuition, experience, knowledge, and input from subordinates, peers, and superiors. Innovative leaders reinforce team building by making everybody responsible for—and stakeholders in—innovation.

D. Interpersonal Tact

Effectively interacting with others is a skill that requires self-awareness. Interpersonal tact is a component of professional behavior. Interpersonal tact relies on understanding the character, reactions, and motives of oneself and others. It can be distilled down to the idea of honestly stating one's views about an idea or another person as diplomatically as possible to ensure it is understood without causing unnecessary offense. Tact should be balanced by professional candor, in terms of saying what needs to be said or done for the good of the mission or the unit. Leaders, who understand how subordinates, peers, and superiors view them, and clearly understand others, have a better idea how to communicate with tact. Candor and tact are important aspects of personal composure:

- **Recognizing Diversity.** Personal perspectives vary within every individual human being and societal groups. Understanding the different backgrounds, qualifications, experiences, and potential of each of the individuals in an organization is an important part of being an effective leader. It is fundamental to knowing your people and harnessing their diverse skills and perspectives to build cohesive teams. Good leaders create conditions where subordinates know they are valued for their individual talents, skills, and perspectives that contribute to mission accomplishment.

- **Composure.** Effective leaders control their emotions. Emotional self-control, balance, and stability enable leaders to make sound, ethical decisions. Leaders must remain calm under pressure and expend energy on things they can positively influence rather than those things they cannot affect. An Army leader's level of self-control greatly influences how they interact with others, particularly during periods of crisis when things are not going well. Leaders understand that emotional energy sparks motivation and endurance. Enthusiastic leaders, who are in control of their emotions, will be able to energize others to rise above difficult conditions.

E. Expertise

Expertise is in-depth knowledge and skill developed from experience, training, and education. Leaders use in-depth knowledge to focus on key aspects of a problem, make effective and ethical decisions, and achieve a high level of performance. Leaders have a moral obligation to those they lead to improve their expertise continuously. Leaders themselves should be open and eager to benefit from others' knowledge to enhance their own tactical and technical expertise. Military professionals require in-depth knowledge in a variety of areas:

- Tactical knowledge
- Technical knowledge
- Joint knowledge
- Cultural and geopolitical knowledge

II. Leader Competencies (Leads, Develops, Achieves)

Ref: ADP 6-22 (w/C1), Army Leadership and the Profession (Nov '19), part two.

Competency-based Leadership for Direct Through Strategic Levels

ADP 6-22 Part Two describes the core leader competencies and their application. Army leaders lead others; develop themselves, their subordinates, and organizations; and accomplish assigned and implied missions. The ten competencies of Army leadership apply across leadership levels as core requirements, while subtle changes occur in purpose and activity at each successive level.

Core Leader Competencies

The core leader competencies are actions that the Army expects leaders to do: lead, develop, and achieve. Competencies provide an enduring, clear, and consistent way of conveying expectations for Army leaders. The core competencies are universal for all Army leaders.

Leader Competencies

A. Leads	B. Develops	C. Achieves
• Leads others	• Prepares self	• Gets results
• Builds trust	• Creates a positive environment	
• Extends influence beyond the chain of command	• Develops others	
• Leads by example	• Stewards the profession	
• Communicates		

Competencies

The core competency categories are—

Leads *(See pp. 1-35 to 1-52.)*

Leads provides purpose, direction, and motivation; builds trust; provides an example; communicates.

Develops *(See pp. 1-53 to 1-68.)*

Develops themselves, creates a positive climate, develops subordinates, and stewards the profession.

Achieves *(See pp. 1-69 to 1-72.)*

Achieves executes, adjusts, and gets results to accomplish tasks and missions on time and to standard.

Core Leader Competencies (Overview)

Ref: ADP 6-22 (w/C1), Army Leadership and the Profession (Nov '19), p. 1-16.

The core leader competencies make up a core set. Figure 1-4 below depicts similarities and distinctions among core leader competencies, demonstrates how competencies fall into three categories and that each represents different leader actions. For instance, Army leaders are expected to develop themselves (prepares self), develop others, ensure unit readiness (create a positive environment) and sustain the Army as a whole (stewards the profession).

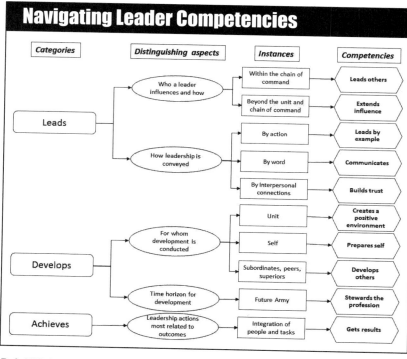

Ref: ADP 6-22 (w/C1), Figure 1-4. Navigating leader competencies.

The core competency categories are—

Leads *(See pp. 1-35 to 1-52.)*
Leads provides purpose, direction, and motivation; builds trust; provides an example; communicates.

Develops *(See pp. 1-53 to 1-68.)*
Develops themselves, creates a positive climate, develops subordinates, and stewards the profession.

Achieves *(See pp. 1-69 to 1-72.)*
Achieves executes, adjusts, and gets results to accomplish tasks and missions on time and to standard.

(Leader Competencies)
IIa. Leads

Ref: ADP 6-22 (w/C1), Army Leadership and the Profession (Nov '19), chap. 5.

Leads consists of five competencies. Leads others includes influencing members in the leader's organization. Influence is central to leadership. Extends influence beyond the chain of command involves influencing others when the leader does not have designated authority or when others may not recognize the leader's authority. Builds trust establishes conditions that lead to mutual confidence among leaders and subordinates. Leader actions and words comprise the competencies of leads by example and communicates. Actions can speak louder than words and leaders who embody standards as role models are generally more effective than those who simply talk about standards. Effective leaders clearly communicate what needs to be done and why.

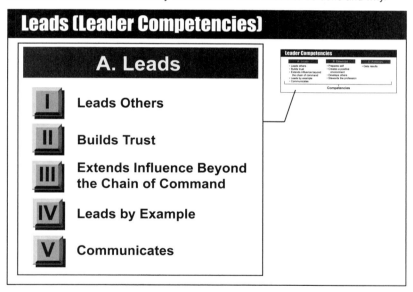

Leads (Leader Competencies)

A. Leads

I Leads Others

II Builds Trust

III Extends Influence Beyond the Chain of Command

IV Leads by Example

V Communicates

Ref: ADP 6-22 (w/C1), Army Leadership and the Profession (Nov '19), chap. 5.

I. Leads Others

Army leaders draw upon their character, presence, and intellect while leading others. Direct leaders influence others person-to-person, such as a team leader who instructs, encourages hard work, and recognizes achievement. Organizational and strategic leaders guide organizations directly through their subordinate leaders, using both direct and indirect means of influence. A company commander directly leads the platoon leaders, who in turn know what the battalion commander wants done, because the lieutenants understand the commander's intent two levels up. The battalion commander does not communicate to the platoon leaders directly, but rather depends upon the company commanders to lead their organizations according to the commander's intent. Intent links higher and lower echelons.

Leads - Summary of Competencies

Ref: ADP 6-22 (w/C1), Army Leadership and the Profession (Nov '19), tables 5-1 to 5-5.

I. Leads Others *(See pp. 1-35 to 1-42.)*

Leaders motivate, inspire, and influence others to take initiative, work toward a common purpose, accomplish critical tasks, and achieve organizational objectives. Influence focuses on compelling others to go beyond their individual interests and to work for the common good.

Uses appropriate methods of influence to motivate others	• Uses methods ranging from compliance to commitment • Applies influence methods to adapt to the followers at a given point in time under the conditions of the situation
Provides purpose, motivation and inspiration	• Inspires, encourages, and guides others toward mission accomplishment. • Emphasizes the importance of organizational goals. • Determines the course of action to reach objectives and fulfill mission requirements. • Communicates instructions, orders, and directives to followers. • Ensures subordinates understand and accept direction. • Empowers and delegates authority to subordinates. • Focuses on the most important aspects of a situation.
Enforces standards	• Reinforces the importance and role of standards. • Performs individual and collective tasks to standard. • Recognizes and takes responsibility for poor performance; addresses it appropriately.
Balances mission and welfare of followers	• Assesses and routinely monitors effects of mission fulfillment on mental, physical, and emotional attributes of subordinates. • Monitors morale, physical condition, and safety of subordinates. • Provides appropriate relief when conditions jeopardize success of the mission or present overwhelming risk to personnel.

II. Builds Trust *(See p. 1-43.)*

Leaders build trust to mediate relationships and encourage commitment among followers. Trust starts from respect among people and grows from common experiences and shared understanding. Leaders and followers share in building trust.

Sets personal example for trust	• Is firm, fair, and respectful to gain trust. • Assesses degree of own trustworthiness.
Takes direct actions to build trust	• Fosters positive relationship with others. • Identifies areas of commonality (understanding, goals, and experiences). • Engages other members in activities and objectives. • Corrects team members who undermine trust with their attitudes or actions.
Sustains a climate of trust	• Assesses factors or conditions that promote or hinder trust. • Keeps people informed of goals, actions, and results. • Follows through on actions related to expectations of others.

III. Extends Influence Beyond Chain of Command *(pp. 1-44 to 1-47)*

Leaders need to influence beyond their direct lines of authority and beyond chains of command to include unified action partners. In these situations, leaders use indirect means of influence: diplomacy, negotiation, mediation, arbitration, partnering, conflict resolution, consensus building, and coordination.

Understands sphere, means, and limits of influence	• Assesses situations, missions, and assignments to determine the parties involved in decision making, decision support, and possible interference or resistance.
Negotiates, builds consensus, and resolves conflict	• Builds effective working relationships. • Uses two-way, meaningful communication. • Identifies individual and group interests. • Identifies roles and resources. • Generates and facilitates generation of possible solutions. • Applies fair standards to assess options.

IV. Leads by Example *(See pp. 1-48 to 1-50.)*

Leaders serve as role models by maintaining standards and providing effective examples through their actions. All Army leaders should model the Army Values. Modeling provides tangible evidence of desired behaviors and reinforces verbal guidance through demonstration of commitment and action.

Displays character	• Sets the example by modeling expected standards of duty performance, personal appearance, military and professional bearing, physical fitness, and ethics. • Makes right decisions and takes right actions, consistent with the leader's intent and bounded by the Army Values. • Completes individual and unit tasks to standard, on time, and within the commander's intent. • Demonstrates determination, persistence, and patience. • Uses sound judgment and logical reasoning.
Exemplifies the Warrior Ethos	• Removes or fights through obstacles, difficulties, and hardships to accomplish the mission. • Demonstrates the commitment to persevere despite adversity, obstacles, and challenges. • Demonstrates physical and moral courage. • Shares hardships with subordinates.
Leads with confidence in adverse situations	• Provides leader presence at the right time and place. • Displays self-control, composure, and positive attitude. • Is resilient. • Remains decisive after discovering a mistake. • Acts in the absence of guidance. • Does not show discouragement when facing setbacks. • Remains positive when situations become confusing or change. • Encourages subordinates.
Demonstrates technical and tactical competence	• Performs duty with discipline and to standards, while striving for excellence. • Displays appropriate knowledge of equipment, procedures, and methods; recognizes and generates innovative solutions. • Uses knowledgeable sources and subject matter experts.
Understands the importance of conceptual skills and models them to others	• Displays comfort working in open systems. • Makes logical assumptions in the absence of facts. • Identifies critical issues to guide decision making and taking advantage of opportunities. • Relates and compares information from different sources to identify possible cause-and-effect relationships.
Seeks diverse ideas and points of view	• Encourages honest communications among staff and decision makers. • Explores alternative explanations and approaches for accompanying tasks. • Reinforces new ideas; demonstrates willingness to consider alternative perspectives to resolve difficult problems. • Discourages individuals from seeking favor through tacit agreement.

IV. Communicates *(See pp. 1-50 to 1-52.)*

Leaders communicate effectively by clearly expressing ideas and actively listening to others. By understanding the nature and importance of communication and practicing effective communication techniques, leaders will relate better to others and be able to translate goals into actions. Followers share information candidly. Communication is essential to all other leadership competencies.

Listens actively	• Listens and watches attentively. • Makes appropriate notes. • Tunes in to content, emotion, and urgency. • Uses verbal and nonverbal means to inform the speaker that they are paying attention. • Reflects on new information before expressing views.
Creates shared understanding	• Shares necessary information with others and subordinates. • Protects confidential information. • Coordinates plans with higher, lower, and adjacent organizations. • Keeps higher and lower headquarters, superiors, and subordinates informed. • Expresses thoughts and ideas clearly to individuals and groups. • Recognizes potential miscommunication and takes corrective action. • Uses appropriate means for communicating a message.
Employs engaging communication techniques	• States goals to energize others to adopt and act on them. • Uses logic and relevant facts in dialogue; expresses well-organized ideas. • Speaks enthusiastically and maintains listeners' interest and involvement. • Makes appropriate eye contact when speaking. • Uses appropriate gestures. • Uses visual aids as needed. • Determines, recognizes, and resolves misunderstandings.
Is sensitive to cultural factors in communication	• Maintains awareness of communication customs, expressions, actions, or behaviors. • Demonstrates respect for others.

All Army leaders are followers; each reports to someone higher in the chain of command, ultimately up to the Secretary of the Army who answers to the President. Leaders inspire and guide subordinates to follow; subordinates react to inspiration and follow guidance while performing their duties. Leaders assess and establish rapport with followers, and followers act in good conscience to follow guidance. Whether serving in the role of leader or subordinate, all are honor bound to perform their duties to the best of their abilities.

Context determines when a Soldier or DA Civilian is a leader or follower. A first sergeant receives guidance from the company commander as a follower and then as a leader translates that guidance to the platoon sergeants. As a leader, the first sergeant does not simply parrot the guidance received. The first sergeant translates the guidance into terms that are appropriate for the company NCOs in the context of other information received from the battalion command sergeant major and issues instructions that best meet the commander's intent. The activity of influencing others depends on the followers' knowledge, skills, and commitment level. The principles of mission command in ADP 6-0 inform the level of control leaders employ in a particular situation.

Effective leadership depends on the alignment of purpose, direction, and motivation among leaders and subordinates. Working with a shared understanding of the operational picture and higher intent generates the unity of purpose, unity of effort, and consistency essential to maintaining a positive leadership climate. Subordinates who see consistency will sense shared purpose and be less prone to distraction by confusing or conflicting guidance from different leaders. Those who align their decisions and activities with their peers, for example during garrison activities and training, may have greater influence than a leader who does not. This unifying aspect of leadership can—

- Ensure attitudes and actions up, down, and across units are aligned around a common vision.
- Enable mission command by delegating authority and control appropriate for the situation.
- Cultivate mutually beneficial relationships with others inside and outside the organization.
- Draw on sources of expertise across a unit.

Leading others requires that leaders influence others to conduct tasks, make decisions, and perform their duty in ways consistent with Army standards. It is the duty of leaders to motivate others to accomplish missions in accordance with the Army Values. Leaders influence others to perform their duties in service of a higher purpose, not personal gain or advantage. Army leaders can draw on a variety of methods to influence others and can use one or more methods to fit to the specific context of any situation. Some tasks only require subordinate compliance for success, such as meeting the requirement for flu shots. Others require building a high level of commitment on the behalf of subordinates to achieve success, such as a platoon seizing a heavily fortified enemy position. Compliance is the act of conforming to a requirement or demand. Commitment is willing dedication or allegiance to a cause or organization. Active opposition to influence denotes resistance.

A. Using Compliance and Commitment

Successful leadership depends upon both the compliance and commitment of those being led. Neither succeeds on its own in most situations; rather, there is a blend of compliance and commitment amongst subordinates in each situation. The best leaders generate a sense of commitment that causes subordinates to go beyond achieving the bare minimum. Compliance to legal and ethical orders, directives, and instructions is always required. Willing and eager agreement is commitment.

Leads Others
(Summary of the Competency)

Ref: ADP 6-22 (w/C1), Army Leadership and the Profession (Nov '19), table 5-1, p. 5-8.

Leaders motivate, inspire, and influence others to take initiative, work toward a common purpose, accomplish critical tasks, and achieve organizational objectives. Influence focuses on compelling others to go beyond their individual interests and to work for the common good.

Uses appropriate methods of influence to motivate others

- Uses methods ranging from **compliance to commitment**
- Applies influence methods to adapt to the followers at a given point in time under the conditions of the situation

Provides purpose, motivation, and inspiration

- Inspires, encourages, and guides others toward mission accomplishment
- Emphasizes the importance of organizational goals
- Determines the course of action necessary to reach objectives and fulfill mission requirements
- Communicates instructions, orders, and directives to subordinates
- Ensures subordinates understand and accept direction
- Empowers and delegates authority to subordinates
- Focuses on the most important aspects of a situation

Enforces standards

- Reinforces the importance and role of standards
- Performs individual and collective tasks to standard
- Recognizes and takes responsibility for poor performance and addresses it appropriately

Balances mission and welfare of followers

- Assesses and routinely monitors effects of mission fulfillment on mental, physical, and emotional attributes of subordinates
- Monitors morale, physical condition, and safety of subordinates
- Provides appropriate relief when conditions jeopardize success of the mission or present overwhelming risk to personnel

See also p. 1-36.

Whereas compliance only affects a follower's behavior, commitment reaches deeper—changing attitudes, beliefs, and behavior. Commitment generally produces longer lasting and broader effects that result in subordinates being willing to expend more effort of their own accord, or even put themselves at personal risk, to accomplish the tasks at hand. Once a leader builds commitment among followers, they will likely demonstrate more initiative, personal involvement, and creativity. Commitment grows from an individual's desire to contribute to the organization. Leaders can strengthen commitment by reinforcing followers' identification with the Nation (loyalty), the Army (professionalism), the unit or organization (esprit de corps), the leadership in a unit (respect), and to the mission (duty).

B. Providing Purpose, Direction, and Motivation

Leaders influence others to achieve some purpose. To be successful at exerting influence, Army leaders have an end or goal in mind. Sometimes the goal will be specific, and at other times, goals are more general, but in both cases, the goal should be valid and meaningful. Leaders should clearly define the 'what' and 'why'. Subordinates should be able to start the mission or task with the end in mind by knowing what success looks like and how they can track their own progress. Motivation increases when subordinates understand how their roles relate to larger and more important outcomes.

Leaders must establish clear understanding of the higher commander's intent to ensure the team understands what must be done and why. Commander's intent is a concise expression of the purpose of an operation and the desired end state. Leaders communicate purpose with implied or explicit instructions so others may exercise initiative. This is important for situations when unanticipated opportunities arise or the original assigned tasks no longer achieve the desired end state.

Besides purpose, leaders provide direction. Direction deals with how to achieve a goal, task, or mission. Subordinates do not always need to receive guidance on the details of execution. A skilled leader will know when to provide detailed guidance or promote subordinate initiative by focusing primarily on purpose.

Motivation is linked to the reason and level of enthusiasm for doing something. Army leaders use the knowledge of what motivates others to influence those they lead. Understanding how motivation works provides insight into why people may take action and how strongly they are driven to act.

Setting achievable goals can shape motivation. Leaders can break larger missions into smaller tasks to keep individuals engaged without being overwhelmed by the scale or scope of what needs to be done. Subordinates require the necessary skills and abilities to perform the tasks they are assigned, have reason to be committed to the goal, and receive feedback to gauge progress. Task assignment and goal setting account for the capabilities and limitations of those performing the tasks a leader directs. Finally, framing performance goals positively produces better persistence and performance than negative framing.

Leaders can encourage subordinates to set goals of their own while setting goals for them in terms of duty performance during counseling and coaching. When subordinates accept goals, they are better able to prioritize, focus their attention, and gauge the amount of effort necessary to achieve them.

Leaders assign responsibility, delegate authority, and allocate resources. Leaders empower subordinates by giving them the necessary resources, authority, and clear intent for success. Subordinates should dutifully accept assigned responsibility, take initiative and accept risk within the limits of their authority, and make disciplined use of the resources entrusted to their care. People value opportunities to be responsible for their own work, be creative, and be respected for their abilities. Leaders apply judgment about when to step aside to let subordinates accomplish a mission. Leaders continually develop subordinates so they are ready to accept ever increasing delegated responsibilities. Empowering others is a forceful statement of trust and one of the best ways of developing subordinates as leaders.

Methods of Influence

Ref: ADP 6-22 (w/C1), Army Leadership and the Profession (Nov '19), pp. 5-3 to 5-5.

Influence is the essential activity of leadership and refers to how people affect the intentions, attitudes, and actions of another person or group of people. Influence depends upon the relationship that develops between leaders and others. Positive rapport and a sense of mutual trust make subordinates more likely to respond positively to a leader's influence. Leaders indirectly influence others by demonstrating integrity, empathy, judgment, expertise, and commitment. Army leaders employ various methods of direct influence based on audience, intent, and context of the situation.

ADP 6-22 discusses nine methods representing different ways to influence: pressure, legitimating, exchange, personal appeals, collaboration, rational persuasion, apprising, inspirational appeals, and participation.

Application of Influence

Creating commitment among subordinates requires that they know their leaders are sincere. Committed subordinates trust their leaders to be doing what is right for the Army, the mission, the team, and each individual Soldier. Leaders who primarily focus on personal gain or recognition are seen by subordinates as self-serving, which undermines trust and erodes motivation. Honorable intentions wrongly perceived by followers as self-serving will yield mere compliance.

The nature of the mission determines which influence method or combination of methods is appropriate. When a situation is urgent and greater risk is involved, eliciting follower compliance through more directive methods may be desirable. Direct-level leaders are often required to coordinate team activities in an expedient manner, meaning that they focus on explaining themselves before or after the activities, and not during execution. In comparison, organizational leaders typically use methods that draw out strong commitment from their subordinate leaders. The degree to which a leader uses commitment or compliance depends on the leader, the led, and the situation. When influencing others, Army leaders understand—

- The reasons for influence should align with the Army Values, the Uniform Code of Military Justice, the Soldier's Creed, and the Army Civilian Corps Creed.
- Commitment emphasizes empowerment and long-lasting trust.
- Compliance focuses on quickly meeting task demands.

Resistance

When leaders experience resistance, the first response is to understand the nature of the relationship and reasons for opposition or non-compliance. Resistance may stem from a lack of trust, lack of understanding, or concerns about well-being. Leaders may need to clarify misperceptions or correct false beliefs. Unfounded rumors can hurt unit cohesiveness and create friction if not confronted at their source. Gossip and rumors reduce focus while increasing the amount of energy leaders must spend on activities other than the mission at hand.

Leaders need to ensure all parties focus on a shared understanding. Overt acknowledgement of resistance can be the first step in reducing it. Leaders should confront resistance quickly to determine the reasons why it exists and how to address the causes constructively. This may be enough to change negative mindsets and build or restore mutual trust within the organization. Leaders can lessen resistance by acknowledging concerns with their own position or requests. This demonstrates that the leaders recognize both the positives and negatives of a given request and that they are approaching the issue even-handedly and fairly.

C. Upholding Standards

Standards provide a mark for performance to assess execution of tasks, as well as compliance with established policy and law. Standards are formal, detailed instructions—observable, measurable, and achievable. Standards and discipline are the point of departure for leading Army organizations. Leaders must enforce Army standards, establish appropriate standards congruent with the Army Ethic where no standards currently exist, and ensure that subordinates understand and adhere to the standards.

When upholding standards, leaders must be sensitive to the reality that not everything can be a number one priority. In practice, leaders establish priorities because it is impossible to accomplish everything at once. A leader's ultimate goal is to train to the standards that ensure mission success; all other matters that consume significant time are of secondary importance. To be successful, leaders use the Army training management process to prepare the organization to meet standards by setting appropriate training goals and to plan, resource, execute, and evaluate training accordingly.

- **Performing Checks and Inspections**. Thorough inspections ensure equipment is mission capable and subordinates are prepared to perform their assigned duties. Mission specific checks and inspections minimize the chances of neglect or oversight that result in mission failure or needless casualties. Inspections give leaders a chance to recognize subordinates preparedness or make on-the-spot corrections.

- **Instilling Discipline**. Leaders who consistently enforce standards instill discipline that will payoff in critical situations. True discipline demands habitual and reasoned obedience. An effective leader instills discipline by training to standard, using rewards and corrective actions judiciously, instilling confidence, building trust among team members, and ensuring they have the necessary technical and tactical expertise to perform their job.

D. Balancing Mission And Welfare

Having genuine concern for subordinate health and welfare generates motivation, inspiration, and influence—it is the right thing for leaders to do. Army members will be more willing to go the extra mile for leaders whom they respect, and they are more likely to respect leaders who respect them. Sending Soldiers or DA Civilians into harm's way to accomplish missions is always in tension with the desire to take care of people. Leaders display genuine concern by preparing subordinates through tough realistic training that prepares them for the hazards and dangers of combat.

- **Taking Care of Subordinates**. Taking care of subordinates is a solemn responsibility. The Army's purpose demands individuals perform their duties even at risk to their lives. Preparing subordinates for combat is the most important leader duty. Preparation entails creating disciplined conditions for learning and growth and enforcing standards in training. Training must be rigorous and simulate mission conditions as much as possible while keeping safety in mind.

- **Identifying High Risk Behavior**. Leaders identify subordinates who exhibit high-risk behavior and take action to reduce it whenever possible. High-risk behavior is a behavioral pattern that intentionally or unintentionally increases an individual's probability of negative consequences. The Army regulates order and discipline through enforcement of statutes (such as the Uniform Code of Military Justice) and policy. Misconduct represents a conscious decision to accept both the risk associated with a prohibited activity and the risk of being caught while violating the standard.

A commander's primary responsibility is to ensure the readiness, health, morale, welfare, and discipline of the unit. Every leader and follower has a role in supporting that responsibility. Leaders must identify at-risk subordinates and intervene to help them.

II. Builds Trust

Ref: ADP 6-22 (w/C1), Army Leadership and the Profession (Nov '19), pp. 5-8 to 5-9.

Trust enables the ability of leaders to influence subordinates and effective command and control. Trust encompasses reliance upon others, confidence in their abilities, and consistency in behavior. People naturally accept the influence of people they trust. When high levels of trust exist among members of an organization, its members are more likely to influence each other up and down the chain of command and laterally with other organizations. Trust increases readiness and is essential for developing the shared understanding of intent that facilitates initiative by everyone within the organization. Trust builds over time through mutual respect, shared understanding, and common experiences. Communication contributes to trust by keeping others informed, establishing expectations, providing feedback, and developing commitment. Sustaining trust depends on meeting expectations and commitments. Leaders and subordinates all contribute to the level of trust that occurs in a unit. Leaders and subordinates earn or lose trust through everyday actions and attitudes.

Importantly, leaders should promote a culture and climate of trust. Teams develop trust through cooperation, identification with other members, and contribution to the team effort. Leaders build trust with their followers and those outside the organization by practicing the leadership competencies and demonstrating character, presence, and intellect. Leaders need to be competent, of good character, and fair and reliable to generate trust.

Leaders who commit to coaching, counseling, and mentoring subordinates build relationships that foster trust. These relationships built on trust enable leaders to empower subordinates, encourage initiative, reinforce accountability, and allow for open communication. Further, these relationships establish predictability and cohesion within the team.

Failure to cultivate a climate of trust or a willingness to tolerate discrimination or harassment on any basis erodes unit cohesion and breaks the trust subordinates have for their leaders.

Builds Trust (Summary of Competency)

Leaders build trust to mediate relationships and encourage commitment among followers. Trust starts from respect among people and grows from common experiences and shared understanding. Leaders and followers share in building trust.

A. Sets personal example for trust
- Is firm, fair, and respectful to gain trust
- Assesses degree of own trustworthiness

B. Takes direct actions to build trust
- Fosters positive relationship with others
- Identifies areas of commonality (understanding, goals, and experiences)
- Engages other members in activities and objectives
- Corrects team members who undermine trust with their attitudes or actions

C. Sustains a climate of trust
- Assesses factors or conditions that promote or hinder trust
- Keeps people informed of goals, actions, and results
- Follows through on actions related to expectations of others

Ref: ADP 6-22 (w/C1), Table 5-2, p. 5-9. See also p. 1-36.

III. Extends Influence Beyond the Chain of Command

Extending influence beyond the chain of command is an essential leader competency. While Army leaders exert influence within their established chains of command, leaders must also be capable of extending influence to others beyond the chain of command. Extending influence beyond the chain of command is critical to achieving success in unified action. Extending influence requires special awareness about how influence works in different groups and different situations.

Extends Influence Beyond Chain of Command

 Building Trust Outside Lines of Authority

 Understanding Sphere, Means, and Limits of Influence

 Negotiating, Building Consensus and Resolving Conflicts

Ref: ADP 6-22 (w/C1), Army Leadership & the Profession (Nov '19), pp. 5-9 to 5-11.

The key element of extending influence and building teams is creating a shared purpose among prospective team members. A unique aspect of extending influence is that those who a leader wishes to influence outside the unit may not recognize or willingly accept the authority of an Army leader. Often, informal teams develop in situations where no official chains of authority exist. In some cases, this may require leaders to establish their credentials and capability for leading others. Credibility of a person or organization may stem from their appearance, conduct, or reputation. The ways Soldiers act and treat others outside the organization contribute to how others perceive the organization and the credibility of its leaders. Leaders ensure subordinates do not diminish the organization's credibility or esteem with external observers.

When extending influence beyond the traditional chain of command, leaders often have to influence without authority designated or implied by rank and position. Civilian and military leaders often find themselves in situations where they must task organize teams to accomplish missions. Leaders, especially commanders, engage and communicate via multiple means (face-to-face, print media, broadcast media, social media, and other emerging collaboration technologies) to influence the perceptions, attitudes, sentiments, and behaviors of key actors and agencies. Leaders should personally engage key players to ensure audiences receive messages as intended.

Leading without formal authority requires adaptation to the conditions and cultural sensitivities of a given situation. Leaders require cultural knowledge to understand different social customs and belief systems and to address issues in those contexts. When conducting operations, for example, small-unit leaders must understand that their interaction with the local populace and their leaders can have dramatic effects on strategic objectives. The manner in which a unit conducts house-to-house

Extends Influence Beyond the Chain of Cmd (Summary of the Competency)

Ref: ADP 6-22 (w/C1), Army Leadership and the Profession (Nov '19), table 5-3, p. 5-11.

Leaders need to influence beyond their direct lines of authority and beyond chains of command to include unified action partners. In these situations, leaders use indirect means of influence: diplomacy, negotiation, mediation, arbitration, partnering, conflict resolution, consensus building, and coordination.

Understand sphere, means and limits of influence

- Assesses situations, missions, and assignments to determine the parties involved in decision making, decision support, and possible interference or resistance

Negotiates, builds consensus, and resolves conflicts

- Builds effective working relationships.
- Uses two-way, meaningful communication.
- Identifies individual and group interests.
- Identifies roles and resources.
- Generates and facilitates generation of possible solutions.
- Applies fair standards to assess options.

See also p. 1-36.

searches for enemy combatants can influence the local population's acceptance of authority or become a recruiting incentive for the enemy

A. Building Trust Outside Lines of Authority

Forming effective, cohesive teams is often a leader's first challenge working outside a traditional command structure. These teams may form from disparate groups unfamiliar with military customs and culture. Successful teams develop an infectious winner's attitude. Problems are challenges rather than obstacles. Cohesive teams accomplish missions more efficiently than a loose group of individuals.

Building coalitions is similar to building teams, but groups maintain generally greater independence in coalitions. Trust is a common ingredient in effective coalitions. Coalitions evolve by establishing contact with others, building relationships, and identifying common interests. An effective strategy for breaking down the barriers among smaller, subordinate group identities is to build or strengthen a common group identity for all members, such as highlighting the common cause shared by all coalition partners.

Training and working together builds collective competence, mutual trust, and promotes interoperability. Mutual trust ultimately permeates the entire organization, embracing every member.

B. Understanding Sphere, Means, and Limits of Influence

When operating within an established command structure and common procedures, the provisions and limits of roles and responsibilities are readily apparent. When leading outside an established organization, assessing the parties involved becomes another part of the operation. Identifying who is who, what role they have, over whom they have authority or influence, and how they are likely to respond to the Army leader's influence are important considerations. Sometimes this is viewed as understanding the limits to the Army's or the leader's influence.

Spanning the boundaries of disparate groups or organizations requires special attention. A key to extending influence outside the chain of command is learning about those organizations. By understanding their interests and desires, the leader will know what methods of influence are most likely to work.

C. Negotiating, Building Consensus, and Resolving Conflicts

Leaders must often resolve conflicts. One method is negotiation. Negotiation is a problem-solving process in which two or more parties discuss and seek to satisfy their interests on various issues through joint decisions. The desired end state of the negotiation process is creation of a suitable choice between a clear, realistic, and satisfactory commitment and a reasonable alternative to a negotiated agreement that better meets the leader's interests. Interests relate to each party's needs, fears, concerns, goals, and motivations. Parties' interests may be shared, different, or in conflict. Effective leaders negotiate around interests rather than positions that tend to be static and unyielding.

Leaders often must use negotiation skills to obtain the cooperation and support necessary to accomplish a mission beyond the traditional chain of command. During complex operations, different unified action partners might operate under constraints of their national or organizational chains. This can result in important negotiations and conflict resolution versus a simpler process of issuing binding orders.

See facing page (p. 1-47) for further discussion of negotiation.

Negotiation

Ref: ADP 6-22 (w/C1), Army Leadership and the Profession (Nov '19), pp. 6-9 to 6-10.

Successful negotiation, employing a joint problem-solving approach, involves building effective relationships, establishing two-way communication, understanding positions to clarify interests, creating possible solutions, using fair standards, and creating a sensible choice from firm, clear commitments, and realistic alternatives. Credible negotiators test their assumptions, measure success appropriately for a given situation, systematically prepare, make deliberate process-oriented decisions in conducting negotiations, and thoroughly review interactions.

Not all partnerships are enduring. Some are intended only for a limited time. Others are expected to last until a specific end state has been achieved. Leaders look ahead, anticipating future scenarios and the conditions under which a partnership will or should dissolve. They help define roles and responsibilities for elements of a post-alliance state to ensure a smooth transition process and set conditions so the desired end state persists after the partnership has ended.

Successful negotiations involve several activities. Leaders should—

- Understand and be willing to challenge assumptions about all parties involved, the desired outcome, the situation, and the negotiation itself.
- Consider the measures of success for negotiation and choose the correct one for the situation.
- Prepare thoroughly in a manner that supports the desired outcome and process for negotiation.
- Build effective working relationships based on genuine rapport, respect, and reputation. Separate relationship issues from substantive issues and address both on their own merits.
- Use meaningful communication among involved parties to inquire, acknowledge, and advocate by demonstrating active listening and understanding while shaping perceptions and emotions of all parties.
- Generate many options or creative solutions that meet the interests of all parties as well as possible. Creating options should be separate from evaluating and deciding.
- Use objective, balanced, and fair criteria, standards, and merit to evaluate options. Apply a reciprocity test: would one party find this aspect fair if they proposed it?
- Determine alternatives to a negotiated agreement. Alternatives are ways that each party can meet their interests without creating an agreement in the current negotiation. What is the best alternative to a negotiated agreement for each party?
- Commit to an agreement only if it is better than alternatives, is the best option, and meets interests based on fair criteria. A commitment should be clearly defined, well planned, and reasonable to implement. Leaders must not promise what they cannot or will not deliver just to reach an agreement.
- Review each negotiation systematically and use lessons to learn from one interaction to the next.

Refer to TAA2: Military Engagement, Security Cooperation & Stability SMARTbook (Foreign Train, Advise, & Assist) for further discussion. Topics include the Range of Military Operations (JP 3-0), Security Cooperation & Security Assistance (Train, Advise, & Assist), Stability Operations (ADRP 3-07), Peace Operations (JP 3-07.3), Counterinsurgency Operations (JP & FM 3-24), Civil-Military Operations (JP 3-57), Multinational Operations (JP 3-16), Interorganizational Coordination (JP 3-08), and more.

IV. Leads By Example

Leads By Example

 Displaying Character

 Demonstrating Competence

Ref: ADP 6-22 (w/C1), Army Leadership &the Profession (Nov '19), pp. 5-12 to 5-14

A. Displaying Character

Leaders are a product of their experiences. What leaders see others do forms their expectations for decisions and actions. Leaders who intentionally live by the Army Values and the Warrior Ethos will consistently display the character and actions that set a positive example. They put the organization and subordinates above personal self-interest, career, and comfort. For the Army leader, it requires putting the lives of others above a personal desire for self-preservation.

Leading with Confidence in Adverse Conditions

A leader who projects confidence is an inspiration to others. Subordinates will follow leaders who are competent and comfortable with their own abilities. Leaders who understand their own abilities can gain greater respect from their subordinates for their honesty, even as they seek to improve.

Displaying confidence and composure when situations are not going well can be a challenge for anyone, but is important for the leader trying to lead others through challenging, stressful, and ambiguous situations. Calm determination reflects confidence and is a key component of leader presence. A leader who shows hesitation or panic in the face of setbacks can trigger a chain reaction among others. A leader who is over-confident in difficult situations may lack the proper degree of care or concern, and risks being viewed as not understanding the seriousness of the problems at hand.

Leading with confidence requires a heightened self-awareness and ability to master one's emotions. Regardless of the situation, developing the ability to remain confident involves—

- Having prior opportunities to experience one's reactions to adverse, high-pressure situations.
- Maintaining a positive outlook when a situation becomes confusing or changes.
- Remaining decisive after making or realizing mistakes.
- Encouraging others when they show signs of weakness.

Displaying Courage

Projecting confidence in combat and other dangerous situations requires physical and moral courage. While physical courage allows Soldiers to face mortal risks to life and limb, moral courage empowers leaders to stand firm on values, principles, and convictions. Leaders who take responsibility for their decisions and actions display moral courage. Morally courageous leaders critically look at themselves, consider new ideas, and implement change when needed.

Moral courage in daily operations is as important as physical courage in combat. Consider a DA Civilian test board director who has the responsibility to determine

Leads by Example
(Summary of the Competency) See also p. 1-37.

Ref: ADP 6-22 (w/C1), Army Leadership and the Profession (Nov '19), table 5-4, p. 5-14.

Leaders serve as role models. They maintain standards and provide effective examples through their actions. All Army leaders should model the Army Values.

Displays character
- Sets the example by displaying high standards of duty performance, personal appearance, military and professional bearing, physical fitness and ethics
- Fosters an ethical climate; shows good moral judgment and behavior
- Completes individual and unit tasks to standard, on time, & within the cdr's intent
- Demonstrates determination, persistence, and patience
- Uses sound judgment and logical reasoning

Exemplifies the Warrior Ethos
- Removes or fights through obstacles, difficulties, & hardships to accomplish mission
- Demonstrates the will to succeed
- Demonstrates physical and emotional courage
- Shares hardships with subordinates

Leads with confidence in adverse situations
- Provides leader presence at the right time and place
- Displays self-control, composure, and positive attitude
- Is resilient
- Remains decisive after discovering a mistake
- Acts in the absence of guidance
- Does not show discouragement when facing setbacks
- Remains positive when the situation becomes confusing or change
- Encourages subordinates

Demonstrates technical and tactical competence
- Performs duty with discipline and to standards, while striving for excellence
- Displays appropriate knowledge of equipment, procedures and methods; recognizes and generates innovative solutions
- Uses knowledgeable sources and subject matter experts

Understands the importance of conceptual skills and models them to others
- Displays comfort working in open systems
- Makes logical assumptions in the absence of facts
- Identifies critical issues to use as a guide in making decisions
- Relates and compares information from different sources to identify possible cause-and-effect relationships.

Seeks diverse ideas and points of view
- Encourages honest communications among staff and decision makers
- Explores alternative explanations and approaches for accompanying tasks
- Reinforces new ideas; demonstrates willingness to consider alternative perspectives to resolve difficult problems
- Discourages individuals from seeking favor through tacit agreement

whether a new piece of military equipment performs to established specifications. Knowing that a failed test may cause the possibility of personal pressure and command resistance from the program management office, a morally courageous tester will be prepared to endure that pressure and remain objective and fair in test procedures and conclusions. Moral courage is fundamental to living the Army Values of integrity and honor, for all civilian or military members

B. Demonstrating Competence

Having the appropriate levels of expertise is vital to competent leaders who display confidence through their attitudes, actions, and words. Subordinates become suspicious of leaders who act confident but do not demonstrate the competence to justify their confidence.

V. Communicates

Competent leadership requires good communication. Communication as a competency ensures more than the simple transmission of information. Communication generates shared understanding and situational awareness. Succinctly communicating information in a clear manner is an important skill for both leaders and subordinates to learn. Leaders cannot lead, supervise, counsel, coach, mentor, or build teams without communication.

Communicates

 Listening Actively

 Create Shared Understanding

Ref: ADP 6-22 (w/C1), Army Leadership & the Profession (Nov '19), pp. 5-14 to 5-16.

A. Listening Actively

An important part of effective two-way communication is active listening. Although the most important purpose of listening is to comprehend the sender's message, listeners should provide an occasional indication to the speaker that they are attentive, such as a head nod when face-to-face or stating "roger" when using radio or telephonic communication. Active listening involves avoiding interruption and keeping mental or written notes (when possible) of important points or items for clarification. Good listeners will understand the message being sent in terms of its content, urgency, and the emotion with which it is communicated.

Leaders should remain aware of barriers to listening that prevent hearing and absorbing what speakers say. Avoid formulating a response before hearing what the person says. Avoid distraction by anger, disagreement with the speaker, or other things that impede focusing on the message itself.

B. Create Shared Understanding

Competent leaders know themselves, the mission, and the message. They owe their organizations and subordinates information that directly applies to their duties, providing context, and purpose. Sharing information contributes to shared understanding. Additionally, sharing information prepares subordinates for future duties and greater responsibility.

Communicates
(Summary of the Competency)
Ref: ADP 6-22 (w/C1), Army Leadership and the Profession (Nov '19), table 5-5, p. 5-16.

Leaders communicate effectively by clearly expressing ideas and actively listening to others. By understanding the nature and importance of communication and practicing effective communication techniques, leaders will relate better to others and be able to translate goals into actions. Communication is essential to all other leadership competencies. A leader:

Listens actively
- Listens and watches attentively
- Makes appropriate notes
- Tunes in to content, emotion, and urgency
- Uses verbal and nonverbal means to reinforce with the speaker that you are paying attention
- Reflects on new information before expressing views

Creates shared understanding
- Shares necessary information with others and subordinates
- Protects confidential information
- Coordinates plans with higher, lower and adjacent organizations
- Keeps higher and lower headquarters, superiors, and subordinates informed
- Expresses thoughts and ideas clearly to individuals and groups
- Recognizes potential miscommunication
- Uses appropriate means for communicating a message

Employs engaging communication techniques
- States goals to energize others to adopt and act on them
- Uses logic and relevant facts in dialogue; expresses well-organized ideas
- Speaks enthusiastically and maintains listeners' interest and involvement
- Makes appropriate eye contact when speaking
- Uses appropriate gestures
- Uses visual aids as needed
- Determines, recognizes, and resolves misunderstandings

Is sensitive to cultural factors in communication
- Maintains awareness of communication customs, expressions, actions, or behaviors
- Demonstrates respect for others

See also p. 1-37.

When leaders keep their organizations informed, they build trust. Shared information contributes to reduced stress and controls rumors. Timely information exchange allows team members to determine requirements and adjust to changing circumstances. Informing subordinates of a decision and the supporting reasons shows respect and conveys the need for their support and input. Good information flow ensures the next leader in the chain is sufficiently prepared to take over, if required.

Leaders use a variety of means to share information: face-to-face talks, written and verbal orders, running estimates and plans, published memos, white board sketches, briefings, email, websites, social media, and newsletters. To create shared understanding, a leader must acknowledge two critical factors:

- A leader is responsible for making sure the team understands what is communicated.
- A leader must consider informing elements outside the formal chain of command.

Any means other than face-to-face communication present some risk for misunderstanding due to the lack of verbal and non-verbal cues. Building rapport and trust is an ongoing, long-term effort that occurs during unit formation, individual unit reception, day-to-day garrison operations, and training exercises. It continues during operational missions. Learning what key leaders and staff mean when they say or write something is key to creating a basis for shared understanding. Taking adequate time to communicate when forming relationships is important to setting the right conditions, as are brief backs to confirm intent. Speaking candidly and asking for clarification when necessary are important steps in creating shared understanding. Email, websites, and social media have increased the volume and speed of available information. However, they minimize verbal cues and lack the non-verbal cues that are vital to clear communications and shared understanding between people. Leaders need to guard against over-reliance upon electronic means to communicate with each other and with subordinates. Leaders should use face-to-face communications with subordinates as much as possible to ensure understanding and to observe the feedback cues given by listeners.

Communication also flows from bottom to top. Leaders find out what their people are thinking, saying, and doing by listening. Effective leaders observe their organizations by circulating among their followers to coach, listen, and clarify. They pass relevant observations to enable planning and decision-making.

To lead an organization effectively, leaders must determine how to reach their superiors when necessary and to build relationships of mutual trust upward. Leaders assess how their direct leader communicates and prefers to receive information. Some use direct and personal contact while others may be more comfortable with weekly meetings, email, or memoranda. Knowing the leader's intent, priorities, and thought processes improves the likelihood of effective communication. A leader who communicates well minimizes friction and improves the overall organizational climate.

To prepare organizations for inevitable communication challenges, leaders may create situations that train subordinates to act with minimal guidance or only the commander's intent. Leaders provide formal or informal feedback to highlight things subordinates did well, what they could have done better, and what they should do differently next time to improve information sharing and processing.

Open communication does more than share information. It shows leaders care about those they work with on a daily basis. Competent and confident leaders encourage open dialogue, listen actively to all perspectives, and ensure others can voice honest opinions without fearing negative consequences.

Chap 1

(Leader Competencies)
IIb. Develops

Ref: ADP 6-22 (w/C1), Army Leadership and the Profession (Nov '19), chap. 6.

Military leadership is unique because the armed forces develop and select their own leaders. The responsibilities of Army members change as they assume new leadership positions. To ensure the quality of our leaders and future leaders does not diminish, all Army Soldiers and DA civilians have a responsibility to develop themselves and their subordinates. In Army leadership, there are four competencies in the category of develops that leaders consider while preparing themselves and their subordinates. A leader—

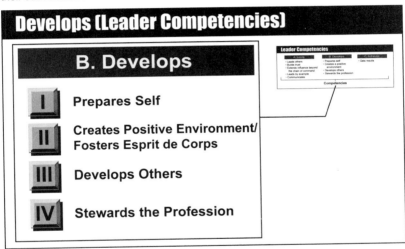

Develops (Leader Competencies)

B. Develops

I Prepares Self

II Creates Positive Environment/ Fosters Esprit de Corps

III Develops Others

IV Stewards the Profession

Ref: ADP 6-22 (w/C1), Army Leadership and the Profession (Nov '19), chap. 6.

Leaders develop their own leadership proficiency through deliberate study, feedback, and practice. Fundamentally, leadership develops when an individual desires to improve and invests effort, their superior supports development, and the organizational climate values learning. Learning to be a leader requires knowledge of leadership, experience using this knowledge, and feedback from one's seniors, peers, and subordinates. It also requires opportunities to practice leading others as often as possible. Formal systems such as evaluation reports, academic evaluation reports, and 360 assessments offer learning opportunities, but the individual must embrace the opportunity and internalize the information. The fastest learning occurs when multiple challenging and interesting opportunities to practice leadership with meaningful and honest feedback are present. These elements contribute to self-development, developing others, and setting a climate conducive to learning.

Leader development of others involves recruiting, accessing, developing, assigning, promoting, and retaining the leaders with the potential for levels of greater responsibility. Leaders develop subordinates when they prepare and then challenge them with greater responsibility, authority, and accountability. It is the individual professional responsibility of all leaders to develop their subordinates as leaders.

Successful leader development is based on five tenets:

- Strong commitment by the Army, superiors, and individuals to leader development.
- Clear purpose for what, when, and how to develop leadership.
- Supportive relationships and culture of learning.
- Three mutually supportive domains (institutional, operational, and self-development) that enable education, training, and experience.
- Providing, accepting, and acting upon candid assessment and feedback.

See chap. 2, Leader Development, for further discussion from FM 6-22.

Committed leaders continuously improve their organization, leaving it better than they found it. They expect other leaders to do the same. Leaders look ahead and prepare subordinates with potential to assume positions with greater leadership responsibility; in turn, subordinates develop themselves to prepare for future leadership assignments. Leaders ensure subordinates know that those who are best prepared for increased responsibility are those they are most likely to select for higher leadership positions.

Army leaders set priorities and weigh competing demands to balance individual and unit goals over various timeframes. They carefully steer their organizations' efforts to develop toward both short-and long-term goals, while continuing to meet immediate requirements. Competing demands that vie for an organization's resources complicate a leader's work. Guidance from higher headquarters may help, but leaders have to make the tough calls to maintain a healthy balance.

I. Prepares Self

Leader preparation begins with self-awareness about one's strengths and limitations, followed by focused self-development. Leaders maintain self-discipline, physical fitness, and mental well-being. They continue to improve their technical, tactical, and leadership expertise. Acquiring the necessary leadership skills to be successful is challenging and critical. In no other profession is the cost of being unprepared to lead so unforgiving in terms of mission failure and loss of life.

Prepares Self

A — **Being Prepared for Expected and Unexpected Challenges**

B — **Expanding Knowledge**

C — **Developing Self-Awareness**

Ref: ADP 6-22 (w/C1), Army Leadership and the Profession (Nov '19), pp. 6-2 to 6-4.

Self-development is continuous and begins with the motivated individual, supplemented by a concerted team effort. Part of that team effort is quality feedback from multiple sources, including peers, subordinates, and superiors to establish self-development goals and self-improvement courses of action. These improve performance by enhancing previously acquired skills, knowledge, behaviors, and experience. Mentorship can focus self-development efforts to achieve professional objectives.

Prepares Self
(Summary of the Competency)

Ref: ADP 6-22 (w/C1), Army Leadership and the Profession (Nov '19), table 6-1, p. 6-4.

Leaders prepare to execute their leadership responsibilities fully. They are aware of their limitations and strengths and seek self-development. Leaders maintain self-discipline, physical fitness, and mental well-being. They continue to improve the expertise required of their leadership roles and their profession. A leader:

Maintains mental and physical health and well being
- Recognizes imbalance or inappropriateness of one's own actions
- Removes emotions from decision making
- Applies logic and reason to make decisions or when interacting with emotionally charged individuals
- Recognizes the sources of stress and maintains appropriate levels of challenge to motivate self
- Manages regular exercise, leisure activities, and time away
- Stays focused on life priorities and values

Expands knowledge of technical, technological & tactical areas
- Seeks knowledge of systems, equipment, capabilities, and situations, particularly information technology systems
- Keeps informed about developments and policy changes inside and outside the organization

Expands conceptual and interpersonal capabilities
- Understands the contribution of concentration, critical thinking, imagination, and problem solving in different task conditions
- Learns new approaches to problem solving
- Applies lessons learned
- Filters unnecessary information efficiently
- Reserves time for self-development, reflection, and personal growth
- Considers possible motives behind conflicting information

Analyzes and organizes information to create knowledge
- Learns about language, values, customary behavior, ideas, beliefs, and patterns of thinking that influence others.
- Learns about results of previous encounters if culture plays a role in mission success.

Maintains relevant cultural awareness
- Learns about relevant societies experiencing unrest
- Recognizes Army influences on unified action partners and enemies
- Understands the factors influencing conflict and peacekeeping, peace enforcing and peacemaking missions

Maintains self awareness: employs self understanding and recognizes impact on others
- Evaluates personal strengths and weaknesses
- Learns from mistakes to make corrections; learns from experience
- Seeks feedback; determines areas in need of development
- Determines personal goals and makes progress toward them
- Develops capabilities where possible but accepts personal limitations
- Seeks opportunities to use capabilities appropriately
- Understands self-motivation under various task conditions

A. Being Prepared for Expected and Unexpected Challenges

Successful self-development concentrates on the key attributes of the leader: character, presence, and intellect. While refining abilities to apply and model the Army Values, Army leaders maintain high levels of fitness and health, not only to set the example and earn the respect of others, but also to withstand the stresses of leading and maintaining their ability to think clearly. Leaders must exploit every available opportunity to sharpen their intellectual capacity and relevant knowledge. A developed intellect enables the leader to think creatively and reason analytically, critically, ethically, and with cultural sensitivity.

When faced with diverse operational settings, leaders draw on their intellectual capacity, critical and creative thinking abilities, and applicable expertise. Leaders create these capabilities by studying doctrine and putting the information into context with personal experiences, military history, and geopolitical awareness. Self-development should include learning languages, the operational environment, military theory, and tactics, techniques, and procedures of potential adversaries. A broad and continuous approach to learning lessens the chances that a leader will face a completely unfamiliar situation, no matter how unexpected.

Civilian and military education is an important part of professional development. Leaders should seek out further education and training opportunities beyond what the Army requires; doing so reflects the intellectual curiosity that the most effective leaders understand being prepared for the unexpected situations they may face. As leaders assume levels of greater responsibility, the problems they face and decisions they make become more complex. This requires that they become life-long learners and develop a keen sense of self-awareness. Leaders who assume they already know everything they need to know set themselves and their organizations up for failure.

B. Expanding Knowledge

Leaders read about, write about, and practice their profession. They prepare themselves for leadership positions through lifelong learning and broadening experiences relevant to their career paths. Lifelong learning involves study to acquire new knowledge, reflection, and understanding about how to apply it when needed. Broadening consists of those education and training opportunities, assignments, and experiences that provide exposure outside the leader's narrow branch or functional area competencies. Broadening should be complementary to a leader's experience, and should provide wider perspectives that prepare the leader for greater levels of responsibility.

Some are fast learners; others must work harder to learn. Becoming a better learner involves—

- Having a plan.
- Focusing on achievable goals.
- Making time to study.
- Absorbing new information.
- Applying what one has learned.

C. Developing Self-Awareness

As a critical element of adaptability, self-awareness enables leaders to recognize their strengths and weaknesses across a range of conditions and progressively employ strengths to correct weaknesses. Awareness of weaknesses also helps leaders rely on others who possess strengths the leader may lack. To be self-aware, leaders must be able to formulate accurate self-perceptions, gather feedback from others, and change their self-concept as appropriate. Being self-aware ultimately requires leaders to develop a clear, honest picture of their capabilities and limitations.

Leaders develop self-awareness though self-critique and self-regulation. Self-aware leaders are open to feedback from others and actively seek it. They possess the humility to ask themselves hard questions about their performance, decisions, and judgment. They are serious about examining their own behavior to determine how to be a better, more effective leader. Self-aware leaders are reflective, hold themselves to higher standards than their subordinates, and look to themselves first when subordinates are unsuccessful. Self-aware leaders use others' strengths to offset their professional shortcomings and are willing to learn from others. Being self-aware ultimately requires leaders to develop a clear, honest picture of their own capabilities and limitations.

Self-aware leaders understand they are a component of a larger organization that demands both adaptability and humility. They understand the importance of flexibility because conditions continuously change. They also understand that the focus is on the mission, not them. Subordinates see leaders who lack self-awareness as arrogant or disconnected. They may be technically competent but lack awareness as to how others see them. This may obstruct their readiness to learn and ability to adapt. Lacking awareness can keep them from creating a positive, learning work climate. Self-aware leaders sense how others react to their actions, decisions, and example.

Competent and confident leaders make sense of their experience and use it to learn more about themselves. Journals and after action reviews (AARs) are valuable tools in gaining an understanding of one's experiences and reactions to changes in conditions. Self-critique can be as simple as posing questions about one's own behavior, knowledge, or feelings or as formal as using a structured set of questions about an event. Critical questions include—

- What happened?
- How did I react?
- How did others react and why?
- What did I learn about myself based on what I did and how I felt?
- How will I apply what I learned?

In rapidly changing conditions, self-awareness is a critical factor in making accurate assessments of changes and a leader's personal capabilities and limitations to operate in those conditions. Self-awareness allows leaders to translate prior training to new conditions and seek the information they need to adapt. Self-aware leaders are more responsive to situational and interpersonal cues regarding actions to take. They are better informed and able to determine what assistance to seek to handle a given situation.

Adjusting one's thoughts, feelings, and actions without prompting from others is self-regulation. Soldiers and DA Civilians self-regulate when they realize that their actions fall short of the standards they have for themselves and take the initiative to close the gap. Leaders who self-regulate have an advantage over those who do not.

II. Creates a Positive Environment/Fosters Esprit de Corps

Army leaders ensure that they create the conditions for a positive environment, build trust and cohesion on their team, encourage initiative, demonstrate care for their people, and enhance esprit de corps by connecting current operations to the unit's traditions and history. Army leaders are approachable when they encourage open, candid communications and observations. Approachable leaders show respect for others' opinions, even if contrary or non-doctrinal. To be approachable, leaders remain objective when receiving bad news and encourage subordinates to be open and candid in their communication.

Creates a Positive Environment

 Establishing a Positive Environment

 Assessing Environment

 Building Trust and Cohesion

 Encouraging Initiative

 Demonstrating Care for People

 Esprit de Corps, Tradition, and History

Ref: ADP 6-22 (w/C1), Army Leadership and the Profession (Nov '19), pp. 6-4 to 6-8.

Culture and Climate

Culture and climate describe the conditions in which a leader leads. Leaders have direct and indirect effects on culture and climate. Culture refers to the environment of the Army as an institution and of major elements or communities within it. All leaders affect the climate at their respective echelon, which may eventually affect the Army's culture.

Culture is a longer lasting and more complex set of shared expectations than climate. Culture consists of shared attitudes, values, goals, and practices that characterize the larger institution over time. The Army's culture is deeply rooted in tradition. Leaders refer to Army's culture to impress on Army personnel that they are part of something bigger than themselves. Soldiers and DA Civilians uphold the Army's culture to honor those who have gone before and those who will come after.

Climate is a shorter-term experience than culture and reflects how people think and feel about their organization. Climate depends upon a network of personalities within a unit that changes as Army personnel come and go. A unit's climate, based on shared perceptions and attitudes, affects mutual trust, cohesion, and commitment to the mission. A positive climate ensures Soldiers and DA Civilians are engaged and energized by their duties, work together as teams, and show respect for each other.

A healthy Army culture and organizational climate will exhibit six overarching characteristics (see AR 600-100):

- The Army culture and unit climate foster unity, cohesion, and trust.
- The culture promotes and rewards mental agility, the ability to break from established paradigms, recognize new patterns or circumstances, and adopt new solutions to problems.
- The Army supports the selection of leaders and rewards members who dem-

Creates a Positive Environment (Summary of the Competency)

Ref: ADP 6-22 (w/C1), Army Leadership and the Profession (Nov '19), table 6-2, p. 6-8.

Leaders establish and maintain positive expectations and attitudes to support effective work behaviors and healthy relationships. Leaders improve the organization while accomplishing missions. They should leave the organization better than it was when they arrived. A leader:

Fosters teamwork, cohesion, cooperation and loyalty
- Encourages people to work together effectively
- Promotes teamwork and team achievement to build trust
- Draws attention to the consequences of poor coordination
- Integrates new members into the unit quickly

Encourages fairness and inclusiveness
- Provides accurate evaluations and assessments
- Supports equal opportunity
- Prevents all forms of harassment
- Encourages learning about and leveraging diversity

Encourages open and candid communications
- Shows others how to accomplish tasks while respectful and focused
- Displays a positive attitude to encourage others and improve morale
- Reinforces the expression of contrary and minority viewpoints
- Displays appropriate reactions to new or conflicting information or opinions
- Guards against groupthink

Creates a learning environment
- Uses effective assessment and training methods
- Encourages leaders and their subordinates to reach their full potential
- Motivates others to develop themselves
- Expresses the value of interacting with others and seeking counsel
- Stimulates innovative and critical thinking in others
- Seeks new approaches to problems
- Communicates difference between professional standards & a zero-defects mentality
- Emphasizes learning from one's mistakes

Encourages subordinates to exercise initiative, accept responsibility and take ownership
- Involves others in decisions and informs them of consequences
- Allocates responsibility for performance
- Guides subordinate leaders in thinking through problems for themselves
- Allocates decision making to the lowest appropriate level
- Acts to expand and enhance subordinate's competence and self confidence
- Rewards initiative

Demonstrates care for follower well-being
- Encourages subordinates and peers to express candid opinions
- Addresses subordinates' and families' needs (health, welfare, and development)
- Stands up for subordinates
- Routinely monitors morale and encourages honest feedback

Anticipates people's on-the-job needs
- Recognizes and monitors subordinate's needs and reactions
- Shows concern for how tasks and missions affect subordinate morale

Sets and maintains high expectations for individuals and teams
- Clearly articulates expectations
- Creates a climate that expects good performance, recognizes superior performance, and does not accept poor performance
- Challenges others to match the leader's example

onstrate the ability to sense and understand the environment quickly to exploit fleeting opportunities or counter unexpected threats.

- The Army requires and rewards delegation of authority on the part of leaders, and the understanding and prompt, thorough execution of leader's intent (two levels up) by subordinates.

- The Army selects and rewards leaders who provide clear priorities and focus their unit's time and organizational energy on their mission.

- The Army culture is one of inclusion that demands diversity of knowledge and perspectives to accomplish missions ethically, effectively, and efficiently

A. Establishing a Positive Environment

Leaders make it a point to dialogue with subordinates about the conditions of their lives and the unit to get a sense of the climate. Communicating goals openly provides subordinates a clear vision to achieve. Communication between subordinates and leaders is essential to achieve and maintain a positive climate. Leaders inspire and motivate subordinates to bring creative and innovative ideas forward and they seek feedback from subordinates about the climate. Openly taking part in unit events and activities increases the likelihood that subordinates perceive leaders are concerned about the group's welfare and has the group's best interests at heart.

Leaders are ethical standard-bearers for the organization, responsible for establishing and maintaining a professional climate wherein all are expected to live by and uphold the Army Values. Other staff specialists—the chaplain, staff judge advocate, inspector general, and equal employment opportunity specialist—assist leaders and assess the organization's climate. Regardless of available expert assistance, the ultimate responsibility to create and maintain an ethical climate rests with the leader.

Setting the right example does not necessarily mean subordinates will follow it. Some may feel that circumstances justify misconduct. Therefore, leaders must monitor the organization's ethical climate and take prompt action to correct any discrepancies. It is important for subordinates to have confidence in the organization's ethical environment because much of what is necessary in combat conflicts with societal values that individuals bring into the Army. Strong commitment to the Army Values, Army Ethic, and Warrior Ethos by the commander fosters a unit's ethical climate.

Leaders need to continually assess the organizational climate, realize the importance of development, and work to limit any zero-defect mentality. Recognizing the importance of long-term sustainability and sharing and encouraging feedback (both positive and negative) should be a priority for all team members. Leaders create positive climates by treating all fairly, maintaining open and candid communications between other leaders and subordinates, and creating and supporting learning environments.

B. Assessing Environment

Leader behavior signals to every member of the organization what is and is not tolerated. The members' collective sense of the group—its organizational climate—is influenced by the leader's values, skills, and actions. Leaders must continuously assess the state of their organizational climates. Feedback from climate assessments (see AR 600-20 and AR 600-100) assist leaders in this effort.

To accurately assess organizational climates, leaders can develop a focused plan of action as follows—

- Assess the unit. Observe those in the unit, gather feedback, and conduct focus group sessions of the workplace. Chaplains may assist with ethical climate assessment through informal means or by use of ethical climate assessment surveys (see GTA 22-06-001).

- Analyze gathered information to identify what needs improvement. After identifying what needs improvement, begin developing courses of action for improvements.

- Select a plan of action to correct identified weaknesses. Gather important information, assess limitations and risks associated with the various courses, identify available key personnel and resources, and verify facts and assumptions. Attempt to predict outcomes for each possible course of action. Based on predictions, select several leader actions to address target issues.

- Execute the plan of action by educating, training, or counseling subordinates; instituting new policies or procedures; and revising or enforcing proper systems of rewards and punishment. Periodically reassess the chosen actions.

C. Building Trust and Cohesion

Trust and cohesion are characteristics of the Army culture that have direct impacts on climate. Leaders encourage subordinates to work together for the greater good while promoting pride in organizational accomplishments. Subordinates trust leaders who underwrite their good faith efforts to act in accordance with their leaders' intents. If the outcome is not what the leader expects, the leader and subordinate discuss the problem and develop a strategy to get back on track.

Trust also follows when a team appreciates a concerted, honest effort even when the results are incomplete. Army members gain confidence in leaders who enable them to achieve standards and demand quality performance. Leaders build cohesive teams by setting and maintaining a collective mindset among team members and enabling successful performance.

Conflict occurs when people disagree about ideas or feel their interests are threatened. Conflict does not require the involvement of two people, nor is it necessarily based on facts. One person may be in conflict with another, without the second person realizing it or being at fault. Leaders should identify and resolve conflict before it affects personal and organizational functioning, good order and discipline, and cohesion.

Leaders should be able to resolve two kinds of conflicts: work-related and personal. Any given conflict is likely to contain some level of both elements. Work-related conflict can stem from disagreement over a course of action, workload perceptions, or the best steps for completing a specific task. Personal conflicts generally stem from people who do not like or respect each other or some perceived grievance based upon individual behavior. Leaders need to develop the skills to address both types of conflicts as rapidly and effectively as possible. Conflicts that simmer lower the morale and duty performance of those involved and can corrode an organizational cohesion when not quickly addressed.

D. Encouraging Initiative

Encouraging subordinates to exercise initiative can be a significant challenge. Those who are not in leadership positions are sometimes reluctant to recognize when a situation calls for them to accept responsibility and step forward. Climate largely shapes the degree to which unit members feel comfortable exhibiting initiative and providing input. Leaders create the conditions for initiative by guiding others in thinking through problems for themselves.

E. Demonstrating Care for People

The nation entrusts the Army leader with its most precious commodity, its sons and daughters. Army leaders embrace this responsibility and keep the well-being of their subordinates and their families in mind. There are times when leaders place their subordinates in harm's way; this is not because they do not care for them, but because they have a duty to the Nation. Leaders also care for subordinates by maintaining their training level so in the event of combat they are well prepared.

Leaders who respect those with whom they work will likely garner respect in return. Simple actions can demonstrate respect and care, such as listening patiently or addressing families' needs. Detecting change in morale and actively seeking honest feedback about the health of individuals and the organization indicate care.

F. Esprit de Corps, Tradition, and History

Historians describing great armies often focus on weapons, equipment, and training. They may mention advantages in numbers or other factors easily analyzed, measured, and compared. However, many historians place great emphasis on two factors not easily measured: esprit de corps and morale.

Esprit de corps is a traditional military expression that denotes the collective camaraderie and cohesion within a unit. Morale is associated with an individual's sense of well-being—mental, spiritual, and physical. Esprit de corps and individual morale are critical factors affecting mutual trust, cohesive teamwork, and the commitment to persevere through adversity, challenges, and setbacks. Focus on customs, courtesies, traditions, and reflection on the organization's history and accomplishments strengthen esprit de corps.

Whether engaging enemy forces, establishing security for a lasting peace, or rebuilding a community devastated by natural disaster, esprit de corps helps organizations overcome adversity and challenges. Leaders who demonstrate genuine concern for the welfare of their subordinates strengthen morale. However, leaders breed cynicism, compromise mutual trust, and degrade morale if they allow disconnects between their words and deeds to occur.

Leaders who foster tradition and an awareness of history build camaraderie and unit cohesion, becoming esprit de corps. Army members draw strength from knowing they are part of long-standing tradition. Many of the Army's everyday customs and traditions remind Soldiers they are the latest addition to a long line of Soldiers. The uniforms, official ceremonies, music, salutes, military titles, organizational history, and the Army Values are reminders of tradition. This sense of belonging lives in many veterans long after they have left service. For many, service to the Nation remains the single most significant experience of their lives.

Unit names such as the Big Red One, All American, Keystone Division, and Rainbow Division carry extensive histories and traditions. To sustain tradition, leaders pass on the history that surrounds unit crests, awards, decorations, and badges. Upholding traditions ensures the Army's culture becomes integral to every member of the Army team.

III. Develops Others

Army leaders, as stewards of the profession, place the needs of the Army as a whole above organizational or personal needs. They have an obligation to be competent in their jobs and train subordinates to be competent in their jobs. Effective leaders balance the long-term needs of the Army, the near-term and career needs of their subordinates, and the immediate needs of their unit's mission. All Army leaders have a duty to prepare subordinates for responsibilities at the next level.

The Army develops leaders through three complementary domains. The institutional domain includes Army centers and schools that provide functional and professional military education such as Airborne school and the Army Management Staff College. The basic knowledge gleaned in the institutional Army develops further through the operational domain. The operational domain encompasses all activities that allow leaders to learn through experiences. Optimizing leader development in the operational domain requires a deliberate approach to leader progression in the context of training events and operational deployments, where leaders apply what they learned from schools to a wide variety of situations and environments. The self-development domain encompasses what individuals do to pursue personal and professional development goals.

Develops Others
(Summary of the Competency)

Ref: ADP 6-22 (w/C1), Army Leadership and the Profession (Nov '19), table 6-4, p. 6-14.

Leaders encourage and support others to grow as individuals and teams. They facilitate the achievement of organizational goals through helping others to develop. They prepare others to assume new positions elsewhere in the organization, making the organization more versatile and productive. A leader:

Assesses developmental needs of others

- Determines strengths and weaknesses of subordinates under different conditions
- Evaluates subordinates in a fair and consistent manner
- Assesses tasks and subordinate motivation to consider methods of improving work assignments, when job enrichment would be useful, methods of cross-training on tasks and methods of accomplishing missions
- Designs ways to challenge subordinates to improve weaknesses and sustain strengths
- Encourages subordinates to improve processes

Counsels, coaches and mentors

- Improves subordinate's understanding and proficiency
- Uses experience and knowledge to improve future performance
- Counsels, coaches and mentors subordinates, subordinate leaders, and others

Facilitates ongoing development

- Maintains awareness of existing individual and organizational development programs and removes barriers to development
- Supports opportunities for self-development
- Arranges training opportunities to help subordinates improve self awareness, confidence, and competence
- Encourages subordinates to pursue institutional learning opportunities
- Provide subordinates information about institutional training and career progression
- Maintains resources related to development

Builds team or group skills and processes

- Presents challenging assignments for team or group interaction
- Provides resources and support for realistic, mission-oriented training
- Sustains and improves the relationships among team or group members
- Provides feedback on team processes

Develops Others

 A   **Empowering Learning**

 B   **Assessing Developmental Needs**

 C   **Counseling, Coaching and Mentoring**

 D   **Operational Development**

 E   **Developing Teams**

Ref: ADP 6-22 (w/C1), Army Leadership and the Profession (Nov '19), pp. 6-8 to 6-14.

FM 6-22 provides techniques about how to create a leader development program and enhance leader development. Effective leader development programs instill in all Soldiers and DA Civilians the desire and drive to improve their professional knowledge and competencies. This approach prepares current and future Army leaders for the challenges they face ahead.

See chap. 2, Leader Development, for further discussion from FM 6-22.

A. Empowering Learning

A leader has the responsibility to foster subordinates' learning. Leaders explain the importance of a particular topic or subject by providing context—how it will improve individual and organizational performance. For instance, leaders discuss the significance of effective counseling with subordinates to help them understand its impact in developing future leaders, achieving goals, managing expectations, and improving organizations.

Learning from experience is not always possible—leaders cannot have every experience in training. Taking advantage of what others have learned provides benefits without having the personal experience. Leaders should share their experiences with subordinates through counseling, coaching, and mentoring sessions; for example, combat veterans can share experiences with Soldiers who have not been in combat. Leaders should also take the opportunity to write about their experiences, sharing their insights with others in professional journals or books.

B. Assessing Developmental Needs

An important step in developing others is to understand which areas are already strong and which should be stronger. Leaders who know their subordinates understand where to encourage development. Leaders observe new subordinates under different task conditions to identify strengths and weaknesses and to see how quickly they pick up new information and skills.

Leaders continuously assess the developmental needs of their subordinates. They evaluate the competence of their subordinates. They assess whether someone can meet the expectations of a new position. They review the organization's policies, status reports, and recent inspection results for indicators of weak areas. They ask outgoing leaders for an assessment and meet with key people outside the organization. Effective leaders periodically update their in-depth assessments since a thorough assessment enables gradual and systematic changes without causing damaging organizational turmoil.

FM 6-22 provides indicators of leader performance and information on determining whether each attribute and competency is a strength, meeting standard, or a developmental need. To objectively assess subordinates over time, leaders—

- Observe and record subordinates' performance in the core leader competencies.
- Determine if their performances meet, exceed, or fall below expected standards.
- Share observations with subordinates and provide an opportunity for them to comment.

Leader development doctrine furnishes detailed information on assessing individual capabilities and expanding them through feedback, study, and practice. FM 6-22 provides learning activities for all leader attributes and competencies. This information is useful whether a leader is developing self or others.

See chap. 2, Leader Development, for further discussion from FM 6-22.

C. Counseling, Coaching and Mentoring

Leaders have three principal roles in developing others. They provide knowledge and feedback through counseling, coaching, and mentoring. Providing feedback is a common element of interacting with others, regardless of developmental role or process. Feedback significantly contributes to development, accelerates learning in day-to-day experiences, and translates into better performance. Providing feedback starts with observation and accurate assessment of performance. Planning to make observations of a subordinate is the first step in feedback. The best observations occur when subordinates engage in critical performance, interact with others, or address a challenging problem. Keeping observation notes is useful when tracking multiple subordinates.

See chap. 3, Counseling, Coaching and Mentoring, for further discussion.

Counseling

Counseling is central to leader development. Counseling is the process used by leaders to guide subordinates to improve performance and develop their potential. Subordinates are active participants in the counseling process. During counseling, leaders help subordinates to identify strengths and weaknesses and create plans of action. To make the plans work, leaders actively support their subordinates throughout the implementation and assessment processes. Subordinates invest themselves in the process by being forthright in their willingness to improve and being candid in their assessment and goal setting. Counseling is an integral part of a comprehensive program to develop subordinates. With effective counseling, no evaluation report— positive or negative—should be a surprise. A counseling program includes all subordinates, not just those thought to have the most potential.

See pp. 3-1 to 3-3 for further discussion from ATP 6-22.1.

Coaching

While a mentor or counselor generally has more experience than the person being supported does, coaching relies primarily on teaching and guiding to bring out and enhance the capabilities already present. Coaching refers to the function of helping someone through a set of tasks or with general qualities. Those being coached may, or may not, have appreciated their potential. The coach helps them understand their current level of performance and guides them how to reach the next level of knowledge and skill.

Coaching is a development technique used for a skill, task, or specific behaviors. Coaches should possess considerable knowledge in the area in which they coach others. An important aspect of coaching is identifying and planning for short- and long-term goals. The coach and the person being coached discuss strengths, weaknesses, and courses of action to sustain or improve.

See pp. 3-4 to 3-5 for further discussion.

Mentoring

Mentorship is the voluntary developmental relationship that exists between a person of greater experience and a person of lesser experience that is characterized by mutual trust and respect (AR 600-100). The following generally characterize mentorship:

- Mentoring takes place when the mentor provides a less experienced leader with advice and counsel over time to aid professional and personal growth.
- The developing leader often initiates the relationship and seeks counsel from the mentor. The mentor takes initiative to check on the well-being and development of the leader.
- Mentorship affects personal development (maturity, interpersonal and communication skills) as well as professional development (technical, tactical, and career path knowledge).
- Mentorship empowers the Army to maintain a highly competent set of leaders.
- The strength of a mentoring relationship relies on mutual trust and respect. Protégés carefully consider assessment, feedback, and guidance; these become valuable for growth to occur.

Mentoring relationships exist outside the superior-subordinate relationship. Supportive mentoring occurs when a mentor does not outrank the person men to red, but has extensive knowledge and experience to share. Mentoring relationships may occur between peers and between senior NCOs and junior officers; thus, mentoring can occur across many levels of rank. Civilian leaders and senior civilian subordinates can provide a substantial mentorship resource for training and integration of military and civilian personnel. Often, this relationship extends past the time where one party has left the other's chain of command.

While many associate mentoring with improving duty-related performance and growth, mentoring may include a spiritual dimension. A chaplain or other spiritually trained individual may play a significant role in advising individuals regarding spiritual issues to help clarify and develop personal and professional identity, purpose, motivation, and resiliency in adversity.

See pp. 3-4 to 3-6 for further discussion.

D. Operational Development

Working in real settings—solving real problems with actual team members—provides challenges and conditions where leaders see the significance of leadership and practice their craft. Good leaders encourage subordinates to develop in every aspect of daily activities and should seek to learn every day themselves. The operational domain includes the three factors of leader, led, and situation and provides real tasks with feedback. This combination provides ideal conditions for development. Planning that includes identification and creation of learning opportunities for leaders promotes development. FM 6-22 provides techniques for how to plan and ensure a mindset to develop leaders. Integrating leader development into the organization creates a positive, learning climate, builds an expectation that leader development is a priority, and produces improved individual and unit readiness.

Good leaders seek ways to define duties to prepare subordinates for responsibilities in their current position or next assignment. Assigning a leader to set up and control a firing range is an opportunity to coach them on working with sister units and ways to train Soldiers. The DA Civilian intern program is another example where duty performance is used for development. Leaders can rotate into special duty assignments to give them broad leadership experiences and be given stretch assignments or tasks to accelerate their development.

Leaders are responsible for ensuring subordinates receive the appropriate education, training, and experiences at the proper time for promotion as well as increasing their potential in current and future assignments. Self-development can occur anywhere, so it is also an important aspect of development in organizations. Individuals must be active participants in their developmental process. They must not wait for a leader or mentor to choose them but have the responsibility to be proactive in their own development. Every Army officer, NCO, Soldier, and DA Civilian should identify personal strengths and areas for improvement. Each individual should then determine a developmental plan. Some strategies to use in planning development are—

- Ask questions and pay attention to experts.
- Read and study.
- Observe those in leadership positions.
- Find educational opportunities (civilian, military, and correspondence).
- Seek and engage in new and varied opportunities.

E. Developing Teams

A team is any collection of people that functions together to perform a mission or collective task. Teams that work well have an advantage of increasing motivation and accountability among members. Developing close teams takes hard work, patience, and interpersonal skill on the part of the leader (see ATP 6-22.6). Because high-functioning teams complete missions on time with given resources and a minimum of wasted effort, they are a worthwhile investment. In war and peace, cohesive teams, operating with mutual trust, accomplish the missions more effectively than those lacking trust and cohesion. Hallmarks of cohesive teams include—

- Trusting each other and being able to predict what each will do.
- Working together to accomplish the mission.
- Executing tasks thoroughly and quickly.
- Meeting and exceeding standards.
- Adapting to demanding challenges.
- Learning from their experiences and developing pride in accomplishments.

Leaders must guide teams through three developmental stages: formation, enrichment, and sustainment. Leaders remain sensitive to the fact that teams develop differently and the boundaries between stages are not absolute. The results can determine what to expect of the team and what improves its capabilities. Understanding the perspectives of team members is important. Leaders understand that the national cause, mission, purpose, and many other concerns may not be relevant to the Soldier's perspective. Regardless of larger issues, Soldiers perform for others on the team, for the Soldier on their right or left. A fundamental truth is that Soldiers accomplish tasks because they do not want to let each other down.

See chap. 4, Army Team Building, for further discussion of teams from ATP 6-22.6.

IV. Stewards the Profession

Leaders take care of the Army profession by applying a mindset that embodies co-operative planning and management of all resources, but especially providing for a strong Army team both now and in the future. Leaders actively engage in sustaining full military readiness and preventing the loss of effectiveness as far into the future as possible. Leaders support developmental opportunities for subordinates such as professional military education attendance, key developmental assignments in other organizations, and attendance at Army schools. Leaders also make decisions and take action to improve the organization beyond their tenure. Table 6-5 summarizes the competency stewards the profession.

Stewards the Profession

Supporting Professional and Personal Growth

Improving the Organization for the Long-Term

Ref: ADP 6-22 (w/C1), Army Leadership and the Profession (Nov '19), pp. 6-14 to 6-15.

A. Supporting Professional and Personal Growth

Developing multiskilled leaders is the goal of preparing self and subordinates to lead. An adaptable leader will more readily comprehend the challenges of constantly evolving conditions, demanding not only warfighting skills, but also creativity Army leaders who reflect upon their experiences and learn from them will often find better ways of doing things. Leaders must employ openness and imagination to create effective organizational learning conditions. Effective leaders are not afraid to under-write mistakes. They allow others to learn from them. This attitude allows growth into new responsibilities and adaptation to inevitable changes.

B. Improving the Organization for the Long-Term

Leaders demonstrate stewardship when they act to improve the organization beyond their own tenure. Improving the organization for the long-term is deciding and taking action to manage people or resources when the benefits may not occur during a leader's tour of duty with an organization

(Leader Competencies)
IIc. Achieves

Ref: ADP 6-22 (w/C1), Army Leadership and the Profession (Nov '19), chap. 7.

I. Gets Results

Gets results is the single achieves competency and relates to actions of leading to accomplish tasks and missions on time and to standard. Getting results requires the right integration of tasks, roles, resources, and priorities. Getting results focuses tasks, priorities, people, and other resources to achieve the desired outcomes. Leaders are ready to take action all the time to achieve outcomes and make necessary adjustments for success. Leaders also work to sustain or improve the organization's performance by assessing and giving feedback as they execute and make adjustments.

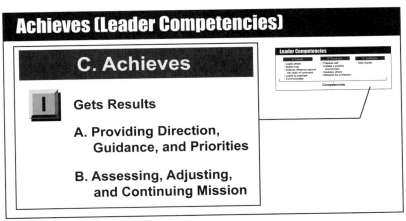

Achieves (Leader Competencies)

C. Achieves

I Gets Results

A. Providing Direction, Guidance, and Priorities

B. Assessing, Adjusting, and Continuing Mission

Ref: ADP 6-22 (w/C1), Army Leadership and the Profession (Nov '19), chap. 7.

A Leader's Purpose

A leader's primary purpose is to accomplish the mission. Leadership builds and guides the effective organizations necessary to do so. Leaders require a focus on the future that views building and maintaining effective organizations as critical to mission accomplishment. Building effective Army organizations serves the larger purpose of mission accomplishment. Mission accomplishment takes priority over everything else, especially in combat where their unit may be at risk of destruction.

Achieves embraces all actions to accomplish tasks on time and to standard by—

- Providing direction, guidance, and priorities.
- Assessing, adjusting, and continuing mission.

Gets Results Competency

Ref: ADP 6-22 (w/C1), Army Leadership and the Profession (Nov '19), table 7-1.

Gets results is the single achieves competency and relates to actions of leading to accomplish tasks and missions on time and to standard. Getting results requires the right integration of tasks, roles, resources, and priorities. Getting results focuses tasks, priorities, people, and other resources to achieve the desired outcomes. Leaders are ready to take action all the time to achieve outcomes and make necessary adjustments for success. Leaders also work to sustain or improve the organization's performance by assessing and giving feedback as they execute and make adjustments.

A Leader's Purpose

A leader's primary purpose is to accomplish the mission. Leadership builds and guides the effective organizations necessary to do so. Leaders require a focus on the future that views building and maintaining effective organizations as critical to mission accomplishment. Building effective Army organizations serves the larger purpose of mission accomplishment. Mission accomplishment takes priority over everything else, especially in combat where their unit may be at risk of destruction.

Achieves embraces all actions to accomplish tasks on time and to standard by—
- Providing direction, guidance, and priorities.
- Assessing, adjusting, and continuing mission.

A leader's ultimate purpose is to accomplish organizational missions. A leader gets results by providing guidance and influence while managing resources, as well as performing the other leader competencies. Gets results focuses on consistent task accomplishment through supervising, managing, monitoring, and controlling work.

Prioritizes, organizes and coordinates taskings for teams or other organizations structures/groups
- Ensures the course of action achieves the desired outcome through planning.
- Organizes groups and teams to accomplish work.
- Ensures subordinates can execute all tasks in the time available and in the correct sequence.
- Limits over specification and micromanagement.

Identifies and accounts for capabilities and commitment to task
- Considers duty positions, capabilities, and developmental needs when assigning tasks.
- Conducts initial assessments to assume a new task or position.
- Keeps followers focused on vision, intent, directive, and plan.

Designates, clarifies, and deconflicts roles
- Establishes and employs procedures for monitoring, coordinating, and regulating subordinate's actions and activities
- Mediates peer conflicts and disagreements

Identifies, contends for, allocates and manages resources

- Tracks people and equipment
- Allocates adequate time for task completion
- Allocates time to prepare and conduct rehearsals
- Continually seeks improvement in operating efficiency, resource conservation, and fiscal responsibility
- Attracts, recognizes, and retains talent

Removes work barriers

- Protects organization from unnecessary taskings and distractions
- Recognizes and resolves scheduling conflicts
- Overcomes obstacles preventing accomplishment of the mission

Recognizes and rewards good performance

- Recognizes individual and team accomplishments; rewards appropriately
- Credits subordinates for good performance; builds on successes
- Explores reward systems and individual reward motivations

Seeks, recognizes and takes advantage of opportunities to improve performance

- Asks incisive questions
- Anticipates needs for actions; envisions ways to improve
- Acts to improve the organization's collective performance
- Recommends best methods to accomplish tasks; uses information and technology to improve individual and group effectiveness
- Encourages staff to use creativity to solve problems

Makes feedback part of work processes

- Gives and seeks accurate and timely feedback
- Uses feedback to modify duties, tasks, procedures, requirements, and goals
- Uses assessment techniques and evaluation tools (such as AARs) to identify lessons learned and facilitate consistent improvement
- Determines the appropriate setting and timing for feedback

Executes plans to accomplish the mission

- Schedules activities to meet commitments in critical performance areas.
- Notifies peers and subordinates in advance of required support.
- Keeps track of task assignments and suspenses; attends to details.
- Adjusts assignments, if necessary.
- Assesses progress toward mission accomplishment, provides additional guidance, or resets the team as necessary.

Identifies and adjusts to external influences on the mission and organization

- Gathers and analyzes relevant information about changing conditions
- Determines causes, effects, and contributing factors of problems
- Considers contingencies and their consequences
- Makes necessary, on-the-spot adjustments

A. Providing Direction, Guidance, and Priorities

Many matters consume a leader's time and attention. Leaders have obligations that are far ranging and at times are contradictory. Leaders make these challenges transparent to their subordinates whenever possible. Leaders are responsible to create conditions that enable subordinates to focus and accomplish critical tasks. They do this by minimizing distractions and prioritizing what they need to accomplish within the commander's intent. Leaders are responsible for anticipating the consequences of any action. Thorough planning is beneficial, but anticipating second-and third-order effects requires imagination, vision, and an appreciation of other people, talents, and organizations.

When communicating the mission, leaders provide clear guidance so subordinates and others understand the mission and their commander's intent. Leaders ensure tasks are within the capabilities of the organization and do not detract from the ability to accomplish the mission. If leaders are unable to deconflict the friction between taskings, they should seek relief by approaching superiors with the impact on their critical task and possible alternative courses of action.

All leaders understand that change is inevitable. Army leaders prepare their organizations to adapt. It does not matter if the unit is on block leave, in a garrison support cycle, or in the most intense firefight. Leaders focus their subordinates on what they need to do to accomplish the mission. This allows subordinates to know where to place effort or what not to do. Leaders monitor their subordinates to ensure they are handling the stress that a task or mission places on them. Even in the most mundane or dangerous situations, there are opportunities to restore or build morale.

All leaders have a responsibility to ensure resources are available and used wisely. Managing resources requires different approaches and different skills. Resources can take the form of money, materiel, personnel, or time. Getting resources can be a relatively straightforward process, such as putting in an ammunition request through established support channels for an upcoming range. Other times, a leader may need to be more creative and resourceful in securing resources for a complex task.

Ultimately, a leader must decide how to best allocate resources to accomplish the mission. Leaders need to deal openly and honestly with their allocation decisions and be prepared to handle reactions from those who feel the leader handled their requests unfairly or ineffectively.

B. Assessing, Adjusting, and Continuing Mission

The ability to assess a situation accurately and reliably against desired outcomes, established values, and ethical standards is a key way for leaders to achieve consistent results and mission success. Assessment occurs continually during planning, preparation, and execution; it is not solely an after-the-fact evaluation. Accurate assessment requires instinct and intuition based on experience and learning. Accurate assessment requires reliable and valid information. Leaders take action based on their assessments to reset or keep tasks and missions on track. Leaders periodically assess individual and organizational weaknesses to prevent mishaps and mission failure. Accurate assessment is essential to developing subordinate leadership, training management, and initiating improvements.

To accomplish missions consistently, leaders need to maintain motivation within the team. One of the best ways to do this is to recognize and reward good performance. Leaders who recognize individual and team accomplishments promote positive motivation and actions for the future. Recognizing individuals and teams in front of superiors and others gives those contributors an increased sense of worth. Leaders seek opportunities to recognize the performance of their subordinates. They do this by crediting their subordinates for the work they do. Sharing credit has enormous payoffs in terms of building trust and teams.

III. Leadership in Practice

Ref: ADP 6-22 (w/C1), Army Leadership and the Profession (Nov '19), chap. 8.

. Leaders and Challenges

Contextual factors and operational challenges affect leaders, their subordinates, and accomplishment of the mission. This chapter builds upon the foundation of attributes and examines dynamic factors—positive and negative—that may arise when applying leadership across different areas and contexts.

The nature of large-scale combat operations creates situations where leaders may send Soldiers and entire units into harm's way knowing they may not survive. Army leaders perform this solemn duty because war demands nothing less than total commitment to accomplish the larger mission. The purpose, direction, and motivation Army leaders provide Soldiers and units is made in good faith that personal sacrifices serve the greater good of the Army and the Nation.

II. Leaders and Courage

Army leaders accept the responsibility to develop and lead others to achieve results. All members of the Army swear an oath to support and defend the Constitution of the United States against all enemies, foreign and domestic. This oath subordinates the military leader to the laws of the Nation and its elected and appointed leaders, creating a distinct civil-military relationship. Fulfilling that oath, leaders will face—and have to overcome—fear, danger, and physical and moral adversity while caring for those they lead and protecting the organization entrusted to them.

Taking the initiative to make something happen requires more personal courage rather than standing by or withdrawing and hoping events will turn out well. Leaders require personal courage in many conditions: confronting problems of discipline or disorderly conduct, leading Soldiers in harm's way, needing innovation or adaptation to do something never done before, being candid with a superior about a risky or improper course of action, deferring to a more technically competent subordinate, or freeing units and personnel to solve problems. Leaders must have the courage to make tough calls, to discipline or demand better when required. Consistent and fair leaders will earn the respect of their followers.

III. Leadership and Management

Leadership and management both cover the actions to influence, motivate, provide purpose and give direction to others, and to sustain and improve the organization. Both add order to situations by planning, controlling, coordinating human, and material resources and by communicating with and gaining commitment from others. Management is complementary to leadership and applies to maintaining order, achieving efficiency, and complying with law. Processes, resources, and systems are things that leaders must manage. Leaders manage personnel as an important resource, but they lead people as individuals and groups to accomplish missions. Management is one of the skills that leaders need more as the scope and scale of their responsibilities increase over the course of a career. Successful management requires understanding about policy, regulations, and the procedural aspects of how an organization functions as part of a larger organization. The leader attributes and competencies apply to management as well as to leadership.

IV. Adaptability and Versatility

The Army recognizes that it faces highly adaptive enemies and operates within dynamic, ever-changing conditions. Sometimes conditions change suddenly and unexpectedly from a calm, relatively safe operation to a close combat situation. Other times conditions differ (such as day to night) and leaders adapt. Adaptability is the ability to influence conditions and respond effectively to changing threats and situations with appropriate, flexible, and timely actions. Leaders develop their skill sets over time and learn what to apply in given situations. This demonstrates versatility. Versatility is having the ability to succeed across a spectrum of demanding, tough situations. Versatility increases the likelihood of effective adaptability by being trained and ready with multiple capabilities. The leader must be willing to deviate from usual, ingrained approaches.

See facing page for further discussion.

V. Challenges of an Operational Environment

Each situation a leader faces is unique and brings new challenges. Some challenges are predictable based on experiences; some are unpredictable, surfacing because of a situation or place in time. Leaders must be prepared to face the effects of stress, changing technology, fear in combat, geopolitical climate, and external influences from the media.

Future leaders must be adept at operating in ambiguity and chaos while possessing technical and professional expertise that enables cognitive overmatch of the enemy. Awareness, proper training, and open, frank discussion mitigate some of these factors. Army leaders must consider these external influences and plan accordingly. An effective leader recognizes the need to adapt in changing situations:

- Evolving Threats
- Media
- Joint and Multinational Conditions
- Geopolitical Situation
- Technology
- Systems
- Health of the Command

VI. Stress of Change

To succeed in conditions of continuous change, leaders emphasize the constants of the Army Values, teamwork, and discipline while helping subordinates anticipate change, adapt, and seek new ways to improve. Competent leadership implies managing change, adapting, and making change work for the team. Leaders determine what requires explicit actions to respond to change. Often, building on what already exists limits stress.

VII. Operational Stress

Stress in response to threatening or uncertain situations occurs across the range of military operations as well as at home, in garrison, and during training exercises. Military experiences expose Soldiers to various operational stresses throughout their careers. Operational stress control does not minimize the experiences faced while engaged in such operations, but provides mechanisms to mitigate reactions to those experiences so Soldiers remain combat effective and maintain the quality of life to which they are entitled. Leaders must understand stress and anticipate Soldiers' reactions. Overcoming obstacles, such as Soldiers becoming wounded or dying, or the enemy attacking unexpectedly, takes mental discipline and resilience.

Refer to ATP 6-22.5 for more information.

Adaptability and Versatility

Ref: ADP 6-22 (w/C1), Army Leadership and the Profession (Nov '19), pp. 8-2 to 8-3.

Adaptability

Adaptable leaders are comfortable with ambiguity. They are flexible and innovative—ready to face the challenges with available resources Adaptability has two key components:

• Ability to identify essential elements critical for performance in each new situation.
• Ability to change practices or the unit to meet the requirement for change.

Experienced leaders recognize when conditions change. As conditions change, leaders apply their experiences to determine a way forward. Leaders exhibit this quality through critical thinking, creative thinking, willingness to accept risk, displaying comfort with ambiguity, and the ability to adjust rapidly while continuously assessing the situation.

Highly adaptable leaders have the proper frame of mind for operating under mission orders. Adaptable leaders can quickly assess the situation and determine skills needed to address it. If skills learned in the past are not sufficient for success under new conditions, adaptable leaders seek to apply new or modified skills.

Adaptive leadership includes being an agent of change. This means encouraging others to recognize conditions are changing and build consensus as change occurs. As consensus builds, adaptive leaders influence the course of the organization. Depending on the immediacy of the problem, adaptive leaders may use several different methods for influencing their organization.

Adaptability takes effort to develop. To become adaptable, leaders must challenge their previously held ideas and assumptions by seeking out novel and unfamiliar situations. Leaders who remain safely inside their comfort zone (current level of education, training, and experience) are less likely to recognize change or understand inevitable changes in conditions. Mindsets affect adaptability. Developing a few systematic ways of thinking encourages adaptability. These include open-mindedness, ability to consider multiple perspectives, not jumping to conclusions about what a situation is or means, willingness to take risks, and being able to overcome setbacks. To become more adaptable, leaders should:

• Embrace opportunities to adapt
• Seek challenges

Versatility

Experiences form the basis of how people react to certain situations. A broader experience base offers greater opportunity to be a versatile leader. Versatile leaders seek opportunities to expand their experiences. They also understand the need to develop these same characteristics and qualities in their subordinates and teams. To promote a climate that promotes versatility, leaders maintain standards and accept constructive feedback without threat of repercussion or blame. Instead, they challenge subordinates to think in new ways and build a broader set of trained and practiced responses.

Leaders lacking adaptability and versatility enter every situation in the same manner and often expect their experience in one position to carry them to the next. Consequently, they may use ill-fitting or outdated approaches that may result in poor performance in new conditions or outright failure. Determining when and how to adapt is important. Adaptability and versatility do not produce certainty that change will improve results. Sometimes, persistence on a given course of action may have merit over change.

VIII. Counterproductive Leadership

Ref: ADP 6-22 (w/C1), Army Leadership and the Profession (Nov '19), pp. 8-7 to 8-8.

The Army expects all leaders to live the Army Values and demonstrate the positive characteristics described by the leader attributes and core leader competencies. Effective leadership is essential for realizing the full potential of an organization's combat power and can compensate for deficiencies in other warfighting functions. The opposite is also true; counterproductive leader behaviors can negate combat power advantages.

Counterproductive leadership is the demonstration of leader behaviors that violate one or more of the Army's core leader competencies or Army Values, preventing a climate conducive to mission accomplishment. Counterproductive leadership generally leaves organizations in a worse condition than when the leader arrived and has a long-term effect on morale and readiness. The term toxic has been used when describing leaders who have engaged in what the Army now refers to as counterproductive leadership behaviors. Counterproductive leadership is incompatible with Army leadership doctrine and Army Values. It often violates regulations and can impede mission accomplishment.

All leaders are susceptible to displaying counterproductive leadership behaviors in times of stress, high operational tempo, or other chaotic conditions to achieve short-term results. Counterproductive leadership decreases followers' well-being, engagement, and undermines the organization's readiness and ability to accomplish the mission in the long term. It can have an adverse effect on the unit with cascading results, such as lowering morale, commitment, cohesion, effectiveness, readiness, and productivity. Counterproductive leadership behaviors prevent establishing a positive organizational climate and interfere with mission accomplishment, especially in highly complex operational settings. Prolonged use of counterproductive leadership destroys unit morale, trust, and undermines the followers' commitment to the mission. Counterproductive leadership can also decrease task performance, physical and psychological well-being, and increase negative outcomes such as depression or burnout.

Army leaders can and will make mistakes, so distinguishing between occasional errors of judgment and counterproductive behavior is important. Counterproductive leadership can include recurrent negative leader behaviors and more serious one-time behaviors that have a damaging effect on the organization's performance and subordinate welfare. Infrequent or one-time negative behaviors do not define counterproductive leadership. Often, counterproductive leadership behaviors have harmful effects on individuals or a unit when several instances occur together or take place frequently.

Counterproductive leadership spans a range of leader conduct that can be organized into several broad categories that are useful to inform strategies for identifying and addressing such behaviors. Counterproductive leadership is not limited to these behaviors listed below. Leaders can demonstrate more than one of the behaviors and their conduct can span multiple categories:

- **Abusive behaviors**—includes behaviors that involve a leader exceeding the boundaries of their authority by being abusive, cruel, or degrading others.
- **Self-serving behaviors**—includes behaviors that result from self-centered motivations on the part of the leader, where they act in ways that seek primarily to accomplish their own goals and needs before those of others.
- **Erratic behaviors**—includes behaviors related to poor self-control or volatility that drive the leader to act erratically or unpredictably.
- **Leadership incompetence**—includes ineffective leadership behaviors that result from a lack of experience or willful neglect. Incompetence can include failure to act or acting poorly.
- **Corrupt behaviors**—includes behaviors that violate explicit Army standards, regulations, or policies.

IV. Organizational Leadership

Ref: ADP 6-22 (w/C1), Army Leadership and the Profession (Nov '19), chap. 9.

Army leaders consistently prepare themselves for greater responsibilities while mastering core leader competencies. By the time they become organizational and strategic leaders, they should be multi-skilled leaders who can comfortably operate at all levels of leadership inside or outside the Army and apply their vast experiences and knowledge for success across the spectrum of operations. They oversee continuous transformation of the Army and respond to evolving operational environments. They mentor and develop the leadership of the future force.

Organizational Leadership

Leading	Developing	Achieving
• Leads others • Extends influence beyond the chain of command • Leads by example • Communicates	• Creates a positive environment • Prepares self • Develops others	• Providing direction, guidance, & clear priorities • Mastering reources and systems • Understanding/Synchronizing Systems for Combat Power • Assessing to Ensure Mission Success & Org. Improvement

I. Leading

Whether they fight for key terrain or work to achieve training readiness, organizational leaders must be able to translate complex concepts into understandable plans their subordinates can execute. Organizational leaders develop the plans and synchronize the systems that allow subordinates to turn ideas into action.

Organizational leaders build teams of teams with discipline, cohesion, trust, and proficiency through personal example, using a wide range of knowledge and applying leader competencies. They focus their organizations down to the lowest level on the mission by disseminating a clear intent, sound concepts, and a systematic approach to execution.

Organizational leaders build on direct leader experiences, reflect the Army Values, and instill pride within organizations. Since they lead complex organizations throughout the Army's generating forces and operating forces, organizational leaders often apply elements of direct and organizational leadership simultaneously

A. Leads Others

Organizational leaders have developed a strong background in fundamentals as well as an appreciation for the geopolitical implications of their situation. From their experiences, they have developed the instincts, intuition, and knowledge that form their understanding of the interrelation of the levels of leadership. Their refined skills allow them to understand, integrate, and synchronize the activities of multiple systems and employ resources and systems across a range of challenges.

B. Extends Influence Beyond the Chain of Command

While organizational leaders primarily exert direct influence through their chain of command and staff, they extend influence beyond their chain of command and organization by other means. These other means include persuasion, empowerment, motivation, negotiation, conflict resolution, bargaining, advocacy, and diplomacy. They often apply such skills when serving as military negotiators, consensus builders, and a direct interface to local populace.

C. Leads by Example

The Army's organizational leaders play a critical part in maintaining focus on fighting the enemy and not the plan. They are at the forefront of adapting to operational environment changes and exploiting emerging opportunities by applying a combination of intuition, analytical problem solving, systems integration, and leadership by example—as close to the action as feasible.

Organizational leaders position themselves with the necessary means to maintain contact with critical elements and headquarters. Proximity to operations provides organizational commanders with the required awareness to apply quick creative thinking in collaboration with subordinate leaders. Proximity facilitates adjustments for deficiencies in planning and shortens reaction time when applying sound tactical and operational solutions to changing realities. Operations require leaders who understand the context of factors affecting the situation, act within that understanding, continually assess and adapt those actions based on the interactions and circumstance of the enemy and conditions, consolidate tactical and operational opportunities into strategic aims, and are able to effectively transition operations.

D. Communicates

Leaders are responsible for ensuring shared understanding. They should share information as much as possible with their organization and subordinates. An open, two-way exchange of information reinforces sharing team values and encourages constructive input.

Communicating openly and clearly with superiors is important for organizational leaders. Understanding the intent, priorities, and thought processes makes anticipating future planning and resourcing priorities easier. Understanding the direction of the higher headquarters reduces course corrections at lower levels, thus minimizing friction and maintaining a stable organizational tempo and climate.

II. Developing

Comparatively, organizational leaders take a long-term approach to developing the entire organization. They prepare their organizations for the next quarter, next year, or five years from now. The responsibility to determine how the Army fights the next war lies with today's Army leaders, especially those at the organizational and strategic levels. Leaders at the organizational level rely more on indirect leadership methods, which can make leading, developing, and achieving more difficult.

A. Creates a Positive Environment

An organization's climate springs from its leader's attitudes, actions, and priorities communicated through choices, policies, and programs. Leaders in organizational leadership positions determine the organizational climate by assessing the organization from the bottom up. An organizational leader can initiate command climate surveys to collect climate input while protecting individual anonymity. Organizational-level leaders ensure company commanders meet requirements for initial and annual climate surveys (see AR 600-20). These leaders should assess subordinate command climate results and supplemental indicators such as instances of misconduct. With a completed assessment, the leader can provide clear guidance and focus (purpose, direction, and motivation) to move the organization toward the desired end state.

Characteristics of successful organizational climates include a clear, widely known purpose; well trained, confident Soldiers and DA Civilians; disciplined, cohesive teams; and trusted, competent leaders. It is a climate that adheres to and promotes the Army Values and fosters the Warrior Ethos, encourages learning, promotes creativity and performance, and establishes cohesion. To create such a climate, organizational leaders recognize mistakes as opportunities to learn, create cohesive teams, and reward leaders of character and competence with increasing responsibilities. Organizational leaders value honest feedback and constantly use available means to maintain a feel for the organization. Special staff members including equal opportunity advisors, chaplains, medical officers, and legal advisors assist the organizational leader with maintaining a positive environment.

B. Prepares Self

The demands on leaders vary at different levels. While leader competencies stay the same across levels, moving from direct to the organizational level requires a shift in approach. What may occupy a great deal of a leader's time at a lower level(for example,face-to-face supervision of Soldiers) involves less time at higher levels. Certain technical skills vital to a direct leader will be of less importance to an organizational leader who must spend time on system-wide issues. Leaders need to accustom themselves to rely on less direct means of direction, control, and monitoring to aid their transition in the scope and breadth of responsibilities.

Organizational leaders keep a focus on where the organization needs to go and what leaders must be capable of accomplishing. As role models, they develop themselves and actively counsel their subordinate leaders about their professional growth. Organizational leaders continue to seek broadening experiences to expand their knowledge, skills, and capabilities. At the organizational level, leaders ensure that systems and conditions are in place for objective feedback, counseling, and mentoring for all organization members, including themselves.

Self-aware organizational leaders who know their organizations generally achieve high quality results and do not shy away from asking close subordinates to give informal feedback as part of an open, transparent assessment and feedback effort. When they are part of official AARs, organizational leaders should invite subordinates to comment on how the leaders could have made things better. Subordinates easily spot errors by organizational leaders since these errors often affect those lead. Consequently, admitting, analyzing, and learning from these errors add value to the training. For the Army's organizational leaders—just as leaders at other levels—reflecting, learning, and applying corrective actions in operations is critical for effectiveness.

C. Develops Others

Organizational-level leaders are stewards of the Army profession. They fulfill this function by placing a high priority upon investment in future leaders at all levels. Leader development is an investment required to maintain the Army as a profession and is a key source of combat power. Organizational leaders set conditions for a robust leader development system and create conditions that enable organization members to learn from their experiences and those of others. They rely on conditions that use learning as well as self-development through various procedures such as 360 assessments. To strengthen learning, organizational leaders can make numerous avenues available for lifelong learning: assignment-oriented training, simulations, learning centers, and virtual training.

Organizational leaders determine the potential of others. This takes awareness of others and flexibility to build on strengths and address weaknesses. Developing others at this level is challenging; the organizational leader has to balance the criticality of the task and the developmental needs of all subordinates. Another consideration for organizational leaders is how and what individuals need to learn. Learning in challenging situations may be a good way for leaders to learn from failure, but others need to experience more successes than failures to develop self-confidence and initiative. Organizational leaders lead, coach, and mentor subordinate leaders.

III. Achieving

For consistent results, organizational leaders have to be competent in planning, preparing, executing, and assessing. They must provide clear focus with their inter so subordinates accomplish the mission, regardless of the original plan.

A. Providing Direction, Guidance, and Clear Priori

Organizational leaders are more likely than direct leaders to provide guidance and make decisions with incomplete information. Part of the organizational leaders' analysis must determine which decisions to make themselves or push to lower levels. While determining the right course of action, they consider possible second- and third-order effects and project into the future—months or years. Organizational leaders must consider the timing of their decisions. In many cases, organizational leaders must exercise patience and not make decisions before allowing subordinates time to overcome the frictions inherent to military operations.

B. Mastering Resources and Systems

During operations, organizational leaders integrate and synchronize available resources. They assign missions and empower their subordinates to execute within the given intent. Effective organizational leaders must be resourcing experts, which requires significant education and self-study. Achieving organizational goals require resources—including time, equipment, facilities, budgets, and people. Organizationa leaders aggressively manage and prioritize the resources at their disposal to ensure optimal readiness of the organization. A leader's situation is more difficult when unanticipated events shift priorities.

Leaders who reach the organizational level should have a comprehensive systems perspective, clearly understanding how all the elements of combat power work together. These systems provide the framework for influencing people and organizations at all levels. They are the foundation for conducting a wide variety of operation and continually improving the organization and the force.

C. Understanding and Synchronizing Systems for Combat Power

Leaders apply a systems perspective to develop and employ their organizations. The ability to understand and effectively employ systems is critical to achieving organizational goals, objectives, and tasks. Organizational leadership, combined with effective information and integration of the warfighting functions, generates combat power.

Effective organizational leaders excel at tactical and operational synchronization. They must arrange activities in time, space, and purpose to mass maximum relative combat power or organizational effort at a decisive point. Organizational leaders further synchronize by applying the complementary and reinforcing effects of joint military and nonmilitary assets to overwhelm opponents. Effective synchronization and integration requires leaders to pull together technical, interpersonal, and conceptual abilities and apply them to warfighting goals, objectives, and tasks.

D. Assessing to Ensure Mission Success and Organizational Improvement

Assessing situations—looking at the state of the organization and its component elements—is critical for organizational leaders to achieve consistent results and mission success. Accurate assessment requires their instincts and intuitions based on the reliability of information and their sources. Quality organizational assessment can determine weaknesses and force focused improvements.

V. Strategic Leadership

Ref: ADP 6-22 (w/C1), Army Leadership and the Profession (Nov '19), chap. 10.

Strategic leaders represent a finely balanced combination of high-level thinkers, accomplished Soldiers, and military experts. Strategic leaders simultaneously sustain what is necessary within current conditions, envision the future, and convey that vision to a wide audience. They often personally spearhead change. Their policies guide lifecycles and talent management of all Army personnel. They guide the design and employment of technological advances and establish programs that care for Army families. They secure resources for facilities and infrastructure, weapons and equipment, supply and maintenance, and manpower and force structure. America's complex national security conditions require strategic leaders with an in-depth knowledge of the diplomatic, informational, military, and economic instruments of national power.

Strategic leadership involves the activities to affect the achievement of a desirable and clearly understood vision. It focuses on influencing Army culture, securing and prioritizing resources, and shaping and supporting organizational and direct level leaders. These goals are realized through directives, policies, programs, systems, and consensus building

Strategic Leadership

Leading	Developing	Achieving
• Leads others • Extends influence • Leads by example • Communicates	• Prepares self • Creates a positive environment • Develops others • Stewards the profession	• Strategic planning and execution • Consistently assess capabilities

Strategic leaders serve inside or outside the Army and must thoroughly understand political-military relationships. Army strategic leaders have responsibilities that extend beyond the Army to the national government, its leaders, and ultimately, to the American people. Senior Army leaders are the strategic stewards of the profession. At the strategic level, senior Army leaders address ends, ways, and means to accomplish global missions. They maintain the trust of the American people by living and upholding the Army Values in their decisions and actions taken in regard to policies, programs, systems and the care they provide to Soldiers, DA Civilians, and Army Families. Those serving in strategic leadership positions may lead complex organizations composed of members of the U.S. Army, other U.S. armed services, and those of other nations, members of federal agencies, and non-governmental entities. Strategic leaders, regardless of position, apply professional expertise and uphold the Army Values.

Strategic leaders have a stewardship responsibility for the relationship between the military and civilian leaders of the Army. Leaders take an oath of office that subordinates the military leader to the laws of the Nation and its elected and appointed leaders, creating a distinct civil-military relationship. Army professionals understand this and appreciate the critical role this concept has played throughout America's history. Equally important, this concept requires military professionals to understand the role of civilian leaders and their responsibilities to the civilian leadership. A critical element of this relationship is the trust that civilian leaders have in their military leaders to represent the military and provide professional military advice. Military professionals have unique expertise, and their input is vital to formulating and executing defense policy. Based on mutual trust, this relationship requires candor and authority to execute the decisions of the civilian leaders. These decisions provide the strategic direction and framework in which strategic military leaders operate.

To maintain focus, strategic leaders survey conditions to understand the context for their roles. Highly developed interpersonal abilities and intergroup relations are essential to building consensus with civilian and military policy makers on national and international levels. Strategic leaders must think in multiple timelines to anticipate change and be agile to manage change. Strategic leaders extend influence in conditions where they interact with other high-level leaders and influential figures over whom they have minimal formal authority or no authority at all.

Strategic leaders are keenly aware of the complexities of national and international security conditions. They operate in intricate networks of overlapping and sometimes competing constituencies. Strategic leaders identify trends, opportunities, and threats that could affect the Army's future and move vigorously to address them. Their actions affect acquisitions, budget constraints, Total Army issues, civilian programs, research, contracting, congressional hearings, and inter-service cooperation. Strategic leaders process information from these areas while assessing alternatives. They formulate practical decisions and garner support.

I. Leading

When leading at the highest levels of the Army, the DOD, and the national security establishment, Army strategic leaders spearhead changes and, at the same time, must balance risks. They balance current operational risks against future institutional or operational risks. To mitigate future institutional risks, these leaders are responsible for providing leadership to the men and women who serve in their organizations and developing their successors to meet future challenges.

A. Leads Others

Strategic leaders influence both the organization and external conditions. Like direct and organizational leaders, strategic leaders lead by example and exert indirect leadership by communicating, inspiring, and motivating. Strategic leaders make decisions balancing delegation, empowerment, and control. A truly effective strategic leader understands the organization from multiple perspectives, transcending from an inside perspective to understanding the views of outsiders. Strategic leaders are able to move beyond their own experiential biases to view the environment and their mission objectively. Through formal and informal networks, strategic leaders actively seek information relevant to their organizations as well as subject matter experts who can help.

B. Extends Influence

Strategic leaders use focused messages to extend influence and to gain support. Whether by nuance or overt presentation, strategic leaders represent the Army and influence other organizations and agencies by communicating what the Army does. Their audience is the Army itself, the Nation, and the rest of the world. Strategic leaders must be proactive in creating relationships. Extending influence requires a shift from direct influence to greater reliance on indirect methods. They focus on increasing engagement with multiple parties or organizations and creating conditions to maximize unity of effort. Strategic leaders rely on writing and public speaking to reinforce their central messages.

C. Leads By Example

Strategic leaders are the ultimate representatives of the organization, its cause, and purpose. As the top leaders for the Nation's military, they also represent our country as diplomats and national representatives. Due to their elevated level of responsibilities and visibility, the Army holds strategic leaders to higher expectations and increased scrutiny. They must exude positivity and confidence. Strategic leaders use multiple outlets to convey strategic messages and set necessary conditions to advance national security interests. Their responsibilities involve spanning the boundaries among the Army and other Services, militaries, coalitions, Congress, industry, and the media.

D. Communicates

Words have international consequences at the strategic level. Communication at the strategic level encompasses a wide array of staffs and functional and operational component teams interacting with each other as well as external agencies. In their interaction with others, strategic leaders need a sharp sense of organizational and personal dynamics. One prominent difference between strategic leaders and leaders at other levels is the greater emphasis on symbolic communication. Strategic leaders must carefully consider the enduring nature of all their communications. Strategic leaders' words, decisions, and actions often have consequences beyond their immediate intent.

Candor and integrity must always be hallmarks of a strategic leader to earn general trust. They must carefully use their authority to identify messages and convey them to the right target audiences. Knowing when to speak and to whom can be just as important as what is said. To achieve desired outcomes, strategic leaders commit to a few powerful and consistent messages that they repeat in different settings. They devise and follow a communications plan outlining how to address each audience. When preparing to address an audience, they determine its composition and agenda beforehand so they know how best to reach its members. They carefully assess the message effect in the categories of medium, frequency, vocabulary, and context. Ensuring the message goes to the right groups with the desired effect is essential.

II. Developing

Strategic leaders make investments with a long-term focus. Most importantly, strategic leaders set the conditions for long-term success by developing subordinates who can take the institution to its next level of capability. This effort calls for initiative to experiment and innovate. Developing the institution, its organizations, and people involves an ongoing balance of operating today and building for tomorrow and, in general, being good stewards of the resources the nation entrusts to its care.

A. Prepares Self

Strategic leaders develop throughout their career. An honest understanding of self is important to be able to draw on strengths and compensate for weaknesses. Neither General Marshall nor General Eisenhower had led troops in combat before assuming strategic leadership positions in World War II, but both were instrumental in preparing and leading the United States and its allies to victory. Eisenhower especially felt disadvantaged by his lack of experience. Both future strategic leaders compensated with professional education between the wars, gaining a strategic appreciation of the conditions and the future that was far better than those with extensive combat experience were.

B. Creates a Positive Environment

Strategic leaders influence the culture of the Army. They, like all leaders, are responsible for creating a positive environment in which to work, where individuals can thrive and be productive. Strategic leaders, by personal example and critical resourcing decisions, sustain the culture and policies that encourage both the individual and the Army to learn and evolve.

Strategic leaders ensure the Army Values and the Warrior Ethos remain fundamental to the Army's culture. They employ culture to support vision, accomplish the mission and improve the organization. Organizational culture that endorses the Army Values should reinforce ethical climates. A healthy culture is a powerful motivational tool. Strategic leaders use culture to guide and inspire large, diverse organizations.

C. Develops Others

Strategic leaders, as all leaders, have the responsibility to actively develop direct subordinates. Strategic leaders are the top-level stewards of the Army, caring for and managing the people, physical, and financial resources entrusted to them. Strategic leaders become enablers as they underwrite the learning, efforts, projects, and ideas of rising leaders. Through developing others, strategic leaders build a team of leaders prepared to fill critical positions in the future.

D. Stewards the Profession

Strategic leaders, as senior stewards of the Army, are responsible for reinforcing trust and ensuring the ethical design, generation, support, and application of land-power. Strategic leaders have the greatest influence on Army policies, regulations, programs, and systems. They balance today's operational requirements against tomorrow's force structure and leadership needs. Their goal is to steward the profession by developing a core of Army leaders with relevant competencies.

III. Achieving

Strategic leaders organize and integrate their efforts to prepare for and achieve the goals of the Army, joint forces, the Nation, and organizations with which they collaborate. Their ability to get results is a function of how well they integrate their leader competencies. The National Security Strategy, National Defense Strategy, and National Military Strategy guide strategic leaders as they develop their visions. Strategic leaders must define for their diverse organizations what success means. They monitor progress and results by drawing on personal observations, organized review and analysis, strategic management plans, and informal discussions.

A. Strategic Planning and Execution

By reconciling political and economic constraints with the Army's needs, strategic leaders navigate to move the force forward using a combination of strategy and budget processes. They spend a great deal of time obtaining and allocating resources and determining conceptual directions, especially those judged critical for future strategic positioning and others necessary to prevent readiness shortfalls. They oversee the Army's responsibilities under Title 10 of the United States Code.

B. Consistently Assess Capabilities

To put strategic vision, concepts, and plans into reality, strategic leaders must employ reliable feedback systems to monitor capabilities and adherence to values and ethics. They must assess many conditions to determine the success of policies, operations, and vision. Other assessment efforts involve understanding the will and opinions of the Nation, expressed through law, policy, leaders, and the media.

Strategic leaders assess a broad range of factors to gain a complete picture of progress toward goals and mission objectives. They rely on performance indicators to signal how well systems and processes balance the imperatives of doctrine, organization, training, materiel, leadership and education, personnel, and facilities. Assessments may also include monitoring such areas as resource use, development of subordinates, efficiency, effects of stress and fatigue, morale, ethical considerations, and mission accomplishment.

Leader Development

Ref: FM 6-22, Leader Development (Jun '15), chap. 1 and 2.

The Army depends upon itself to develop adaptable leaders able to achieve mission accomplishment in dynamic, unstable, and complex environments. A robust, holistic leader development program is essential. Through a mix of education, training, and experience, Army leader development processes produce and sustain agile, adaptive, and innovative leaders who act with boldness and initiative in dynamic, complex situations to execute missions according to doctrine, orders, and training. Furthermore, it also produces leaders that possess the integrity and willingness to act in the absence of orders, when existing orders, doctrine or their own experience no longer fit the situation, or when unforeseen opportunities or threats arise.

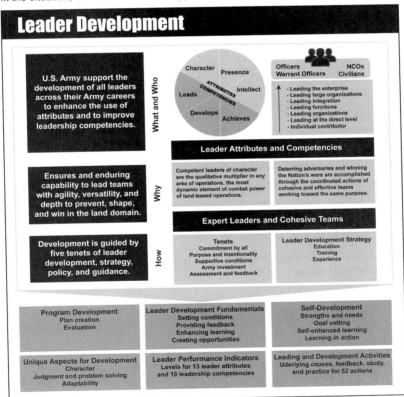

Ref: FM 6-22 (Jun '15), Introductory Figure 1. Integrating diagram.

The goal of leader development programs is to develop Army leaders who clearly provide purpose, direction, motivation, and vision to their teams and subordinates while executing missions to support their commander's intent. Leaders at all levels need to be prepared to understand the strategic context for execution and success of any mission.

Leader development is fundamental to our Army—leader development is the deliberate, continuous, sequential, and progressive process—founded in Army values—that grows Soldiers and Army Civilians into competent and confident leaders capable of decisive action. Leader development is achieved through the life¬long synthesis of the knowledge, skills, and experiences gained through the training and education opportunities in the institutional, operational, and self-development domains (AR 350-1). A key component of leader development is remaining focused on the professionalism of our leaders and those they lead. By developing and promoting a professional force, the Army develops trust on several levels: between Soldiers; between Soldiers and leaders; between Soldiers and Army Civilians; between the Soldiers, their families and the Army; and between the Army and the American people. This is why the Army is committed to providing quality institutions of education and training along with challenging experiences throughout a career.

I. Tenets of Army Leader Development

The tenets of Army leader development provide the essential principles that have made the Army successful at developing its leaders. The tenets also provide a backdrop for the Army principles of unit training. The overarching tenets of Army leader development are—

- Strong commitment by the Army, superiors, and individuals to leader development.
- Clear purpose for what, when, and how to develop leadership.
- Supportive relationships and culture of learning.
- Three mutually supportive domains (institutional, operational, and self-development) that enable education, training, and experience.
- Providing, accepting, and acting upon candid assessment and feedback.

Development of people is an Army priority. Commitment represents intention and engagement from the individual, from supportive leaders, and from the Army. Beyond their directed responsibility to develop subordinates, leaders want to serve in an organization that values camaraderie and teamwork and improves the capabilities of others. Leaders have a directed responsibility to develop their subordinates; accountability for implementation follows responsibility. Leaders must be committed to the development of others and themselves. Teams change and organizations change when individuals choose to engage and improve.

Development depends on having clear purpose for what, when and how to develop. Good leader development is purposeful and goal-oriented. A clearly established purpose enables leaders to guide, assess, and accomplish development. The principles of leader development describe goals for what leaders need to be developed to do: leading by example, developing subordinates, creating a positive environment for learning, exercising the art and science of mission command, adaptive performance, critical and creative thinking, and knowing subordinates and their families. The core leader competencies and attributes identified in ADRP 6-22 and the Army Leader Development Strategy (ALDS) provide additional detail of what leaders need to be able to do.

Supportive relationships and a culture of learning recognize that for development to occur a willingness to engage with others must exist. This tenet relates to two of the principles of leader development: creating a learning environment and knowing subordinates and their families (see ADRP 7-0). Leaders, organizations, and the entire Army must set the conditions for development to occur. Leader development is a mindset incorporated into all organizational requirements and mission accomplishment. Leaders must balance leader development against organizational requirements and mission performance. In operational units and other organizations, development can occur concurrently with training and mission performance, especially when leaders create an environment that places real value and accountability on leader development activities and the Soldiers and civilians to be developed.

Development occurs through both formal systems and informal practices. Reception and integration, newcomer training, developmental tasks and assignments, individual and collective training, educational events, transition or succession planning, and broadening are all activities where development occurs and should be encouraged. Development involves experiential learning that is consistent with the principle of train as you fight. The performance of duties is always an opportunity for learning while doing. Any experience that shapes and improves performance enhances development.

Feedback is necessary to guide and gauge development. Formal and informal feedback based on observation and assessment provide information to confirm or increase self-awareness about developmental progress. The Army established performance monitoring, evaluation reports, coaching, mentoring, and growth counseling processes to engage leaders and individuals. Each is essential for development.

II. Growth Across Levels of Leadership

Leaders develop the confidence, leadership, and the competence needed for more complex and higher-level assignments through education, training, and experience gained throughout a career. The Army balances education, training, and experience to develop leaders at all ranks and in all cohorts (officer, warrant officer, NCO, and Army Civilian). While the core leader competencies and attributes remain the same across levels, fine points in application and of expectations change. See ADRP 6-22 for discussions on leadership at the direct, organizational, and strategic levels.

The processes and expectations for each cohort are similar, while the outcomes are slightly different. Grounded in the Army Values, the Army expects all cohorts to be resilient, adaptive, and creative throughout careers of service to the Nation.

The Army develops officers, at all echelons, to understand and practice the mission command philosophy to lead and execute unified land operations. The Army expects officers to integrate leader development practices with collective and individual training to accomplish the Army's missions and develop subordinates for future responsibilities. They routinely operate at direct-level interactions with others and work at the organizational and strategic levels to plan, prepare, execute, and assess leader development policies, systems, and practices. Warrant officers serve at all echelons as the primary integrators and managers of Army systems. They bring an unequalled depth of knowledge, experience, and perspective in their primary areas of expertise. Warrant officers, at all echelons, understand and practice the mission command philosophy to execute unified land operations. See DA PAM 600-3 for descriptions of the full spectrum of developmental opportunities throughout a career.

NCOs are responsible for setting and maintaining high-quality standards and discipline while conducting daily missions and making intent-driven decisions. NCOs serve as standard-bearers and role models vital to training, educating, and developing subordinates. Through training, coaching, mentoring, counseling, and informal interaction, they guide the development of Soldiers in an everyday basis and play a role in the development of junior officers. NCOs, at all echelons, understand and practice the mission command philosophy to execute unified land operations. NCOs advise officers at all levels and are an important source of knowledge and discipline for all enlisted matters. See DA PAM 600-25 for professional development opportunities.

Army Civilians provide crucial continuity that complements the roles of Soldiers. Army Civilian leaders require a broad understanding of military, political, and business-related strategies, as well as, high levels of managerial, leadership, and decision-making skills. Army Civilians create and practice leader development for other Army Civilians and support the development of military personnel while serving as supervisors, mentors, and instructors. At all echelons, Army Civilians should understand and exercise the mission command philosophy while providing mission-based capabilities to support Army missions.

Refer to DOD Instruction 1430.16 and AR 690-950 for specifics.

III. Leadership Requirements

Ref: FM 6-22, Leader Development (Jun '15), pp. 1-3 to 1-5.

An Army leader, by virtue of assumed role or assigned responsibility, inspires and influences people to accomplish organizational goals. Army leaders motivate people both inside and outside the chain of command to pursue actions, focus thinking, and shape decisions for the greater good of the organization (ADP 6-22). These occur through leadership—the process of influencing people by providing purpose, direction, and motivation to accomplish the mission and improve the organization (ADP 6-22). The nation and the Army has articulated the expectations of leaders in the Army. The Army leadership requirements model (see figure 1-1) illustrates expectations of every leader, whether military or civilian, officer or enlisted, active or reserve. This model aligns the desired outcome of leader development activities and personnel practices to a common set of characteristics valued throughout the Army. It covers the core requirements and expectations of leaders at all levels of leadership. Attributes are the desired internal characteristics of a leader—what the Army wants leaders to be and know. Competencies are skills and learnable behaviors the Army expects leaders to acquire, demonstrate, and continue to enhance—what the Army wants leaders to do.

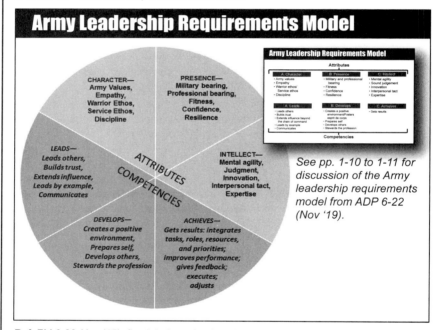

Ref: FM 6-22 (Jun '15), fig. 1-1. Army leadership requirements model.

The competency of getting results requires special mention to counter beliefs that only the end result matters. While the other elements in the model address enablers, conditions, and processes, the achieves category is where leadership is most direct and most challenging. The actions for gets results integrate all other components in a way that brings people, values, purpose, motivation, processes, and task demands together to make the difference in outcomes related to the mission. The integrating actions of this competency also affect all other attributes and competencies. Getting results must simultaneously address improvements to the organization, Soldier and civilian well-being and motivation, adjustments due to situational changes, ethical mission accomplishment, and so on. All the competencies and attributes together lead to trust between the leader and the led, trust that lays the foundation for mission command and effective teamwork.

The leadership requirements and principles of mission command are mutually supportive. Understanding and practicing the principles of mission command are imperative for all leaders: officers, warrant officers, noncommissioned officers (NCOs), and Army Civilians. Mission command is the exercise of authority and direction by the commander using mission orders to enable disciplined initiative within the commander's intent to empower agile and adaptive leaders in the conduct of unified land operations (ADP 6-0). While commanders exercise mission command, the actions of subordinates influence effectiveness.

Through practices in all domains of leader development, the philosophy of mission command becomes ingrained in the Army's ethos and culture. Army leaders, Soldiers, and Civilians at every echelon throughout the operating force and the institutional Army apply mission command principles in the conduct of routine functions and daily activities.

To best prepare leaders for the uncertainty associated with Army operations, leaders must develop and create opportunities to understand and become proficient in employing the mission command principles. This development requires continual assessment and refinement throughout the individual's service. Leaders who fail to assess or develop their people or teams will not have prepared them to take disciplined initiative. Additionally, the leaders will not understand what individuals and teams are capable of doing and will not be in a position to capitalize on using mission orders.

Army leaders exercise mission command. Table 1-1 below shows the linkage between the principles of mission command and the competencies and attributes of Army leaders in the leadership requirements model. Leader development activities must maintain the vision of developing leaders to execute mission command.

Principles of Mission Command	Army Leadership Requirements (ADRP 6-22)
Build cohesive teams through mutual trust	Develops others—builds effective teams. Builds trust—sets personal example; sustains a climate of trust. Demonstrates the Army Values and decisions consistent with the Army Ethic. Leads others—balances subordinate needs with mission requirements. Extends influence beyond the chain of command—builds consensus and resolves conflict. Creates a positive environment—fosters teamwork.
Create shared understanding	Communicates—creates shared understanding. Demonstrates interpersonal tact—interaction with others. Leads others—provides purpose, motivation, and inspiration. Extends influence beyond the chain of command—uses understanding in diplomacy, negotiation, consensus building. Builds trust—uses appropriate methods of influence to energize others. Creates positive environment—supports learning. Gets results—designates, clarifies and deconflicts roles.
Provide a clear commander's intent	Leads others—provides purpose. Communicates—employs engaging communication techniques. Gets results—prioritizes taskings.
Exercise disciplined initiative	Leads others—influence others to take initiative. Demonstrates the Army Values—duty. Demonstrates self-discipline—maintains professional bearing and conduct. Demonstrates mental agility—anticipates uncertain or changing conditions. Gets results—accounts for commitment to task.
Use mission orders	Leads others—provides purpose without excessive, detailed direction. Develops others—expands knowledge. Gets results—executes plans to accomplish the mission the right way.
Accept prudent risk	Leads others—assesses and manages risk. Gets results—identifies, allocates, and manages resources. Stewardship—makes good decisions about resources.

Ref: FM 6-22 (Jun '15), table 1-1. Principles of mission command linkage to Army leadership requirements.

IV. Transitions Across Organizational Levels

Cultural and individual mindsets that promote continuous learning are the cornerstone for creating and sustaining an agile Army. Through activities in the institutional, operational, and self-development domains, personnel obtain education, training, and experiences in order to grow and be able to succeed at positions of greater responsibility. As Army leaders progress in leadership responsibilities, it is necessary for them to develop new mindsets and to refine how they will lead at the next level.

Understanding key shifts in requirements across the progression of levels, helps individuals prepare for what may be ahead of them and helps prepare others to acquire capabilities for their next level. For the Army, the refinement of requirements across levels helps with management of talent. The Army provides opportunities for developmental experience before assigning leaders to positions of greater responsibility.

The timing of development is especially important in the military because personnel join and move through a series of alternating and progressive education, training, and operational experiences. The approach applies to Army Civilians as well; however, Army Civilians understand that federal service does not program advancement opportunities for most positions. Army Civilians move across positions based on the governing regulations and laws relating to applying for and filling vacated or newly created positions. Ideally, the best of the direct-level leaders are developed into organizational level leaders and ultimately into strategic and enterprise level leaders.

A clear framework of leadership requirements provides leaders the basis to assess their strengths and developmental needs and to determine goals for improvement. Created through lengthy study and practice, the Army's leadership requirements model (figure 1-1) specifically provides leaders with an enduring set of attributes and competencies expected of them. The model provides a consistent reference point throughout the progression of professional and personal development. Leaders must improve in all the leader competencies, become more knowledgeable about the way the military operates, and understand how to operate in complex geopolitical situations. In addition to the leadership requirements model, leaders must grow in their ability to understand, visualize, describe, direct, lead, and assess under differing conditions that change at each level of leadership. As leaders progress, they will experience greater challenges based on the scope of the situation, the consequences and risks involved, and the time horizon. As the scope increases, the number of people and outside parties involved also increases. The consequences of decisions increase, as do the risks that leaders must address. The length of time that leaders' decisions apply tend to increase at higher levels as well as the time over which leaders can apply influence.

Transitioning to the next stage in a career can be difficult, regardless of demonstration of performance and potential at prior levels. When moving into new positions with different demands, individuals may not perform at a previous high level. Individuals must have a developmental mindset to improve what is within their capability and be motivated to do their best. The Army endorses a culture where individuals continually strive to learn, broaden personal skills, and improve regardless of whether such efforts lead to promotion.

Army Organizational Transitions

Ref: FM 6-22, Leader Development (Jun '15), pp. 1-8 to 1-9.

For military leaders there are six transition points spanning the full range of organizational levels. The changing requirements across levels are illustrative of the relative amount of emphasis needed on certain skills or attributes. Not all levels and transitions apply to all cohorts, military fields, or functions and there will be positions that do not fit neatly into the model. For Army Civilians, there are similar transition points, each of which requires additional leadership skills at progressive levels of responsibility. Six transitions that apply to Army organizations are—

- **Leading at the direct level.** Initial-entry Soldiers and civilians transition from a focus on self to providing direct leadership to others. Junior leaders learn how to plan daily tasks and activities, understand organizational constructs, and how to interact with subordinates, peers, and superiors.

- **Leading organizations.** The second transition occurs when leaders begin to lead at the organizational level. This level begins at company, battery, troop, staff, and similar organization levels for Army Civilians. Direct level leadership still occurs at this level, but the leaders become leaders of leaders and will rarely be performing individual tasks, unless out of emergency or in undermanned organizations. Coaching subordinate, direct-line leaders and setting a positive example as a leader are two characteristics that stand out for managers.

- **Leading functions.** The third transition is from leading an organization (as a leader of direct-line leaders) to leading functions. This level involves directing functions beyond a single individual's experience path. Operating with other leaders of leaders and adopting a longer-term perspective are key characteristics of this phase. Functional leaders typically include majors, mid-level warrant officers, and mid-level NCOs.

- **Leading integration.** A fourth transition occurs when leaders assume command and leadership responsibility for battalion and similar sized generating force organizations. These leaders must become more adept at establishing a vision, communicating it, and deciding on goals and mission outcomes. They need to find more time for reflection and analysis and value the importance of making trade-offs between future goals and current needs. Positive attitudes related to trust, accepting advice, and accepting feedback will pay dividends during this phase and into the future.

- **Leading large organizations.** A fifth transition happens when leaders operate at the brigade-equivalent and higher levels of operational and institutional organizations. These leaders develop strategy for organizational and strategic-level operations. They are operating outside of their experience paths while leading others operating beyond theirs as well. Leaders in this phase will only be successful by valuing the expertise and success of others and operating within the multiple layers of their organization. Humility is a desired characteristic of organizational and strategic leaders who should recognize that others have specialized expertise indispensable to success. A modest view of one's own importance helps underscore an essential ingredient to foster cooperation across organizational boundaries. Even the most humble person needs to guard against an imperceptible inflation of ego when constantly exposed to high levels of attention and opportunities.

- **Leading the enterprise.** A final step occurs in the transition to serving as an enterprise leader. Enterprise leaders must be long-term, visionary thinkers who spend considerable time interacting with agencies beyond the military. This level of leader must be willing to relinquish control of the pieces of the enterprise to strategic and lower-level leaders.

V. Cohesive and Effective Teams

Ref: FM 6-22, Leader Development (Jun '15), pp. 1-5 to 1-7.

Teams are an essential configuration of how people come together to accomplish missions. In the Army, teams occur throughout every structure level of the organization. The Army as a whole is teams of teams. It begins with buddy teams—two military members who look after each other in a variety of positions and environments. The missions of the Army demand that leaders and teams be developed and ready. It is proven that a team is more effective than an individual when members work together, using their unique skills, experiences, and capabilities. The Army leadership competency categories cover how Army leaders lead; develop themselves, their subordinates, and organizations; and bring efforts together to achieve results. Army leaders are charged with developing others and conducting team building. Holistic leader development programs contribute to unit cohesion, resilience, and agility by producing leaders and teams that are creative, life-long learners, adaptable, and capable of exercising mission command.

The mission command philosophy helps to set the conditions for developing teams. Creating a shared understanding is the first step and most important in developing a team. It gives the team a unifying purpose. The leader sets the tone; in a team-focused climate, members understand how they contribute to the overall success of the organization. Knowing the 'why' drives each action taken. Developing an overall sense of team and building an effective high quality team are two separate actions that should be parts of the overall leader development program. The goal of team building is to improve the quality of the team and how it works together to accomplish the mission.

The Army relies on effective teams to perform tasks, achieve objectives, and accomplish missions. Building and maintaining teams that operate effectively is essential to both internal and external organizations. To do this, Army leaders employ Army team building, a continuous process of enabling a group of people to reach their goals and improve their effectiveness through leadership and various exercises, activities, and techniques.

Ineffective Teams	Effective Teams
Fail to listen to relevant input of a team member.	Emphasize what is common among members rather than focus on characteristics that could cause subgroups to form.
Speak despairingly about other members.	
Fail to enforce or encourage discipline in the team.	
Compete, rather than cooperate, with other team members.	Hold a shared vision about operating as a team.
Argue with other team members in front of counterparts or other individuals.	Share information that may be useful to other team members.
Fail to act or make decisions on issues that have implications for the team.	Ensure team members periodically engage in group activities (such as sports, meals, or other off-duty activities).
Focus more on self-interest than the well-being of the team.	Act quickly to promote togetherness when schisms in the group appear or morale drops.
Give less than full effort because of low morale or lack of confidence in other team members.	Show appreciation and concern for team members.
	Act as a team instead of individuals; take pride in team accomplishments.

Ref: FM 6-22 (Jun '15), table 1-2. Signs of ineffective and effective teams.

Three qualities measure good teamwork: identity, cohesion, and climate. Team identity develops through a shared understanding of what the team exists to do and what the team values. Cohesion is the unity or togetherness across team members and forms from mutual trust, cooperation, and confidence. Teamwork increases when teams operate in a positive, engaging, and emotionally safe environment. An engaging environment is one where team members desire to work together on required missions; they feel a sense of self-worth and they are accomplishing something more important than they are. A safe environment occurs when team members feel they can be open and are not threatened by unwarranted criticism.

See chap. 4, Army Team Building, for further discussion.

I. Program Development

Leader
Development

Ref: FM 6-22, Leader Development (Jun '15), chap 2.

Leader development occurs for the benefit of both individuals and the organization. The Army is known for its success in developing leaders rapidly. Multiple leader development opportunities occur in organizations, though not always used for their learning value. Without intent, plans, or a program for leader development, organizational emphasis on learning is based on commander interest and unit climate. Leader development programs leverage the opportunities for development to address individual and organizational goals for development.

Commanders are responsible for training and leader development in their units and for providing a culture in which learning takes place. They must deliberately plan, prepare, execute, and assess training and leader development as part of their overall operations. Commanders and leaders must integrate leader development into their organizational training plans or leader development programs.

Developing Army leaders at all levels, military and civilian, is the best means to ensure the Army can adapt to the uncertainties the future holds. Individuals who feel that the Army and their leaders are interested in them are motivated to demonstrate greater initiative and to engage fully in leader development. Leader development programs that are individualized and that have a multi-leveled aspect are the most effective. The content of leader development programs need to account for the individual's levels of competence, character, and commitment.

Organizational leader development plans must nest in purpose and guidance of the higher organization's plan. Plans should be consistent with Army enterprise concepts, strategy, and guidance on leader development. Leader development plans should provide guidance to subordinate units yet allow them freedom to determine practices and schedules most conducive to their missions. Plans up and down an organizational structure need to align to create synergy and unity of effort. A battalion leader development plan or equivalent-sized unit will identify specific processes supporting leader development. Generating force organizations headed by a colonel or similar ranking Army Civilian are a good target for leader development plans that detail specific processes. The battalion plan should anticipate the needs of and execution by its subordinate units.

Variations in programs will occur across echelons depending on the type and size of the organization. For example, a division has greater latitude in selecting leaders for special assignments than does a battalion due to the wider scope of opportunities and larger number of leaders. A Reserve Component unit has fewer training days to plan and schedule team building events, so there may be a greater role for self-development and mentoring. Detached and dispersed units have fewer organic assets to prepare and conduct special events but may have access to external opportunities, such as a training detachment on a university campus.

The Army holds commanders accountable for unit leader development by regulation (see AR 350-1). Accountability can be included as part of the organizational inspection program (see AR 1-201). Responsibility for leader development cuts across all leader and staff roles. Some examples of roles and responsibilities for developing leaders are—

- Each leader develops subordinates.
- The senior warrant officer, noncommissioned officer, and civilian leaders take

ownership for their cohorts' leader development in the organization.

- Each leader (as well as those who aspire to positions of leadership) takes responsibility for their own leader development.

The next-higher echelon commander, human resources and operations staff, and senior cohort leaders must clarify leader development roles and responsibilities. These individuals directly and indirectly affect the efficiency and effectiveness of leader development.

Delineating Responsibilities

Efficient implementation of leader development programs depends on a clear definition and allocation of responsibilities across leaders and staff both in and outside the organization. Develop a matrix to document notes on the roles and responsibilities for developing leaders in the organization.

I. Unit Leader Development Programs

Leader development is a mindset and process, not merely an event, reflected by everything leaders do. An opportunity for leader development exists in every event, class, assignment, duty position, discussion, physical training formation, briefing, and engagement. Leader development is a continuous and purposeful process. It is an ongoing process intended to achieve incremental and progressive results over time.

Plan Creation

Various types and echelons of commands and organizations label their leader development guidance with different descriptions such as strategy, philosophy, policy, memorandum, plan, or standing procedure. The title and format are less important than having a good plan—one that aligns with the tenets of leader development: committed organization; clear purpose; supportive learning culture; enabler of education, training, and experience; and feedback. The plan helps to inspire and guide the organization to engage in leader development. Plans that incorporate leader development into daily operations without creating extra events will be well received and have the greatest chance for effective implementation. The imperative of having a plan is to bring attention to leader development, provide focus and purpose, encourage the mindset, set the conditions, show how development should occur, and coordinate efforts across the organization.

Developing a leader development plan follows the same steps used in the operations process (see ADP 5-0). Planning involves understanding a situation, envisioning a desired future, and planning effective ways of achieving that future. The plan should allow for disciplined initiative by subordinate units and individual leaders. A leader development plan is specific because the outcomes need to address both organizational and individual goals as well as both short-term and long-term goals. The long-term focus extends beyond a military commander's tour and beyond the military personnel's time in the unit. Most Army Civilian leaders are not reassigned based on time, though leader development plans similar to those in operational units can serve their needs. Once the commander's visualization is described and the plan is developed, it directs preparation and execution of the unit's leader development program. The commander and unit leaders lead the execution of the program and assess its progress. The leader development program will create change in the organization and in individuals—it is a living document. As the program creates change and as leaders develop, the plan can be updated.

A. Understand

To aid in understanding, command teams can use formal assessments such as command climate surveys, unit Multi-Source Assessment and Feedback (MSAF) 360 assessments, training center after action review (AAR) take-home packages, and

Assessment Considerations

Ref: FM 6-22, Leader Development (Jun '15), p. 2-3.

Planning a holistic leader development program starts with an assessment. Leaders gain the information needed to shape and inform an assessment from multiple external and internal sources. These are some sources for leaders to consider when developing an assessment:

External

- Review the Army Leader Development Strategy, Army Campaign Plan, and command guidance.
- Meet with personnel who focus on the organization's well-being such as the higher headquarters' chaplain, Staff Judge Advocate, Inspector General, other staff, and support agencies.
- Review higher headquarters' leader development guidance, programs, and plans.
- Review prior command inspection program results.

Internal

- Mission essential task list assessment.
- Exercise or deployment results and after action reviews.
- Operational and training exercise performance records.
- Upcoming events or training calendars.
- Organizational climate surveys.
- Multi-Source Assessment and Feedback unit rollup report.
- Personnel roster and personnel qualification records.
- Personal assessment of subordinates' education and experience.
- Social media.
- Tour work areas and facilities.
- Evaluations and support forms.
- Initial counseling feedback.
- Individual development plans.

The leadership team may not always have existing formal assessments to use. Additionally, the unit mission or composition may change so those sources may no longer apply. In these cases, leaders align goals with their observational assessments and any changes to organizational mission and goals.

One source to determine an organizational developmental baseline is to schedule and complete a unit-level MSAF event. The unit rollup report provides information on organizational leadership strengths and developmental needs that can focus planning and identifying developmental priorities. In addition, assessed leaders receive an individual feedback report highlighting personal leadership strengths and developmental needs. Individuals can use this information to develop their individual development plan (IDP). During periodic developmental counseling sessions, leaders can review subordinate IDPs to gain insight on current developmental priorities and possible program improvements.

command inspection program results to focus on conditions indicating unit strengths and developmental needs. The command team takes these various sources of information along with their own observations and discussions with subordinates and colleagues to determine an appropriate focus.

B. Visualize

There are several sources to inform decisions about setting the desired future end states for leader development. For the philosophy aspects, the team can examine the ALDS, Army Campaign Plan, and the intent in higher and sister organization's leader development plans. The most important and enduring outcomes are stated in a statement of vision or intent, depending on the preference of the commander.

An organizational leader development plan establishes the goals for specific end states. Each leader development plan has four mutually supporting purposes. The leader of each organization has a designated responsibility to 1) accomplish the mission, 2) improve the organization, 3) enable personnel to be prepared to perform their current duties and 4) develop leaders for future responsibilities and other as-signments. Different from unit training plans, the leader development plan addresses long-term outcomes for individuals and the organization (see table 2-1).

	Individual	Organization
Short-term outcomes	Improve personnel capabilities for unit duties	Accomplish the mission
Long-term outcomes	Increase personnel capabilities beyond current assignment	Improve the organization

Ref: FM 6-22 (Jun '15), table 2-1. Goals and end states of the leader development plan.

Outcomes should address at least these four areas. The planning and execution of the leader development program is a responsibility of the leaders in the organization and the individual. The vision or intent helps to focus and synchronize the leader development actions across the organization to achieve the greatest effects.

Leaders who recognize and approach leader development as a process are able to balance the long-term needs of the Army, the short-term and career needs of their subordinates, and the immediate needs of their organizations to determine how and when to integrate leader development opportunities in already-busy schedules

C. Plan

To start a plan, the leadership team goes through a conceptual process to consider how to achieve its desired end state. The end state and enduring purpose help guide the detailed phase of planning that involves the selection of activities to emphasize in the unit's program.

See facing page for further discussion.

From considering the learning enablers and developmental opportunities, the com-mand team will create a plan for scheduling events. The schedule assists those leading and supporting the execution. The schedule maintains a reasonable number of activities and direction of emphasis to help ensure quality. Some events are required, such as performance evaluations and professional growth counseling, and the plan's emphasis triggers other activities. The plan should encourage a mindset where leaders take the initiative to incorporate development into daily activities.

Successful programs integrate formal, semiformal, and informal practices. Policy or regulation direct formal techniques. Addressed in doctrine, semiformal activities are commonly practiced and may be required, but failure to conduct them does not carry punitive consequences. Informal leader development consists of opportunities with a focus on learning.

Planning Leader Development Programs

Ref: FM 6-22, Leader Development (Jun '15), pp. 2-4 to 2-5.

To start a plan, the leadership team goes through a conceptual process to consider how to achieve its desired end state. The end state and enduring purpose help guide the detailed phase of planning that involves the selection of activities to emphasize in the unit's program.

Leaders with a mindset, clear-cut vision, and a passion for developing others, themselves, and teams are the most important elements of a successful leader development program. They capitalize on every opportunity. The activities cover both unit and individual development for short-term and long-term development. The following factors provide ways to structure a plan:

- Phases of a leader's cycle within a unit.
  - Reception.
  - Integration.
  - Utilization.
  - Assignment rotation within the unit.
  - Transition.
- Unit cycles.
  - Sustainable readiness model.
  - Deployment schedule.
  - Green-amber-red time management and training cycles.
- Cohort programs.
  - Sergeant's time.
  - Preparation for Soldier and sergeant excellence boards.
  - NCO professional development.
  - Warrant officer professional development.
  - Officer professional development.
  - Command team.
  - Civilian leader development seminars.
  - Combined leader development programs.
- Developmental focus—common core for the team and all leaders.
  - Essential characteristics of the profession (see ADRP 1).
  - Command climate (see AR 600-20).
  - Mission command principles (see ADRP 6-0).
  - Core leadership competencies (see ADRP 6-22).
  - Core leader attributes (see ADRP 6-22).
  - Performance qualities, such as adaptability, resilience, versatility, creativity.
  - Core unit mission and functions.
- • Developmental focus—career paths for groups of leaders.
  - Career leadership responsibilities (see DA PAM 600-3, DA PAM 600-25, Army Civilian Training, Education, and Development System (ACTEDS)).
  - Career Management Field.
  - Functional area.
  - Army Civilian Career Programs.

D. Execute

Once completed, the leaders distribute the plan throughout the unit to direct program preparation and execution. Depending on the echelon, the leaders will review subordinate unit plans for leader development. The leadership team sets, directs, and leads the organizational goals, shaping the conditions for individual development. Individual leader development is based on the interest and the effort of individuals who develop others and themselves. It is up to each individual to learn, grow, and develop as an Army professional. An individual's IDP is a personal version of a unit leader development plan. Ideally, individuals and their raters work together to develop the IDP. Execution of the leader development plan can become a regular reported item in reviews, situation reports, and training briefs.

Leaders must ensure the plan affects development positively. The plan is a way to emphasize leader development and desired outcomes for individuals and for units. Leaders develop the plan with an intent to seeing it through. Reviewed, assessed, and updated periodically, the plan is a living document. Leaders commit to creating an open learning environment where leader development becomes second nature. This occurs when leaders integrate leader development into daily administrative and training events, as well as deployed operations.

E. Assess

The leadership team needs to ensure that individual development stays the main effort and that the focus does not become the plan or running events. The documented plan can be either an enabler or a detractor to successful execution and achievement of the desired outcomes depending on the degree of mission command and disciplined initiative.

Leaders assess implementation and execution against the established vision and end states. Just as assessments help set goals for the unit leader development plan, assessments focused on implementation and execution provide useful information on how well the end states are being achieved and areas for adjustment. The leadership team can also assess whether the vision and end states were adequate or need improvement.

Leaders must conduct required leader development activities such as performance evaluations, professional growth counseling, IDPs, and command climate surveys. Assessment of a leader in developing others can occur through reviewing how leaders used formal, semi-formal, and informal activities in the program. The leadership requirements model establishes the expectations for these functions and performance evaluations have provided the mechanism for checking. The 360° leader assessments provide personal feedback to the leader on what they have done to establish a positive climate, engage in developing others, and steward the profession. The 360° feedback provides an opportunity to leaders to address and improve their approaches before evaluation.

Leader development is a holistic process that occurs every day aligning training, education, and experience to prepare leaders to improve. Leader development is critical to all cohorts—enlisted, officer, and civilian—the source of the Army's future leaders. The process balances long-term Army needs, short-term and career needs of subordinates, and immediate needs of the organization.

Refer to FM 6-22 (Figures 2-1 through 2-5) for examples of leader development guidance and programs for units. Figure 2-1 (p. 2-8) is a sample battalion plan template followed by an example using that template (figure 2-2, p. 2-10). Program guidance may have annexes for special events or specific cohort programs. Figures 2-3 through 2-5 show example development programs for battalion NCOs, platoon sergeants, and lieutenants.

Learning Enablers and Opportunities

Ref: FM 6-22, Leader Development (Jun '15), tables 2-2 and 2-3 (pp. 2-5 to 2-6).

Table 2-2 lists ways to enable learning. Setting conditions for development, goal setting, assessments, and advice and counsel all contribute to improved learning.

Learning enablers	Formal	Semiformal	Informal
Setting conditions	• Integration and reception counseling. • Initial performance counseling.	• Understand individual differences in strengths, interests, potential, and development methods.	• Getting to know and understand subordinates. • Build rapport to enable supportive development.
Goal setting	• Individual Development Plan.	• 5-year plan.	• Short-term and long-term personal and professional goals. • Stretch goals.
Assessment	• Performance evaluation. • Certifications. • Inspection program. • Command climate. • Commander 360° assessment. • General Officer 360° assessment.	• Organizational certifications. • Unit acculturation program. • Core unit mission and functions review. • Multi-Source Assessment and Feedback-Leader 360° for self-assessment. • Unit 360° assessment.	• Day-to-day observations. • Asking others about a leader. • Sensing sessions.
Advice and guidance	• Performance counseling. • Professional growth counseling.	• Mentoring. • Coaching. • Training center counterpart feedback. • Instructor feedback.	• 5-minute feedback. • Peer discussions. • Indirect questioning (What have you planned or done for your development lately? What have done to help a Soldier today?).

Table 2-3 provides additional opportunities and developmental activities. Both tables separate various techniques into formal, semiformal, and informal categories.

Developmental opportunities	Formal	Semiformal	Informal
Challenging experiences	• Broadening assignments.	• Unit succession planning/ Talent management: • Stretch assignments. • Developmental assignments. • Rotational assignments.	• Opportunities to operate in unfamiliar situations. • Broadening tasks, casualty assistance, staff duty, food service duty.
Group leader development	• Leader Training Program. • After action reviews.	• Officer professional development. • Noncommissioned officer professional development. • Combined events. • Team building events.	• Professional reading and writing program. • Sharing experiences. • Excellence competitions.
Education	• Professional military education courses. • Functional, branch, career program, or special training.	• Scheduling or supporting leaders to attend institutional education	• Encourage utilization of new skills and knowledge of recent graduates.
Self-development	• Structured self-development.	• Guided self-development.	• Self-assessment. • Reflective journaling. • Personalized self-development. • Study and practice.
Collective training	• Incorporate leader development goals and processes into training objectives.	• Team building exercises.	• Shared stories of development.

II. Evaluation of Leader Development Programs

Developing a set of formal and informal indicators that accurately assess the health of unit leader development in the organization is essential. Leaders can use these locally developed indicators to develop a leader development scorecard (see figure 2-6). Indicators may be different for different types of units, such as operational vice institutional. Employing a red/amber/green status suggests indicators requiring further investigation, which may or may not relate directly to unit leader development efforts. The purpose is to identify trends over time and not react adversely to a single occurrence of an indicator.

Add locally-developed leader development indicators to the unit training brief for subordinate units to track and report on indicators of leader development like other key unit systems (such as training, maintenance, or budget). Refine the measures to those that accurately indicate the health of leader development.

Unit Indicators	Status (red/amber/green)	Action Needed
All key leader positions are filled	amber	Review succession plan for first sergeants
Unit leader changes have little or no detrimental effect on unit performance	green	Sustain job shadow
Multiple qualified candidates competed for last leadership position vacancy	amber	Talk with sergeant major to increase platoon sergeant candidates
A subordinate leader shared a challenge they are experiencing	red	Share a personal challenge
Leader(s) express interest in joining this unit	green	Follow up with G1
Leader(s) express a desire to stay in the unit	amber	1 - Yes; 1 - no - talk with chain of command
Last leader with option to leave the Army was retained	amber	Interview captains on career intentions
Other units requested a leader from this unit	green	Commander selected as general's aide
Unsolicited Soldier comments about their leaders	amber	Talk with sergeant major about unit leaders
A new idea or innovation was implemented	red	Implement feedback from brown bag lunch session
Initial performance of new leaders is high	green	Sustain role models running certification
Overall unit performance is high; no sub-unit is a consistent low performer	amber	Increase unit visits to HHC
Leaders and their units demonstrate lessons learned; few repeat mistakes	green	Sustain personal AARs
Leaders want to discuss strengths and developmental needs	green	Sustain IDP use with counseling
Surveys indicate good morale and climate	amber	Follow-up on climate surveys

Ref: FM 6-22 (Jun '15), fig. 2-6. Example unit leader development scorecard.

II. Fundamentals of Development

Ref: FM 6-22, Leader Development (Jun '15), chap 3.

Every part of the Army is vested in maximizing its human capital to prevent, shape, and win in the land domain. Every individual that makes up this capital is—or can become—a pivotal leader. While the Army employs many strategies in the development of leaders, the most influential of these coincide with the time spent in operational assignments for Soldiers and while at work for Army Civilians. Working in real settings—solving real problems with actual team members—provides the challenges and conditions where leaders can see the significance of and have the opportunity to perform leadership activities.

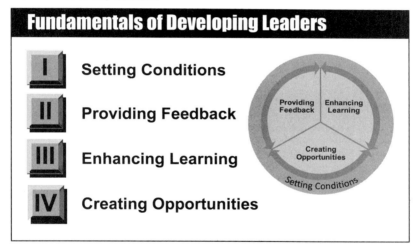

Fundamentals of Developing Leaders

I Setting Conditions

II Providing Feedback

III Enhancing Learning

IV Creating Opportunities

Ref: FM 6-22 (Jun '15), fig. 3-1. Fundamentals of developing leaders.

The following sections focus on the fundamentals of leader development:

- **Setting conditions for leader development**. Leaders personally model behaviors that encourage leader development, create an environment that encourages on-duty learning, apply principles that accelerate learning, and get to know the leaders in the organization.

- **Providing feedback on a leader's actions**. Provide opportunities for observation, assessment, and feedback. Immediate, short bursts of feedback on actual leader actions enhance leader development in operational assignments as well as regular counseling.

- **Enhancing learning.** Use leaders as role models in the organization. Encourage mentoring, training, reflection, and study. Learning from other leaders is one of the most effective and efficient methods of development.

- **Creating opportunities.** Modify position assignments to challenge leaders. Be deliberate about the selection and succession of leaders. Integrate leader development across day-to-day activities. Evaluate its effectiveness.

Leaders encourage development and learning in their subordinates in every aspect of daily activities and should seek to learn something new every day. Self-development can occur anywhere, so it is an important aspect of development in organizations. Other settings, such as education, can apply the principles that are effective and efficient for development in units. Units and organizations operate in a more decentralized manner than educational and training centers. Decentralization makes the sharing of effective practices necessary and beneficial. Educational institutions and training centers are organizations that can adopt these same leader development principles for their own staffs, students, and trainees.

The fundamentals of development simplify and span the formal leader development activities that the Army has advocated, such as assessing, counseling, coaching, mentoring, broadening, and team building. The fundamentals are common across formal and informal leader development activities and serve to reinforce an Army developmental culture and a developmental mindset.

Other sources provide guidance on techniques associated with the formal activities, such as AR 350-1 on MSAF assessments, AR 623-3 on the evaluation process, ATP 6-22.1 on the counseling process, ADRP 6-22 and MSAF resources on coaching, AR 621-7 and DA PAM 600-3 on broadening, and emerging doctrine on team building.

Efforts to implement leader development will yield better results if the focus is on methods that have already proven effective. Army leadership requires the establishment of interpersonal relationships based on trust and setting the example for everyone—subordinates, peers, and superiors. In leader development surveys, leaders ranked leading a unit, personal examples, and mentoring as the three most effective ways to develop their leadership qualities. Integrating the fundamentals of leader development into the organization creates a positive, learning climate and builds a mindset among leaders that development is a priority. Experience is a powerful learning tool, however, learning from experience is not guaranteed. As the tenets of leader development convey, learning requires commitment and purpose. For learning to occur, experiences need to be interpreted.

I. Setting Conditions

Establishing a culture that promotes leader development throughout the organization is necessary. The organizational culture needs to embrace leader development to reinforce it as an expected part of daily operations. The culture is affected by leaders who share a mindset that leader development is important and is achievable as part of what they do each day. Leaders need to designate and protect time for leader development and develop a culture that encourages and rewards professional development.

Leaders create a pro-development culture through the same behaviors they use for any task. Individuals will accomplish what leaders view as important. How leaders react under pressure or during organizational crises will shape what the organization views as important. Leaders' assignment and prioritization of resources also speaks to what is valued and important. What coaching, teaching, mentoring, and counseling that leaders do sends a message of what is important. Leaders' treatment of others through rewards, recognition, and feedback is another sign of what is important. Leaders who demonstrate behaviors supportive of learning and development create a learning environment for the whole organization. ADRP 6-22 describes the importance of leaders setting the example.

Two other keys are addressed as part of setting conditions:

- Leaders establish a learning environment by encouraging subordinates to take reasonable risks, grow, and develop on their own initiative.
- Leaders gain knowledge of subordinates in the organization as individuals with unique skills, abilities, backgrounds, and goals.

A. Learning Environment

Setting the Conditions for Development

Leaders set the conditions for leader development by performing their tasks and missions in ways that signal to subordinates throughout the organization that leader development is important. It can have a big effect in return for minimal personal time and resource investment.

> *Be receptive to individuals input, recommendations, and advice. Be receptive and shut down others who belittle someone's suggestion to take a different or creative approach. Good leaders back subordinates trying to do the right thing and learn something new at the same time. A positive leadership climate encourages a learning environment.*

See following page (p. 2-21) for discussion of leader actions for setting the conditions for development.

Techniques For Creating Conditions Conducive to Development

Subtle actions on the leader's part build trust and communicate the role of trainer and developer. Experienced leaders use the following techniques to create a developmental culture:

- Be present to observe enough key activities without smothering the leader. After initial observations, give them time and space to exercise leadership without being under the observation spotlight. This helps establish the leader's role as a supportive resource rather than an evaluative note taker. It also builds trust, self-confidence, and creativity in the follower.

- Take an indirect approach. Start by providing descriptions of observations along with positive and negative outcomes. Allow the subordinate to understand what is going well and what needs improvement. The opposite of an indirect approach is to be micromanaging and overly prescriptive, outlining specifics for completion.

- Give each leader a fresh, objective start. Make comparisons between subordinates and an objective standard. Avoid subjective comparisons to past leaders or units (including personal experiences). It is appropriate to reflect on and use personal experience. The bottom line is to observe and assess each leader on individual merit. Avoid thinking of the observation process to grade leaders.

> *Mistakes occur in all organizations and operational environments. Leaders foster a learning environment by acknowledging that honest mistakes come with challenging missions. Tell leaders about a time you took on a risky, challenging mission. Recount the mistakes made in trying to accomplish it. Wrap up the discussion with the lessons learned from the experience.*

Learning Principles

Development is a process of change. Developmental growth is the same as learning. Learning is gaining knowledge or skill through study, practice, experience, or instruction. Knowing ways to promote learning is key to those who set up and conduct leader development. Applying learning principles throughout leader development practices will accelerate and improve learning. Table 3-1 presents common principles used to design instruction to promote effective, efficient, and appealing learning.

Principles	How each principle works to encourage development
Being task- or problem-centered	Learners are engaged in solving real-world problems. Intellect is stimulated with learning that will affect leader and unit performance.
Activation	Existing knowledge is activated as a foundation for new knowledge.
Demonstration	New knowledge is demonstrated to the learner.
Application	The learner applies new knowledge. Repetition and practice across varying conditions enhances application—through interaction with role models and mentors, from feedback and reflection, and by studying other leaders.
Integration	New knowledge is integrated into the learner's world.

Ref: FM 6-22 (Jun '15), table 3-1. Learning principles.

These principles are important for Army leader development because they are compatible and supportive of learning that occurs while completing duties or during professional development sessions or other modes of learning. Opportunities that challenge the individual and allow learning to occur enhance development in operational assignments, as well as in generating force assignments. Learning best occurs when the area to be learned has real-world relevance; what an individual learner already knows related to the subject is activated; new knowledge and skills are demonstrated to the learner; the skills are actually tried and applied by the learner; and the learner has the opportunity to integrate, absorb, or synthesize new insights or create their own take on the knowledge. Training and developmental projects enhance learning when the learner has an interest in the material and sees its relevance. Learning can accelerate when existing, related knowledge that an individual has comes to mind. Providing an example and using new knowledge enhance learning. The mind absorbs knowledge better when there is time for integration by the learner.

> Survey subordinates on the top three skills they need to improve unit performance or review their Individual Development Plans (IDPs) to determine what they need to learn. In doing so, subordinates are motivated and increase their reception to the leader skills they need to learn.

Purposeful learning starts when learners are challenged to know more and do better. Purposeful learning occurs when practice at mastery of tasks and skills are integrated into leaders' day-to-day activities. Applying the learning principles will result in leaders who actively engage in learning, quickly retain and recall information, and transfer learning to novel situations.

B. Knowledge of Subordinates

For effective leader development, individual relationships with each subordinate are necessary. Leaders who interact with subordinates on-and off-duty better understand their subordinates' backgrounds and experiences. This may enable discovery of special skills and experiences to support specific mission requirements. Likewise, leaders must avoid establishing or being perceived as having improper relationships. Generally, getting to know subordinates communicates a genuine interest in them as individuals. This builds confidence and generates trust. Trust is key to having candid talks with leaders about their development needs.

There are boundaries to what leaders should know about the personal lives of organization members. Some personal issues may be sensitive and leaders must be aware and understand the sensitivity. Interacting with subordinates in varied on- and off-duty situations enables leaders to build appropriate relationships and develop the trust necessary to discuss sensitive situations.

Team Trust and Unit Cohesion

An initial and ongoing objective of a leader is to create a culture that supports leader development. A key accomplishment is for subordinates to accept you as part of

Setting the Conditions for Development

Ref: FM 6-22, Leader Development (Jun '15), pp. 3-3 to 3-4.

Leaders set the conditions for leader development by performing their tasks and missions in ways that signal to subordinates throughout the organization that leader development is important. It can have a big effect in return for minimal personal time and resource investment.

Being a role model—setting the example—for leader development is essential. Leaders who model these leader actions encourage effective development in others and signal that leader development is valued:

- Encourage development.
  - Are you actively and directly engaged in the development of others.
  - Are leaders visibly present and actively engaged in the development of others?
  - Are leaders inspiring others through genuine concern for their growth?
  - Are leaders readily available to provide guidance and answer questions?
  - Do leaders defer to others to develop their subordinates?

- Encourage learning.
  - Do leaders feel free to ask themselves what went right and wrong in planning and executing an operation? Is there tolerance for discussing mistakes?
  - Do others observe you engaged in learning? Do you develop yourself? Are you prepared to meet mission challenges as they arise?
  - Do you actively listen to what others have to say? Are followers encouraged to provide candid feedback?
  - Do you create a positive environment? Do you enjoy being a leader and does your example motivate subordinates to emulate you?
  - Do you develop subordinates? Do you know their strengths, developmental needs, goals, and life activities that extend beyond the workday? Are you serving as a teacher and mentor?

- Promote learning from mistakes.
  - When mistakes occur, is the focus on assigning blame or on why the mistakes occurred and how to reduce the likelihood of a reoccurrence? Do you avoid criticizing individuals publicly?
  - Do you speak openly about personal leadership mistakes and lessons learned?

- Encourage innovation.
  - Are leaders restricted to operating strictly according to standing operating procedures? Do leaders dismiss new ideas in favor of tried and true practices?
  - Do you promote innovation? Can leaders debate with you, exchange issues, or challenge each other's perspectives?
  - Allow for risk taking and encourage exercise of disciplined initiative.
  - Do you delineate the boundaries or prioritize the areas where subordinates can take risk? Is it clear what is or is not acceptable?
  - Are leaders willing to accept the challenges in unit performance that come with new ideas?
  - Do you show empathy? Do you consider the situations of others relating to their challenges?
  - Encourage effective decisionmaking.
  - Are leaders well informed when they make important decisions? Do they consider and understand the relevant consequences for Soldiers, Army Civilians, and the mission?

the team. This means they trust you as an advisor and coach who facilitates their success. Starting with the first encounter, leaders position themselves as trusted advisors by communicating and modeling attributes and competencies to create a developmental culture. Initial communications might start like this—

- "The only thing I want out of this is to help you (or your staff or unit) maximize capability."
- "I am a developmental resource. The measuring stick for success here is for you to look back when it's all over and see the progress you have made"
- "Tell me a little about yourself—what have you been going through leading up to this assignment? How much experience do you have in your current leadership role? What comes next for you?

The objective of engaging in this communication with subordinates is as much about listening to their response and understanding their situation as it is about clarifying your role and willingness to be a developmental resource. It is important to build rapport by sharing something about yourself.

> *From a master sergeant: Without trust, Soldiers will not level with you—at best, you learn either non-truths or part truths. The best way to start building trust is to take the time and talk to your Soldiers from the first day that you become their leader.*

Early in interactions with subordinates, briefly share personal experiences—including areas of specialized expertise and areas of less experience. Candor helps build credibility while at the same time role modeling that it is okay to bring up personal leader developmental needs. It is important to establish trust and a developmental culture. Subordinates have to be receptive, engaged, and ready to develop. With some individuals, it may take extra interaction time to build the necessary level of rapport. Some individuals will seek additional attention and feedback and some will want less.

Individual Development Plan (IDP)

Counseling and feedback provide clear, timely, and accurate information concerning individual performance compared to established criteria. As a part of professional growth counseling and feedback sessions, leaders should help subordinates in identifying strengths and developmental needs. As part of this process, leaders should help subordinates design an IDP. IDPs enable developing an objective approach to professional development. Army Career Tracker (ACT) provides the central location to develop and track IDPs over a service career for both military members and Army Civilians. Reserve Component IDPs should include career development plans that relate to the individual's civilian career as well as Army career and focus on balancing Army careers with civilian careers and family life. Figure 3-2 provides an example IDP.

IDP TIMEFRAME							
Status	Draft		Last Updated				
Start Date	01 Sep 2015		End Date	30 Jun 25	Rank		2LT
Name	Daniel R. Christopher	SSN	xxx-xx-xxxx	Rank			
Duty Position	Rifle platoon leader	DOR	24 May 2015	MOS			11A
MOS Description	Infantry	UIC	WABCAA	Date Assigned			14 Nov 2015
ASI	5P Parachutist	SQI		LSI			

SHORT TERM IDP GOALS						
Goal Description	Activity Type	Range	Targeted Completion Date	Actual Completion Date	Status	
Handgun certification	Personal	Short	30 Jul 2016		Pending	
Scout platoon leader	Professional	Short	15 Mar 2017		Pending	
Battalion Supply Officer	Professional	Short	15 Mar 2018		Pending	
Maneuver Captain's Career Course	Professional	Short	30 July 2019		Pending	

LONG TERM IDP GOALS					
Goal Description	Activity Type	Range	Targeted Completion Date	Actual Completion Date	Status
Hindi-Urdu proficiency	Personal	Long	30 July 2020		Pending
Company command	Professional	Long	30 July 2021		Pending
Complete master's degree	Personal	Long	30 May 2023		Pending
Complete Command & General Staff College	Professional	Long	30 June 2025		Pending

Ref: FM 6-22 (Jun '15), fig. 3-2. Example IDP.

Inspiration Sources

Ref: FM 6-22, Leader Development (Jun '15), pp. 3-7 to 3-8.

To maintain the momentum of leader development activities, leaders need to reinforce purpose and provide inspiring examples. The Army promotes three reasons for leader development:

- To sustain and improve the immediate performance of the organization. Better leaders translate into better performing teams and units, and better units accomplish their mission.

- To improve the long- and short-term performance of the Army. Better-prepared leaders will be better equipped to fulfill the Army's leadership needs in the future.

- For the well-being of the individual leader. Leader development will let good leaders know that the Army values them and fulfill their desire to learn and to meet personal goals.

Personal experiences with leaders and leader development that provide inspiration are—

- An exceptional leader, peer, or subordinate who deliberately puts you in challenging situations to grow and learn.

- A leadership challenge where prior experiences prepared you.

- An exemplary professional role model who inspires and motivates others.

- Leaders who, at their own initiative, took responsibility for their own development.

Personal Inspiration

Note sources of personal inspiration for investing in leader development. Use these notes to communicate with others and personally understand the importance of developing leaders when distractions threaten implementation.

Sharing Experiences

Learning from the experiences of others can be invaluable. The purpose of this discussion is to give leaders the opportunity to share their experiences in terms of the leader competencies (see ADRP 6-22).

Discussion Questions:

- Choose a competency. Discuss the listed behaviors that support it. Describe a situation where you or someone you observed demonstrated the competency well.

- What actions did they take?

- What was the outcome?

- Why do you consider this a good demonstration of the competency?

- Describe a situation where you or someone you observed did not demonstrate this competency well, but could have.

- What actions did they take?

- What was the outcome?

- What actions would have been more effective?

II. Providing Feedback

Leaders need to learn how to observe subordinates and provide developmental feedback. Using multiple methods of assessment and feedback provides a robust and more accurate picture of the individual and provides better developmental opportunities.

A leader's ability to provide feedback to subordinates will significantly contribute to their development. It will enhance and accelerate learning from the day-to-day work experience—the most valued and effective environment for leader development. Timely, accurate feedback should translate into better leader performance, which will in turn have an effect on unit performance and mission success. Providing accurate feedback starts with planned observation and accurate observation and assessment.

A. Observation Planning

The first step to having a legitimate role in a subordinate's leader development process is to observe them. To use available time productively, plan to—

- See them challenged by a developmental need.
- See them excel by applying a personal strength.
- Observe their actions during critical times of unit performance.
- See them reach their limits of strength and endurance.
- Observe decisionmaking and conduct.
- Observe their effect on subordinate leaders and Soldiers.
- See them relaxed and available for conversation.

Do not draw a lasting impression of a leader from a single observation. It usually takes multiple observations before a pattern of behavior emerges. Take time to gather information from others observing the same leader, as different people focus on different aspects.

B. Accurate Observations and Assessments

Observing other leaders may seem like a difficult task. However, it is a valuable outcome once a leader is familiar with the methods for making accurate observations and providing feedback.

The Army possesses tools and measures for unit readiness and performance. Training briefs are full of these metrics and leaders generally receive continual feedback on their units' performance. This performance assessment and feedback, however, does not provide leaders with an assessment of their leadership behaviors. Leadership assessment—

- Speaks to the leader behaviors that contributed to the unit's performance.
  - Combines perception and reality, with reality best confirmed by multiple sources.
  - Occurs through two-way communication between leader and the led.
  - Has a common language defined by the doctrinal language of ADRP 1 and ADRP 6-22.

Effective commanders observe training, participate in operations, and interact with subordinates and their units. Personnel other than the commander or rater make observations contributing to leader development. Peers, trainers, operations officers, first sergeants, and others can all make accurate observations that can contribute to assessment and coaching.

See following pages (pp. 2-26 to 2-27) for discussion of accurate, descriptive observations.

C. Feedback Delivery

When experienced leaders reflect on their own leader development, they place high importance on day-to-day, two-way communication with their senior leaders because they do the same with their subordinates. Feedback is less effective if a leader waits until there is time for a formal sit-down counseling session to provide feedback. Leaders should provide feedback as soon as possible after observing a particular leader behavior to encourage positive effects.

Day-to-day informal feedback makes sitting down with subordinates for developmental counseling much easier. This informal feedback develops a shared understanding of the subordinate's strengths and developmental needs. Still, many leaders find it difficult to sit down with a subordinate to engage in developmental counseling.

See chap. 3 for extensive discussion of the counseling process from ATP 6-22.1.

Leader
Development

Providing feedback on every observed act, response, or behavior will overwhelm a subordinate. Provide feedback based on established competencies and attributes. Focus feedback on a few key behaviors that, if changed, will contribute the most to improved leader and unit performance. Having a focus for improvement will also motivate the subordinate to implement change.

Ask the observed leader for a self-assessment before providing personal views. Do this by first recounting back to the leader the situation and observation (the first two parts of the SOAR format). Then ask the leader to provide an assessment and recommendation. This reinforces three important leader development principles: leader self-assessment and self-awareness, individual leader responsibility for leader development, and leader ownership of the recommendation.

Giving Feedback In 60 Seconds Or Less

Day-to-day feedback is important to ensure improved leader and unit performance. The following example can guide feedback delivery.

Situation: Commander walks in on a patrol debriefing that one of his company commanders is conducting. He approaches CPT Philips after the debriefing.

Commander provides brief description of the situation: "CPT Phillips, I was in the back of the room while you debriefed the platoon. Let's talk for a minute."

Commander describes the leader behavior observed: "When I came in, Sergeant Jones was describing the suspects he had detained. You listened intently to his general descriptions and asked some pretty probing questions to get details."

CPT Phillips: "Yes sir, I want patrol leaders to understand how important their gathering information is to developing our intelligence efforts."

Commander: "That's a great technique to ask a few questions to confirm what Sergeant Jones is saying and probe for details. He said the suspects were not local. You noticed that. From the excitement in Sergeant Jones's voice, I think he knows the suspects are up to something, but he wasn't sure just what."

Delivery of Observations for Effect

It is important to plan how a leader will deliver observations to a subordinate. The delivery methods that follow, when done correctly, provide a leader with an understanding of the effect behaviors have on consequences, all based on careful and planned observations. The two-way communication techniques used for delivering an observation should motivate subordinates to start acting in ways that improve leader and unit performance.

See pp. 2-28 to 2-29 for discussion and examples of providing feedback.

Accurate, Descriptive Observations

Ref: FM 6-22, Leader Development (Jun '15), pp. 3-8 to 3-11.

Observing leadership requires an understanding of leadership, ability to discern the quality of behaviors, and practice. Observing leader behaviors occurs by watching how a leader interacts with and influences others. These observations focus on what was done well, what was not done well, and what could be done differently. Written directives, verbal communications, and leader actions all provide indications of how a leader influences others. Leaders learn about their subordinate's leadership by observing reactions by peers, subordinates, and superiors.

Three key components ensure observations are accurate and descriptive:

Observations Planned around Key Events

Leaders can use the training calendar to identify events that are likely to compel a leader to demonstrate a considerable number of leadership competencies and attributes.

Observations for Patterns of Behavior (SOAR Feedback)

With time and frequent observation, leaders gain confidence and start to see a consistent pattern of behavior. It is a judgment call as to when to consider an observation as a pattern of behavior. To observe for a pattern, make a note of how often a leader exhibits the same behavior in a given time. The frequency of behavior may indicate a pattern. If sufficient time has passed and the observer can predict the leader's actions, then a pattern of behavior has likely emerged.

When observing leadership, it is important to frame observations in a context consistent with Army doctrine (refer to performance indicators for the competencies and attributes from ADRP 6-22). A way to capture observations and assessment is to use a quick, accurate, and complete way to take notes that makes for an effective feedback session such as a situation, observation, associate and assess, and reinforce and recommend (SOAR) format. Details for the SOAR elements are—

- **(S) Situation**—Describe the situation and conditions of the assessment. This should include the time, location, event, or other context of the situation. If known, capture the prevailing leadership relationship or climate between the leader and the led. In later discussions, this information will help leaders and subordinates recall the event and circumstances surrounding it.

- **(O) Observation**—Describe the leadership behaviors that the leader exhibits. Focus on competencies within the lead, develop, and achieve categories. Likewise, note evidence of the attributes in the character, presence, and intellect categories. Leaders use this section to note both strengths and developmental needs and the effect of the subordinate's behavior on the mission or Soldiers.

- **(A) Associate and Assess**—Identify and associate the competency or attribute that best describes the leader actions. Leaders assess the subordinate's actions to determine whether they meet the standard or represent a strength or developmental need. Leaders record the competency and observed behaviors.

- **(R) Reinforce and Recommend**—Record how to reinforce the leader's behavior through praise or correction. The supervisory leader will identify actions for the subordinate to sustain or improve and other recommendations for change. Recording these notes help plan the feedback to discuss with the subordinate.

Often a leader will not directly observe the leadership behavior of a subordinate, but will receive a report on unit performance. Leader assessment in this situation requires the leader to communicate the performance indicator to the subordinate. Then, together, move the discussion to the causes of the unit performance. Ask, "What part did your leadership play in the unit's performance?"

Background:
At FOB Bender, an observer is paired with SFC Olson, who is about to lead a 9 vehicle convoy to an assembly area 12 km away. SFC Olson's mission is to successfully deliver all 9 vehicles to the assembly area. He leads 5 subordinate NCOs and 8 junior enlisted Soldiers.

Situation: (Describe behavior and impact on mission and or Soldiers)

1900 14MAR - FOB Bender
SFC Olson leads convoy of 9 vehicles
9 drivers and 13 other troops (5 NCOs and 8 junior enlisted)
High morale and enthusiasm among the section

Observation: (Describe behavior and impact on mission and or Soldiers)	Associate & Assess: (Identify competency - attribute and assess proficiency)
Provided initial guidance and followed-up; ensured everyone understood objective and requirements and kept in contact	Communicates + Creates Pos. Environment √ Leads Others √
Promoted optimistic expectations and attitudes among troops	Leads by Example (DN)
Ensured PCI were completed by all drivers Improperly wore kneepads around ankles	Develops Leaders (DN) Gets Results √
Missed opportunities to delegate leadership responsibility to subordinates during this task	[Assess: + Strength; √ Standard; (DN) Need]
Mission completed	

Reinforce & Recommend: (Note appropriate feedback, praise, or correction, and recommendations for action to sustain/improve leader behavior)

Reinforce- Troops and drivers were prepared, well informed, and motivated
Recommend- (Leads by Example) Several junior enlisted Soldiers wore kneepads around ankles violating the standard

Reinforce - Mission completed successfully but missed opportunities to delegate/develop subordinate leaders

Ref: FM 6-22 (Jun '15), fig. 3-3. Example SOAR feedback notes.

Recording Important Observations

Important details of a leadership observation may be lost or be inaccurately recorded if not written down soon after they occur. Accurate and complete notes are useful when providing leaders with feedback. As described earlier, using the SOAR format is one way to record observations.

- **Use words that depict action**. A leader needs to describe what the subordinate is doing when they are in the act of leading. By writing down an observation using action words, the leader can be sure the subordinate will be able to recognize it when communicating it back to them.

- **Link to effects and outcomes.** The immediate effect of a subordinate's leadership may be observed in the verbal and nonverbal reactions of others in direct proximity. Leaders and Soldiers in subordinate echelons will feel the positive or negative consequences of a leader's action. Leadership can affect task or mission accomplishment. Trace mission results and look for leader actions that contribute to success or lack of success.

Providing Feedback (Examples)

Ref: FM 6-22, Leader Development (Jun '15), pp. 3-12 to 3-15.

Feedback During Training

Before the start of training, leaders should explain the SOAR format or any feedback tool to the unit and its leaders. Leaders should emphasize the developmental nature of the feedback. Armed with this knowledge, unit leadership should be supportive of efforts to deliver of feedback.

The timing of a discussion of leadership observations can be critical and a deciding factor between whether perceiving a situation as evaluative or developmental. Ultimately, determining the appropriate time for the delivery of an observation is at the discretion of the leader. Consider whether delivery should occur during the action, at a break in action, or at the end of the day or event completion.

During the Action.
Sometimes, leaders deliver observations as they occur. Part of guided discovery learning relies on "during the action" feedback. This is especially true when pointing out to the leader that actions must occur "in the moment" while they can be observed. However, care must be taken not disrupt the training exercise.

Finding a Break in the Action.
Find the right 'break' in the action to deliver observations. This could be during a lull after a major event has occurred (a major success or a failure).

End-of-Day or at Completion of a Major Event.
Consider waiting until the end of the day, especially if observations are lengthy and require discussion. To enable better collective learning, wait until after conducting the unit or team AAR. Then, deliver observations to the subordinate privately, as a mentoring session away from others. This also allows aligning the delivery of observations of the subordinate's strengths and areas for improvement with those of the unit or team as identified in the AAR, assuming they are compatible.

If observation delivery is best done at the completion of an event, consider letting the subordinate set the time for the discussion. At a minimum, provide a "heads up" about a situation or circumstance to be discussed. This allows the leader an opportunity to reflect and psychologically prepare to listen and receive. This approach reduces the likelihood the subordinate will be preoccupied, nervous, or defensive. Examples of a leader employing this approach include—

- "I'll be back in about 30 minutes and I'd like to talk about how things went this morning. I'm going to ask about how you led the team through the scenario and some of the approaches you took during the decision-making task." [SOAR, Situation]
- "The simulation you led the staff through this afternoon was successful, though I've noted some areas that you could work on. Is there a time you'd prefer to talk later today so I can share my observations and discuss with you?" [SOAR, Situation]

Observation Delivery

The following steps are an effective way to deliver an observation. These steps represent an indirect approach to providing leadership observations. Once the SOAR outline is completed, leaders are ready to discuss observations and reinforce and recommend actions. The following steps provide a framework for delivering observations.

Confirm the Situation.
Start by orienting the subordinate's attention to the observed situation. State the situation and clarify that the observation is about leadership. Reiterate the information recorded: "I would like to discuss the actions you took in the battlefield simulation you just led with your staff." [SOAR, Situation]

Ask for a Self-Assessment.
Ask the subordinate for a self-assessment of the situation and personal leader actions. Guide questioning to the subordinate's leadership during the given event or situation. The subordinate's response should match the leader's assessment. If it does not, the leader should ask additional specific questions:

- "How effective was the communication between you and the subordinates you were leading? And how could you tell?" [SOAR, Associate and Assess]
- "What factors did you observe that may have contributed to miscommunication or a vague understanding among the troops?" [SOAR, Associate and Assess]

Clarify and Come to an Agreement.
Leaders confirm the subordinate either agrees with the assessment or acknowledges a difference in opinion if the subordinate does not share the assessment. Confirm agreement or acknowledgement before proceeding to the assessment, linkages, and observations:

- "That is what I saw as well"
- "Actually, in my observations I noted that you were directive in your message and didn't ask for questions. Would you agree that this is the approach you took?"

Add your Observations.
Leaders may include observations that the subordinate is not aware. Leaders build on what the subordinate has already said to increase personal self-awareness. Specific behaviors that had an effect on the consequence or outcome include—

- "Your assessment is correct. When you asked for other viewpoints, a good sharing of information followed." [SOAR, Observation]
- "It was clear some of the staff had differing opinions or other points to add, though the opportunity to share really didn't arise." [SOAR, Observation]

Ways to Further Engage Leaders
Leaders raise questions that will prompt subordinates to think about how to act or respond in the future. Leaders should ask for recommendations about how the subordinate will take better actions in the future, avoid problems, and take advantage of an opportunity. Here are some possible questions—

- "How will you handle a similar situation next time?" [SOAR, transition to Reinforce and Recommend]
- "What steps can you take to avoid this outcome in the future?" [SOAR, transition to Reinforce and Recommend]

Reinforce—Validate a Strength.
Once the leader and subordinate agree on the behaviors that contributed to a consequence and a recommendation for the future, the leader should provide reinforcement on what the subordinate is doing correctly. Here are some examples—

- "Your influencing strategies are working for you, keep it up."
- "Consider closing out staff meetings with opportunities for questions or discussion. Your pre-meeting planning and organizing is effective—you should continue that."

Additional Tips for Providing Feedback.
There are several other items to consider when providing feedback:

- Focus on the leader's behavior and actions.
- Identify what the leader has control over to change.
- Use focused questions as a form of feedback to create discovery learning.
- Give the leaders the opportunity to come up with a recommendation to the observation. This promotes their taking ownership and responsibility for it.
- Be familiar with improvement actions (FM 6-22, app A)and offer appropriate ones. Remind leaders that this source is available to guide development, including improving their understanding of positive and negative behaviors and underlying causes.

D. Lessons from Delivering Observations

Leaders should avoid delivering some kinds of feedback to a subordinate. These are especially important to avoid—

- Vague and general ideas: "You are a good leader."
- Using absolutes or generalities, such as always or never: "You never follow-up after meetings."
- Observations applied to general traits or the total person: "Your personality is that of an introvert."
- Untimely feedback that the leader is unable to apply: "Two days ago you gave ambiguous instructions at the mission rehearsal."

It is also important for leaders to learn from the delivery of their observations and realize it takes practice. It is helpful after an interaction for leaders to reflect on their delivery. Self-reflective questions include—

- Was my subordinate receptive to what we discussed?
  - Based on my questions, how easily did they identify the behaviors that needed to change?
  - Did my subordinate ask for techniques or ideas on how to change or improve?
  - Is there agreement on the next step of development and its timeframe?
  - Is there evidence that my subordinate is taking action on the observations?

After delivering observations, leaders look for the next opportunity to observe the subordinate's leadership. Then, gauge how well the subordinate received the observation, what steps the leader has taken to change behavior, and what effect the change is having on unit outcomes.

E. Subordinate Receptiveness to Feedback

Trust and a developmental culture are critical to ensuring reception of leader observations. If subordinates perceive a leader to be genuinely interested in helping subordinates, the subordinate will be receptive to observations than if there is doubt or mistrust about motives.

To gauge receptiveness, leaders must remain attuned to verbal and nonverbal cues. These may occur as verbal disagreement or resistance, or nonverbal gestures such as folded arms, rolling eyes, or a lack of attentiveness. Refocus the subordinate by—

- Reaffirming the intent of your feedback is to maximize the subordinate's capabilities to achieve optimal unit performance.
- Reminding the subordinate that your observations are for development—not evaluation or judgment. You are a developmental resource for the leader and the unit.
- Reiterating what went well and note any incremental progress made thus far.

III. Enhancing Learning

Setting conditions and providing feedback and advice are two of the fundamentals of development. Applying practices to enhance learning will make development more effective. Enhancing learning draws on the developmental value from learning opportunities. Learning from experience can be enhanced by facilitating what an experience means. Making sense of an experience requires interpretation of the event to create personal understanding. This process requires observation, feedback, dialogue, and reflection. A leader-subordinate pair, coach, or mentor can use these four steps with a leader, any group, or adapted for an individual learner. At the individual level, experiential learning is learning while doing. At the organizational level, experiential learning is improving while doing. Experiential learning is consistent with the principle of train as you fight.

Practical approaches to enhance learning include leader role models, mentoring, guided discovery learning, and individual and group study. These practices are not events that come up on a schedule. They are powerful ways to integrate and promote learning in the day-to-day operations of the organization.

A. Leader Role Models

Because leaders vary in their skill and experience level, an effective way to learn is directly from unit role models. Positive role models exhibit leadership behaviors that others should emulate. Leveraging role models for leader development is an efficient use of time and resources. They are a resource right in the organization. Supervisors should identify role models for each key position (such as company commander or platoon sergeant) and may want to identify role models possessing special skills that other leaders need to master. Leaders should resource these role models appropriately for the responsibilities. Likewise they should create opportunities for less experienced individuals for interaction. For example, supervisors may assign—

- A role model to new leaders for their reception and integration.
- A role model to coach a leader due to possessing a particular skill or expertise.
- Role models to run leader certification programs.
- An inexperienced leader to shadow a role model for a specified period.

THE 5-MINUTE SHADOW

Bring in a subordinate to observe or participate in an aspect of work that will make them a better leader. To maximize the experience—

- Communicate the situation, decision, or issue.
- Convey the importance of acting appropriately or making the right decision.
- Describe possible consequences, second- and third-order effects.
- Discuss the decision or actions and reasoning behind them.

B. Mentorship

Mentoring can benefit leader development efforts. Mentorship is the voluntary developmental relationship that exists between a person of greater experience and a person of lesser experience that is characterized by mutual trust and respect (AR 600-100). A mentor is a leader who assists personal and professional development by helping a mentee clarify personal, professional, and career goals and develop actions to improve attributes, skills, and competencies. A mentee is the individual receiving mentorship. Individuals are encouraged to participate in mentoring as a voluntary experience. Age or seniority is not a prerequisite for providing mentoring. A junior individual may mentor a senior individual based on experience or specialized expertise as a subject matter expert.

Mentoring will occur while individuals are in operational and institutional assignments; however, the mentor-mentee connections are best if they occur outside the chain of command. This is not contrary to the requirement that superiors have the responsibility to develop subordinates. It is differentiating between the role of a mentor and the role of a leader to develop, counsel, teach, and instruct subordinates. Supervisors should refrain from appointing mentors or formally matching individuals with mentors. Participant self-selection leads to the most effective mentoring relationship. Leaders foster mentorship by—

- Educating leaders in the organization on mentor responsibilities.
- Participating as a mentor.
- Inviting experienced leaders to visit and share their mentoring experiences.

See following pages (pp. 2-32 to 2-33) and pp. 3-4 to 3-6 for further discussion.

Mentor Roles and Responsibilities

Ref: FM 6-22, Leader Development (Jun '15), pp. 3-18 to 3-20.

Selection as a mentor is a compliment to one's professional abilities and competence. Table 3-2 highlights the general roles and responsibilities of mentors.

Role	Responsibility
Provides	Encouragement and motivation. Candid feedback about perceived strengths and developmental needs. Advice on dealing with obstacles. Guidance on setting goals and periodically reviews progress.
Shares	Experiences that contributed to personal success. An understanding of the Army, its mission, and formal and informal operating processes.
Encourages	Appropriate training and developmental opportunities. Sense of self-awareness, self-confidence, and adaptability. Efficient and productive performance.
Serves	As a confidant, counselor, guide, and adviser. As an advisor for career development ideas or opportunities. As a resource for enhancing personal and professional attributes.

Ref: FM 6-22 (Jun '15), table 3-2. Mentor roles and responsibilities.

Mentoring is a powerful tool for personal and professional development. Mentoring generally improves individual performance, retention, morale, personal and professional development, and career progression. Mentoring offers many opportunities for mentors and mentees to improve their leadership, interpersonal, and technical skills as well as achieve personal and professional objectives.

It is not required for leaders to have the same occupational or educational background as those they coach or counsel. In comparison, mentors generally specialize in the same area as those they mentor. Mentors have likely experienced what their mentees are experiencing or will experience. Consequently, mentoring relationships tend to be occupation-specific, focused primarily on developing a better prepared leader.

Mentoring Relationships

The appearance of favoritism or creating conflict with raters or senior raters should keep leaders from mentoring subordinates within their chain of command. Subordinates should avoid approaching superiors in their chain of command to be mentors.

Mentoring relationships can be described by purpose and relationship:

- **Traditional mentoring.** Focuses primarily on the mentee, examining the career path through goal setting, with overall development of the individual as the focus. This mentoring is a process where the mentor and mentee join by their own volition.

- **Peer mentoring.** Occurs when a mentor has extensive knowledge and experience but not higher rank or grade than the mentee. Mentoring relationships may occur between peers and often between senior NCOs and junior officers. This relationship can occur across many grades or ranks.

Regardless of purpose, a successful mentoring relationship is based on several elements:

- **Respect.** Established when a mentee recognizes desirable attributes, skills, and competencies that the mentor has and when the mentor appreciates the attitude, effort, and progress of the mentee.

- **Trust.** Mentors and mentees should work together to build trust through open communication, forecasting how decisions could affect goals, frequent discussion of progress, monitoring changes, and expressing enthusiasm for the relationship.

- **Realistic expectations and self-perception.** A mentor may refine the mentee's self-perception by discussing social traits, intellectual abilities, talents, and roles.

It is important for the mentor to provide honest feedback. A mentor should encourage the mentee to have realistic expectations of their own capabilities, present and potential position opportunities, and the mentor's offerings.

- **Time**. Set aside specific time to meet; do not change times unless necessary. Meet periodically to control interruptions. Frequently check in with each other via calls or e-mail.

Soldiers and Army Civilians who seek feedback to focus their development, coupled with dedicated, well-informed mentors, will embed the concepts of life-long learning, self-development, and adaptability into the Army's culture. The benefits are threefold: for the mentor, the mentee, and the organization.

Mentor Benefits

Serving as a mentor can provide many benefits, such as—

- **Professional development**. Becoming identified as someone who develops or mentors well-known performers can attract qualified, high-potential individuals who will look for opportunities to work for the mentor. Developing others to follow in a mentor's footsteps can facilitate the mentor's own personal and professional development and career progression.

- **Knowledge**. Mentees can be a source of general organizational data, feedback, and fresh ideas. Because higher-level positions isolate some executives and managers, mentees can serve as an important link in keeping communication lines open. While the mentor might possess facts about issues, mentees often provide important feedback about views at different levels of the Army.

- **Personal satisfaction**. Mentors generally report a sense of pride in watching mentees develop and a sense of contribution to the Army. It is an opportunity to pass on a legacy to the next generation.

- **Sharpened skills**. Mentors sharpen management, leadership, and interpersonal skills as they challenge and coach the mentee.

- **Source of recognition**. Good mentors are well respected.

- **Expanded professional contacts**. Mentors develop rewarding professional contacts by interacting with other mentors, supervisors, and contacts made through the mentorship relationship.

Mentee Benefits

Mentees gain tremendously from a mentoring relationship. Such benefits include—

- Increasing self-awareness through candid feedback.
- Building confidence and encouragement to grow beyond usual expectations.
- Having a role model and a trusted advisor.
- Gaining better understanding of the Army and what is required to succeed and advance.
- Gaining visibility through opportunities to try advanced tasks and demonstrate expanded capabilities.
- Reporting greater career satisfaction with higher performance and productivity ratings.

Organizational Benefits

The organization and the Army as a whole benefit in the following ways—

- Increased commitment and retention.
- Improved performance.
- Leader development.
- Leadership succession.
- Recruitment.

C. Guided Discovery Learning

Underpinning all developmental activity is the accurate observation of performance. Armed with accurate observations, the senior leader engages the subordinate in effective two-way communication to deliver observations on actions and behaviors. Effective delivery techniques foster leader acceptance, ownership, and action.

Besides directly delivering an observation, leaders can use indirect methods. Indirect methods place increased responsibility on the subordinate to identify personal strengths and developmental needs. Indirect methods employ the techniques of guided discovery learning. The techniques are designed to engage subordinates to discover their learning needs, supported by the senior leader.

Guided discovery learning is an advanced technique that experienced leaders employ to help the subordinate learn. The technique can be used in coaching, counseling, and mentoring situations. Guided discovery learning is effective because—

- It is the subordinate's responsibility to make sense of incoming information and integrate it with their personal base of experience and knowledge of relevant doctrine. It is a process of discovery for the leader.

- Subordinate learning and transfer of knowledge are maximized because the supervisor generally keeps the subordinate on track through hints, direction, coaching, feedback, or modeling.

- Guided learning enables deep understanding of targeted concepts, principles, and techniques.

Pure discovery learning is less effective than guided discovery learning. With discovery learning alone—

- The subordinate merely executes based on personal experience or knowledge.

- The subordinate makes sense of incoming information using whatever criteria they feel is relevant.

- The supervisory leader is passive, providing no guidance or feedback concerning the rules or criteria that the subordinate is using for problem solving.

Guided discovery learning is more effective than prescriptive methods where the leader gives the subordinate the correct answer to a problem. Prescriptive methods require neither thinking nor deep learning by the subordinate. They merely execute the prescribed solution given by the supervisory leader.

Guided Discovery Learning Techniques

Guided discovery learning techniques are an effective way to deliver leadership observations. These methods are commonly employed when developing the leadership skills of subordinates:

- Positive reinforcement.
- Open-ended questioning.
- Multiple perspectives.
- Scaling questions.
- Cause and effect analysis.
- Recovery from setbacks.
- Use experience.

D. Coaching

Coaching helps another individual or team through a set of tasks or with improving personal qualities. A coach gets the person or team to understand their current level of performance and guides their performance to the next level. A central task of coaching is to link feedback interpretation with developmental actions. The role of the coach is to advise the individual or team on what levels can be reached and what to do to reach them.

Similar to other development processes, there are a number of components to coaching:

- **Building rapport**. The coach builds a strong rapport to facilitate trust and open communications.
- **Gathering and analyzing information**. Performance indicators or the leader or team's perceptions are reviewed to determine an accurate picture of capabilities.
- **Addressing the gaps**. Specific issues are discussed in light of similarities and differences with what are normal expectations.
- **Narrowing focus**. The coach helps guide the leader to identify the directions to strengthen and develop.
- **Setting goals**. The coach assists the leader in establishing development goals.
- **Planning development**. Together the coach and leader determine paths of development, desired outcomes, and specific developmental actions.
- **Promoting action**. The coach sets conditions that help to sustain developmental action and establish accountability for development.

Coaches can draw on the guided discovery learning techniques to establish and maintain rapport and to build commitment. The coach tailors how directive feedback and guidance are depending on the situation of those being coached and the performance level. If coaches are involved in developmental actions, they look for a good balance between challenge and the learner's perception of ability to achieve incremental improvement.

To prepare for coaching, leaders will study and apply the fundamental guidelines for leader development. They will be passionate learners in the area being coached. They will arm themselves with tips, techniques, and practice routines to advise subordinates. Developmental actions for leadership include observing other leaders, modeling what good leaders do, and practicing new techniques or approaches. Leaders can apply techniques in the conduct of their duties, look for different on-the-job opportunities, or identify outside opportunities. Other actions include reading, research, consulting, and formal coursework. Sometimes applying different mindsets and ways of thinking provide enough development to meet established goals.

See pp. 3-4 to 3-5 for further discussion.

E. Study

Leader development processes in the organization should establish an expectation for each leader to spend personal time seeking sources of knowledge and opportunities to grow and learn. If a supervisor's personal involvement and unit resources were always prerequisites for leader development, it would be a limited effort indeed. Organization leaders should develop distinct ways of studying their chosen profession and identifying ways to improve the unit.

Encourage subordinates of the same position or similar grade to form a community-of-practice group that fosters excellence. Provide the groups reachback capability to Web-based forums. Provide each group with an opportunity to present recommendations or new methods to the leadership team.

Professional Reading Programs

Professional reading programs broaden leader knowledge, understanding, and confidence. Leaders gain a refined understanding of the material and develop critical thinking skills through pertinent discussion with others. Discussing ideas and topics with peers, subordinates, and leaders who may offer significantly different perspectives exposes all participants to new ideas and potentially broadens their outlook.

Successful reading programs depend on how they are structured—what readings are chosen and what purpose is integrated into the program. If you want to encourage tactics, then select readings on operational tactics. If you want to develop skills for which interesting readings do not exist, then design questions that trigger reflection about engaging material. For example, to stimulate critical thinking assign questions about the materials that require consideration of underlying assumptions, alternative courses of action, and application of lessons to other situations.

Organizations and individuals can implement professional reading programs; a wealth of materials are available to support topic determination, such as the U.S. Army Chief of Staff's Professional Reading list or the U.S. Center of Military History Professional Reading List. Determining the frequency, such as monthly or quarterly, will be dependent on organizational missions, but the unit must allocate and protect time for effective implementation.

For personal professional reading, topics may come from established reading lists, stem from personal interests, or follow from determining strengths and developmental needs. As part of a personal reading program, leaders should maintain a reading journal to take notes and record key passages, insights, and reflections. Leaders who record thoughts on paper can gain clarity and develop new ideas. The journal could record titles of related books and articles for further investigation.

Professional Writing Programs

Army leaders consider how they can contribute to the body of thought in their fields of expertise by researching and writing about topics that interest them. By writing and publishing papers, they can advance their profession, their mastery of their discipline, and their writing skills. Writers of scholarly papers study their topics in depth and in breadth. They take formal classes in research and in writing so they can master appropriate standards. They use appropriate writing processes. Before submitting papers to professional or academic journals, they ensure their submissions meet the publications' requirements. In addition, the unit security office should screen items for publication to prevent the spillage of classified information. Writers scrupulously adhere to intellectual property rights rules and shun plagiarism.

For developing leaders, a developmental writing program serves as a significant complementary companion to a professional reading program. Length and time given for completion should vary based on the requirement. Some ideas and suggested lengths for professional writing include:

- Leadership philosophy—an opportunity to codify what you believe as a leader such as expectations, what is important, and what is non-negotiable (2-3 pages).
- Personal experiences:
    - Significant experience, whether good or bad, and how it affected you including lessons learned (5-7 pages).
    - Routine experiences, describing how you handle them and possible improvements for consideration (2-3 pages).
- Historical person or event related to your branch, regimental affiliation, or organization (5-7 pages).
- Opinion piece explaining changes affecting your branch through a particular person, policy, or equipment (5-7 pages).

Individuals should consider writing for publication as a complementary element to the professional reading program. Writing increases self-development as well as develops others who gain from the lessons learned and stimulated thought. Papers created through the writing program could be considered for publication in branch journals or as blog entries.

V. Creating Opportunities

Creating opportunities for development or using existing experience opportunities is a fourth way of creating a culture of development. An organizational culture develops based on shared values, beliefs, and learning. These cultural values, when consistent with the mission, affect an organization's performance.

Leaders foster a positive culture by providing a supportive command climate that values member involvement and learning. Likewise, the selections for and responsibilities of key positions of leadership will have implications for developing leaders far into the future. Integrating these efforts into a holistic program will establish lasting operating norms. Developing leaders to this level requires an investment of time and effort, but leaves a lasting legacy of trained and ready leaders for the Army of tomorrow.

Selection and screening of leaders can be useful in leader development efforts. Forming leadership teams where strengths in one complement developmental needs in another is a common selection goal. Developing leaders is often about preparing them for responsibilities in the next position. Creating opportunities for leader development involves—

- Creating challenging experiences.
- Sharpening leader selection.
- Planning leader succession.
- Tracking career development and management.

A. Challenging Experiences

Experience is a developmental tool. Leaders can create learning opportunities by placing subordinates into challenging assignments to stretch their thinking and behavior. Challenging experiences are characterized by pressure, complexity, novelty, and uncertainty. Challenge creates learning situations that are interesting and motivating. Leaders can also create these experiences or ensure opportunities are used as learning experiences.

All Army assignments inherently provide a degree of developmental challenge. Leader development will happen even if supervisors do nothing at all. Creating the right challenges in a position for a particular leader can dramatically increase development.

Some missions or circumstances may not offer key developmental opportunities. Supervisors may need to shape position responsibilities to allow a subordinate to enhance personal leadership skills. Before adjusting a position's requirements, leaders should consider unit and mission demands.

Leaders should be deliberate placing subordinates in special missions and organizational assignments. Experienced leaders implicitly know the defining tasks early in an assignment and should be deliberate about identifying these tasks and ensuring each leader gains experience from them. Sometimes, supervisors must assign subordinates to positions for which they do not have the requisite skills or experience. Supervisors should consider modification of position requirements and providing additional support or resources.

Not all leaders develop on the same timelines. Supervising leaders should be willing to adjust how much time each subordinate stays in a position. Supervisors should involve human resources staff early in these discussions as decisions may have implications beyond the organization. When making such determinations, supervisors should weigh the effects on—

- Unit performance.
- Stability of the leadership team.
- Leadership needs of adjacent units, higher units, and the Army.
- The leader's well-being and personal growth.

B. Leader Selection and Succession

Ref: FM 6-22, Leader Development (Jun '15), pp. 3-30 to 3-32.

Supervising leaders should foster an attitude that leadership positions are not necessarily automatic appointments. It is a privilege, not an entitlement, to serve in a leadership position. Selections for key leadership positions require thorough consideration. Each step in the screening and selection process should narrow the field of acceptable candidates. For key leadership positions, a deliberate selection process should be followed:

• Forecast potential position openings.

• Identify key leader characteristics.

• Build a pool of candidates by working with higher, adjacent, and subordinate units, as applicable.

• Use selection tools to screen out applicants such as—

 - Conducting a career file review to identify prerequisite experiences and training; review files and rate candidates against career indicators.

 - Reviewing disciplinary or derogatory information in personnel and intelligence files.

 - Obtaining references or recommendations on the leader from trusted sources.

 - Conducting structured interviews with candidates for the position—structure the interviews to assess values, attributes, and responses to situations.

 - Organizations may develop minimum prerequisite knowledge or skills requirements for particular positions. Final candidates may demonstrate capabilities by conducting a task that proves their qualifications for the position (such as leading a patrol or leading a convoy).

• Select and appoint approved candidates.

If creating a pool of qualified candidates is not possible, supervising leaders should consider modifying the position or providing additional support or resources to available candidates.

These processes fall within the realm of talent management, which complements leader development. Talent management takes into account the individual talents of an officer, NCO, or Army Civilian—the unique distribution of personal skills, knowledge, abilities, and behaviors and the potential they represent. The Army looks to develop and put to best use well-rounded leaders based on the talents they possess—talents that derive not only from operational experience but also from broadening assignments, advanced civil schooling and professional military education, and demonstrated interests.

Consider the leadership team when selecting leaders. For example, pair a technically strong warrant officer with a tactically strong officer. Pair a strong operations officer with an intelligence officer willing to challenge the operational plan by forcefully presenting the enemy point of view. Pair an experienced NCO with an inexperienced lieutenant.

Leader Succession

Succession planning is a developmental activity for the individual leaders that focus deliberate planning to provide opportunities for experience in key developmental assignments and to prepare for future assignments beyond the unit. Unit leaders do not have total input into succession planning but with forethought can have plans developed to rotate leaders within the unit. Succession planning is a localized version of talent management. Senior leaders plan the systematic rotation of subordinates within the organization so that trained and qualified leaders are ready to assume vacancies, proven leaders move on to positions of greater responsibility, and marginal leaders receive opportunities to improve. Succession planning serves individual leaders by looking beyond the replacement interests of the organization. It helps develop leaders with the potential to succeed in future positions beyond their current unit and returns a benefit to the Army by optimizing development opportunities and duration across the unit's leaders.

Understanding the projected career paths and timing for leader branches and specialties is an important factor in succession planning. Moving leaders into and out of positions should be a factor of—

- **Unit performance**. Keeping leaders in positions long enough so that their stability promotes high unit performance.
- **Army need**. Providing experienced leadership back to the Army to fulfill its requirements.
- **Individual leader developmental goals and readiness**. Determining when the leader has achieved development goals and is ready to take on new responsibilities and challenges.

Supervising leaders should work with human resources staff to predict accurate leader gains and losses to the unit. Be sure to—

- Account for leader needs for career and position-specific training before position assumption.
- Assess leaders during their initial assignments to drive subsequent position assignments.
- Use leader vacancies due to schooling, special assignment, or leave as leader development opportunities; assign less experienced leaders temporarily to the vacancies.

Identify the key leadership positions that trigger succession planning and management. Chart the timing and sequencing of leaders into and out of unit leadership positions. Account for prerequisite schooling and plan primary and alternate candidates for each position.

C. Career Development and Management

Individuals should understand and actively manage their own career paths while supervisors should consider the career paths and influence their subordinates to gain breadth in development. Commanders and other senior leaders should encourage their developing subordinates to take challenging assignments. Reserve Component leaders should be aware of subordinates' civilian development plan as this may affect their ability to take on new and challenging assignments.

The Army provides ACT and other online tools to help leaders in collaborating with their subordinates in professional development planning discussions. Supervisors must provide opportunities for subordinate's personal and required individual learning. ACT enhances personnel counseling by providing a framework to create IDPs and the ability to monitor career development while allowing leaders to track and advise subordinates on personalized leadership development.

Balance Of Army Needs With Personal Choices

The gravity of the Army mission and the dynamic nature of the world make continuous learning and self-development crucial to personal success and national security. Rapid changes in geopolitical affairs, technology, and general knowledge require individuals to repetitively seek current information. Army and civilian schools provide basic knowledge, frameworks, and techniques that individuals need to continue to review and update after they leave those schools. To thrive professionally and personally, individuals must engage in life-long learning and self-development.

Finding the proper balance between professional work and personal life while planning career development challenges professionals at all stages of their careers. Most career planning models have the following common steps—

- Perform a self-assessment to determine strengths and developmental needs (based on abilities, characteristics, needs, responsibilities, or interest or goals)
- Weigh the possibilities to choose goals and milestones for self-development efforts.
- Make a self-development plan that uses effective methods of learning.
- Implement the plan, overcoming obstacles, and measuring progress.

Ask the organizational leaders to describe their most valuable leader development experience. Give them a few days to think about it before they respond. Have them briefly write the experience down or tell it to a group of their peers. Use their experiences to help prioritize implementation.

Providing a first, second, third, and fourth priority reflects the understanding that leaders may not be able to implement every idea or method. Some methods of leader development provide a leader with a higher return in performance for less investment of resources.

Civilian Training and Development Programs

The Civilian Education System is a structured program with central funding for all Army Civilian personnel and serves as the foundation for civilian leader development. Army Civilians have developmental opportunities afforded by their duty series, grouped into career programs. Each career program makes available career planning tools to enable the development of core competencies. ACTEDS provides a planned course of professional development, using a combination of formal training and education and progressively challenging work experiences. ACTEDS is a resource for both individuals and for their supervisors. Through ACTEDS, Army Civilians have the opportunity to plan and conduct their own development.

Information is available for each Army Civilian career program at Civilian Personnel Online and ACT. For example, Career Program 34 is a 14,000-member group of Information Technology Management personnel. Development programs and op-

D. Professional Development Programs

Ref: FM 6-22, Leader Development (Jun '15), p. 3-34.

Leader professional development programs bring an organization's leaders together for a specific developmental purpose. Leader development programs are an effective vehicle for leader development when consistently applied. Common elements of successful programs include—

- Mission-essential leader task training when a common need exists across the organization.
- Required orientation or education sessions (such as equal opportunity and safety).
- Cohesion-building activities that foster esprit de corps (such as a dining-in, sports, or adventure training).
- Opportunities for the commander, command sergeant major, or first sergeant to emphasize key guidance to all leaders.
- Education sessions on leader career path topics (assignments, schooling, or promotions).
- Education sessions on the mission command philosophy, culture, and geopolitical issues.

Professional development sessions, conducted to facilitate discussion and collaboration, are extremely valuable in gaining a greater understanding and application of specific information or skills in a unit. The sources of information and means of conducting these sessions are endless and allow for creativity. Instructors should not rely solely on dry briefings. Scenarios and materials should be tailored to the grades and ranks present. These sessions can be great team building opportunities to bring together groups of different ranks and responsibilities.

All of these applications fulfill the training and development needs of the leaders in the organization. To implement leader development programs effectively, leaders should invoke the following guidelines—

- Link training and professional development.
- Clearly communicate purpose and relevance.
- Gather all leaders together only when doing so is the most effective learning method.
- Consider prior listed applications as integral to leader development programs.

portunities for Career Program 34 include academic degree training in such areas technology management, information technology management, information security and computer science. Short–term training is available in areas such as project management, cloud computing, system administration, and software development. Some opportunities are competitive and slots are filled through application, nomination and screening of candidates. Management programs are available from Office of Personnel Management development centers, executive leadership development and executive potential programs.

Developmental assignments are encouraged to broaden knowledge of how different organizations conduct information technology and cyber missions. Training with industry is available to higher-ranking personnel where they learn about information technology practices outside the Army. Distributed learning resources are extensive for the Career Program 34 population, predominantly through Army e-Learning courses and certifications. Each career program has similar opportunities to guide the professional development of Army Civilians.

Opportunities During Training Events

Training is an organized, structured, continuous, and progressive process based on sound principles of learning designed to increase the capability of individuals, units, and organizations to perform specified tasks or skills. The objective of training is to increase the ability of competent leaders to perform in a variety of training and operational situations. Individual task training builds individual competence and confidence to perform these tasks to support collective training and operations.

Leaders contribute substantially to the unit's mission success or lack of success. Therefore, the Army devotes considerable resources to foster leader development during exercises. Leader development is an important duty of supervisory leaders and the leader's chain-of-command. Their responsibility is to provide leaders with accurate observations of their abilities and the effects on unit performance. Providing leadership feedback is a difficult, yet essential, part of training exercises. Without it, the assessment of an important contributor to a unit's mission accomplishment, namely its leadership, is left undone.

Leaders have a specific task to observe subordinates during planning and executing missions. Some may feel unqualified to observe and provide feedback on leadership actions. However, understanding how to treat leadership as a set of skills that can be developed and improved is essential.

Guided discovery learning is an important underpinning of developing leaders. To the extent possible, leaders ought to use guided discovery learning. Doing so places the observed leader in charge of their learning, with the chain of command in a supporting role. Using guided discovery learning during training exercises makes the leader better prepared to be a self-guided learner in any contemporary operational environment. Providing feedback falls in the larger context of guided discovery learning methods.

III. Self-Development

Ref: FM 6-22, Leader Development (Jun '15), chap 4.

Self-development bridges the gaps between the operational and institutional domains and sets the conditions for continuous learning and growth. Military and Army Civilian personnel engage in self-development to improve their capabilities for current and future positions. Self-knowledge is an important part of a leader's development. Several tools, such as the Army MSAF program, are available to leaders to understand strengths and obtain insights into developmental needs.

Self-Development Process

The self-development process consists of four major phases. They are—

Strengths and Developmental Needs Determination

Goal Setting

Self-Enhanced Learning

Learning In Action

Self-development is an individual's responsibility but it is important for leaders to set conditions and support self-development. Leaders need to be actively involved in developing themselves and each other. Development happens through study and practice. Leaders can support others' self-development through the exchange of professional development information, discoveries, and opinions.

Self-development supports planned, goal-oriented learning to reinforce and expand the depth and breadth of what a person knows to include themselves and situations they experience and how they perform their duties. The Army acknowledges three types of self-development:

- **Structured self-development** includes mandatory learning modules required to meet specific learning objectives and requirements.
- **Guided self-development** is recommended, optional learning intended to enhance professional competence.
- **Personal self-development** is self-initiated learning to meet personal objectives such as pursuing a college education or an advanced degree.

To help subordinates learn from their experiences, leaders should provide opportunities for them to pause, reflect, and process the experience for what was learned. Reflecting on an experience—

- Keeps leaders from repeating the same mistakes.
- Helps leaders consider effects in future decisionmaking.
- Helps leaders to link their actions with the resulting effects on unit performanc

Working environments can be chaotic, noisy, and filled with activity. However, prioritizing time for reflection and consolidation of thoughts enhances self-development.

I. Strengths and Developmental Needs Determination

The first step in determining strengths and developmental needs is to think about what you do and how well you do it. At a minimum, this information comes from self-examination. Outside opinions and information on strengths and developmenta needs are useful. Feedback can come from formal or informal assessments and from other leaders, peers, or subordinates. Keep this in mind during a self-examination.

Understanding current strengths and developmental needs is necessary before setting self-development goals. This is part of being self-aware. These methods help identify strengths and developmental needs:

A. Information Collection

Formal assessments such as evaluations and tests are a good place to start gaining insight into strengths and developmental needs, since they measure individual performance and compare it to a standard. Individuals use the information and results from relevant assessments to inform understanding of personal strengths an developmental needs. Formal assessments include—

- Performance evaluations.
- Counseling sessions (formal and informal).
- Skills tests (such as the Expert Field Medical Badge and Expert Infantryman Badge tests).
- Tests administered in resident and non-resident schools.
- Field performance evaluations such as those at the combat training centers.
- Intelligence and aptitude tests (such as Armed Services Vocational Aptitude Battery or Defense Language Aptitude Battery).
- MSAF program feedback (360-degree assessment) where superiors, peers, and subordinates provide anonymous feedback.
- Occupational interest inventories.

B. Feedback Gathering

Hearing what peers, subordinates, superiors, mentors, family, and friends think can help identify strengths and developmental needs that went unnoticed or you have been reluctant to acknowledge. There are two ways to get feedback: observe how others interact with you or ask them directly. Supervisors have an explicit role in subordinate development. Subordinates should consult supervisors for guidance about development goals or any other aspect of self-development.

Compare the feedback received from different sources to look for common themes. These themes will help to identify strengths and developmental needs. Army leaders must try to avoid the natural inclination to reject or minimize responses that do not confirm self-perceptions or attribute them to the situation instead.

Gathering Feedback

Ref: FM 6-22, Leader Development (Jun '15), pp. 4-2 to 4-3.

After considering these questions, analyze the answers to determine the opinions that each person considered may have of your strengths and developmental needs:

Supervisors, raters, and superiors.
- Who gets the most challenging assignments?
- The supervisor relies upon whom during emergencies or tough problems?
- The supervisor praises whom the most?
- What kinds of tasks does your supervisor give you versus others?
- How does your supervisor react to your suggestions compared to others' suggestions?
- Does your supervisor listen to your opinions on certain subjects much more or much less than the opinions of others? If so, what are those subjects?

Peers and Subordinates.
- Do peers and subordinates come to you for help or advice? In what topics?
- Do they understand you or seem confused or overwhelmed by what you say?
- Do they repeatedly contact you for help or are they one-time interactions?
- Does their interest and enthusiasm increase or diminish when they interact with you?
- What does their body language communicate? Is it relaxed, apprehensive, or reserved?

Asking for Feedback

To gain perspective, talk to others who know you in different ways, such as one's rater, enlisted or officer counter-part, mentor, instructor, or family member. The goal is to find out—
- What a person actually saw and their impressions of your action(s).
- That person's impression of how well you performed during the interaction(s).
- How you react in certain situations. For example, "When a subordinate challenges your authority in front of others, you seem to get flustered."

Who to Ask

These are items to consider when determining who to ask for feedback—
- Who has been able to observe you enough to offer useful information?
- Who has observed you from different perspectives?
- Who has experience in an area of interest (former or current supervisor, mentor)?

Things to Remember When Asking for Feedback

When asking for feedback, keep the following in mind—
- Be respectful of others' time—prepare questions ahead of time.
- Approach with an open mind to accept uncomfortable or critical feedback without offense.
- Listen carefully and respectfully.
- Ask for clarification and examples when points are unclear.
- Summarize the points to make sure that you understand the person correctly.
- Thank the feedback providers for their time and assistance.

These ideas may help you focus on what to ask:
- Get descriptions of your behaviors and opinions of those behaviors.
- For feedback about a recurring issue, ask about the situation, your actions, and the usual outcomes.
- Ask for suggestions for other ways of handling situations.

Observe Others

Observing how others act toward you and the decisions they make affecting y
will give an idea of what they think about your skills and expertise. When obse
ing others:

Make observations on different occasions. Watching the same person several
times will help you see trends that may be a sign of a firmly held opinion of you
One observation is not reliable, as that behavior may have been a result of oth
issues.

Consider the circumstances. What outside factors influenced the person's deci
sions and actions? For example, if your supervisor selected someone else to
perform an important task, was it because you were too busy or unavailable?

C. Self-Analysis

After gathering the information from outside sources through formal assessments,
observing others, and requesting feedback, it is time to reflect on personal behavio
and performance. Examining personal situations and experiences can reveal things
to change or improve. The situation analysis exercise will help analyze experiences
to help identify personal strengths and developmental needs.

After recording the information, look for key factors that influenced the situation
progression and the overall outcome. Keep in mind that if the same factor occurs in
multiple situations, it may suggest a significant strength or developmental need that
may be developed.

By knowing how personal actions affected the situation and the thoughts and feelings associated with those actions, leaders can work to become more self-aware
and choose the most productive actions. In addition, a self-analysis may suggest
broader interests to pursue or issues to avoid.

See facing page for further discussion.

D. Strengths and Developmental Needs Identification

The final step is to take the information gathered from formal assessments, information gathered from observing others and asking others, and results of the situation
and self-analyses and analyze it to determine strengths and developmental needs.

Instead of taking all of the feedback as fact, look for recurring themes or patterns
of feedback heard from more than one person. Look at what others identified as
strengths and developmental needs and compare that to personal knowledge (from
the self-exam) and the results of formal assessments.

Usually, repeated success or expertise in a particular activity indicates a strength.
These abilities may come easily even though others find them difficult:

- What are your favorite things to do or learn about?
- What do others turn to you for help with?
- What do recent assignments show as strengths?

Developmental needs are tasks that are a struggle to learn or difficult to perform:

- What was noted as being hard or not fun to do?
- What did others suggest as a limitation?
- Did formal assessments point out any deficiencies?

Identify where these descriptions apply and make a list of strengths and developmental needs. This list will enable setting clear goals for self-development efforts.

Self-Analysis Process

Ref: FM 6-22, Leader Development (Jun '15), pp. 4-4 to 4-5.

Complete a Situation Analysis for Self-Development

After gathering the information from outside sources through formal assessments, observing others, and requesting feedback, it is time to reflect on personal behavior and performance. Examining personal situations and experiences can reveal things to change or improve. The situation analysis exercise will help analyze experiences to help identify personal strengths and developmental needs.

Think of experiences over the past two years that give insight into personal strengths and developmental needs—maybe a critical decision, an important task you led or were a part of, or a significant personal interaction. Use these questions to analyze each situation:

What was the situation? What was happening? Who was there?

What was the goal and did you reach it? What were you trying to accomplish? What resources or skills did you have or not have that you needed?

What did you say and think? Were you able to find the right words to make your point? What were you thinking at the time? What made you feel good (confident, excited) or bad (confused, worried)?

What did you do? How did you act (including your body language)? Why did you choose to act the way you did? How did others react? Did you help or hurt the situation? Did you adjust your actions based on how others were reacting?

Why did you act the way you did? What knowledge and skills led you to act the way you did?

What could have helped you handle the situation better? How could you have used your strengths to reach a better outcome? Are there any developmental needs that you should make a high priority for personal self-development efforts?

After recording the information, look for key factors that influenced the situation progression and the overall outcome. Keep in mind that if the same factor occurs in multiple situations, it may suggest a significant strength or developmental need that may be developed.

By knowing how personal actions affected the situation and the thoughts and feelings associated with those actions, leaders can work to become more self-aware and choose the most productive actions. In addition, a self-analysis may suggest broader interests to pursue or issues to avoid.

Complete a Self-Analysis

Consider the following items and be as specific as possible. Use the items as necessary to identify unique aspects of personal strengths and developmental needs.

Strengths

The skill or ability at which I am best is— The personal quality that I rely on most for my success is—I am most knowledgeable about— The activities I look forward to include— I would love to learn more about— The accomplishment I am most proud of is— Others usually come to me for help with— Others think the best position for me would be—

Developmental needs

The skill or ability that is always difficult for me is— I don't know as much as I should about— I usually go to others for help on— The situation that causes me the most frustration is— I am most hesitant when I try to— I am most concerned about my— Others think I am not skilled at— I would become a more valued member of my organization if I—

II. Goal Setting

To make the most of self-development efforts and avoid wasting time and energy, it is crucial to set self-development goals—identify personal and professional goals and decide where to go. This section outlines procedures to—

A. Information Gathering

An understanding of strengths and developmental needs is an important place to start when determining where to focus self-development efforts. Other areas to analyze for self-development opportunities include—

- Roles and responsibilities (personal and work-related).
- The needs of the Army.

Roles and Responsibilities

Roles and responsibilities at home and at work may offer opportunities for self-development, such as being a spouse, parent, teacher, Soldier, or other roles. Each role has different responsibilities, skill and knowledge requirements, and expectations. Reserve Component leaders have a unique opportunity to improve both civilian and military profession skills by linking self-development goals to skills shared by both professions. ADRP 6-22 describes expectations for key roles as Army military and civilian leaders.

Chosen roles usually reflect personal interests and values, but even assigned roles will affect the value of different self-development paths. When roles and responsibilities align with talents and interests, leaders are likely to succeed and be satisfied.

Needs of the Army

Another way to identify satisfying goals for personal self-development efforts is to align personal interests with Army needs. This ensures that the acquired knowledge and skills are personally interesting but benefit the Army.

Soldiers and Army units must be ready to deploy to any part of the world and accomplish diverse missions. Some requirements may be unforeseen and untrained, requiring Soldiers to use their knowledge, skills, and creativity to accomplish the mission. As members of a unit develop expertise in a variety of areas, the unit and the Army as a whole become stronger. The range and depth of expertise gives the unit resiliency and an increased ability to adapt to specific challenges.

B. Self-Development Goals

Self-development activities aim at learning new knowledge, gaining or enhancing skills, changing attitudes or values, or a combination of these. It is often easier to improve upon strengths rather than developmental needs. Learning is quicker and greater when strengths are used as a path to improvement rather than developmental needs. However, if a particular developmental need is an obstacle to development, consider improving it.

No set formula exists in choosing personal development goals. However, key considerations include—

- Personal strengths.
- Personal developmental needs.
- Family roles and responsibilities.
- Current or future roles.
- Army needs.
- Personal interests.

Personal experiences and goals, as well as personal interests, needs, and resources should influence the determination of self-development goals. Ideally, self-development goals will provide a long-term professional aim to work toward through a variety of activities.

Planning Milestones

Ref: FM 6-22, Leader Development (Jun '15), pp. 4-8 to 4-9.

After establishing self-development goals, create one or more milestones to get started and gauge progress. Use an IDP to document goals and milestones. Use each milestone to stretch you. Milestones can be a mix of short-term or long-term—whatever personally works and encourages progress. Milestones should—

- **Be specific and measurable:** They need to state what to accomplish so you can tell if you have met the milestone or not.

- **Be meaningful:** They should help achieve self-development goals.

- **Provide a challenge:** Milestones should stretch personal abilities and be challenging to accomplish. Challenging milestones increase motivation; being too easy or hard can hurt motivation.

- **Have a time limit:** Time limits provide motivation and will help gauge success.

- **Be flexible**: Build in some flexibility to overcome obstacles or revise milestones if necessary.

- **Be realistic**: Ensure milestones are reachable with available resources. For example, if a deployment will occur in the next 12 months, do not set a milestone requiring college attendance during that time. Keep in mind that unforeseen obstacles may occur along the way.

- **Be cost effective:** The benefits gained must be worth the effort, resources, risk, and other costs of reaching the milestone.

Every milestone requires at least a minimal amount of planning. After setting the first milestone, create a plan to achieve it. A plan can increase chances of success by—

- Identifying all required actions.
- Identifying the resources needed to meet the milestones.
- Establishing time estimates and deadlines that help track progress.
- Dividing large tasks into smaller parts to reduce being overwhelmed.
- Identifying possible obstacles and the actions and resources needed to overcome them.
- Making the best use of personal time and other resources.

Plan to Meet Milestones

Develop a plan by listing the first milestone and identify the main steps needed to reach it along with associated timelines to meet those milestones. Consider all of the developmental resources the Army has to offer as well as other sources to reach each milestone. Identify potential enablers and obstacles before beginning to better prepare for difficulties along the way. Collaborating through online forums and interest groups may help personal development and provide encouragement.

C. Milestone Planning

After establishing self-development goals, create one or more milestones to get started and gauge progress. Use an IDP to document goals and milestones. Use each milestone to stretch you. Milestones can be a mix of short-term or long-term– whatever personally works and encourages progress.

See previous page (p. 2-49) for further discussion.

III. Self-Enhanced Learning

Self-development requires learning. Knowing how to learn is the most important skill require for self-development. Self-understanding, setting self-development goals, and planning milestones all influence a personal ability to learn. Beyond that, effective learning requires–

A. Motivation and Persistence

Self-development may require hard work over a long period, especially if the goal is t become an expert in an area or undergo significant personal growth. It takes motiva- tion and effort to keep self-development efforts alive. Genuine motivation provides lasting energy because it is the internalization of goals and the desire to achieve ther

B. Learning Opportunities

Learning stems from deliberate planned activities or from the unplanned experience of daily life. Make the most of each learning opportunity, whether planned or not.

Leaders can embed planned learning into routine duties by using normal events as learning opportunities or it can be a completely separate, scheduled activity for a specific item. Prepare for the unexpected times by having appropriate learning materials available. It is a good idea to take advantage of time that opens up such a from transportation delays, waiting for appointments, or cancellations.

Unplanned learning happens when something unexpectedly captures your attention. Interest in the topic causes you to pay attention and learn. Attune your mind to draw at tention to information related to self-development aims by thinking about developmen- tal aims in detail—what you are trying to accomplish and why you want to accomplish these things. Review what you know and what you need to learn. Remind yourself of key terms and ideas related to the subject as well as who the experts in the field are.

Personal After Action Review (AAR)

A personal AAR is an in-depth self-assessment of how leadership contributes to task and unit performance. Leaders should conduct their own personal AARs after a task is complete, or even while it is playing out, by asking themselves:

What happened and what were the consequences?

How were my leader actions supposed to influence the situation?

What were the direct results or consequences of my leader actions?

How did my actions benefit or hinder mission accomplishment?

How should I change my leader actions for better results next time?

What did I learn?

A good time to encourage personal AARs is following the unit AAR process. The unit AAR will clarify for the leader what happened and accurately assess mission accomplishment. Commanders can reinforce personal AARs by:

• Walking less experienced leaders through the personal AAR.

• Asking individuals what they learned from their personal AARs.

• Telling subordinates the outcome of their personal AARs.

Effective Learning Methods

Ref: FM 6-22, Leader Development (Jun '15), pp. 4-12 to 4-13.

The purpose of each learning activity will help determine the learning principles to use to make the most of learning. The purpose may be to learn new knowledge, a new skill, or a new attitude about something. No matter the purpose, there are general principles of learning that apply:

- **Use multiple senses.** Moore senses used while learning enable better memory and information recall. Involve multiple senses by taking notes, highlighting, reciting, and observing.
- Space out learning sessions. Do not try to learn a large amount of information or a complex skill in one long session—try to break the material into multiple, manageable sections.
- Study the information or practice the skill on multiple occasions.
- Know the time of day when you learn best and study the most difficult material during that time.
- Design learning activities so that they mimic reality as much as possible. If the expected conditions to use the information cannot be duplicated, try to imagine the conditions as vividly as possible.
- Familiarize information through self-study prior to formal instruction. Reinforce learning by reviewing the information after instruction. This is a good way to review and test memory skills.
- When learning an entirely new field, go slow at first to ensure thorough understanding of the basics—it is important to have a solid foundation to build on.
- Learn in layers. Start with what you know to determine what is the first level of understanding, information, or skill needed. Learn that level then determine what the information just learned suggests to learn next.
- Learn like a scientist. Adopt the attitude that the best knowledge is subject to change and that new discoveries may prove old beliefs or assumptions wrong.

Principles for Specific Types of Learning

While the general learning principles apply to all types of learning, some learning principles apply based on whether the learning activity focuses on learning a new skill, a new attitude, or new knowledge.

Learning or improving a skill requires repeated, deliberate practice. Deliberate practice is not just repetition of a skill. Deliberate practice involves—

- Making your best attempt at performing the skill.
- Analyzing the results of the attempt (sometimes with the help of a coach or instructor) to identify ways of improving personal performance.
- Attempting the skill again using the identified improvements.

Learning a new attitude about something requires repeated exposure to and testing of the attitude. Taking on a new attitude might involve realizing that a prior viewpoint is counterproductive to obtaining goals. Changing attitude can be done in two ways:

- Behave as if you have already adopted the new attitude. If done often with positive results, it is likely that you will actually adopt the attitude.
- Observe another person behaving in a way that reflects the attitude. If you respect this person as a role model and you see the person gaining some benefit from the behavior, you may eventually come to accept and adopt the attitude for yourself.

Learning new knowledge requires linking the new information to already known information. This occurs by deeply processing the information that you want to learn.

C. Effective Learning Methods

The purpose of each learning activity will help determine the learning principles to use to make the most of learning. The purpose may be to learn new knowledge, a new skill, or a new attitude about something.

See previous page (p. 2-51) for further discussion.

D. Deep Processing

The ability to learn and recall information depends upon what someone does with the information while trying to learn it. Deep processing requires analyzing the new information, picking it apart, using it, and connecting it to already-known information

Critical Thinking and Reflective Thinking

Using critical and reflective thinking skills is essential to being an effective learner and gaining subject expertise. Critical thinking and reflective thinking do not apply solely to learning but are essential practices and important ways of deeply processing information for duties across the range of military operations.

E. Learning through Focused Reading and Analysis

Books and other written materials may be key learning resources for self-development. To maximize learning, approach reading for learning differently than casual reading. Deep processing of written materials is essential to the ability to understand, recall, and use the information contained in the books and other documents. Even though books may present information in a logical way, you must take an active role in teaching the information to yourself.

The **Survey-Question-Read-Recite-Review** method uses the deep processing principles. Developed over 70 years ago, these activities comprise one of the most widely recommended and effective ways of learning from written materials.

Personal Reading

Documents often suggest related information to expand knowledge of the subject. The end of a chapter or book may list related documents. The bibliography or footnotes identify information sources the author used. To help narrow the search, make notes of any reference that sounds interesting and relevant.

Reflective Journaling

A journal may track and record the occurrence, actions, and outcomes of various situations. Reflective journaling goes beyond a personal AAR including periodic entries on self-awareness of personal strengths, developmental needs, values, feelings and perceptions, and questions and ideas about leadership situations. A leader may track personal successes and lessons learned by recording their experiences in leading others, the chosen actions, the resulting outcomes, and any insights. The journal may serve as a reference to pass along lessons learned to others. Key leader references also may be recorded.

IV. Learning in Action

Self-development efforts take time and effort. To stay on track—

A. Let Milestones Guide

Use the milestones as a guide to—

- Avoid impulsive actions that may be ineffective and discouraging.
- Keep the big picture in mind.
- Work effectively toward self-development goals.
- Take advantage of resources and overcome obstacles.
- Measure success.

Adjust the plan as needed to reach milestones. Be willing to update the plan to improve it, change goals, address obstacles, take advantage of resources, and reflect upon accomplishments.

B. Self-Development Obstacles

In developing a milestone plan, obstacles to reaching the first milestone were identified. There is always the possibility of encountering internal and external obstacles, despite thorough preparation.

Internal Obstacles

Procrastination, apathy, and pride are major obstacles to self-development and occur for many reasons. Some come to realize their milestones are too ambitious, complex, unclear, or difficult. Others hesitate because of the effort or discomfort that the work requires or lack the motivation to start. Poor attitude also can interfere with learning and make it difficult to understand and remember information. For example, thinking that math is hard or disliking history can interfere with an ability to learn anything related to math or history. Other attitudes, such as closed mindedness, inflexibility, or rigid adherence to beliefs and assumptions, can interfere with learning. To combat poor attitudes, identify a productive replacement. Practice thinking and behaving with a positive attitude until it feels natural and becomes a habit.

External Obstacles

External factors such as workload or other personal or professional obligations may hinder self-development efforts. Resistance may also come from others, such as a spouse who resents time spent away from the family or friends who may pressure you to spend time with them.

A lack of resources is another common roadblock. Resources include anything needed for self-development including people (such as teachers, coaches, and mentors), facilities (such as schools, libraries, and museums), and things (such as training programs, books, and equipment). Learners best handle external obstacles through careful planning and creativity.

C. Work Efficiently

By efficiently managing workload and personal life, one can increase how much time is available to spend on self-development. To increase efficiency—

- Take care of yourself. Proper food, exercise, and rest enable functioning at your best.
- Manage time and energy efficiently. Keep a running 'to do' list. Prioritize each task according to its importance, required work, and completion date. Remove low-priority tasks from the list.
- Look for ways to accomplish daily activities and routines in less time. For example, combine several errands in a single trip instead of making individual trips.
- Learn to quickly locate and obtain the information needed for self-development and other requirements of daily life.
- Organize work and living areas so that required information, tools, and work-space are available.

D. Forward Momentum

It is important to keep the developmental momentum moving forward. There may be a tendency to slow down after completing an important self-development step or be discouraged by setbacks. Resting after a strong effort is natural, but too much rest may make it hard to restart. Maintain momentum by—

- **Keeping a positive attitude**: Let go of setbacks and start each day with re-
newed enthusiasm. Each morning offers an opportunity for a fresh start.
- **Making consistent progress**: Try to accomplish something, however small,
related to self-development milestones and goals each day.
- **Recognizing benefits**: Benefits can be tangible results such as increased pay,
awards, and abilities or intangible results such as pride, a sense of accomplishment, and satisfaction. Remember that important benefits often require hard work

E. Progress Assessment

Assessing progress can provide encouragement to keep going if things are going w
or to guide changes if they are not. Individuals can assess progress at any time—
while working toward a milestone or after completing one. To assess progress—

- Use objective and subjective measures.
- Compare the milestone plan with what actually happened and adjust the
remainder of this milestone plan or future milestones to account for lessons
learned.
- Decide if you are satisfied with your progress or if the milestones or general
self-development goals need changes.

F. Course Corrections

Self-development occurs over time in a dynamic environment that includes professional and personal responsibilities. At some point, obstacles or other challenges wi
force a change of plans. If the progress assessment indicates course corrections are
needed, determine what correction is warranted:

- **Goal**: A self-development goal or milestone may have turned out to be too difficult, too easy, or just not what was hoped. Examine other possible self-development goals or milestones. Identify why the unsatisfactory goal or milestone
was selected and avoid repeating any missteps.
- **Action Steps**: If the actions taken to achieve milestones were not effective,
figure out why they did not work, and then develop actions that are more effective. To be effective, you must be capable and willing to perform the actions
with available resources. If a course correction is required due to obstacles
then create new action steps that avoid or solve these obstacles. Action steps
should form a logical path from where you currently are to achievement of the
milestone.
- **Resources**: The identified milestone resources may have been inappropriate,
inadequate, or unavailable. If so, analyze planned action steps to determine
the resources (such as time, money, equipment, facilities, or help) needed to
perform these steps. Determine if they can be obtained.

G. The Next Milestone

With the first self-development milestone achieved, a full cycle of self-development
is completed. It is now time to continue the self-development process by setting and
pursuing the next milestone.

IV. Unique Aspects for Development

Ref: FM 6-22, Leader Development (Jun '15), chap 5.

Character, judgment and problem solving, and adaptability are capabilities that are especially valuable to leaders and team members in special situations. They allow leaders and teams to address the demands of complex, ambiguous, and chaotic environments of military operations. Whether making the tough moral decision, thinking critically to resolve uncertainty, thinking from a broad and strategic perspective, or adapting to unexpected changes, expert leaders find the way to do what is right. This chapter describes these capabilities and identifies unique aspects of developing, enhancing, or fostering them in leaders and teams.

I. Character

Character is a critical component of being a successful Army leader. Character is one's true nature including identity, sense of purpose, values, virtues, morals, and conscience. Character is reflected in an Army professional's dedication and adherence to the Army Ethic and the Army Values. Character is the essence of who an individual is, what an individual values and believes, and how they behave. Doing the right thing the right way for the right reasons demonstrates character. Demonstrating character often means resisting the easier wrong in favor of the tougher right. Making the right choices involves discipline. Discipline can be thought of as the foundation of character. Team character is the melding of individuals' character in a team.

As the uncertainty of operating environments dictate, junior leaders need to be capable of independent decisions using sound discretionary judgments founded in moral character. Character is also such an important quality of a leader because decisions and actions of the leader are viewed by others. The demonstrated character of the leader greatly influences how other people either emulate their conduct or disapprove of it. These can, in turn, add to or detract from team trust and cohesion.

Character forms over time through education, training, and experience in a continuous, iterative process. Leaders employ character when all decisions, big or small, are analyzed for ethical consequences. One must have the knowledge of how to address the consequences. This knowledge comes from the Army Ethic, personal experience, and others' guidance. Internalizing the moral principles of the Army Ethic as personal beliefs is essential for character development. An individual demonstrates character when they correctly identify the ethical implications of a decision, possesses knowledge to act, and acts accordingly.

II. Judgment and Problem Solving

Intellect enables a leader to understand, visualize, and decide and is essential in unfamiliar and chaotic settings. Judgment, as a key component of intellect, is an ability to make considered decisions and come to sensible conclusions. Leaders can reflect on how they think and better foster the development of judgment in others. Problem solving, critical and creative thinking, and ethical reasoning are the thought processes involved in understanding, visualizing, and directing. Problem solving involves situation assessment (understanding), imagining (visualizing), and converging on a solution (directing). Thinking critically involves analytical, cautious, and convergent judgment. It checks on the sensibility, relevance, and relationship of meaning and possibility. Creative thinking is generative, daring, and divergent. Critical thinking considers what might be wrong, while creative thinking considers what possible. The two complementary processes—evaluation and generation—occur in a free-flowing manner depending on what ideas and conclusions stem from thinking in specific situations.

A goal of all leaders and teams is to think as well and as thoroughly as time permits. The brain encodes experience as expertise that allows automatic and intuitive responses, which frees up time to apply to other thinking or provides a reserve capacity for addressing the most complex problems. Intuition can operate rapidly, but the downside is that it can be misapplied. Intuition operates based on the best or closest match, having no built-in or automatic process that checks on mismatches in cues, and no repair of ill-fitting ideas. Evaluation, repair, and design are roles of deliberate thinking processes.

Leaders draw on their knowledge and expertise in the context of each part of a problem. However, most situations will always have incomplete knowledge. Thinking is a technique to identify gaps in knowledge. Experience or a hunch can be used to facilitate a new way of framing (seeing or structuring) a problem or a solution. Leaders test ideas through visualization or a war-gaming process. The thought process judges how well ideas meet goals. (See emerging doctrine on the Army Design Methodology.)

Everyday thinking switches back and forth from a subconscious process of intuition to deliberate, effortful thought. The active monitoring of one's own thinking guides the process, keeping it on track. Thinking about thinking is metacognition. Metacognition and deliberate thought are processes that people can learn to improve. Intuition develops through the natural accumulation of experiences. Individuals develop judgment intentionally through overt attention to the deliberate side of thinking. The following sections describe these deliberate processes.

III. Adaptability

A key outcome of development of an individual leader or unit is building increased capability to adapt to meet mission challenges. Adaptability for the purpose of performance is an effective change in behavior in response to an altered or unexpected situation. The Army stresses the importance of adaptability due to the rapid pace of world events and the dynamic change that occurs across related military operations. Military history is replete with accounts of adaptation, hinging on a leader's ability to have uncanny insight into the situation, to be keenly self-aware, and to have a mindset and knowledge that promotes adaptation.

Adaptability for an individual means having broad and deep knowledge and a good mix of skills and characteristics (see table 5-3). Critical and creative thinking skills are needed when new situations are encountered and the team does not have existing knowledge to use in adaptation.

Skills	Characteristics
Quickly assess the situation.	Open-minded.
Recognize changes in the environment.	Flexible, Versatile, Innovative.
Identify critical elements of new situation.	Sees change as an opportunity.
Apply new skills in unanticipated contexts.	Passionate learner.
Change responses readily.	Comfortable in unfamiliar environments.
Use multiple perspectives through critical and creative thinking.	Comfortable with ambiguity.
Avoid oversimplification.	Maintain appropriate complexity in knowledge.

Ref: FM 6-22 (Jun '15), table 5-3. Skills and characteristics of adaptability.

Adaptability for a team means having a variety of skills within the team to enable adaptation. Adaptability is enhanced when members of the team apply unique knowledge to a problem in new ways. Developing expertise is important to enable adaptable performance later.

V. Leader Performance Indicators

Ref: FM 6-22, Leader Development (Jun '15), chap 6.

Accurate, descriptive observations of leadership are important to assess performance and provide feedback that produce focused learning. Assessing an individual's performance into the categories of developmental need, meets standard, and strength informs the individual about what needs development or sustainment. It will also provide motivation to develop. The behavior indicators in this chapter provide some general performance measures for varying levels of proficiency for the leader attributes and core leader competencies. Understanding the behavior indicators and observation methods provides a strong base for providing feedback to subordinates.

Accurate and Descriptive Observations

Observing leadership occurs by watching how a leader interacts with others and influences them. Written directives, verbal communications, and leader actions all provide indications of how a leader performs. Raters also learn about their subordinates' leadership by observing reactions to the subordinate among peers, subordinates, and other superiors.

When observing leadership, these key components ensure observations are accurate and descriptive:

- Plan to take multiple observations over several months or during a rating period. Use both key events and routine operations.
- Make observations based on ADRP 6-22, ADRP 1, and the individual's duty descriptions and performance objectives. Look for patterns of behavior. Seek to confirm initial impressions. Be alert to changes in performance and causes for strengths, inconsistencies, or developmental needs.
- Record important observations immediately for later use in performance and professional growth counseling and for evaluations.
- Consider dimensions on which performance can be differentiated such as the extent of demonstration of a desired behavior, the ability and initiative shown in learning to improve or engage in a desired behavior, and the extent and duration of effects that the behavior has on individual or unit performance.

Application of the Performance Indicators

Performance indicators are grouped according to the doctrinal leadership requirements model in categories of leader attributes (character, presence, and intellect) and leader competencies (lead, develop, and achieve). The performance indicators provide three levels of proficiency: a developmental need, the standard, and a strength. For developmental purposes, these three categories are sufficient and apply across cohorts. A developmental need is identified as a specific need for development when the observed individual does not demonstrate the leader competency. Strength indicators are associated with successful performance of a leader attribute or competency. Strengths include a consistent pattern of natural talents, knowledge gained through learning, and skills acquired through practice and experience.

Leader Performance Indicators

Ref: FM 6-22, Leader Development (Jun '15), pp. 6-2 to 6-6.

Editor's Note. An overview of leader attribute and leader competency categories/ tables from FM 6-22 are provided below. In the interest of space, rather than duplicate material essentially referenced elsewhere in this SMARTbook, page jumps are provided for related discussion of these attributes/competencies from ADP/ADRP 6-22.

I. Attribute Categories

The leader attributes are presented in three categories: character, presence, and intellect. *See pp. 1-19 to 1-32 (from ADP 6-22).*

Character

ADRP 6-22 defines character as factors internal and central to a leader, which make up an individual's core and are the mindset and moral foundation behind actions and decisions. Leaders of character adhere to the Army Values, display empathy and the Warrior Ethos/Service Ethos, and practice good discipline.

See pp. 1-22 to 1-28 (from ADP 6-22).

Presence

Presence is how others perceive a leader based on the leader's appearance, demeanor, actions, and words. Leaders with presence demonstrate military and professional bearing, fitness, confidence, and resilience.

See pp. 1-28 to 1-30 (from ADP 6-22).

Intellect

Intellect is comprised of the mental tendencies or resources that shape a leader's conceptual abilities and affect a leader's duties and responsibilities. Leaders with high intellect are mentally agile, good at judgment, innovative, tactful around others, and expert in technical, tactical, cultural, geopolitical, and other relevant knowledge areas.

See pp. 1-30 to 1-32 (from ADP 6-22).

II. Core Leader Competency Categories

The core leader competencies are presented in three categories: lead, develop, and achieve. *See pp. 1-33 to 1-72 (from ADP 6-22).*

Lead

Leaders set goals and establish a vision, motivate or influence others to pursue the goals, build trust to improve relationships, communicate and come to a shared understanding, serve as a role model by displaying character, confidence, and competence, and influence outside the chain of command.

See pp. 1-35 to 1-52 (from ADP 6-22).

Develop

Leaders foster teamwork; express care for individuals; promote learning; maintain expertise, skills, and self-awareness; coach, counsel and mentor others; foster position development, and steward the profession of arms.

See pp. 1-53 to 1-68 (from ADP 6-22).

Achieve

Leaders achieve by setting priorities, organizing taskings, managing resources, developing thorough and synchronized plans, executing plans to accomplish the mission, and achieving goals.

See pp. 1-69 to 1-72 (from ADP 6-22).

VI. Learning & Development Activities

Ref: FM 6-22, Leader Development (Jun '15), chap. 7.

FM 6-22, chapter 7 provides a guide for all Army leaders to develop themselves or to develop others. These activities follow the same organization as the leader competencies found in the Army leadership requirement model (see ADRP 6-22): ten leader competencies grouped in the categories of lead, develop, and achieve.

Learning & Developmental Activities

 A **Capability EVALUATION**

- **Strength Indicators**
- **Need Indicators**
- **Underlying Causes**

 B **Capability EXPANSION**

- **Feedback**
- **Study**
- **Practice**

To best use this information, first identify the competencies and behaviors for developmental focus. An individual may already have an IDP that documents goals and a plan for development or have an idea of what leadership competency or skill to develop. A coach, rater, counselor, or mentor can use this material to help focus leaders or subordinates on specific developmental goals. Different sources and events inform the identification of developmental goals as illustrated in table 7-1.

Source or event providing identification of developmental goal	Example
Interest to the developing leader	'I want to get better at setting a positive climate that encourages subordinates to promote development.'
360° assessment and feedback report and/or coaching session	Communication skills make up the lowest assessed area relative to all other areas.
Performance evaluation and developmental growth counseling session	'You are good at motivating your Soldiers, you could grow into an even better leader by learning to better integrate tasks, resources and priorities to achieve results.'
Mentor's advice	'To move to the next level you could learn additional ways to operate with others outside the Army and to extend influence.'
Self-realization during institutional education course	'My fellow students generally seem more knowledgeable than me about world affairs affecting our Army.'
Counterpart feedback received during a training center rotation or home station training	'Under stress you are overly directive which doesn't align fully with mission command; you could learn to use commitment-building actions to expand your toolkit of influence.'

Ref: FM 6-22 (Jun '15), table 7-1. Identification of developmental goal.

Capability Evaluation and Expansion

Ref: FM 6-22, Leader Development (Jun '15), pp. 7-1 to 7-3.

To start using any of the developmental action tables, there are a few guidelines to consider for the most benefit from them. Each section is designed to help a leader understand and act on strengths as well as developmental needs. Some leaders may experience greater growth by focusing on improving strengths rather than focusing on developmental needs or using strengths to address developmental needs.

A. Capability EVALUATION

Evaluating capabilities involves identifying personal practices that support or hinder successful performance. Each table includes diagnostics to enable evaluation of how well an individual is doing on that behavior and provides examples of why they may or may not be excelling. Consider if the strength and need indicators represent personal behaviors. Each diagnostic section includes:

- **Strength Indicators**: Behaviors and actions that contribute to or support successful performance.
- **Need Indicators**: Behaviors and actions that reduce or hinder successful performance.
- **Underlying Causes**: Examples of why an individual may not be excelling at a particular leader behavior.

B. Capability EXPANSION

To build on an individual's current level, review the developmental activities for each capability area and personalize them. Table 7-2 outlines methods to engage in developmental activities. The developmental activities include:

- **Feedback**. Sources and methods for obtaining feedback to guide self-development.
- **Study**. Topics and activities to learn more about a behavior.
- **Practice**. Actions to improve skill and comfort in performing a leader behavior.

Developmental Step	Options to take	Method
Feedback	Ask for feedback...	From others about how you are doing with specific issues and areas of performance.
	Gain support...	From peers, colleagues, friends, or other people who can provide encouragement or recognize success.
	Consult...	With friends, supervisors, peers, subordinates, coaches, mentors, or other professionals to give advice on strengths or areas of concern.
Study	Observe...	Other leaders, professionals, and similar organizations. Note the most or least effective behaviors, attributes, and attitudes.
	Make time to reflect on...	Personal or situational characteristics that relate to the strength or need. Consider alternative perspectives.
	Read...	Books, articles, manuals, and professional publications.
	Investigate...	A topic through internet or library searches, gathering or asking questions, and soliciting information and materials.
Practice	Practice...	A skill or behavior that needs improvement in a work situation or away from the unit.
	Participate in training...	Including Army schools, unit training programs, outside seminars, degree programs, and professional certifications.
	Teach...	A skill you are learning to someone else.
	Accept an opportunity...	That stretches personal abilities, such as giving presentations, teaching classes, volunteering for special duty assignments, position cross-training, and representing the unit at meetings.
	Explore off-duty events...	Such as leading community groups, trying a new skill in a volunteer organization, or presenting to schools and civic organizations.

Ref: FM 6-22 (Jun '15), table 7-2. Methods to implement developmental activities.

Developmental Activities

Table 7-3 will assist an individual in determining where to start development activities. If the individual needs greater understanding to direct development, they should first seek feedback and follow with study and practice. If a developmental need is understood but knowing how to address that need is unknown, the individual should start with study and follow with practice. If the only unknown is what to practice, then the individual should focus on the practice activities. Applying the if-then logic in table 7-3 to each developmental goal will help individuals get the most from their development efforts.

If...	Then...
I need more insight into how well I am demonstrating a competency or component and what I can do to improve...	I should seek *Feedback*. Feedback is an opportunity to gain information about how well you are doing. Feedback can include direct feedback, personal observations, analysis of response patterns, and acknowledgement of outcomes.
I need to gain or expand my understanding of theory, principles, or knowledge of a leader competency or component...	I should *Study*. Study facilitates an intellectual understanding of the topic. Study can include attending training courses, reading, watching movies, observing others on duty, and analyzing various sources of information.
I need more experience to build or enhance my capability through opportunities to perform a leader competency or component...	I should *Practice*. Practice provides activities to convert personal learning into action. Practice includes engaging in physical exercises, team activities, rehearsals, and drills.

Ref: FM 6-22 (Jun '15), table 7-3. Evaluation model.

View all suggestions for developmental activities through a personal lens. The following questions are sample questions to ask when refining a development activity to fit personal needs and situation. Depending on the chosen activity, other considerations may be important too. Be willing to take risks and choose activities outside personal comfort zones to challenge yourself and accelerate development.

Determining Developmental Activities

Answer these to focus selection of appropriate developmental activities.

Developmental Activity: What do I want to do?

Desired Outcome: What do I hope to achieve?

Method: How am I going to do this? What resources do I need?

Time available: When will I do this? How will I monitor progress (such as identifying and monitoring milestones, rewarding success, or identifying accountability partners)? Limits: What factors will affect or hinder successful implementation of this activity?

Controls: What can minimize or control the factors that hinder implementation of this activity?

Table 7-4 on the following page provides a listing of appropriate developmental activities from FM 6-22. The MSAF 360° feedback reports detail individual or unit strengths and developmental needs. Learners and coaches will select a few actions at a time to guide development.

Leadership Competencies and Actions

Ref: FM 6-22, Leader Development (Jun '15), pp. 7-4 to 7-64.

Table 7-4 below provides a listing of appropriate developmental activities from FM 6-22. The MSAF 360° feedback reports detail individual or unit strengths and developmental needs. Learners and coaches will select a few actions at a time to guide development.

Competency	To find developmental activities for…	Go to…
Leads others	Uses appropriate methods of influence to energize others.	Table 7-5.
	Provides purpose.	Table 7-6.
	Enforces standards.	Table 7-7.
	Balances mission and welfare of followers.	Table 7-8.
Builds trust	Sets personal example for trust.	Table 7-9.
	Takes direct actions to build trust.	Table 7-10.
	Sustains a climate of trust.	Table 7-11.
Extends Influence	Understands sphere, means, and limits of influence.	Table 7-12.
	Negotiates, builds consensus, and resolves conflict.	Table 7-13.
Leads by example	Displays Army Values.	Table 7-14.
	Displays empathy.	Table 7-15.
	Exemplifies the Warrior Ethos/Service Ethos.	Table 7-16.
	Applies discipline.	Table 7-17.
	Leads with confidence in adverse situations.	Table 7-18.
	Demonstrates tactical and technical competence.	Table 7-19.
	Understands and models conceptual skills.	Table 7-20.
	Seeks diverse ideas and points of view.	Table 7-21.
Communicates	Listens actively.	Table 7-22.
	Creates shared understanding.	Table 7-23.
	Employs engaging communication techniques.	Table 7-24.
	Sensitive to cultural factors in communication.	Table 7-25.
Creates a positiv eenvironment/ esprit de corps	Fosters teamwork, cohesion, cooperation, and loyalty (esprit de corps).	Table 7-26.
	Encourages fairness and inclusiveness.	Table 7-27.
	Encourages open and candid communications.	Table 7-28.
	Creates a learning environment.	Table 7-29.
	Encourages subordinates.	Table 7-30.
	Demonstrates care for follower well-being.	Table 7-31.
	Anticipates people's duty needs .	Table 7-32.
	Sets and maintains high expectations for individuals and teams.	Table 7-33.
Prepares self	Maintains mental and physical health and well-being.	Table 7-34.
	Expands knowledge of technical, technological, and tactical areas.	Table 7-35.
	Expands conceptual and interpersonal capabilities.	Table 7-36.
	Analyzes and organizes information to create knowledge.	Table 7-37.
	Maintains relevant cultural awareness.	Table 7-38.
	Maintains relevant geopolitical awareness.	Table 7-39.
	Maintains self-awareness.	Table 7-40.
Develops others	Assesses developmental needs of others.	Table 7-41.
	Counsels, coaches, and mentors.	Table 7-42.
	Facilitates ongoing development.	Table 7-43.
	Builds team skills and processes.	Table 7-44.
Stewards the profession	Supports professional and personal growth.	Table 7-45.
	Improves the organization.	Table 7-46.
Gets results	Prioritizes, organizes, and coordinates taskings.	Table 7-47.
	Identifies and accounts for capabilities and commitment to task.	Table 7-48.
	Designates, clarifies, and deconflicts duties and responsibilities.	Table 7-49.
	Identifies, contends for, allocates, and manages resources.	Table 7-50.
	Removes work obstacles.	Table 7-51.
	Recognizes and rewards good performance.	Table 7-52.
	Seeks, recognizes, and takes advantage of opportunities.	Table 7-53.
	Makes feedback part of work processes.	Table 7-54.
	Executes plans to accomplish the mission.	Table 7-55.
	Identifies and adjusts to external influences.	Table 7-56.

I. Counseling, Coaching, Mentoring

Ref: ATP 6-22.1, The Counseling Process (Jul '14) and ADP 6-22 (w/C1), Army Leadership and the Profession (Nov '19), pp. 6-10 to 6-11.

Leaders have three principal ways of developing others. They can provide knowledge and feedback through counseling, coaching, and mentoring.

Counseling-Coaching-Mentoring

*Leaders have three principal ways of **developing others**. They can provide others with knowledge and feedback through counseling, coaching, and mentoring:*

 Counseling

 Coaching

 Mentoring

Ref: ADRP 6-22, pp. 7-10 to 7-12.

See pp. 1-63 to 1-67 for related discussion of the leader competency "develops others."

Providing feedback is common to interacting with others during development. Feedback significantly contributes to development, accelerates learning in day-to-day experiences, and translates into better leader performance. Providing feedback starts with observation and accurate assessment of performance. Planning to make observations of a subordinate is the first step in feedback. The best observations occur when subordinates engage in critical performance, interact with their subordinates or other Soldiers, or address a challenging problem. Keeping observation notes is useful when tracking multiple subordinates.

See following page (p. 3-3) for a counseling, coaching and mentoring comparison.

I. Counseling

Counseling is central to leader development. Leaders who serve as designated raters have to prepare their subordinates to be better Soldiers or Army Civilians. Good counseling focuses on the subordinate's performance and issues with an eye toward tomorrow's plans and solutions. Leaders expect subordinates to be active participants seeking constructive feedback. Counseling cannot be an occasional event but should be part of a comprehensive program to develop subordinates. With effective counseling, no evaluation report—positive or negative—should be a surprise. A consistent counseling program includes all subordinates, not just the people thought to have the most potential.

Counseling is the process used by leaders to guide subordinates to improve performance and develop their potential. Subordinates are active participants in the counseling process. Counseling uses a standard format to help mentally organize and isolate relevant issues before, during, and after the counseling session. During counseling, leaders help subordinates to identify strengths and weaknesses and create plans of action. To make the plans work, leaders actively support their subordinates throughout the implementation and assessment processes. Subordinates invest themselves in the process by being forthright in their willingness to improve and being candid in their assessment and goal setting.

Approaches to Counseling

Counsel, Coach, Mentor

Inexperienced leaders are sometimes uncomfortable when confronting a subordinate who is not performing to standard. Counseling is not about leader comfort; it is about correcting the performance or developing the character of a subordinate. To be effective counselors, Army leaders must demonstrate certain qualities: respect for subordinates, self-awareness, cultural awareness, empathy, and credibility.

One challenging aspect of counseling is selecting the proper approach for a specific situation. To counsel effectively, the technique used must fit the situation. Some cases may only require giving information or listening. A subordinate's improvement may call for just a brief word of praise. Other situations may require structured counseling followed by specific plans for actions. An effective leader approaches each subordinate as an individual. Counseling includes nondirective, directive, and combined approaches. The major difference between the approaches is the degree to which the subordinate participates and interacts during a counseling session.

See p. 3-14 to 3-15 for related discussion (adaptive approaches to counseling).

Nondirective Approach
The nondirective approach is preferred for most counseling sessions. Leaders use their experiences, insight and judgment to assist subordinates in developing solutions. Leaders partially structure this type of counseling by telling the subordinate about the counseling process and explaining expectations.

Directive Approach
The directive approach works best to correct simple problems, make on-the-spot corrections, and correct aspects of duty performance. When using the directive style, the leader does most of the talking and tells the subordinate what to do and when to do it. In contrast to the nondirective approach, the leader directs a course of action for the subordinate.

Combined Approach
In the combined approach, the leader uses techniques from both the directive and nondirective approaches, adjusting them to articulate what is best for the subordinate. The combined approach emphasizes the subordinate's planning and decision-making responsibilities.

Counseling, Coaching and Mentoring Comparison

Ref: ADP 6-22 (w/C1), Army Leadership and the Profession (Nov '19), table 6-3, p. 6-11.

Leaders have three principal roles in developing others. They provide knowledge and feedback through counseling, coaching, and mentoring.

Counseling-Coaching-Mentoring

	Counseling	Coaching	Mentoring
Purpose	Review past or current performance to sustain and improve current or future performance.	Guide learning or improvement skills.	Provide guidance focused on professional or personal growth.
Source	Rater, chain of command.	Assigned coach or trainer with special knowledge.	Those with greater experience.
Interaction	As a formal or informal conversation between superior and subordinate.	During practice or performance between a coach/trainer and the individual, observation, guidance.	Conversation on a personal level.
How it works	The counselor identifies the need, prepares for the session, conducts counseling to encourage subordinate's active participation, sets goals, and checks on progress.	The coach demonstrates a skill, observes performance, and provides guidance and feedback.	The mentor applies experience to guide the protégé, shares knowledge, provides challenges, and addresses questions.
Outcome	Formal (Individual Development Plan) or informal goals for sustainment and improvement.	Behaviors identified for improvement, higher performance level.	Personal commitment to career choices, intent to improve, or better knowledge.
Requirement	Required—develop and counsel all subordinates.	Required or voluntary.	Voluntary, mutual agreement.
Occurrence	Prescribed times IAW performance evaluation or upon event when rater determines a need.	Training or performance events.	Initiated by either party.

Ref: ADP 6-22 (w/C1), table 6-3. Counseling—Coaching—Mentoring Comparison.

Providing feedback is a common element of interacting with others, regardless of developmental role or process. Feedback significantly contributes to development, accelerates learning in day-to-day experiences, and translates into better performance. Providing feedback starts with observation and accurate assessment of performance. Planning to make observations of a subordinate is the first step in feedback. The best observations occur when subordinates engage in critical performance, interact with others, or address a challenging problem. Keeping observation notes is useful when tracking multiple subordinates. Table 6-3 provides a concise comparison of each approach to development

II. Coaching

While a mentor or counselor generally has more experience than the person being supported does, coaching relies primarily on teaching and guiding to bring out and enhance the capabilities already present. Coaching refers to the function of helping someone through a set of tasks or with general qualities. Those being coached may or may not, have appreciated their potential. The coach helps them understand their current level of performance and guides them how to reach the next level of knowledge and skill.

Coaching is a development technique used for a skill, task, or specific behaviors. Coaches should possess considerable knowledge in the area in which they coach others. An important aspect of coaching is identifying and planning for short- and long-term goals. The coach and the person being coached discuss strengths, weaknesses, and courses of action to sustain or improve.

Note: See facing page for a discussion of coaching tools.

III. Mentoring

Current and anticipated operations place additional pressures on developing leaders rapidly. To help leaders acquire the necessary abilities, the Army relies on a leader development system that compresses and accelerates development of professional expertise, maturity, and conceptual and team-building skills. Mentoring is a developmental tool that can effectively support many of these learning objectives.

It is not required for leaders to have the same occupational or educational background as those they coach or counsel. In comparison, mentors generally specialize in the same area as those they mentor. Mentors have likely experienced what their protégés are experiencing or are going to experience. Consequently, mentoring relationships tend to be occupation-specific, with the mentor having expertise in the particular area. Mentoring focuses primarily on developing a more experienced leader for the future.

Mentorship is the voluntary developmental relationship that exists between a person of greater experience and a person of lesser experience that is characterized by mutual trust and respect (AR 600-100). Mentorship is generally characterized by the following:

- Mentoring takes place when the mentor provides a less experienced leader with advice and counsel over time to help with professional and personal growth
- The developing leader often initiates the relationship and seeks counsel from the mentor. The mentor takes the initiative to check on the well-being and development of that person.
- Mentorship affects personal development (maturity and interpersonal and communication skills) as well as professional development (technical, tactical, and career path knowledge)
- Mentorship helps the Army maintain a highly competent set of leaders
- The strength of the mentoring relationship relies on mutual trust and respect. Protégés carefully consider assessment, feedback, and guidance; these become valuable for growth to occur.

Supportive mentoring occurs when a mentor does not outrank the person being mentored, but has extensive knowledge and experience. Contrary to common belief, mentoring relationships are not confined to the superior-subordinate relationship. They may occur between peers and often between senior NCOs and junior officers. This relationship can occur across many levels of rank. In many circumstances, this relationship extends past the time where one party has left the chain of command.

Coaching Tools

Ref: ADP 6-22 (w/C1), Army Leadership and the Profession (Nov '19), pp. 6-10 to 6-11.

Coaching relies primarily on teaching and guiding to bring out and enhance capabilities already present. Coaching is a development technique used for a skill, task, or specific behaviors. The coach helps them understand their current level of performance and guides them to reach the next level of development. Coaches should possess considerable knowledge in the area in which they coach others.

Coaches use all or some of the following approaches depending on the subordinate and situation:

Focus Goals

This requires the coach to identify the specific purpose of the coaching session. Both the person being coached and the coach need to discuss expectations. The coach communicates to the individual the developmental tasks for the coaching session, which can incorporate results of the individual's 360-degree assessment and feedback report.

Clarify the Leader's Self-Awareness

The coach works directly with the individual to define both strengths and developmental needs. During this session, the coach and the individual communicate perceived strengths, developmental needs, and focus areas to improve performance. Both the coach and the individual agree on areas of developmental needs.

Uncover Potential

The coach facilitates self-awareness of the individual's potential and developmental needs by guiding the discussion with questions. The coach actively listens to how the individual perceives potential. The aim is to encourage the free flow of ideas. The coach also assesses the individual's readiness to change and incorporates this into the session.

Eliminate Developmental Barriers

The coach identifies developmental needs with the individual and areas that may hinder self-development. The coach helps the individual determine how to overcome barriers to development and implement an effective plan to improve performance. The coach helps identify potential sources of support for implementing an action plan.

Develop Action Plans

The coach and the individual develop an action plan defining actions that can improve performance within a given period. The coach uses a developmental action guide to communicate those self-directed activities the individual can accomplish to improve performance in a particular competency.

Follow-Up

After the initial session, the coach should conduct a follow-up as part of a larger transition. Additionally, participants should provide feedback concerning the effectiveness of the assessment, the usefulness of the information received, and progress made. Coaches provide frequent informal feedback and timely, proactive, formal counseling to regularly inspire and improve subordinates.

See also pp. 2-34 to 2-35 for discussion of coaching from FM 6-22.

Individuals must be active participants in their developmental process. They must not wait for a mentor to choose them but have the responsibility to be proactive in their own development. Every Army officer, NCO, Soldier, and Civilian should identif personal strengths and areas for improvement. Each individual should then determine a developmental plan. Some strategies that may be used are:

- Ask questions and pay attention to experts
- Read and study
- Watch those in leadership positions
- Find educational opportunities (civilian, military, and correspondence)
- Seek and engage in new and varied opportunities

Soldiers can increase their chances of mentorship by seeking performance feedback and by adopting an attitude of lifelong learning. These self-development actions enable mentoring opportunities. Soldiers who seek feedback to focus their development, coupled with dedicated, well-informed mentors, will embed the concepts of lifelong learning, self-development, and adaptability into the Army's culture.

While mentoring is generally associated with improving duty-related performance and growth, it may include a spiritual dimension. A chaplain or other spiritually trained individual may play a significant role in helping individuals cope with operational stress to find better professional balance and purpose.

See pp. 2-31 to 2-33 for discussion of mentor roles and responsibilities from FM 6-22.

II. Developmental Counseling

Ref: ATP 6-22.1, The Counseling Process (Jul '14), chaps. 1 and 2.

Counseling is the process used by leaders to review with a subordinate the subordinate's demonstrated performance and potential. Counseling, one of the most important leadership development responsibilities, enables Army leaders to help Soldiers and Army Civilians become more capable, resilient, satisfied, and better prepared for new responsibilities. Counseling is one process within the developing others competency and benefits from techniques of other competencies: getting results, communicating, and creating a positive environment. Counseling is required of raters and occurs at prescribed times while the related developmental processes of coaching and mentoring may be done voluntarily by others. The Army's future and the legacy of today's Army leaders rest on the shoulders of those they help prepare for greater responsibility.

Types of Counseling

 Event Counseling

 Performance Counseling

 Performance Growth Counseling

Leaders at all levels must understand the counseling process. More importantly, Army leaders must understand that effective counseling helps achieve desired goals and effects, manages expectations, and improves the organization. Regular counseling provides leaders with opportunities to:

- Demonstrate genuine interest in subordinates
- Help subordinates understand their role in accomplishing the unit's mission
- Acknowledge and reinforce exceptional work or dedication
- Evaluate subordinates' potential for development
- Provide subordinates with assistance or resources to address issues or further strengths
- Empower subordinates to identify and solve issues on their own so they become more self-reliant
- Identify issues before they become significant problems
- Identify causes of sub-standard performance

I. Types of Developmental Counseling

Developmental counseling is categorized by the purpose of the session. Understanding the purpose and types of counseling enables the leader to adapt the counseling session to the individual subordinate's needs in order to achieve desired outcomes and manage expectations. Counseling is not a one-size-fits-all endeavor.

While these categories can help organize and focus counseling sessions, they should not be viewed as separate or exhaustive. For example, a counseling session that focuses on resolving an issue may also address improving duty performance. A session focused on performance often includes a discussion on opportunities for professional growth. Regardless of the purpose or topic of the counseling session, leaders should follow a basic format for preparation and execution. The Developmental Counseling Form, DA Form 4856, provides a useful framework to prepare for counseling. It helps organize the relevant issues to cover during counseling sessions.

Types of Counseling

 Event Counseling

 Performance Counseling

 Performance Growth Counseling

A. Event Counseling

See following pages (pp. 3-10 to 3-11) for discussion on event counseling.

Event-oriented counseling involves a specific event or situation. It may precede events such as participating in promotion boards, attending training courses, and preparing for deployment or redeployment. It also addresses events such as noteworthy duty performance, an issue with performance or mission accomplishment, or a personal issue. Examples of event-oriented counseling include:

- Specific instances of superior or substandard performance
- Reception and integration counseling
- Crisis counseling
- Referral counseling
- Promotion counseling
- Separation counseling

B. Performance Counseling

Performance counseling is the review of a subordinate's duty performance during a specified period. The leader and the subordinate jointly establish performance objectives and clear standards for the next counseling period. The counseling focuses on the subordinate's strengths, areas to improve, and potential. Effective counseling includes providing specific examples of strengths and areas needing improvement and providing guidance on how subordinates can improve their performance. Performance counseling is required under the officer, noncommissioned officer, and Army Civilian evaluation reporting systems.

During performance counseling, leaders conduct a review of a subordinate's duty performance over a certain period. Simultaneously, leader and subordinate jointly establish performance objectives and standards for the next period. Rather than dwelling on the past, leaders focus on the future: the subordinate's strengths, areas for improvement, and potential.

Counseling at the beginning of and during the evaluation period ensures the subordinate's personal involvement in the evaluation process. Performance counseling communicates standards and is an opportunity for leaders to establish and clarify the expected values, attributes, and competencies. Army leaders ensure that performance objectives and standards focus on the organization's objectives and the individual's professional development. They should also echo the objectives on the leader's support form as a team member's performance contributes to mission accomplishment.

C. Professional Growth Counseling

Professional growth counseling includes planning for the accomplishment of individual and professional goals. During the counseling, leader and subordinate conduct a review to identify and discuss the subordinate's strengths and weaknesses and to create an individual development plan that builds upon those strengths and compensates for (or eliminates) weaknesses. Leaders can assist subordinates in prioritizing development efforts based upon those perceived strengths and weaknesses.

As part of professional growth counseling, the leader and subordinate may choose to develop a pathway to success with short- and long-term goals and objectives. The discussion includes opportunities for civilian or military schooling, future duty assignments, special programs, available training support resources, and reenlistment options. Each individual development plan varies as every person's needs and interests are different.

II. The Leader as a Counselor

To be effective, developmental counseling must be a shared effort. Leaders assist their subordinates in identifying strengths and weaknesses and creating plans of action. Once an individual development plan is agreed upon, leaders support their Soldiers and Army Civilians throughout implementation and continued assessment. To achieve success, subordinates must be forthright in their commitment to improve and candid in their own assessments and goal setting.

Army leaders evaluate Army Civilians using procedures prescribed under civilian personnel policies. Use of DA Form 4856 is appropriate to counsel Army Civilians on professional growth and career goals. The servicing civilian personnel office should be consulted when using a DA Form 4856 to counsel an Army Civilian concerning misconduct or poor performance.

Army leaders conduct counseling to help subordinates become better team members, maintain or improve performance, and prepare for the future. While it is not easy to address every possible counseling situation, leader self-awareness and an adaptable counseling style focusing on key characteristics will enhance personal effectiveness as a counselor. These key characteristics include:

- **Purpose:** Clearly define the purpose of the counseling
- **Flexibility:** Adapt the counseling style to each subordinate, situation, and relationship desired
- **Respect:** View subordinates as unique, complex individuals, each with a distinct set of values, beliefs, and attitudes
- **Communication:** Establish open, two-way communication with subordinates using spoken language, nonverbal actions, gestures, and body language. Effective counselors listen more than they speak
- **Support:** Encourage subordinates through actions while guiding them through their problems

Event Counseling

Ref: ATP 6-22.1, The Counseling Process (Jul '14), pp. 1-2 to 1-3.

Event-oriented counseling involves a specific event or situation. It may precede events such as appearing before a promotion board or attending training. It can also follow events such as noteworthy duty performance, a problem with performance or mission accomplishment, or a personal issue.

1. Counseling for Specific Instances

Sometimes counseling is tied to specific instances of superior or substandard duty performance. The leader uses the counseling session to convey to the subordinate whether or not the performance met the standard and what the subordinate did right or wrong. Successful counseling for specific performance occurs as close to the event as possible. Leaders should counsel subordinates for exceptional as well as substandard duty performance. The key is to strike a balance between the two. To maintain an appropriate balance, leaders keep track of counseling for exceptional versus substandard performance.

Although good leaders attempt to balance their counseling emphasis, leaders should always counsel subordinates who do not meet the standard. If the Soldier or civilian's performance is unsatisfactory because of a lack of knowledge or ability, leader and subordinate can develop a plan for improvement. Corrective training helps ensure that the subordinate knows and consistently achieves the standard. When counseling a subordinate for a specific performance, take the following actions:

- Explain the purpose of the counseling—what was expected, and how the subordinate failed to meet the standard
- Address the specific unacceptable behavior or action—do not attack the person's character
- Explain the effect of the behavior, action, or performance on the rest of the organization
- Actively listen to the subordinate's response
- Remain neutral
- Teach the subordinate how to meet the standard
- Be prepared to do some personal counseling, since a failure to meet the standard may be related to or be the result of an unresolved personal problem
- Explain to the subordinate how an individual development plan will improve performance and identify specific responsibilities in implementing the plan. Continue to assess and follow up on the subordinate's progress. Adjust the plan as necessary.

2. Reception and Integration Counseling

Caring and empathic Army leaders should counsel all new team members when they join the organization. Reception and integration counseling serves two important purposes:

- It identifies and helps alleviate any problems or concerns that new members may have, including any issues resulting from the new duty assignment.
- It familiarizes new team members with the organizational standards and how they fit into the team. It clarifies roles and assignments and sends the message that the chain of command cares.

Reception and integration counseling should among others include the following discussion points:

- Chain of command familiarization
- Organizational standards
- Security and safety issues
- Noncommissioned officer (NCO) support channel (who is in it and how it is used)
- On- and off-duty conduct
- Personnel/personal affairs/initial and special clothing issue
- Organizational history, structure, and mission
- Soldier programs within the organization, such as Soldier of the Month/Quarter/Year, and educational and training opportunities
- Off limits and danger areas
- Functions and locations of support activities
- On- and off-post recreational, educational, cultural, and historical opportunities
- Foreign nation or host nation orientation, as applicable
- Other items of interest as determined by the leader or organization

3. Crisis Counseling

Crisis counseling includes getting a Soldier or employee through a period of shock after receiving negative news, such as the notification of the death of a loved one. It focuses on the subordinate's immediate short-term needs. Assisting can also mean referring the subordinate to a support activity or coordinating for external agency support, such as obtaining emergency funding for a flight ticket or putting them in contact with a chaplain.

4. Referral Counseling

Referral counseling helps subordinates work through a personal situation. It may or may not follow crisis counseling. Referral counseling aims at preventing a problem from becoming unmanageable if the empathic Army leader succeeds in identifying the problem in time and involves appropriate resources, such as Army Community Services, a chaplain, or an alcohol and drug counselor.

5. Promotion Counseling

Army leaders must conduct promotion counseling for all specialists and sergeants who are eligible for advancement without waivers but not recommended for promotion to the next higher grade. Army regulations require that Soldiers within this category receive initial (event-oriented) counseling when they attain full promotion eligibility and then periodic (performance/personal growth) counseling thereafter.

6. Adverse Separation Counseling

Adverse separation counseling may involve informing the Soldier of the administrative actions available to the commander in the event substandard performance continues and of the consequences associated with those administrative actions.

Developmental counseling may not apply when an individual has engaged in serious acts of misconduct. In those situations, leaders should refer the matter to the commander and the servicing staff judge advocate. When rehabilitative efforts fail, counseling with a view towards separation is required. It is an administrative prerequisite to many administrative discharges, while sending a final warning to the Soldier: improve performance or face discharge. In many situations, it is advisable to involve the chain of command as soon as it is determined that adverse separation counseling might be required. A unit first sergeant or the commander should inform the Soldier of the notification requirements outlined in AR 635-200.

III. The Qualities of the Counselor

Army leaders must demonstrate certain qualities to be effective counselors. These qualities include respect for subordinates, self-awareness and cultural awareness, empathy, and credibility.

One challenging aspect of counseling is selecting the proper approach to a specific situation. To counsel effectively, the technique used must fit the situation, leader capabilities, and subordinate expectations. Sometimes, leaders may only need to give information or listen, while in other situations a subordinate's improvement may call for just a brief word of praise. Difficult circumstances may require structured counseling followed by definite actions, such as referrals to outside agencies.

Self-aware Army leaders consistently develop and improve their own counseling abilities. They do so by studying human behavior, learning the kinds of problems that affect their followers, and developing their interpersonal skills. The techniques needed to provide effective counseling vary from person to person and session to session. However, general skills that leaders will need in almost every situation include active listening, responding, and questioning.

A. Active Listening

Active listening helps communicate reception of the subordinate's message verbally and nonverbally. To capture the message fully, leaders listen to what is said and observe the subordinate's manners.

See facing page for a discussion of key elements of active listening.

B. Responding

A leader responds verbally and nonverbally to show understanding of the subordinate. Verbal responses consist of summarizing, interpreting, and clarifying the subordinate's message. Nonverbal responses include eye contact and occasional gestures such as a head nod.

C. Questioning

Although focused questioning is an important skill, counselors should use it with caution. During professional growth counseling, leaders should ask open-ended questions to obtain information or to get the subordinate to think deeper about a particular situation. Questions should evoke more than a yes or no answer and not lead towards a specific answer or conclusion. Well-posed questions deepen understanding, encourage further discussion, and create a constructive experience. Too many questions can aggravate the power differential between a leader and a subordinate and place the subordinate in a passive mode. The subordinate may also react to excessive questioning, especially if it resembles an interrogation, as an intrusion of privacy and become defensive.

Active Listening

Ref: ATP 6-22.1, The Counseling Process (Jul '14), pp. 2-1 to 2-3.

Active listening helps communicate reception of the subordinate's message verbally and nonverbally. To capture the message fully, leaders listen to what is said and observe the subordinate's manners. Key elements of active listening include:

Eye contact
Maintaining eye contact without staring helps show sincere interest. Occasional breaks of eye contact are normal and acceptable, while excessive breaks, paper shuffling, and clock-watching may be perceived as a lack of interest or concern.

Body Posture
Being relaxed and comfortable will help put the subordinate at ease. However, a too-relaxed position or slouching may be interpreted as a lack of interest.

Head Nods
Occasionally head nodding indicates paying attention and encourages the subordinate to continue.

Facial Expressions
Keep facial expressions natural and relaxed to signal a sincere interest.

Check for Understanding
Paraphrase or summarize points back to the subordinate for confirmation; for example, "What I heard was…".

Verbal Expressions
Refrain from talking too much and avoid interrupting. Let the subordinate do the talking, while keeping the discussion on the counseling subject. Active listening implies listening thoughtfully and deliberately to capture the nuances of the subordinate's language. Stay alert for common themes. A subordinate's opening and closing statements as well as recurring references may indicate his priorities. Inconsistencies and gaps may indicate an avoidance of the real issue. Certain inconsistencies may suggest additional questions by the counselor.

Pay attention to the subordinate's gestures to understand the complete message. By watching the subordinate's actions, leaders identify the emotions behind the words. Not all actions are proof of a subordinate's feelings but they should be considered. Nonverbal indicators of a subordinate's attitude include—

- **Self-confidence**. Standing tall, leaning back with hands behind the head, and maintaining steady eye contact
- **Interest, friendliness, and openness**. Be aware that leader actions must be context and situation specific. For example, leaning towards the subordinate may be considered as expressing interest or being aggressive.
- **Anxiety**. Sitting on the edge of the chair with arms uncrossed and hands open
- **Boredom**. Drumming on the table, doodling, clicking a ballpoint pen, or resting the head in the palm of the hand
- **Defensiveness**. Pushing deeply into a chair, glaring at the leader, and making sarcastic comments as well as crossing or folding arms in front of the chest
- **Frustration**. Rubbing eyes, pulling on an ear, taking short breaths, wringing the hands, or frequently changing total body position

Leaders consider each indicator carefully. Although each may reveal something about the subordinate, do not judge too quickly. When unsure look for reinforcing indicators or check with the subordinate to understand the behavior, determine what is underlying it, and allow the subordinate to take responsibility.

Adaptive Approaches to Counseling

Ref: ATP 6-22.1, The Counseling Process (Jul '14), pp. 2-4 to 2-5 and table 2-1, p. 2-4.

Leaders plan each counseling session, tailoring the counseling session to the individual and situation. Part of the planning process includes identifying the counseling approach, assessing the individual's situation and reputation, and identifying any likely resistance. An effective leader approaches each subordinate as an individual. Different people and different situations require different counseling approaches. Three approaches to counseling include nondirective, directive, and combined.

IV. Counseling Techniques

The Army leader can select from several techniques when counseling subordinates. These techniques may cause subordinates to change behavior and improve upon their performance.

	Advantages	Disadvantages
Nondirective	■ Encourages maturity ■ Encourages open communication ■ Develops personal responsibility	■ More time-consuming ■ Requires greatest counselor skills
Combined	■ Moderately quick ■ Encourages maturity ■ Encourages open communication ■ Allows counselors to use their experience	■ May take too much time for some situations
Directive	■ Quickest method ■ Good for those needing clear, concise direction ■ Allows counselors to use their experience	■ Does not encourage subordinate to be part of solution ■ Treats symptons, not issues ■ Tends to discourage subordinates from talking freely ■ Solution is the counselor's, not the subordinates

Nondirective and Combined Approaches

- **Suggesting Alternatives**. Discuss alternative actions that the subordinate may take. Leader and subordinate together decide which course of action is most appropriate.
- **Recommending.** Recommend one course of action, but leave the decision to accept it to the subordinate.
- **Persuading.** Persuade the subordinate that a given course of action is best, but leave the final decision to the subordinate. Successful persuasion depends on the leader's credibility, the subordinate's willingness to listen, and mutual trust.
- **Advising.** Advise the subordinate that a given course of action is best. This is the strongest form of influence not involving a command.

Directive Approach to Counseling

- **Corrective Training.** Teach and assist the subordinate in attaining and maintaining the required standard. A subordinate completes corrective training once consistently meeting standards.
- **Commanding.** Order the subordinate to take a given course of action in clear, precise words. The subordinate will face consequences for failing to execute.

V. Counseling Practices

Dominating the counseling by talking too much, giving unnecessary or inappropriate advice, not truly listening, and projecting personal likes, dislikes, biases, and prejudices all interfere with effective counseling. Competent leaders avoid rash judgments, stereotyping, losing emotional control, inflexible counseling methods, or improper follow-up. Leaders conduct effective counseling sessions and improve their counseling skills when they follow these general guidelines:

- Determine the subordinate's role in the situation and what has been done to resolve the issue
- Focus attention on the subordinate. Listen to what is said and how it is said to understand what the subordinate says and feels
- Encourage the subordinate to take the initiative and speak aloud
- Remain objective; avoid confirming a subordinate's prejudices
- Display empathy when discussing the issue. Be receptive to the subordinate's emotions without feeling responsible
- Ask open-ended questions for relevant information; avoid interrogating the subordinate
- Listen more and talk less; avoid interrupting
- Keep personal experiences out of the counseling session
- Draw conclusions based on all information, not just the subordinate's statement
- Enable the subordinate to help himself or herself
- Know what information to keep confidential and what to present to the chain of command, if necessary

VI. Accepting Limitations

Army leaders cannot help everyone in every situation. Army leaders should recognize their personal limitations and seek outside assistance when required. When necessary, refer a subordinate to an agency more qualified to help.

Although it is generally in an individual's best interest to begin by seeking help from his or her first-line leaders, leaders should respect an individual's preference to contact support agencies.

VII. Addressing Resistance

Resistance in counseling may stem from either the leader or subordinate and may occur in several ways. Identifying and understanding the possible forms of resistance is essential. A leader may be reluctant to counsel subordinates because the leader has not been counseled, has had no effective role modeling for what is involved in the process, or does not understand how to conduct counseling. Additionally, leaders may feel there is no time to do counseling, counseling will not be a constructive use of time, or counseling will violate a regulation or policy. They may associate counseling with only negative issues such as dispensing punishment or correcting poor performance. Further, leaders may not want to confront a subordinate. Other typical reasons for leader reluctance involve a lack of respect for the subordinate, believing the subordinate lacks potential, or encountering constant issues with the subordinate.

See following page (p. 3-16) for further discussion of addressing resistance.

Addressing Resistance

Ref: ATP 6-22.1, The Counseling Process (Jul '14), pp. 2-3 to 2-4.

Counsel,
Coach, Mentor

Resistance in counseling may stem from either the leader or subordinate and may occur in several ways. Identifying and understanding the possible forms of resistance is essential. A leader may be reluctant to counsel subordinates because the leader has not been counseled, has had no effective role modeling for what is involved in the process, or does not understand how to conduct counseling. Additionally, leaders may feel there is no time to do counseling, counseling will not be a constructive use of time, or counseling will violate a regulation or policy. They may associate counseling with only negative issues such as dispensing punishment or correcting poor performance. Further, leaders may not want to confront a subordinate. Other typical reasons for leader reluctance involve a lack of respect for the subordinate, believing the subordinate lacks potential, or encountering constant issues with the subordinate.

Subordinate resistance often occurs as a reaction to the purpose or message of the counseling session. They may be embarrassed, misunderstand the intention of the counseling session, or disagree with the leader's assessment of the situation. Subordinates may not want to change, may blame the leader for the issue or behavior at hand, may dislike being held accountable, or may defy being disciplined. In some cases, the subordinate may not respect or trust the leader.

Leaders may preempt potential resistance by opening the counseling session with a discussion of the purpose of the session, expectations of the session, and how they relate to the subordinate's short- and long-term goals. Through regular periodic counseling, leaders should understand and be aware of the subordinate's goals. For the session to be effective, leaders must focus on the issue and adapt the counseling session to the subordinate's needs and understanding.

Once a leader understands that counseling subordinates is a significant leader responsibility in developing subordinates' potential, leader reluctance can be overcome through self-education about the counseling process and preparation. Overcoming subordinate resistance is a process and draws upon the positive counseling practices. After the leader identifies the source of a subordinate's resistance, then the counseling process can be adapted to accommodate and overcome the resistance.

To overcome resistance in counseling, leaders can employ several techniques to redirect the subordinate:

- **Keep the discussion professional and balanced in tone**—do not argue or place blame on any party.

- **Discuss the suspected resistance openly** with the subordinate and respect his or her response.

- **Slow the tempo of the session**— rely on pertinent open-ended questions to give the subordinate the appropriate time and ability to reveal information and be an active participant in the counseling session.

- **Reconfirm the counseling session purpose**—be specific and keep focused on the details (such as conditions, triggers, and outcomes) of the situation; refrain from any personal attacks on the subordinate.

- **Focus on one specific behavior, its effect, and the consequences** to minimize overwhelming the subordinate. It may be necessary to divide the session into multiple meetings to address each area adequately. Further, the leader should prioritize these discussions based on the needs of the individual and unit.

III. The Four-Stage Counseling Process

Ref: ATP 6-22.1, The Counseling Process (Jul '14), pp. 2-5 to 2-10.

Effective Army leaders make use of a four-stage counseling process:

The Four-Stage Counseling Process

 Identify the Need for Counseling

 Prepare for Counseling
1. Select a suitable place
2. Schedule the time
3. Notify the subordinate well in advance
4. Organize information
5. Outline the counseling session
6. Plan counseling strategy
7. Establish the right atmosphere

 Conduct Counseling
1. Open the session
2. Discuss the issue
3. Develop a plan of action
4. Record and close the session

 Follow Up
1. Support plan of action implementation
2. Assess the plan of action

Ref: ATP 6-22.1, The Counseling Process (Jul -14), pp. 2-5 to 2-10.

STAGE 1: Identify the Need for Counseling

Usually organizational policies, such as counseling associated with an evaluation or command directed counseling, focus a counseling session. However, leaders may also conduct developmental counseling whenever the need arises for focused, two-way communication aimed at subordinate's development. Developing subordinates consists of observing the subordinate's performance, comparing it to the standard, and providing feedback through counseling.

STAGE 2: Prepare for Counseling

Successful counseling requires preparation in the following seven areas:

- Select a suitable place
- Schedule the time
- Notify the subordinate well in advance
- Organize information
- Outline the counseling session components
- Plan the counseling strategy
- Establish the right atmosphere

1. Select a Suitable Place

Conduct the counseling in an environment that minimizes interruptions and is free from distracting sights and sounds. The location should allow for privacy as the counseling session may cover personal issues not intended for public knowledge.

2. Schedule the Time

When possible, counsel a subordinate during the duty day. Counseling after duty hours may be rushed or perceived as unfavorable. Select a time free from competition with other activities. Consider that important events occurring after the session could distract a subordinate from concentrating on the counseling. The scheduled time for counseling should also be appropriate for the complexity of the issue at hand. Generally, counseling sessions should last less than an hour.

3. Notify the Subordinate Well in Advance

Counseling is a subordinate-centered, two-person effort for which the subordinate must have adequate time to prepare. The person being counseled should know why, where, and when the counseling takes place. Counseling tied to a specific event should happen as closely to the event as possible. For performance or professional development counseling, subordinates may need a week or more to prepare or review specific documents and resources, including evaluation support forms or counseling records.

4. Organize Information

The counselor should review all pertinent information, including the purpose of the counseling, facts, and observations about the person to be counseled, identification of possible issues, and main points of discussion. The counselor can outline a possible plan of action with clear obtainable goals as a basis for the final plan development between counselor and the Soldier or Army Civilian.

5. Outline the Components of the Counseling Session

Using the available information, determine the focus and specific topics for the counseling session. Note what prompted the counseling requirement, aims, and counselor role. Identify possible comments and questions to keep the counseling session subordinate-centered and which can help guide the subordinate through the session's stages. As subordinates may be unpredictable during counseling, a written outline can help keep the session on track and enhances the chance for success

6. Plan the Counseling Strategy

There are many different approaches to counseling. The directive, nondirective, and combined approaches offer a variety of options that can suit any subordinate and situation.

See pp. 3-14 to 3-15 for further discussion.

Counseling Outline (Sample)

Ref: ATP 6-22.1, The Counseling Process (Jul '14), fig. 2-1, p. 2-7.

Types of counseling

Initial NCOER counseling for SFC Taylor, a recently promoted new arrival to the unit.

Place and time

The platoon office, Tuesday at 1500.

Time to notify the subordinate

Notify SFC Taylor one week in advance of the counseling session.

Subordinate preparation

Instruct SFC Taylor to develop a list of goals and objectives to complete over the next 90 to 180 days. Review the values, attributes, and competencies of ADRP 6-22.

Counselor preparation

Review the NCO Counseling Checklist/Record

Update duty description; fill out the rating chain and duty description on a working copy of the NCOER.

Review each of the values and responsibilities in Part IV of the NCOER and the values, attributes, and competencies in ADRP 6-22. Think how each applies to SFC Taylor's duties as platoon sergeant.

Review the actions necessary for a success or excellence rating in each area.

Make notes in blank spaces on relevant parts of the NCOER to assist in counseling.

Role as a counselor

Help SFC Taylor to understand the expectations and standards associated with the platoon sergeant position. Assist SFC Taylor in developing the values, attributes, and competencies that enable him to achieve his performance objectives consistent with those of the platoon and company. Resolve any aspects of the job that SFC Taylor does not clearly understand.

Session outline

Complete an outline following the counseling session components based on the draft duty description on the NCOER. This should happen two to three days prior to the actual counseling session.

7. Establish the Right Atmosphere

The right atmosphere promotes open, two-way communication between a leader and subordinate. To establish a more relaxed atmosphere, leaders may offer the subordinate a seat or a cup of coffee. If appropriate, choose to sit in a chair next to or facing the subordinate since a desk can serve as a barrier.

Some situations require formal settings. During counseling to correct substandard performance, leaders seated behind a desk may direct the subordinate to remain standing. This reinforces the leader's role and authority and underscores the severity of the situation.

STAGE 3: Conduct Counseling

Caring Army leaders use a balanced mix of formal and informal counseling and learn to take advantage of everyday events to provide subordinates with feedback. Counseling opportunities often appear when leaders encounter subordinates in their daily activities in the field, motor pool, barracks, and wherever else Soldiers and civilians perform their duties. Even during ad-hoc counseling, leaders should address the four basic components of a counseling session:

- Opening the session
- Discussing the issues
- Developing a plan of action
- Recording and closing the session

1. Open the Session

In session opening, the leader counselor states the purpose and establishes a subordinate-centered setting. The counselor establishes an atmosphere of shared purpose by inviting the subordinate to speak. An appropriate purpose statement might be "SFC Taylor, the purpose of this counseling is to discuss your duty performance over the past month and to create a plan to enhance performance and attain performance goals." If applicable, start the counseling session by reviewing the status of the current plan of action.

2. Discuss the Issues

Leader and counseled individual should attempt to develop a mutual and clear understanding of the counseling issues. Use active listening and invite the subordinate to do most of the talking—encourage the subordinate to participate fully in the session. Leaders respond and ask questions without dominating the conversation but help the subordinate better understand the subject of the counseling session: duty performance, a situation and its effects, or potential areas for growth.

To reduce the perception of bias or early judgment, both leader and subordinate should provide examples or cite specific observations. When the issue is substandard performance, the leader must be clear what did not meet the standard. During the discussion, the leader must clearly establish what the subordinate must do to meet the standard. It is very important that the leader frames the issue at hand as substandard performance and prevents the subordinate from labeling the issue as unreasonable. An exception would be when the leader considers the current standard as negotiable or is willing to alter the conditions under which the subordinate can meet the standard.

3. Develop a Plan of Action

A plan of action identifies a method and pathway for achieving a desired result, limited to one or two realistic goals tied to work or life events with milestones that allow for monitoring progress. The plan of action must be specific, showing the subordinate how to modify or maintain specific behaviors to reach goals set during the counseling session. For example: "PFC Miller, next week you'll attend the map reading class with 1st Platoon. After class, SGT Dixon will coach you through the land navigation course and help you develop your compass skills. After observing you going through the course with SGT Dixon, I will meet with you again to determine if you need additional training."

4. Record and Close the Session

Although requirements to record counseling sessions vary, a leader always benefits from documenting the main points of a counseling session, even informal ones. Documentation serves as a ready reference for the agreed-upon plan of action and helps the leader track the subordinate's accomplishments, personal preferences, or issues. A good record of counseling enables the leader to make proper recommendations for professional development, promotions, and evaluations. The Developmental Counseling Form (DA Form 4856) is designed to help Army leaders conduct and record counseling sessions. Leaders must decide when counseling, additional training, rehabilitation, reassignment, or other developmental options have been exhausted.

Army regulations require specific written records of counseling for certain personnel actions, such as barring a Soldier from reenlisting, processing an administrative separation or placing a Soldier in the overweight program. When a Soldier faces involuntary separation, the leader must maintain accurate counseling records. Documentation of substandard actions often conveys a strong message to subordinates that a further slip in performance or discipline could require more severe action or punishment.

When closing the counseling session, summarize the key points and ask if the subordinate understands and agrees with the proposed plan of action. With the subordinate present, establish any follow-up measures necessary to support the successful implementation of the plan of action. Follow-up measures may include providing the subordinate with specific resources and time, periodic assessments of the plan and additional referrals. If possible, schedule future meetings before dismissing the subordinate.

STAGE 4: Follow-Up

1. Support Plan of Action Implementation

The counseling process does not end with the initial counseling session. It continues throughout the implementation of the plan of action consistent with the observed results. Sometimes the initial plan of action will require modification to meet its goals. Leaders must consistently support their subordinates in implementing the plan of action by teaching, coaching, mentoring, or providing additional time, referrals and other appropriate resources. Additional measures may include more focused follow-up counseling, informing the chain of command, or taking more severe corrective measures.

2. Assess the Plan of Action

During assessment, the leader and the subordinate jointly determine if the desired results happened. They should determine the date for their initial assessment during the initial counseling session. The plan of action assessment provides useful information for future follow-up counseling sessions.

Example Counseling Session

Ref: ATP 6-22.1, The Counseling Process (Jul '14), fig. 2-2, p. 2-9.

1. Open the Session

- To establish a relaxed environment for open exchange, explain that discussing and understanding the importance of the Army Values, leader attributes and competencies makes it easier to develop and incorporate them for success into an individual leadership style.
- State the purpose of the initial counseling: what SFC Taylor must do to be a successful platoon sergeant. Agree on the duty description and specific performance requirements. Discuss related values, competencies, and standards for success. Explain subsequent counseling will address developmental needs and how well performance objectives are met. Urge SFC Taylor to identify developmental needs during the next quarter.
- Ensure that SFC Taylor knows the rating chain. Resolve any questions about the duty position and associated responsibilities. Discuss the close relationship that must exist between a platoon leader and a platoon sergeant including the importance of honest, two-way communication.

2. Discuss the Issue

- Jointly review the draft NCOER duty description including all associated responsibilities such as maintenance, training, and Soldier welfare. Relate the responsibilities to leader competencies, attributes, and values. Revise the duty description, if needed. Highlight areas of special emphasis and additional duties.
- Discuss the meaning of value and responsibility on the NCOER. Discuss the values, attributes, and competencies noted in ADRP 6-22. Ask focused questions to check understanding of these items as part of the platoon sergeant role.
- Explain that character, presence, and intellect are the basis for competent leadership; developing the desired leader attributes requires that Army leaders adopt them through self-awareness and lifelong learning. Emphasize that the plan of action to accomplish major performance objectives must include the appropriate values, attributes, and competencies.

3. Assist in Developing a Plan of Action (During the Counseling Session)

- Ask SFC Taylor to identify tasks to facilitate accomplishing the performance objectives. Describe each by using the values, responsibilities, and competencies found on the NCOER and in ADRP 6-22. Discuss specific examples of success and excellence in each area. Ask for suggestions to make the goals objective, specific, and measurable.
- Ensure that SFC Taylor has at least one example of a success or excellence statement for each area. Discuss SFC Taylor's promotion goals and ask what he considers as strengths and weaknesses. Obtain the last two master sergeant selection board results and compare stated goals and objectives.

4. Close the Session

- Verify SFC Taylor understands the duty description, performance objectives, and expectation to assist in your development as a platoon leader.
- Stress the importance of teamwork and two-way communication.
- Remind SFC Taylor to perform a self-assessment during the next quarter.
- Set a tentative date during the next quarter for the follow-up counseling.

Army Team Building

Ref: ATP 6-22.6, Army Team Building (Oct '15), chap. 1.

A team is any group that functions together to accomplish a mission or perform a collective task. A team's work is interdependent and team members share responsibility and accountability for attaining results. There is no size limit to a team. Teams are complex, dynamic groups that range from two people to thousands of individuals. In the Army profession, Soldiers and Department of the Army Civilians are a part of different teams, and sometimes they can be a part of many teams simultaneously.

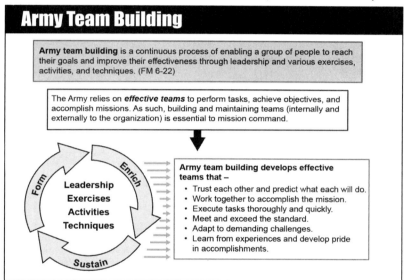

Army Team Building

Army team building is a continuous process of enabling a group of people to reach their goals and improve their effectiveness through leadership and various exercises, activities, and techniques. (FM 6-22)

The Army relies on **effective teams** to perform tasks, achieve objectives, and accomplish missions. As such, building and maintaining teams (internally and externally to the organization) is essential to mission command.

Form — Leadership, Exercises, Activities, Techniques — Enrich — Sustain

Army team building develops effective teams that –
- Trust each other and predict what each will do.
- Work together to accomplish the mission.
- Execute tasks thoroughly and quickly.
- Meet and exceed the standard.
- Adapt to demanding challenges.
- Learn from experiences and develop pride in accomplishments.

Ref: ATP 6-22.6 (Oct '15), fig. 1-1. Army team building process.

Fundamentals of Army Team Building

Army organizations rely on effective teams to complete tasks, achieve objectives, and accomplish missions. The ability to build teams through mutual trust and maintain effective, cohesive teams throughout military operations is an essential skill for all Army commanders, staffs, and leaders. Faced with many different types of missions and joint operations in an operational environment, building and maintaining effective teams is a constant challenge for leaders. Building a successful team is challenging, but the positive benefits of teamwork in a cohesive, effective team are well worth the effort and time it takes. These benefits enhance the performance of the team, improve the skills of the individual team members, and build important relationships with other organizations and unified action partners for the present and future.

Building cohesive teams through mutual trust and creating a shared understanding within those teams are two principles that guide commanders in exercising mission command. Mission command is the exercise of authority and direction by the commander using mission orders to enable disciplined initiative within the commander's intent to empower agile and adaptive leaders in the conduct of unified land operations

II. Team Building Stages

Ref: ATP 6-22.6, Army Team Building (Oct '15), pp. 1-2 to 1-3.

Developing cohesive teams is a process that transforms groups of people into effective teams that are able to accomplish missions and perform tasks. This continuous process helps newly formed teams from initial orientation and integration through mission accomplishment. Team leaders and team members must know and understand the stages in this process so they can identify them as the team develops and progresses. Identifying and monitoring each stage allows the team to move toward the next step.

Team Building Stages

The three stages of team building are the:

 Formation Stage

 Enrichment Stage

 Sustainment stage

I. Formation Stage

Team leaders have an instrumental role in how a team works together, beginning with team formation. Team leaders assemble the team and provide the team direction. The formation stage is important because the team members get to know one another, exchange some personal information, and make new friends. This is also a good opportunity to see how each member of the team works as an individual.

Formation begins with receiving new team members. The new member reception and orientation creates the first impression that affects the person's opinion of the team. Having a good experience when joining an organization makes it easier for a new member to fit in and to contribute to the team effort. The team leader prepares the team to work, which involves orienting team members to the team's mission, goals, and objectives. The team leader sets the team on a path to success by assigning team roles and responsibilities appropriately to team members with the right capabilities.

The principal work for the team during the formation stage is to create a team with a clear structure, goals, direction, and roles so that members begin to build trust, understand how to collaborate, and learn to communicate effectively.

See pp. 4-7 to 4-16 for discussion of the formation stage.

II. Enrichment Stage

During the enrichment stage, the team members build commitment to the team. Commitment is the foundation for synergy in groups when individuals put aside personal needs for the benefit of the team. The team begins to work together effectively as individual am members focus more on the team as a whole. Team members feel an increasing acceptance of others, recognizing that the variety of opinions and experiences make the team stronger. Because of this, there is increased cohesion and more collaboration.

The enrichment stage focuses on how to strengthen relationships and motivate team members. A leader's role in motivation is to understand the needs and desires of others, to align and elevate individual desires into team goals, and to inspire others to accomplish those larger goals. Team leaders use different techniques to motivate the team to improve the team's effectiveness.

During the enrichment stage, team members develop accountability focused at the team rather than the individual level. This means that the members of the team feel mutually accountable to each other. The team as a whole accepts accountability for the results of the team's actions. Team members begin to develop shared competence and shared confidence. Shared competence is important to the success of a cohesive, effective team. Competence is evident when people perform their work at or above an established standard. Shared confidence is the product of working as a team to execute an understood, shared mission, vision, goal, objective, or purpose with a competent team. Small team successes develop shared confidence, which in turn causes teams to undertake new and even more difficult challenges. With each accomplishment, a team builds confidence and increases its effectiveness.

As members begin to feel like a part of a team, and there is increased trust and commitment, a team becomes more cohesive. Cohesion is the bonding together of team members and their leaders in such a way as to develop and sustain their commitment to their unit and their resolve to accomplish the mission. Cohesion characterizes this stage of team building. A cohesive team puts aside any interfering differences and chooses to work together. Every new mission gives the team leader a chance to challenge the team to reach new levels of accomplishment and confidence.

See pp. 4-17 to 4-22 for discussion of the enrichment stage.

III. Sustainment Stage

At the sustainment stage, team members will do what is necessary without direction. The team's attitude about its capabilities elevates motivation and increases its ability to overcome adversity. Teams can have challenges in the sustainment stage. Effective team leaders will watch for signs of complacency and intervene when it occurs by reinforcing good interaction practices and holding the team to standard. Changes for which the team is not prepared can be another challenge for the team leader. Shared experiences and regular training help teams address unexpected changes in situations. Empowering the team to improve coordination can strengthen its ability to handle change.

Learning how to manage conflict is important in all of the stages of team building, but it is especially relevant in the sustainment stage. When conflict arises or trust is broken, team members disregard commitments, team members are not accountable, or work goes undone. At this point, the leader steps in and gets the team back on track. Team members handle these things during the sustainment stage. (See chapter 4 for a detailed discussion of the sustainment stage.)

The Army relies on effective teams to perform tasks, achieve objectives, and accomplish missions. Thus, building and maintaining effective teams is essential to mission command. To build an effective team, it is important to have an understanding of the characteristics of an effective team.

See pp. 4-23 to 4-26 for discussion of the sustainment stage.

(ADP 6-0). Through dedication and understanding of how to apply team-building principles to their organization, Army leaders create cohesion and accomplish missions.

A key to effective teamwork is the cooperative or coordinated effort of individuals acting together as a group or in the interests of a common goal. Teamwork is built on mutual trust and commitment to the team. The individual strengths and skills of each member combine in the pursuit of a common direction or cause, producing results for the team members and the organization. The support a team provides to individual team members reflects teamwork.

Understanding team dynamics is an important aspect of building and maintaining effective teams. Team dynamics are the behavioral relationships between members of a group who connect within an organization. The dynamics of a team will depend on the personalities of each team member and can affect how a team performs. Many factors influence team dynamics, such as team members' personalities, how the team operates, the team's identity, and the team's organizational environment.

Army team building is a continuous process of enabling a group of people to reach their goals and improve their effectiveness through leadership and various exercises activities and techniques (FM 6-22). The goal of Army team building is to improve the quality of the team and how it works together to accomplish the mission. Team building is essential for the Army to function and perform, and success for the team depends on the work and cooperation of every member. The Army's process for team building includes forming, enriching, and sustaining teams

III. Categories of Teams

The Army is a team of teams composed of numerous organizations with one overarching common mission: win the nation's wars. Brigade combat teams, command teams, planning teams, and fire teams are just a few examples of teams. Each of these is a team established through a permanent organizational structure or temporarily selected for a specified mission. Members of the Army are familiar with teams in the traditional context of squads, platoons, companies, or battalions. Team members share the same values, interests, experiences, training, climate, and Army culture in these intact organizations.

There are two categories of teams in the Army that leaders, Soldiers, and Department of the Army Civilians are part of and participate in. These are internal teams and external teams. All military teams fall into these two categories according to the commander task of the mission command warfighting function, titled "Develop teams, both within their own organizations and with joint, interagency, and multinational partners." Team members may be members or leaders in one or both categories of teams simultaneously, depending on the operation.

Internal Teams

Internal teams are teams comprised of leaders, Soldiers, and Department of the Army Civilians assigned to a specific unit or organization. Internal teams are the most common types of teams. These teams do not include individuals from outside organizations, unified action partners, or other nations. Higher headquarters assign members of these teams to the organization. Army squads, platoons, companies, battalions, brigades, and divisions are all examples of internal teams.

External Teams

External teams are teams whose members are from different organizations, cultures, agencies, or backgrounds and who bring specific knowledge, skills, and attitudes to the team. Most leaders do not have the option to select their team members. They must be prepared to build and develop the team with the assigned members. These teams have members with different expertise and can cross boundaries such as distance, time zones, functions, or cultures. Some examples of external teams include a security force assistance team, a working group, or a provincial reconstruction team.

IV. Characteristics of Effective Teams

Ref: ATP 6-22.6, Army Team Building (Oct '15), pp. 1-5 to 1-6.

Knowing the characteristics of effective teams help team leaders and team members build and maintain effective teams throughout the Army. Effective teams—

Trust Each Other and Predict What Each Will Do

For a team to work effectively, all team members establish trust. Teams with solid trust among their team members are better equipped to predict what each team member will do. Team leaders foster trust and commitment through shared experiences to build relationships that result in trust. In an effective team, members become able to predict each other's behaviors and respond quickly in changing circumstances.

Work Together to Accomplish the Mission

The teamwork necessary for cohesive, effective teams requires individuals to work together. A good team supports and enhances the skills and learning of its members, and brings out the best in them. Individual strengths and skills combine with teamwork, in the pursuit of a common direction or cause, to produce results.

Execute Tasks Thoroughly and Quickly

Cohesive, effective teams execute their plans thoroughly and quickly and focus on achieving collective results. Teams that execute tasks in this manner have high levels of motivation. Motivation is the will and initiative to do what is necessary to accomplish a mission. To execute tasks thoroughly and quickly, team leaders maintain motivation.

Meet and Exceed the Standard

Team members on effective teams readily meet and exceed the standards. An effective team leader instills discipline and builds esprit de corps by training to the standards, sensibly using rewards and punishment, instilling confidence, and ensuring team members have the necessary technical and tactical expertise. Effective team members know the standards and strive to meet and exceed them.

Adapt to Demanding Challenges

The Army's operational requirements are changing. Teams react to a wide range of potential missions. Team building develops agility and adaptability by focusing on training events and exercises that require creative solutions. Leaders develop a team's ability to focus and concentrate as the team's environment changes. Effective teams are flexible and able to adapt to changing conditions.

Learn From Their Experiences and Develop Pride in Their Accomplishments

Effective teams celebrate their successes together, just as they identify the special performances and contributions of each individual. Teams look upon first-time mistakes as opportunities for learning, rather than criticism and punishment. Teamwork reflects the pride in the outcomes of the team. Team members honor the contribution that each member makes to the total work of the team, which develops pride throughout the team.

The Armed Forces of the United States—including every military organization to the lowest level— are a team. Deterring adversaries and winning the Nation's wars are the team's common goals. While there are many different types and varieties of teams, the Army functions with two categories of teams: internal and external.

Refer to appendix B-3 of JP 1 for a discussion of professionalism and teamwork.

V. Team Roles and Responsibilities

A team consists of two components—a team leader and team members. Each component has roles and responsibilities in the formation, enrichment, and sustainment of the team.

Team Leaders

The team leader is the individual who provides guidance, instruction, and direction to a group of individuals to achieve a common goal. The leader enables the team to work together. Dynamic leaders build groups into teams and help personnel understand the fundamentals of team building. This type of leader knows how to build teams and set the stage for team success by establishing a positive atmosphere. Team leaders set goals to strengthen team connections, sense of purpose, commitment, and communication. Team leaders create an environment that fosters teamwork, promotes cohesion, and encourages initiative.

The team leader has a distinct and critical role in developing effective teams. Some of the responsibilities of a team leader include (but are not limited to)—

- Establishing a positive climate.
- Creating a shared vision and team identity.
- Providing clearly stated goals.
- Establishing roles and responsibilities.
- Establishing an environment of collaboration and dialogue.
- Establishing an environment that embraces learning.
- Knowing the strengths and weaknesses of team members.

Team Members

Effective team members are disciplined, task-oriented, and have a strong work ethic. They are open-minded, adaptable, and eager to learn. As a successful and capable member of a team, each person develops individual self-awareness to be a productive member of a team. This self-awareness allows team members to identify the positive attributes they seek in themselves and in other team members.

An exceptional team member has enthusiasm for the organization and the mission. These team members bring a positive attitude to the team and inspire others to do the same. Other positive attributes include being a reliable, trustworthy person. Reliable team members consistently get the work done. They work hard, follow through, and always deliver a good performance.

Some team members are especially critical of others and continually try to bring a team down. They will often take pleasure in the failure of others. They often look on the negative side of things, and will be the first to criticize others. This type of criticism is not meant to improve team efforts, but the overly critical team member seeks to hurt other people's feelings to make themselves feel better. Some other attributes of team players that are negative include being selfish, controlling, and egotistical.

Team members understand what they are able to contribute and understand the individual responsibilities that make people effective members of a team. Some of those responsibilities include—

- Building relationships.
- Demonstrating flexibility and adaptability.
- Cooperating with other team members.
- Having a willingness to help others.
- Respecting others.

I. Formation Stage

Ref: ATP 6-22.6, Army Team Building (Oct '15), chap. 2.

The formation stage is critical to the success of the team. During this stage, team members build confidence and trust in each other. Team members show characteristic behaviors in each stage, and each phase has unique highs and lows, as individuals assume their roles and come to a greater understanding of themselves and each other.

Formation Stage

There are three critical components of the formation stage of team building:

 Assemble the Team

 Build Trust

 Communicate Effectively

In the formation stage, team members may not know one another very well. Communication among members is functional and noncontroversial. The team is thinking short term and members' focus is more on the task at hand than on process improvement. Team members may have conflicting opinions and different approaches to solving problems. They may even resist the team leader as the team develops. Strong team leaders address the needs of team members at each stage to minimize conflict and reach higher performance levels quickly.

I. Assemble the Team

In the early stage of a team's development, leaders face the task of assembling the individuals who will comprise the team. In most cases, leaders will not have the opportunity to select some or all of the team members who will become part of the team. When operating internally, leaders select team members, but this is rare when working with joint, interagency, and multinational partners.

Whatever the involvement is in forming the team, team leaders determine how to organize a collection of individuals into an effective team. To assemble a group of individuals into a team, leaders manage a number of considerations. To assemble a team, a team leader must be prepared to—

- Integrate new team members.
- Get the team ready to work.
- Understand team dynamics.
- Manage the team's workflow.

A. Integrate New Team Members

The reception and orientation steps during the formation stage are important to bu[ld] an effective team. Teams work best when new members quickly feel that they are [a] part of the team. How thoroughly and thoughtfully the team leader welcomes and c[ri]ents new team members influences how quickly they develop trust and commitmer[t]. Teams build trust and commitment from the beginning by sharing the team's vision and ensuring that team members understand their roles and responsibilities. There[ ]are two critical steps to integrating new team members—reception and orientation.

Reception

The reception step establishes a cohesive team, and it establishes a positive first ir[n]pression of the team. The reception step should be such that the new member wan[ts] to become part of the team. Reception includes the team leader welcoming the nev[ ]member to the organization. The team-building process starts with reception and integration counseling. Reception and integration counseling identifies and helps fi[x] any problems or concerns that new members have, and it explains the standards. It[ ]clarifies responsibilities and sends the message that the leaders of the team care. Reception and integration counseling should begin immediately upon arrival, so the[ ]new team member quickly integrates into the organization.

Developing a standardized plan for all new members ensures that all team member[s] receive the same information. Before a new team member's arrival, team leaders can send a welcome letter including sponsor information and in-processing information. Once new team members arrive, they will begin reception. This includes assign[ ]ment to a specific duty position, timely and accurate in-processing to the installation[ ]and issue of additionally authorized personal equipment.

Orientation

Orientation takes place after most administrative in-processing is complete. An effective orientation program is essential. New team members have many questions, and a well-designed orientation program will help get them integrated into the team quickly and efficiently. During orientation, a new member meets the team, learns the workplace layout and schedule, and learns about the environment. The orientation step communicates team standards and values, goals and missions, and should include the team's history.

The orientation step starts new members out in the right direction. Whether the orientation is conducted with a group or individually, it is important that the team leader spend time in a face-to-face conversation with the new team members. Getting to know each team member establishes the trust necessary for team cohesiveness. Orientation solidifies new members' relationship with the team. It fuels their enthusiasm and guides their steps into a positive relationship with other team members. If done poorly, reception and orientation leave new team members with concern about their future with the team. A good experience joining the team makes it easier for the new member to fit in and to contribute to the team effort.

Socialization Process

New team members go through a socialization process. During socialization, they learn what the team expects of them, and they learn accepted norms and standards. The socialization process begins before a new team member reports to the unit. Corresponding with a new arrival gives the team leaders the opportunity to explain team values and standards. As part of integrating into the team, new members are individually committed to the team and internalize the values of the team. This helps them establish a bond with other members of the team.

The first goal of socialization is commitment, and it is comparable to the amount of selfless service a team member contributes to the team effort. The second goal of socialization is for new team members to adopt and internalize the values and attitudes of the team. Innovation is the third goal of the socialization process. If a leader demands too much conformity, innovation is stifled. Conformity may lead to boredom, loss of focus, over familiarity with tasks, contempt, and ultimately, defeat. Recognizing when to conform and when to be innovative is critical to the socialization process. The fourth goal of socialization is for the team member to develop a cohesive bond with the team. This bond is the ultimate goal of the socialization process.

One way to socialize new team members is to provide them with rewarding jobs that are challenging, but not impossible. This provides them the opportunity to learn new skills and advance to the next skill level. Another important way to socialize new members is to establish social support systems. Joining a new team can be an uncomfortable and stressful experience. Most new team members are hesitant to bring problems to the team leader. There are additional actions team leaders take to socialize individuals into their teams. Team leaders—

- Express acceptance so that new members know the team leader accepts them.
- Create supportive group expectations.
- Communicate positive expectations.
- Clarify the team member's role on the team.

B. Get the Team Ready to Work

Getting ready involves learning how the team will work together. It also involves lining up resources and tools and configuring the team's physical work areas. To get a team ready to work entails helping team members prepare their minds for the work ahead. Two of the components to get the team ready to work are—

- Prepare the team for likely challenges.
- Prepare the mental workspace.

Team leaders might face some challenging factors. The team leader provides the team with some direction without defining or prescribing a set of processes the team follows. The difference is providing guidance versus providing rules. While it is important to avoid dictating what the process is, the team needs an awareness of how the team's activities will unfold.

Prepare the Team For Likely Challenges

Another challenge is to understand that there are practical considerations that impose on the team's work. Teams have to work with time, personnel, materials, equipment, and information constraints. It is important to balance the team's recognition of these constraints against the team's needs. There are techniques to help team leaders with getting the team ready to work. They include—

- Clearly articulating the team's goals to provide the team with a sense of the team's goals. This helps the team manage the uncertainty it faces during the mission.
- Developing a charter document to capture the team's mission and goals and to promote shared understanding between the team leader and the team.
- Providing a process outline or standard operating procedures. While the team leader avoids providing too much structure, there is significant value in providing the team with a general process outline it can follow to get started.
- Providing examples of previous problems or situations. Team leaders and other team members offer examples of previous problems or situations that they have tackled in the past and provide approaches to dealing with them now.
- Developing ground rules for team interaction. Team members work together as a team to develop and establish a set of ground rules. Then, the team documents and posts the team's ground rules as a reminder.

Team leaders prepare the team for the challenges they are likely to experience wh working together on a complex, unfamiliar mission or problem set. Team leaders explain that it is not unusual for teams to experience periods of significant ambigu and confusion. Team leaders remind their teams that confusion can be informative and a sign of progress. One technique that team leaders have used to prepare for the probable moments of confusion and frustration is to tell the team to expect confusion. Team leaders describe the confusion and disorientation that occurs whe working on complex, unfamiliar problems.

Team leaders let the team know that there will be times when their understanding the mission or problem seems to fall apart and when members feel as though they are making little progress. Also, team leaders note that these confusing moments can be an exciting time where significant learning happens and team members achieve new insights. Setting this expectation can help prepare team members an provide reassurance when team members find themselves getting frustrated.

Prepare the Mental Workspace

Team members think and explore problems in different ways. Making sense of a problem requires many team members to adapt their typical ways of thinking, and t think critically, creatively, holistically, reflectively, visually, and from multiple perspec tives. This allows team members to see important connections and influences and articulate key aspects of a problem.

Team leaders should know how team members think and approach problems. This helps the team members with critical thinking skills to begin reflecting on and becoming more aware of the perspectives and attitudes they bring to the team. Tea leaders should also help team members become more confident and aware of their own abilities to be innovative and creative. This is important for team members who are resistant to different ways of thinking and exploring problems because they be lieve they are not creative. In exploring problems as a team, team members should engage in different ways of thinking.

- Think About Thinking
- Think Holistically
- Understand Others' Motivations
- Think Visually

C. Understand Team Dynamics

A central aspect of the team leader's role when assembling the team is under- standing the internal workings of the team. While all team members monitor the team's process and dynamics, the team leader helps the team maintain a positive and productive tone and maintain progress. This includes understanding diverse personalities and competing personal agendas. This also requires anticipating when conflicts or clashes could arise due to differences in personalities. Being prepared to handle these challenges facilitates a sense of team cohesion and productivity. These techniques can help teams with their team dynamics by—

- Discussing and establishing the dynamic for the team.
- Learning about team members.
- Addressing difficult personalities.
- Monitoring and reflecting on the team's dynamic.

A key challenge in managing the team's dynamics is awareness of the diverse personalities within the team. Diversity is important and advantageous for the team, but diversity within the team can also lead to considerable challenges. Another major challenge involves ensuring that everyone's ideas and perspectives are considered. Some team members are comfortable speaking up and sharing their views. Other team members may be more comfortable listening than talking. On teams where certain people dominate the conversation, access to the full range of viewpoints and perspectives can be reduced. It is everyone's responsibility to create opportunities for those who are less vocal to contribute their ideas. In most cases, the strength of the team is dependent on the diverse skill sets of each individual member.

D. Manage the Team's Workflow

Effective leaders are able to observe their team and recognize when team members are frustrated or unfocused. In these moments, effective team leaders recognize the need for a change in activity and shift the team's attention in a way that creates opportunities for members to be most engaged. Monitoring the team requires the team leader to consciously step back at moments to assess the team's overall tone and energy level. The following paragraphs discuss some techniques to help team leaders to manage the team's workflow.

Set Expectations

Teams work collectively to create a schedule and expected flow of activity. The schedule includes key milestones for work to continue to a next phase. While the schedule is flexible, it provides members with a vision of what to expect and how to manage their productivity. This will help the team anticipate and mentally prepare for work.

Know Indicators of Mental Fatigue

There can be indications that the team needs to restructure its activity. Some cues that indicate it is time to shift activities include low energy, excessive yawning, eyes glazing over, or fidgeting. Some other clues may not be as obvious. One indicator is when the team is stuck generating the same ideas, or the discussion is circular. Another indicator is when there are significant lulls in the discussion, and members become disagreeable over relatively insignificant issues. Being attuned to these cues helps the team leader and other team members recognize when the team needs a break, a change in activity, or a different work setting.

Conduct Periodic Checks on Team Process

Planning for time to step away from the work itself to discuss how the team is functioning is a way for team leaders to check on the team. When the team is in the midst of the work itself, it can be easy to forget about how the team is working together. Regular process checks can be particularly helpful in managing the team's workflow and productivity. Process checks do not focus on content. They are discussions about work style, work processes, and progress toward the team's goals.

. Build Trust

A key aspect in forming a team is building trust. Trust is the degree of confidence and reliability that people have in one another. Trust is a belief that another person or group will act or behave in a certain manner, and it is one of the foundations of successful teams. Trust facilitates a bond between leaders, Soldiers, and Department of the Army Civilians that enables mission success. In order for the team to work effectively, members should have established trust with each other. With trust, there is confidence among the team that the intentions of all members are good. Team members who trust each other are more willing to resolve differences of opinion and fact. Having trust in each other allows members to suspend any doubts, concentrate on duties, and accomplish the mission.

Among the meanings associated with trust is the expectation that a person has a high level of integrity and dependability. People put themselves at risk because of their confidence that the other person will do what they expect. Direct experience with each other over time allows team members to develop more informed, deeper levels of shared trust. This development of trust, combined with building on small successes, results in improved confidence across the team.

Building Trust

Ref: ATP 6-22.6, Army Team Building (Oct '15), pp. 2-6 to 2-9.

Successful leaders—and fellow team members—build trust over time by behaving consistently and predictably and by showing that the needs of the team come before their personal needs. Team leaders have a key role in building and maintaining a climate of mutual trust within the team. Some techniques to build trust include—

Expressing Mutual Trust In The Team

The simple expression of confidence in team members can engender mutual trust. Team leaders affirm their trust in their team members and in the team with statements such "I trust you," or "I have faith in your judgment and the judgment of the team."

Providing Opportunities For Social Interaction

Social events are great opportunities for team members to know one another on a more personal level and provide a needed reprieve from intense work and discourse. However, social events are not mandatory, as they can possibly backfire on the trust-building inte

Taking Advantage of Breaks

Breaks provide opportunities for team members to talk about the issues they address in an informal, non-threatening way. Not only do team members release tension and recharge during breaks, they also get to know each other, on a professional as well as a personal level. Breaks should be consistent, but team leaders do not allow breaks to become excessive and have a negative effect on the workload.

Facilitating Relationship Building When Receiving New Team Members

New team members may arrive at any moment as a replacement for a current team member, to increase the size of the team, for a specific skill set, or on a temporary ba for a specific task. If possible, it is helpful to discuss the addition of a new member with the team ahead of time. This prepares the team for the addition, so team members ca integrate the new member into the team. The team leader introduces the new membe to the team by describing their backgrounds, skills, expertise, experiences, and why the new members are coming to the team. Teams can also consider a version of the personal storytelling activity that provides the new team members an opportunity to te the team a little about themselves.

Increasing Difficulty of Training Sessions

During training, team leaders develop exercises and training situations that increase th difficulty and complexity of the scenarios as the team becomes familiar with one anoth With increased difficulty and complexity, mutual trust among team members expands, the team's comfort level increases. Team leaders increase the freedom of action perm ted to team members and broaden each team member's range of authorized action. T indirectly increases mutual trust between the team leader and other team members.

Recognizing Importance of Maintaining or Rebuilding Tru

2-44. Attention is often given to mutual trust-building activities. However, maintaining tual trust or rebuilding trust after it has been damaged is equally important, and consi able time must be dedicated to these activities and techniques. Rebuilding trust once is broken is different and often much more difficult than building and maintaining mutu trust. If trust is damaged, it takes significant effort and time to mend. Thus, attention t maintaining good mutual trust is very important. A few ways to support the maintenan of mutual trust in the team include monitoring and evaluating the level of trust within t team. Team leaders can discuss the importance of trust in the team and task the tean members to monitor trust relationships. Team members should actively note or engag the issue when a breakdown in trust is imminent.

Providing Feedback to Team Members

Teams who have worked together for a sustained period may find it helpful to discuss the key strengths and weaknesses for each individual on the team. In other words, what does the team member bring to the team that offers the greatest benefit, and what does the team member bring that could potentially harm the team? Discussing these strengths and weaknesses alert the individual team members personally and as a group, so that the team can make adjustments. Team leaders ensure feedback is constructive and not personal, as negative feedback has the potential of doing more harm than good.

Building Trust by Increasing Transparency

When team members have a low level of trust in each other or the team leader, it may be because they feel the information they need is not being fully shared with them or the entire team. This is particularly likely to be the case when the team is operating under a high tempo or a stressful combat situation. Under these conditions, team members become more distrustful of being excluded from the information loop because of the fast pace of the operations. Team leaders or team members identify the need for greater informational transparency in this environment.

Mitigating Distrust

When team members do not trust each other, they are more likely to hold grudges and find reasons to avoid spending time together. There are ways that team members can prevent distrust from surfacing within a team. One way is to foster information sharing. Information sharing facilitates cooperation and communication between team members. On teams in which distrust might become a problem, it is important for the team members to prevent information from becoming a tool to leverage advantages over other team members. Team leaders communicate instructions and expectations clearly to the whole team and try to avoid giving more information to one team member than another.

Repairing Trust

If an incident occurs that breaks trust within a working relationship, team leaders should address the behaviors that created distrust. Action must be taken immediately after the violation. Each person responsible for the violation of trust should apologize and explain the violation. These team members should also be sincere, take action through their own volition, and make sure to show a genuine desire to earn the person's trust again. The team leader can ask each party to restate and renegotiate expectations for one another for the future and agree to the terms.

Identify and Evaluate Barriers to Trust

There can be obstacles and challenges to building mutual trust. One obstacle to promoting a positive climate can be the Army culture itself. Army personnel conform to a command structure. However, if teams operate using the standard Army modes of interaction, many junior members of a team may fear asking questions. Another obstacle is the time and opportunities for the interaction that building mutual trust requires. In some teams, members may be working with team members whom they already know and trust. In other teams, members will likely be working with others for the first time. Having the necessary time and shared experiences for building mutual trust can be particularly challenging when the team is operating under time constraints with limited opportunity to develop relationships. This is often the case with a team that is convened quickly for purposes of crisis response.

Lastly, integrating external personnel into a team might create challenges to building and maintaining trust within that team. These personnel may come from organizations and agencies with differing agendas, different organizational cultures, differing views of the military, and different norms for interacting and conducting business. All of these differences have the potential to create challenges to trust development and information sharing within a team.

Successful leaders—and fellow team members—build trust over time by behaving consistently and predictably and by showing that the needs of the team come before their personal needs. Team leaders have a key role in building and maintaining a climate of mutual trust within the team. Some techniques to build trust include—

- Expressing mutual trust in the team.
- Providing opportunities for social interaction.
- Taking advantage of breaks.
- Facilitating relationship building when receiving new team members.
- Increasing difficulty of training sessions.
- Recognizing the importance of maintaining or rebuilding trust.
- Providing feedback to team members.
- Building trust by increasing transparency.
- Mitigating distrust.

See previous pages (pp. 4-12 to 4-13) for further discussion.

III. Team Communication

Communication is the process by which two or more people clearly and accurately exchange information. It is the exchange of thoughts, messages, or information through words, tone of voice, or body language. Effective communicators clarify or acknowledge the receipt of information, listen to other team members, and share their understanding of others. Communication is central to all human behavior, and it is one of the essential elements of team building. All individuals, especially leaders of teams, should be able to present information in a manner that is clear and concise to be effective in groups or organizations they lead. Informal communication, in which team members freely communicate with each other, is also important to team success.

Acknowledge Differences

Team members acknowledge differences in communication style between themselves and other team members. Team leaders should encourage all team members to remember that they each have differences in communication styles. Anticipating variances will help increase awareness of distinctions that may not be immediately obvious.

Understand Non-Verbal Communication

Communication is not just speaking and listening. It is a holistic process including verbal and non-verbal communication. Body position, gestures, and eye movements reflect a person's feelings as much as verbal communication. Team members should use non-verbal communication appropriately. Awareness of non-verbal communication is critical as team members from different cultures may use non-verbal signals in ways not familiar to all members of the team. Team leaders and team members must understand differences in non-verbal signals to know if their information is being received the same by every other team member. This also includes looking for and listening for indirect messages.

Clarify

Team leaders and team members clarify communication within the team to ensure all team members understand it. Spending a little extra time to verify understanding early on can save a lot of time and frustration later. Some ways to clarify communication are to repeat information as necessary, request and provide clarification when needed, and ensure statements are direct and unambiguous.

Be An Active Listener

Effective team leaders are active listeners. Actively listening helps leaders detect problems early to avoid misunderstandings. A way to do this is to ask questions that reflect active listening and understanding of the speaker's perspective. The most important purpose of listening is to comprehend the speaker's thoughts and internalize them. Both listening and questioning help build direct communication, which means using language that is clear and direct while maintaining a nonjudgmental stance. Active listening summarizes or mirrors the meaning of what another person has said to ensure mutual understanding. It also distinguishes between the words, tone of voice, and non-verbal cues.

Acknowledge Communication With Feedback

Feedback confirms the receipt of the message being sent. It also confirms whether the receiver understands the message or not. This includes both verbal and nonverbal responses to another person's message. Non-verbal feedback quickly lets the sender of a message know that the receiver is listening and is either getting the message or not. This can be done with a simple nod of the head or a thumbs up. Verbal feedback is another method. There are several types of verbal feedback techniques. Parroting is a feedback communication technique in which the receiver repeats the message to the sender word for word. Parroting can come across as condescending or patronizing, so team members must use it carefully. However, parroting may be very helpful when speaking on the phone with someone who is giving detailed information. Paraphrasing is another way of checking to make sure that the listener understood the other person's ideas, information, or suggestions. Paraphrasing illustrates two areas of communication—the information or content and how the person feels about the information or content.

Communicate With Stakeholders

A critical aspect of a team's effectiveness is the exchange that occurs between the team and those who have specific interests in the team's mission. Teams must often convey their understanding of the mission to stakeholders. A primary issue that makes conveying understanding to stakeholders challenging is figuring out how to package the information in a way that is meaningful and has an impact. A related challenge is getting to know the way stakeholders would prefer to receive and absorb information from the team. Some will prefer a visual representation. Getting to know the stakeholders helps the team tailor its communications.

An additional factor relevant to communicating with stakeholders is the team leader's involvement with the team. Due to an enormous array of competing demands, the team leader may have very little engagement in the day-to-day workings of the team. In these situations, teams need alternative strategies for keeping the team leader apprised of the team's work. Team leaders may use the following techniques to convey the teams' understanding and insights to stakeholders:

- Study the Team's Stakeholders
- Socialize Ideas with Stakeholders
- Recognize that Simple does not Equal Simplistic
- Seek External Feedback
- Build In Opportunities For Discussion and Exchange With Key Stakeholders

Rapidly Formed Teams

Ref: ATP 6-22.6, Army Team Building (Oct '15), pp. 2-11 to 2-13.

A rapidly formed team is composed of two or more individuals who come together due to either environmental demands or the need for people with specific expertise. For example, a team may be needed to accomplish a specific goal, such as rescue someone who is wounded, or respond to the scene of a vehicular accident. Other rapidly formed teams may come together to solve a specific problem, such as brainstorming for mission analysis, or they may become an Army design planning team.

Rapidly formed teams must be ready to work very soon after forming, whether in just a few hours or up to several weeks after they are created. They often face high stakes problems because they operate in dynamic, temporally constrained situations. These dynamic situations are characterized by the need to make complex decisions quickly, evolving and ambiguous situations, information overload, strict time pressures, adverse physical conditions, or severe consequences for error.

Teams developed rapidly may or may not be composed of team members that understand one another and have performed together before. Either way, they must be ready to function as a cohesive whole in a short period. To rapidly integrate individuals into a team, team leaders may—

- Use a personal histories exercise to introduce team members.
- Identify commonalities among team members.
- Share leadership responsibilities with team members to instill personal responsibility.
- Formulate operating guidelines to promote open discussion.
- Provide feedback on the team's process and performance on a regular basis.
- Get team members invested in the task—link the task to their personal values and goals.
- Make sure all members are present for the first meeting.

These activities do not need to take long to conduct, but they are critical to performance. Spending even just a few minutes getting team members familiar with one another's experiences and getting them invested in the purpose of the task can be critical for subsequent performance. If there is not much time available, team leaders concentrate on identifying commonalities, getting team members invested, and continuing to provide feedback on how the team is doing throughout the life of the team. To rapidly develop a team, team leaders may—

- Define the goal.
- Work collaboratively.
- Recognize differences.
- Determine motivation.
- Clarify roles and responsibilities.
- Develop shared understanding.
- Develop team goals and expectations.

II. Enrichment Stage

Ref: ATP 6-22.6, Army Team Building (Oct '15), chap. 3.

Enrichment is the process of enhancing teamwork, improving cohesion, and developing team norms. All team members must be committed to working as a team and realize that others depend on them. It is important to build commitment and keep the team motivated during the enrichment stage, as the team continues to learn how to work together.

Enrichment Stage

I   Build Commitment

II Build Shared Competence

III Motivate Team Members

IV Build Shared Confidence

V   Build Shared Accountability

VI Develop Cohesion

During the enrichment stage, teams will usually build commitment and develop shared competence and shared confidence, which will allow them to develop cohesion. A team that has commitment creates clarity around direction and priorities, which aligns the entire team around common objectives. Effective teams develop the ability to learn from mistakes and take advantage of opportunities. They are able to move forward or change direction without hesitation.

I. Build Commitment

Commitment is an individual's motivation and willingness to belong to the team and help achieve the defined goals. Building commitment is a process involving everyone on the team. Soldiers and Department of the Army Civilians foster an enduring commitment to the Army, its mission, its people, and the continued practice of the fundamental aspects of the Army culture. Commitment to the purpose and values of an organization provides a clear sense of direction.

Commitment relies on acceptance, the degree to which team members are committed to the team's vision and mission, and the degree to which they believe in what the team is trying to accomplish. Team members who have acceptance take ownership of the team's direction and put out the extra effort to ensure the team's success. Effective teams make clear and timely decisions and move forward with complete acceptance from every member of the team. The following paragraphs describe supportive team-based techniques and suggested actions for building and maintaining commitment. Teams can use these techniques and modify them as required for each unique team organization and team missions.

Encourage Team Identification

Team leaders encourage a sense of self-identification by articulating the team vision and defining the values that the team should have. This ensures that the team vision incorporates the skills of the whole team. Articulating the mission will encourage team members to view the team and its goal positively, and then they will define their own role within the team.

Reward Cooperation

Team leaders reward cooperation and acknowledge that teamwork is part of performance. Rewarding cooperation will encourage team members to interact with each other to accomplish goals. This allows a team to foster a sense of belonging.

Provide the Team with a Clear Vision

For team members to make a substantial commitment to success, they must feel that they are working toward a joint outcome that is meaningful, and they are contributing to the success and support of the team and its mission. Providing the team with a good visualization of the desired future for the team and the team's mission is an important technique for building commitment with the team members.

The important starting point is a clear vision and mission statements that team members have helped create, are able to understand, use, and commit to achieving. Team members must also see the natural linkage between the work they are performing and the long-term goals of their higher organization. The last element is the creation of well-defined goals that are both challenging and support the overall mission of the team.

Communicate Team Commitments

A lack of communication and communication breakdowns are normal and will happen from time to time. However, most, if not all, communication problems are avoidable, if team leaders and team members are aggressive about clearly communicating team commitments and information routinely.

Mitigate Challenges

A team that fails to develop commitment creates ambiguity among team members about its direction and priorities. This type of team may watch as windows of opportunity close due to excessive analysis and unnecessary delay. This often leads to a lack of confidence and a fear of failure, and it encourages second-guessing among team members. A team can ensure commitment by taking specific steps to maximize clarity and achieve acceptance.

II. Build Shared Competence

Competence is an Army professional's demonstrated ability to perform duties successfully and to accomplish the mission despite adversity, obstacles, and challenges. Shared competence means the team collectively can perform its duties and accomplish the mission. Team members accept one another and their leaders when they are satisfied with each other's knowledge of the job and ability to apply that knowledge. Nothing deteriorates teamwork more quickly than the perception that team

III. Motivate Team Members

Ref: ATP 6-22.6, Army Team Building (Oct '15), pp. 3-3 to 3-5.

Motivation supplies the will and initiative to do what is necessary to accomplish a mission. Motivation comes from within, but others' actions and words can affect it. There are two kids of motivation, intrinsic and extrinsic.

Intrinsic Motivation

Intrinsic motivation refers to the drive within an individual that comes from personal interests. This type of motivation resides within a person and does not come from external pressures. When a person finds an activity satisfying, the activity itself is intrinsically motivating.

Extrinsic Motivation

Extrinsic motivation refers to the motivation that comes from external influences. Team leaders often use extrinsic motivation to encourage behaviors that a team member would not develop from internal motivation. When a team member discovers that engaging in an activity will result in a reward or other desired outcome, that team member can become extrinsically motivated.

Group Motivation

Group motivation refers to those team processes in which the team defines objectives, and then the team becomes energized to achieve those objectives. The extent to which team members identify with the team also contributes to the groups' motivation. Articulating a team's vision is fundamental to developing an effective team. This vision is what motivates and directs a team to reach its goal. Loyalty, dedication, and enthusiasm are important factors that contribute to the effectiveness of a team and the team's motivation.

- **Account for Common Needs.** Team members sometimes need help to meet their needs. Most people want to feel competent, connected to others, and empowered in their ability to complete a task. One way to motivate team members is to make their needs coincide with unit tasks and missions. People have a natural desire to work to satisfy their own needs.

- **Understand Individual Motivational Differences.** Different things motivate different individuals. What motivates people differs from one person to the next, whether it is a person's values, self-interests, a cause, or another force. An example of internal motivation is a fear or belief. An external motivation could be danger, the environment, or pressures from other people.

- **Establish Goals.** Goals help to focus attention and action. They increase the effort that is expended to master new skills. Goals help provide motivation for the team members to persist, even in the face of failure, until the goal is accomplished. Team leaders collaboratively establish goals that are challenging and specific. They follow up with team members and provide feedback about their work toward meeting those goals. Team leaders ensure that there are multiple feedback mechanisms in place.

- **Reward and Recognize Team Members.** Team leaders who recognize individual and team accomplishments shape positive motivation and actions for the future. Team leaders reward individual and team behavior that supports unit tasks and missions. Recognition and feedback for team members is valuable in increasing motivation, and recognition should be used when someone achieves a high performance standard.

- **Planning Events.** Participating in the planning of future events can be a highly motivating experience. By contributing ideas to a plan, team members then have a personal interest in seeing the plan succeed. Participating in planning improves communication, which improves teamwork.

members do not know their jobs and leaders do not know how to lead. The development of shared competence is important because team members rely on each othe for team expertise. The sum of the team's skills is greater than the separate parts.

Competency may be initially assumed, but it must be proven to increase trust and confidence. Effective teams display competence by meeting or exceeding team goals and expectations. Shared competence means that each member of the team has the competence to complete all the required tasks to accomplish the mission. there are tasks associated with mission accomplishment, each member of the tean is competent in the team tasks that are required to realize or accomplish the missic

IV. Build Shared Confidence

Shared confidence is the product of shared trust from working as a team to execute a fully understood and agreed upon vision with a competent team. Team leaders sometimes assume confidence among team members with common backgrounds, values, and beliefs (such as among team members in the military). However, in mo complex environments with unified action partners, such an assumption of shared confidence comes at the risk of degraded performance. A team may include members whose parent organizations have historically shared little faith in one another, in which case personal interaction and relationships between team members are critical to success.

It is the team leader's responsibility to build confidence in the team members' abilities. The team leader establishes the conditions that foster taking initiative and encourage team development. Team members and leaders develop mutual confidence by sharing difficult, challenging, and realistic training. Mutual confidence multiplies combat power as it forms personnel into cohesive teams.

Being part of a team that performs well during challenging training instills confidence and pride. Team members who lack pride in themselves and their performance cannot feel pride in their team or their leaders. It is necessary for team leaders to show respect for each team member and encourage pride and self-confidence in their team. Shared confidence grows once team members have developed shared trust and are working together to accomplish an understood, agreed-upon vision or mission. Confident team members are self-assured, comfortable taking prudent risks, creative when solving problems, share pride in their accomplishments, and work together to continue to win.

V. Build Shared Accountability

Accountability means accepting the responsibility for one's actions. This includes a person's ability to accept the consequences for the results of those actions. In order for a team to promote shared accountability, team leaders should reinforce the team's mission and vision. Team leaders hold team members accountable by identifying problems that arise from a lack of teamwork. By noting these problems, team members can work together to solve them.

One way that team leaders can foster shared accountability is to have the team members describe their purpose and define the teams' roles and responsibilities. A team leader should also ensure that each team member understands what the standards are. Holding teams accountable for their combined results will only work if the team members are able to influence each other's behavior. When teammates participate in the shaping of the team's vision, they are more likely to accept responsibility and accountability for the team's success.

When a team holds itself accountable, then the team members can handle the consequences of their actions together. This means the whole team is accountable for each member's performance. The team connects real consequences to a team's actions. Team leaders should not shield their teams from the consequences of what they fail to accomplish together.

Self-Correction

Effective teams learn through self-correction. Self-correction means the team leader and team members identify, admit, and learn from individual and group mistakes and use this information to adjust their course of action. On self-correcting teams, team members develop goals and tasks to help everyone succeed and accomplish the mission. Additionally, on self-correcting teams, interpersonal conflict is resolved between team members without escalating the conflict to the team leader or other team members.

Climate of Accountability

Creating a climate of accountability means developing a climate in which people can speak openly and admit to mistakes without fear. The biggest fear people have about accountability is that they will be punished for their actions. In successful teams, team members view mistakes as learning opportunities. Creating a climate of accountability for mistakes allows team leaders to foster a learning organization. All team members should be able to admit to mistakes and accept the consequences for them. When mistakes occur, teams should focus on how to correct problems and how to prevent them from happening again.

I. Develop Cohesion

Cohesion is the bond of relationships and motivational factors that help a team work together. A cohesive team puts aside interfering differences and chooses to work together. Every new mission gives the team leader a chance to strengthen internal bonds and challenge the team to reach new levels of performance, accomplishment, and confidence. A team's positive attitude about its capabilities elevates motivation and the team's desire to meet new challenges.

Teams develop cohesion through three elements: bonding, commitment, and resolve. Bonding is the development of strong interpersonal relationships among team members and their leaders. Bonding results from shared experiences through which interpersonal relationships are developed. The collective levels of mutual respect, trust, and confidence that develop between units is a form of bonding. Commitment is dedication to the team and what it represents and to the values and goals of the Army. All team members must be committed to working as members of the team and realize that others depend on them. Resolve is the shared determination and motivation of teammates to work interdependently to accomplish the mission and to sustain this capability over a long period.

Improve the Level of Cohesion

There are seven areas where team leaders can improve the level of cohesion within a team:

- Leadership.
- Group characteristics.
- Individuals on the team.
- Team socialization.
- Team and individual goals and objectives.
- Team activities.
- Team identification and history.

See following page for further discussion.

Improving the Level of Cohesion

Ref: ATP 6-22.6, Army Team Building (Oct '15), pp. 3-3 to 3-5.

Team leaders can improve the level of cohesion within a team in following areas:

Leadership. The most critical factor in developing team cohesion is leadership. Cohesion cannot be created from the top down. It is developed within a team and involves all members of that team. Leaders create the climate for cohesive growth. Leaders who encourage and provide opportunities to develop a sense of ownership in the mission develop teams that are more cohesive. Team leaders must ensure that all team members are treated with respect and communicate standards and expectations clearly.

Group Characteristics. Groups identify with customs, traditions, and values. Cohesive teams form groups along organizational lines. Team leaders ensure their team has sufficient members to accomplish its missions. Group characteristics help teams build group and team pride. Cohesive teams recognize that group membership satisfies member needs and will create the conditions that require group interaction. Team leaders should recognize and reinforce groups that have a positive influence on the team.

Individuals on the Team. A team leader's attention must be directed on the development of each team member. The team leader must know and respond to the personal interests and needs of the team. The individuals in a team affect the cohesion of that team. When each member of a team becomes a valuable, contributing member, team cohesion is enhanced. Team leaders make the effort to know each team member and ensure team members perform all tasks to standard. Team leaders should also encourage and recognize individual initiative.

Team Socialization. An individual becomes a team member through a socialization process. Socialization is the process by which a new team member acquires the skills, knowledge, and attitudes unique to a team and is accepted by that team. The stages of team development outline this process. The team leader must recognize that informal groups within a team establish socialization processes as well. The goal of socialization is commitment to the team and the internalization of the team's mission. Team socialization is an important component of team development and cohesion. Cohesive teams reinforce actions and attitudes that support the professional Army ethic, and they set and maintain high standards.

Team and Individual Goals and Objectives. One of the most important factors of team cohesion is the integration of team and individual goals. When team members work together to accomplish goals, they develop the belief that they can accomplish almost anything. One way to develop this belief is to establish clear and achievable, yet challenging, goals. Team leaders should involve team members in the goal and objective setting process and relate individual goals to team goals. Additionally, team leaders should ensure that team goals support the team's mission.

Team Activities. Team leaders should conduct team activities that are interesting and include all team members. Possible activities include everything from field training exercises and crew qualification tests to organization days and social events. Team leaders plan these activities with cohesion in mind. Some ways that team leaders can build cohesion through team activities are to train as a team and make training challenging and realistic. When appropriate, the team leader may also involve family members.

Team Identification and History. A cohesive team draws some of its strength from the achievements and experiences of those who have previously served. A cohesive team will include unit history in the orientation program and use mottos or sayings correctly and with pride.

III. Sustainment Stage

Ref: ATP 6-22.6, Army Team Building (Oct '15), chap. 4.

During the sustainment stage, teams develop a sense of pride and ownership in the team and its goals. However, teams often have difficulties during the sustainment stage. Effective team leaders watch for signs of complacency and intervene when it occurs by reinforcing good interaction practices and maintaining team standards.

Sustainment Stage

 Adapt to Change

 Manage Conflict

 Sustain Resilient Teams

Changes for which the team is not prepared can be another challenge for the team leader. Shared experiences and regular training help teams address unexpected changes in situations. Empowering the team to improve coordination can strengthen its ability to handle change.

I. Adapt to Change

Team leaders recognize that what works for them when leading a team in one organizational context may not be the best fit for the team within the current organization. Team leaders elicit the team members' views about what will (or will not) be accepted within the current organizational climate. Team leaders work with team members to adapt their leadership style, the team's approach, and the work process accordingly.

As teams adapt to change, they must continually reassess their goals and priorities. As missions change, team leaders must ensure the goals and priorities of the team are in line with the mission. If several things need to be accomplished at the same time, team leaders should set priorities and allocate time to complete each task. Team leaders inform their team of changes, explain to their team why the mission has changed, how they will work to accomplish the new mission, and the standards expected of them. Cohesive teams adjust quickly when they understand the goal.

Effective teams handle change. As team leaders respond to situations that threaten sustained teamwork and cohesion, they must realize that team growth and stability are often uneven. A team may reach a peak, seem to slump, and then build to a new level of performance. This may occur when new members are added to the team. Successful leaders guide the team to peak performance with it faces critical tasks or combat actions. The effectiveness of the team changes when team members change. The efficiencies teams establish as members working together must be reestablished when new members join the team. This also applies when team members leave with no replacement.

Some techniques that can help adapt to changes in the team are listed from table 4-1 on the facing page.

II. Manage Conflict

Conflict is the tension between individuals or groups because of real or perceived differences. It is built on an individual's or group's perception of a problem, whether that be a perceived difference in views or ideas, interpersonal incompatibilities, or one individual or group interfering with another group's goals or interests. Sometimes conflict is necessary to bring about a change or resolve a problem. In this way, conflict can be positive and constructive, but only when it is managed properly. To manage conflict, a team leader must address the other side's perception of the issue, which may be completely different from that team leader's perception. There are different ways to manage conflict. The approach used will depend on the time available, the degree and impact of the conflict, and the underlying goal.

A. Approach To Conflict Resolution

When conflicts occur, team leaders acknowledge the problem and determine the best way to resolve it. The team leader should gain understanding of the situation from both sides in order to remain unbiased. The conflict resolution process should stay focused on the issue and ways to resolve it. The most desired method for resolving conflict is by collaboration. This method allows both sides of the conflict to contribute to solving the problem. Once the team leader identifies the source of conflict, both sides must show an interest in working together to solve the problem. After they have developed ideas together on how to come to a resolution, the team leader helps them to choose a solution.

Another approach to conflict resolution is consensus building, a form of negotiation in which everyone agrees to the solution. While the idea of a unanimous decision may seem unlikely, building consensus within a team helps set the conditions for a collective decision to solving a problem.

B. Types Of Conflicts

There are generally two types of conflicts found in teams: task conflicts and personal conflicts. Task conflicts refer to disagreements about work. Task conflicts can be beneficial to team performance, while personal conflicts are usually harmful. Team leaders cannot ignore personal conflicts. If the team does not confront the problem, the team will develop a negative climate. When personal conflicts occur, teams must communicate with each other to resolve the problem. Using conflict positively and constructively can help build a strong foundation of trust and respect among team members.

At some point, most teams will encounter team conflicts. Accordingly, it is helpful to spend some time during team development to establish team ground rules for working through difficult team issues.

- Avoid Personal Attacks
- Prevent Heated Outbursts
- Approach Other Team Members Directly
- Never Assume Hostile Intent
- Act to Control Conflict

Adapting to Team Member Changes

Ref: ATP 6-22.6, Army Team Building (Oct '15), table 4-1, p. 4-2.

New Team Member Techniques

- Identify, contact, and integrate new team members as early as possible.
- Acquire rapid access to e-mail and operating sites.
- Introduce the new team member to the team.
- Determine what areas the new member will lead.
- Introduce the new team member to team processes.
- Implement a standard training plan.
- Explain how key decisions are made.

Loss of a Team Member Techniques

- Identify a backup for everyone and cross-train on responsibilities.
- Conduct focused exit interviews.
- Capture knowledge, including file transfers and continuity books.
- Obtain new contact information.
- Recognize the outgoing team member and formally say goodbye.

Mission Change Techniques

- Update vision and purpose.
- Identify new competencies required.
- Reform the team (as needed).
- Identify processes from previous missions that will remain relevant or become outdated.
- Rebuild trust and confidence.

Introducing New Technology to the Team Techniques

- Identify experienced users. If there are any, they take the lead until the team is proficient.
- Formulate a training and implementation plan.
- Identify the impact on mission and capabilities.

C. Avoiding Conflict

Teams can engage in constructive conflict and know that the purpose is to construc the best solution in the shortest time. When team members avoid conflict and do nc discuss their opinions, poor decisions are the result. The desire to avoid a fight may prevent situations in which productive conflict would be useful. A team can develop the ability and willingness to engage in healthy conflict.

The important point is to understand that many teams have a tendency to avoid conflict, even though it can be productive. One way for a team to make conflict easy to handle is to appoint a team member who can identify disagreements and bring them out in the open. This team member will also need to recognize that the people engaged in conflict are becoming uncomfortable and stop to remind them that conflict is sometimes necessary.

D. Teams that Fail to Meet the Standard

Team leaders need to recognize when a team is not meeting the standard and identify the source of the problem. In some cases, there are team members who will not work together regardless of the circumstances. In other cases, the team leader needs to plan additional training. A lack of planning often leads to a team not meeting the standard as well. The team leader must figure out what the problem is and respond appropriately to bring the team up to standard.

III. Sustain Resilient Teams

To have resilience, team members have to be able to build and sustain positive relationships. Team members need strong bonds with people who allow them to be themselves and help them to become stronger people. Social resilience is not just about being the strongest fighting force. It also includes having a team in which members can have fun with each other and confide in each other. During stressful times, teams find out whom they can count on. Experiences in combat can test relationships. When experiences are good, they can contribute in a powerful way to helping to become more socially resilient. They can help to recover quickly from traumatic events and overcome difficult obstacles that stand in the way.

A. Social Resilience

Social resilience is the capability to foster, engage in, and sustain positive social relationships as well as to endure and recover from stressors and social isolation. Building social resilience within a team means working together to be a cohesive unit.

The resilience of the unit can be beneficial to the team climate. Even during the most painful experiences, by continuing to connect with other team members and sharing thoughts and feelings, bonds become stronger, and team members are able to bounce back much more quickly from painful or traumatic events.

B. Team Diversity

Diversity is the things that make people different and unique, including differences in roles, ethnicity, gender, physical size, and ability. A team that is bonded in its efforts and diverse in its approaches will be more resilient and effective in responding to any unexpected or adverse situations. Differences can make teams more adaptable, and help build more cohesion, trust, mutual respect, and effectiveness within the team. Each team member has a unique skill and role that enhances the team's effectiveness. Unfortunately, there are natural impulses that compete with desire to work together as a diverse team. Two natural tendencies that prevent teams from capitalizing on diversity are the desire to bond with people who are most like them and a desire to seek agreement.

I. Training to Fight & Win

Ref: ADP 7-0, Training (Jul '19), chap. 1.

Training Readiness

The Army trains to fight and win. To do this, the Army trains by developing proficiencies in mission-essential tasks, weapon systems, and the effective integration and employment of both. These components of training readiness provide the backbone to the development of unit readiness—the Army's first priority.

Training prepares Soldiers to execute missions which shape operational environments, prevent conflict, and conduct large-scale ground combat against peer threats with chemical and nuclear capabilities. Army forces must be organized, trained, and equipped to meet worldwide challenges. The Army provides these forces by planning for and executing tough, realistic training. Unit training occurs continuously—while at home station, at combat training centers, and while deployed.

Training prepares the Army to conduct prompt and sustained operations across multiple domains. Units train all the time—while deployed, at home station, and at combat training centers. Through effective, battle-focused training, units, leaders, and Soldiers achieve the tactical and technical competence that builds confidence, adaptability, and effectiveness. Army forces train using proven training doctrine that sustains their operational capabilities. The Army trains units, Soldiers, and Army Civilians to achieve proficiency in individual and collective tasks under challenging and realistic conditions. Training continues in deployed units to sustain skills and adapt to continual changes in an operational environment.

Readiness is the Army's top priority. Training is the most important activity units do to achieve and maintain readiness. **ADP 7-0** establishes the principles and concepts of training and introduces the training procedures further expanded upon in **FM 7-0**.

As part of decisive action, Army units must be capable of simultaneously employing the offense, defense, and stability or defense support of civil authorities (known as DSCA) across multiple domains. The Army does this to shape operational environments, prevent conflict, prevail in large-scale ground combat, and consolidate gains as part of unified action. The expansive scope of possible tasks to conduct complex and sustained operations demands that commanders provide subordinates with clearly prioritized training guidance that aligns with missions and the resources necessary to train.

Commanders ensure Soldiers and units train under challenging and realistic conditions that closely replicate an operational environment. Deployed units continue training to sustain their skills and facilitate their adaptation to changes in tactical and demanding operational environments. Candid and objective assessments made as a result of evaluated training and feedback, and the rapid application of lessons learned, produce effective, versatile, and adaptive units and leaders.

The core of training readiness centers on tasks that Soldiers and units train to fight and win as cohesive and effective teams. It is the progressive development and sustainment of these tasks that form the basis of a unit's ability to conduct unified land operations.

II. Individual Training

Individual Soldier skills and proficiencies establish a solid foundation for unit collective training proficiency. Soldiers train to individual tasks which are clearly defined, observable, and measurable activities accomplished by an individual. These individual tasks enable Soldiers to master the necessary fundamental skills to fight and win. Training and education prepares Soldiers to perform assigned tasks to standard. Training and education also provides the skills and confidence that individuals need in order to perform duties and accomplish missions under a wide range of circumstances, some of which may be unfamiliar. Training individual tasks occurs in the institutional, operational, and self-development training domains. (See AR 350-1 for a discussion of the training domains). Individual skill proficiency is the basis for collective task proficiency.

Individual training also includes the training that Soldiers receive and the proficiencies achieved on the individual weapons they are assigned. In addition to individual task proficiency, individual weapons proficiencies form the backbone of the unit's ability to execute more complex and dynamic collective training under live-fire conditions and ultimately the unit's ability to successfully execute operational missions.

Unit noncommissioned officers (NCOs) ensure Soldiers meet individual task and weapons proficiencies and work to ensure those proficiencies are sustained. Unit NCOs constantly monitor—as well as constantly train and retrained as necessary—the underlying proficiencies at the individual level. In units where Soldiers cannot perform individual skills to standard, the unit cannot effectively execute collective tasks to standard.

III. Collective Training

Units train collective tasks which are clearly defined, observable, and measurable activities or actions. Collective tasks require organized team or unit performance, leading to the accomplishment of a mission or function. Based on the accomplishment of individual task proficiencies, units progress to more complex collective training. Collective training is the essence of teamwork, and develops the mutual trust essential to developing effective, cohesive teams.

An integral component of collective training includes the successful and lethal employment of a unit's weapons systems. This training is tied not just to the Soldier's proficiency with individually assigned weapons, but also to the proficiencies gained as part of collective teams. Proficiencies in both crew-served and platform weapon systems require the same level of constant attention and training as those at the individual level.

There are never sufficient resources or time to train every collective task equally well. Commanders and other leaders ensure training is planned for the long-range and communicated to subordinates in training guidance and unit training plans (UTPs) that prioritize battle-focused training as the unit's first training priority. Battle-focused training is that training that develops skills and proficiencies tied to unit capabilities and mission requirements. Unit training priorities are based upon the guidance provided by the next higher commander with consideration to the mission, time, and available training resources.

Collective training also capitalizes on a multiechelon approach, unified action partners, and multinational force training opportunities whenever possible. Multiechelon training is a training technique that allows for the simultaneous training of more than one echelon on different or complementary tasks. Combined arms training consists of tasks conducted jointly by associated warfighting functions and functional units.

Department of the Army Civilians train to support both operating forces and the institutional force. They provide unit continuity and fill positions that make it possible to man, equip, resource, and train units. Commanders ensure the civilian workforce gets the training, education, and experience necessary to hone skills and prepare for future positions and responsibilities. Generally, Department of the Army Civilians enter the Army with the skills and knowledge required for their positions. They continue to enhance their knowledge, skills, and abilities through the civilian education system, functional training, self-development, and progressive assignments.

Training (Logic Chart)

Ref: ADP 7-0, Training (Jul '19), introduction and introductory figure.

ADP 7-0 describes the fundamentals of how the Army trains to conduct operations as a unified action partner employing the Army's operational concept—unified land operations. Developing and sustaining readiness is the Army's number one priority. Training represents the most important activity units do every day to achieve readiness. The Army does this by conducting tough, realistic, standards-based, and performance-oriented training.

ADP 7-0 is founded on the concept that unit training is a logical extension of the Army's operations process. The ideas and concepts of planning, preparing, executing, and assessing operations is fundamentally the same whether the unit trains to achieve readiness at home station or trains to operate when deployed. Learning and applying the concepts, ideas, and terminology of the operations process as units train makes the transition from training to operations more seamless for both leaders and their units—and improves the overall readiness of the force.

> ## Unified Land Operations
> ### (The Army Operational Concept)
> Simultaneous execution of offense, defense, stability, and defense support of civil authorities across multiple domains to shape operational environments, prevent conflict, prevail in large-scale ground combat, and consolidate gains as part of unified action.

Prepare Soldiers and units for conducting decisive action, guided by mission command and the following principles, processes, and procedures:

Principles of Training	Executed through	Training
• Train as you fight • Train to standard • Train to sustain • Train to maintain		• Plan • Prepare • Execute • Assess

> Unit Training Management (UTM)
> located on the
> Army Training Network (ATN)
> (https://atn.army.mil)

IV. Commander's Activities in Training

Ref: ADP 7-0, Training (Jul '19), chap. 2.

Central to training, commanders perform specific and recurring activities that facilitate training to achieve and sustain proficiencies. These activities—understand, visualize, describe, direct, lead, and assess— ensure that the commander drives training. As commanders plan, prepare, execute, and assess training, they ensure that all training is done to Army standards. (See figure 2-1.) As the unit's primary trainers, commanders determine what need to be trained and ensure subordinates understand the standards to meet. This shared understanding between the commander and subordinates is fundamental to Army training. The commander then encourages initiative and innovation in subordinates as they determine the most effective ways to achieve standards, training objectives, and meet the commander's intent for training.

Commander's Activities to Guide Unit Training

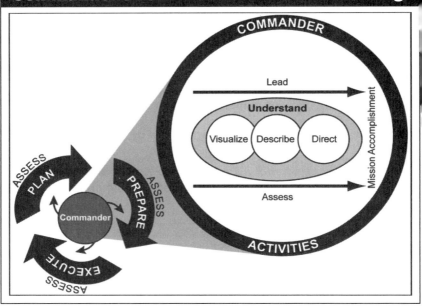

Ref: ADP 7-0 (Jul '19), fig. 2-1. Commander's activities to guide unit training.

The Operations Process (as the Framework for Unit Training)

ADP 7-0 is founded on the concept that unit training is a logical extension of the Army's operations process. The ideas and concepts of **planning, preparing, executing, and assessing** operations is fundamentally the same whether the unit trains to achieve readiness at home station or trains to operate when deployed. Learning and applying the concepts, ideas, and terminology of the operations process as units train makes the transition from training to operations more seamless for both leaders and their units—and improves the overall readiness of the force.

See pp. 6-1 and 6-8 for further discussion.

Understand

Unit commanders understand the next higher commander's training guidance, which gives the tasks the unit trains. The first step in devising effective UTPs, unit commanders analyze the next higher commander's training guidance and determine the tasks and weapons the unit must train to meet that guidance. This is done with an understanding of the current state of unit training readiness. During the entire process, the unit commander maintains a continuous dialogue with the next higher echelon to ensure a shared understanding of training expectations as training plans are formulated. Additionally, commanders read and understand operations and training doctrine. They also familiarize themselves with and use web-based training resources such as the Army Training Management System (known as ATMS).

Visualize

Commanders visualize how their units should conduct training based on their understanding of next higher commander's training guidance. Drawing on their own training, education, and experience, commanders develop a mental model as the unit progresses through training events to attain the desired end state. Visualization should encompass the environment, potential for improvement, and resources likely to be required to train.

Describe

Commanders describe the desired end state of training to their subordinate leaders by providing clear, detailed, and unambiguous training guidance. They ensure that subordinates understand what tasks and weapons proficiencies to achieve, when to attain them, and how long to sustain them. In providing training guidance, the next higher commander empowers subordinate commanders to develop their own training plans based on this guidance and backbrief these plans for concurrence.

Lead

Commanders influence unit training with their presence and leadership by providing purpose, direction, and motivation. During every aspect of unit training, commanders give the unit the benefit of their experience, knowledge, and guidance from planning training to execution. By setting the example for all subordinates to follow, the commander sends the message that unit training is key to operational success.

Assess

Once training has concluded, the commander considers the results of observed training—in particular evaluations. These evaluations along with other sources of feedback—to include the commander's own observations—provide the information necessary to accurately and objectively assess whether the unit can perform tasks to standard. Assessment is a continual process that not only considers task performance, but also the other factors that directly affect unit training. These factors include assessing the efficacy of training plans, the effectiveness of after action reviews, and the achievement of training objectives, among others. Based on the commander's assessment of these factors, unit training evolves and improves as the unit progresses toward training readiness.

Refer to BSS6: The Battle Staff SMARTbook, 6th Ed. for further discussion of commander's activities from ADP 5-0. BSS6 covers the operations process; commander's activities; Army planning methodologies; the military decisionmaking process and troop leading procedures; integrating processes (IPB, information collection, targeting, risk management, and knowledge management); plans and orders; mission command, C2 warfighting function tasks, command posts, liaison; rehearsals & after action reviews; and operational terms and military symbols.

V. Principles of Training

Ref: ADP 7-0, Training (Jul '19), chap. 3.

Units employ effective training based on the Army's principles of training. Training must embody all the principles to be effective.

Principles of Training

- **Train as You Fight**
- **Train to Standard**
- **Train to Sustain**
- **Train to Maintain**

Train as You Fight

Units train as they intend to operate. This means replicating the complex and uncertain operational environments in training that the unit will likely face in combat and other operations. Leaders ensure that Soldiers and the unit train to cope with the complex, stressful, and lethal situations they will likely encounter in combat.

Just as in operations, unit commanders drive training through their personal engagement and presence. A commander's actions and activities for training communicate a clear message to the unit that training and the mission is a priority. Commanders effectively resource training and protect subordinates' valuable training time. They create stability and predictability throughout the organization by protecting approved training plans from unnecessary and unprogrammed training distracters. Commanders and other leaders ensure subordinates understand the end state of training while empowering them to develop the best plan to achieve and then execute it. Commanders create a positive and effective training culture by listening to and rewarding subordinates who are bold and in-novative. Commanders challenge the organization and individual Soldiers to train to their full potential. By challenging Soldiers and leaders, commanders foster a can-do training culture to attain not just task standards but to attain task mastery.

The Army fights and trains as a combined arms team by training tasks and weapons conducted jointly by associated warfighting functions and functional units. The Army also trains using multiechelon training techniques capitalizing on the inherent relationships among higher, lower, and adjacent units that habitually operate together. In this way, units conduct training employing more than one echelon, multiple warfighting functions, and functional units in a manner that closely replicates how they will fight.

In operations, Soldiers and units are led by trained and qualified leaders—officers and NCOs. These leaders have a direct and decisive role in unit training. NCOs are directly responsible for training individual Soldiers, crews, and small teams. Additionally, NCOs coach other NCOs, advise senior leaders, and help develop junior officers. Leaders implement a strong chain of command, high ésprit de corps, and good discipline. As the unit trains, leaders mentor, guide, listen to, and offer solutions by thinking with subordi-nates to challenge their depth of knowledge and understanding. Commanders ensure their subordinates know how to think instead of what to think. This type of training builds trust among Soldiers and between Soldiers and their leaders. Commanders develop their subordinates' confidence and empower them to make independent, situational-based decisions. Ultimately, commanders aim to develop subordinates who have agile and adaptive mindsets that easily translate to operations.

Train to Standard

The Army is task and standards based as it trains. Through mission analysis, leaders at every level identify the right tasks to train with their associated standards. A standard is the minimum proficiency required to accomplish a task under a specified set of conditions. The goal in training is achieving task mastery, not just proficiency. Task mastery means Soldiers and units can perform a task to standard repeatedly under increasingly challenging, stressful, and varying conditions. Soldiers and units rarely achieve task standards on the first attempt or even after a few initial attempts. Leaders continually vary task conditions and conduct multiple iterations of task execution to make achieving standards more challenging. This technique builds Soldiers' confidence that they can perform tasks under the most demanding conditions.

Leaders know and enforce standards. Standards include measures of performance leaders use to evaluate the ability of individuals and organizations to accomplish tasks. Standards are found in current doctrine and other Army approved and published materials. These products provide leaders with basic principles and correct tactics, techniques, and procedures so training is done to standard. Standards also provide Soldiers and leaders with a common framework of understanding including terminology and symbology. Doctrine establishes standard operating procedures so units and Soldiers can rapidly adjust when operating anywhere in the world and in challenging operational environments. Leaders and Soldiers find current Army doctrine at the Army Publishing Directorate (known as APD) website (https://armypubs.army.mil/).

Leaders train to standard, not to time by allocating sufficient time to train tasks to standard. When the unit achieves task standards in less time than expected, it can conduct more iterations of the task by changing the conditions, moving on to the next task, or moving on to a more complex task. Good leaders understand that they cannot train on everything; therefore, they focus on training the most important tasks. Leaders do not accept substandard performance. They prefer units to train a few tasks to standard over training many tasks below standard. Achieving the standard may require repeating tasks or restarting a training event when appropriate. Leaders always allocate time for retraining tasks during training events.

Train to Sustain

Sustaining unit training proficiencies takes solid planning and insightful execution. Unit proficiencies naturally fluctuate because of the many factors that cause task atrophy. These factors include training frequency, key personnel turnover, new equipment fielding, and resource constraints. Leaders work to sustain training proficiencies within a band of excellence. This common sense approach precludes significant fluctuations in task and weapon proficiencies that would require excessive time and resources to regain. Sustaining training proficiency within a band of excellence is the key to consistent performance and combat readiness.

Train to Maintain

Maintenance is essential for continuous operations and is an integral component of unit training. Maintenance includes maintaining personnel, equipment, and systems over extended periods. Leaders create conditions that require units to do this as they train. Maintenance training is designed to keep equipment in the fight and ensures Soldiers are expert in its use. Training to maintain personal and unit equipment is fundamental to ensuring that units retain capabilities and accomplish missions. Units train maintenance tasks continuously according to Army standards under a variety of conditions that replicate the challenges of combat operations.

Additionally, individual and unit maintenance tasks represent important training opportunities that leaders must exploit. Disciplined units conduct disciplined maintenance to Army standards in garrison, during training, and when deployed. Training to maintain also means leaders train subordinates to be good stewards of Army resources. Building a sense of stewardship and frugality conditions leaders and units to operate more effectively in austere operational conditions.

VI. Readiness through Training

Ref: ADP 3-0, Operations (Jul '19), pp. 1-12 to 1-13. See also pp. 2-34 to 2-35.

Training is the most important thing the Army does to prepare for operations. It is the cornerstone of combat readiness and the foundation for successful operations. Effective training must be commander driven, rigorous, realistic, and to the standard and under the conditions that units expect to operate in during combat. Realistic training with limited time and resources demands that commanders focus their unit training efforts to maximize repetitions under varying conditions to build proficiency. Units execute effective individual and collective training based on the Army's principles of training as described in ADP 7-0. Through training and leader development, units achieve the tactical and technical competence that builds confidence and allows them to conduct successful operations across the competition continuum. Achieving this competence requires specific, dedicated training on offensive, defensive, and stability or defense support of civil authorities (DSCA) tasks. Training continues in deployed units to sustain skills and to adapt to changes in an operational environment. (See ADP 7-0 for training doctrine.)

Army training includes a system of techniques and standards that allows Soldiers and units to determine, acquire, and practice necessary skills. The Army's training system emphasizes experiential practice and learning to build teamwork and cohesion within units. It recognizes that Soldiers ultimately fight for one another and their units. Training instills discipline. It conditions Soldiers to operate within the law of war and rules of engagement. Training prepares unit leaders for the harsh reality of land combat by emphasizing the fluid and disorderly conditions inherent in land operations. Effective training accounts for cyberspace, space, and information-related capabilities that influence the warfighting functions. Well-rounded training includes candid assessments, after action reviews, and applied lessons learned to ensure improved readiness. Adversaries assess the training readiness of Army forces continuously, which is how training helps to shape operational environments. Training creates combat credibility, which contributes to deterrence.

Regardless of the importance of technological capabilities, success in operations requires Soldiers to accomplish the mission. Demanding operational environments require professional Soldiers and leaders whose character, commitment, and competence represent the foundation of a values-based, trained, and ready Army. Soldiers and leaders adapt and learn while training to perform tasks both individually and collectively. Soldiers and leaders develop the ability to exercise judgment and disciplined initiative under stress.

The complexity of integrating all unified action partners into operations demands that Army forces maintain a high degree of proficiency that is difficult to achieve quickly.

U.S. responsibilities are global and Army forces prepare to operate in any environment. Because Army forces face diverse threats and mission requirements, commanders adjust their training priorities based on a likely operational environment. As units prepare for deployment, commanders adapt training priorities and conditions to best address tasks required by actual or anticipated operations. The Army as a whole trains to be flexible enough to operate successfully across the range of military operations. Units train to be agile enough to adapt quickly and shift focus across the competition continuum.

Refer to AODS6-1 (w/SMARTupdate 1): The Army Operations & Doctrine SMARTbook (Guide to FM/ADP 3-0 Operations & the Elements of Combat Power). Completely updated with the Jul 2019 ADPs, Chg 1 to the 400-pg AODS6 includes operations (ADP 3-0), large-scale combat operations (FM 3-0 w/Chg 1), and refocused chapters on the elements of combat power: command & control (ADP 6-0), movement and maneuver (ADPs 3-90, 3-07, 3-28, 3-05), intelligence (ADP 2-0), fires (ADP 3-19), sustainment (ADP 4-0), & protection (ADP 3-37).

II. Training Proficiency & Battle Focus

Ref: FM 7-0, Train to Win in a Complex World (Oct '16), chap 1

The Army trains to win in a complex world. To fight and win in a chaotic, ambiguous, and complex environment, the Army trains to provide forces ready to conduct unified land operations. The Army does this by conducting tough, realistic, and challenging training. Unit and individual training occurs all the time—at home station, at combat training centers, and while deployed.

Army forces face threats that will manifest themselves in combinations of conventional and irregular forces, including insurgents, terrorists, and criminals. Some threats will have access to sophisticated technologies such as night vision systems, unmanned systems (aerial and ground), and weapons of mass destruction. Some threats will merge cyberspace and electronic warfare capabilities to operate from disparate locations. Additionally, they may hide among the people or in complex terrain to thwart the Army's conventional combat overmatch. Adding to this complexity is continued urbanization and the threat's access to social media. This complex environment will therefore require future Soldiers to train to perform at the highest levels possible.

Principles of Training

- **Train As You Fight**
- **Training Is Commander Driven**
- **Training Is Led By Trained Officers and Noncommissioned Officers (NCOs)**
- **Train To Standard**
- **Train Using Appropriate Standard**
- **Training Is Protected**
- **Training Is Resourced**
- **Train To Sustain**
- **Train To Maintain**
- **Training Is Multiechelon and Combined Arms**

Ref: FM 7-0 (Oct '16), p. 1-4 provides this list of training principles. The newer ADP 7-0 (2019) narrows the list to four (primary) training principles. See p. 5-6.

Training is the most important thing the Army does to prepare for operations. Training is the cornerstone of readiness. Readiness determines our Nation's ability to fight and win in a complex global environment. To achieve a high degree of readiness, the Army trains in the most efficient and effective manner possible. Realistic training with limited time and resources demands that commanders focus their unit training efforts to maximize training proficiency.

I. Training Proficiency

Proficiency in individual, leader, and collective tasks is measured against published standards. Proficiency is recognized as complete task proficiency, advanced task proficiency, basic task proficiency, limited task proficiency, and cannot perform the task.

A. Sustaining Proficiency - the Band of Excellence

A unit's training readiness is directly tied to its training proficiency. That proficiency naturally fluctuates over time and in response to various factors. Each unit encounters and adjusts to these factors, including training frequency, key personnel turnover, new equipment fielding, and resource constraints. Well-trained units seek to minimize significant variances in achieved training proficiency over time. This is training in a band of excellence. This common sense approach precludes deep valleys in proficiency that occur when units lose their training proficiency. Failing to sustain proficiency requires more resources and time to retrain the unit. Training within a band of excellence is the key to sustaining long-range training readiness.

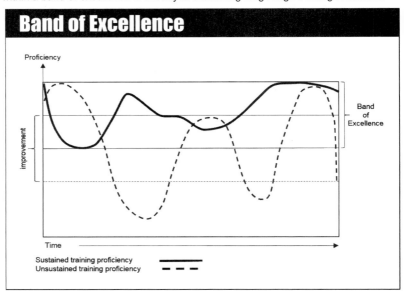

Ref: FM 7-0 (Oct '16), fig. 1-1. Sustaining proficiency within a band of excellence.

Effective commanders take the unit from a training start point, attain the required training proficiency, and maintain that proficiency over time. Once training proficiency is attained, the unit strives to maintain that proficiency within a band of excellence. The commander who understands factors that negatively affect training proficiency can better plan so that unit training skills do not atrophy to a less than acceptable level.

To adjust to the anticipated highs and lows of training proficiency, commanders continually assess training plans and strategies to keep the unit mission-ready over long periods. This assessment may cover individual memory degradation, skill degradation, unit personnel turnover, changes in crew assignments, and changes in key leadership. Maintaining high levels of proficiency may prove more difficult than building proficiency from a training start point. By understanding and predicting the factors that affect training proficiency, commanders can mitigate those effects and maintain higher levels of training readiness longer.

Training Proficiency Ratings

Ref: FM 7-0, Train to Win in a Complex World (Oct '16), p. 1-2.

The proficiency ratings are as follows:

- T is fully trained (complete task proficiency).
- T- is trained (advanced task proficiency).
- P is practiced (basic task proficiency).
- P- is marginally practiced (limited task proficiency).
- U is untrained (cannot perform the task).

T (Fully Trained)

A T proficiency rating means a unit is fully trained. It has attained task proficiency to the Army standard, achieved a GO in 90% or more of both performance measures and leader performance measures, and has met 100% of all critical performance measures. The task is externally evaluated and meets the remaining requirements as outlined in the training and evaluation outline (T&EO) in accordance with the objective task evaluation criteria matrix. (See appendix B for a detailed explanation of the objective task evaluation criteria matrix.)

T- (Trained)

A T- proficiency rating means a unit is trained. It has attained advanced task proficiency free of significant shortcomings, achieved a GO in 80% or more of both performance measures and leader performance measures, and has met 100% of all critical performance measures. The unit's shortcomings require minimal training to meet the Army standard. The task is externally evaluated and meets the remaining requirements as outlined in the T&EO in accordance with the objective task evaluation criteria matrix.

P (Practiced)

A P proficiency rating means a unit is practiced. It has attained basic task proficiency with shortcomings, achieved a GO in 65% or more of all performance measures, achieved 80% or more of all leader performance measures, and has met 100% of all critical performance measures. The unit's shortcomings require significant training to meet the Army standard. The task is not externally evaluated and meets the remaining requirements as outlined in the T&EO in accordance with the objective task evaluation criteria matrix.

P- (Marginally Practiced)

A P- proficiency rating means a unit is marginally practiced. It has attained limited task proficiency with major shortcomings, achieved a GO in 51% or more of all performance measures, achieved less than 80% of all leader performance measures, and has met less than 100% of all critical performance measures. The unit's shortcomings require complete retraining of the task to achieve the Army standard. The task is not externally evaluated and does not meet the remaining requirements as outlined in the T&EO in accordance with the objective task evaluation criteria matrix.

U (Untrained)

A U proficiency rating means a unit is untrained. The unit cannot perform the task. It achieved a GO in less than 51% of all performance measures, less than 80% in all leader performance measures, and less than 100% in all critical performance measures. The unit requires complete training on the task to achieve the Army standard.

B. Top-Down/Bottom-Up Approach to Training

A top-down/bottom-up approach to training reflects a team effort with commanders and their subordinate leaders. Commanders provide top-down guidance in the training focus, direction, and resources while subordinate leaders provide feedback on unit task proficiency, identify needed training resources, and execute training to standard. This team effort helps maintain training focus, establishes training priorities, and enables effective communication between command echelons.

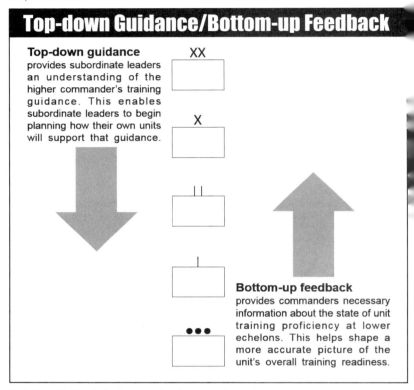

Top-down Guidance/Bottom-up Feedback

Top-down guidance provides subordinate leaders an understanding of the higher commander's training guidance. This enables subordinate leaders to begin planning how their own units will support that guidance.

Bottom-up feedback provides commanders necessary information about the state of unit training proficiency at lower echelons. This helps shape a more accurate picture of the unit's overall training readiness.

Ref: FM 7-0 (Oct '16), fig. 1-2. Top-down training guidance and bottom-up feedback.

Training guidance flows from the top down and results in subordinate units' identification of specific collective and individual tasks that support the higher unit's mission. Subordinates provide bottom-up feedback. This input from the bottom up identifies the current state of training proficiency for collective and individual tasks at lower echelons. This input helps the commander objectively determine unit training readiness.

C. Training Subordinates in Mission Command

Mission command is the exercise of authority and direction by the commander using mission orders to enable disciplined initiative within the commander's intent to empower agile and adaptive leaders in the conduct of unified land operations (ADP 6-0). As the Army's philosophy of command, mission command emphasizes that command is essentially a human endeavor. Successful commanders understand that their leadership directs the development of teams and helps establish mutual trust and shared understanding throughout the force. Commanders provide clear guidance that directs subordinates' actions while promoting freedom of action and initiative.

Subordinates, by understanding the commander's guidance and the overall common objective, can adapt to rapidly changing situations and exploit fleeting opportunities. They are given the latitude to accomplish assigned tasks in a manner that best fits the situation. Commanders influence the situation and provide direction and guidance while synchronizing operations. Likewise, subordinates understand they have an obligation to act and synchronize their actions with the rest of the force. Commanders encourage subordinates to take action, accept prudent risks to create opportunity, and seize the initiative.

To exercise mission command successfully during operations, leaders in units understand, foster, and frequently practice the principles of mission command during training. Using these principles during training enables subordinates to overcome obstacles. The principles of mission command apply to all levels of command.

Commanders aggressively train to overcome institutional obstacles that the Army's operational pace and personnel turbulence present. These obstacles can include frequent deployments of an organization comprised of units that have not trained together, personnel turbulence caused by operational commitments, and constrained financial resources. In particular, training creates common and shared experiences that increase trust and allow commands to acquire competence in mutual understanding. This training builds teams who can communicate explicitly and implicitly, conduct decentralized operations, and achieve unity of effort in uncertain situations.

II. The Role of Leaders

All unit leaders are responsible for quality training. Primary roles involve training subordinate leaders and developing teams.

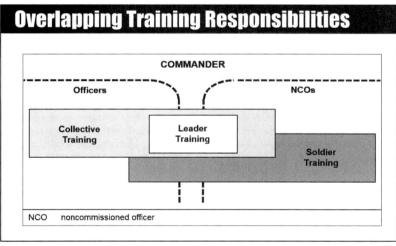

Ref: FM 7-0 (Oct '16), fig. 1-3. Overlapping training responsibilities.

Train and Develop Subordinate Leaders

Successful leaders build cohesive organizations with a strong chain of command, high ésprit de corps, and good discipline. As the unit trains, leaders mentor, guide, listen to, and think with subordinates to challenge their subordinates' depth of knowledge and understanding. These actions build trust among Soldiers and between Soldiers and their leaders. Commanders ensure that their subordinates know how to think instead of what to think. They develop their subordinates' confidence and empower them to make independent, situational-based decisions. Effective commanders develop subordinates with agile and adaptive approaches to problem solving that more easily translate to operations.

Leader Roles in Training (Overview)

Ref: FM 7-0, Train to Win in a Complex World (Oct '16), pp. 1-5 to 1-7.

A. Commanders

In addition to the unit commander's activities—understand, visualize, describe, direct, lead, and assess—in training, commanders at all echelons fulfill their role in unit training with their continuous attention, physical presence, and energy to—

Develop and Communicate a Clear Vision

Published training guidance provides the vision, direction, purpose, and motivation necessary to prepare individuals and organizations to win. It is based on a comprehensive understanding of—

- Task proficiencies to attain—the what to train.
- Commander's guidance.
- Operational environments.
- Organizational and personnel strengths and weaknesses.
- The training environment.

Personally Engage in Training

Commanders are engaged in every aspect of training. Commanders are physically present to the maximum extent possible during the planning for and execution of training. As stewards of the Army Profession, they effectively resource training and protect subordinates' training time. They create a sense of stability throughout the organization by protecting approved training plans from training distracters. Commanders are responsible for executing the approved training to standard. Effective commanders provide timely, valuable feedback to all participants.

Demand Training Standards Be Achieved

Leaders anticipate that units may not perform some tasks to standard. When designing the training calendar, leaders allow time during training events for additional training for those tasks not performed to standard. It is better to train to standard on a limited number of tasks rather than attempt and fail to achieve the standard on too many tasks. Soldiers will remember the enforced standard, not the one that leaders discussed. Leaders cannot assume that time will be available to train to standard next time. Rationalizing that corrective action will occur during some later training period sets units up for failure rather than success.

Foster a Positive Training Culture

Commanders create a training culture that listens to and rewards subordinates who are bold and innovative leaders and trainers. Commanders challenge the organization and each individual to train to their full potential. Such a challenge fosters a training culture so that organizations and individuals strive to not just attain task standards but to attain higher levels of task mastery.

Limit Training Distracters

Commanders plan and resource training events while limiting potential distractions. They ensure participation by the maximum number of Soldiers. Although commanders cannot ignore administrative support burdens, commanders can manage those burdens using an effective time management system. Additionally, commanders must support subordinates' efforts to train effectively by managing training distracters and reinforcing the requirement for all assigned personnel to be present during training.

Enforce a Top-Down/Bottom-Up Approach to Training

Senior commanders provide the lead in a top-down/bottom-up approach to training. Commanders provide the training focus, direction, and resources, while subordinate leaders provide feedback on unit training proficiency, identify specific training needs, and execute training to standard. This team effort maintains training focus, establishes training priorities, and enables effective communication between command echelons.

Training guidance flows from the top down and results in subordinate units' identification of the individual and collective tasks that support the higher unit's mission. Input from the bottom up is essential because it identifies training needs to achieve task proficiency. Leaders at all echelons communicate with each other about requirements as well as about planning, preparing, executing, and assessing training.

Commanders centralize planning to provide a consistent training focus from the top to the bottom of the organization. They decentralize execution to promote subordinate leaders' initiative to train their units. Commanders do not relinquish their responsibilities to supervise training, develop leaders, and provide feedback.

See ADRP 7-0 for more on the commander's activities in training.

B. Noncommissioned Officers

The NCO Corps has an enduring and foundational role in unit training. NCOs are responsible for the individual training of Soldiers, crews, and small teams. NCOs conduct standards-based, performance-oriented, battle-focused training. They—

- Identify specific individual, crew, and small-team tasks that support the unit's collective mission-essential tasks (METs).
- Plan, prepare, and execute training.
- Evaluate training and conduct after action reviews (AARs) to provide feedback to the commander on individual, crew, and small-team proficiency.
- Fulfill an important role by assisting in the professional development of the officer corps.

C. Unit Leaders

In addition to the commander and NCO roles and responsibilities, all leaders must require their subordinates to understand and perform their roles in training. The commander assigns primary responsibility to officers for collective training and to NCOs for Soldier training. The commander is responsible to meld leader and Soldier training requirements into collective training events using multiechelon techniques. Additionally, all leaders must—

- Train the combined arms team to be proficient on its METs. This includes training Soldiers, leaders, subordinate units, and supporting elements. Proficiency requires training the leader with the unit. Additionally, leaders pay special attention to training newly assigned lieutenants and sergeants as they train with their platoons as well as to newly promoted sergeants as they train with their sections, squads, teams, and crews.
- Centralize training planning to maintain unit focus on the mission.
- Decentralize execution to allow subordinate leaders the flexibility to focus training on their units' strengths and weaknesses.
- Establish effective communications at all levels.
- Talk to and exchange information with other leaders. Guidance on missions and priorities flows down while Soldier, leader, and collective training requirements flow up. Training meetings, briefings, and AARs serve as the primary forums for exchanging training information among leaders.
- Demand units achieve training standards.

Effective Army leaders develop others and conduct team building. Holistic leader development plans contribute to unit cohesion, resilience, and agility by producing teams and leaders that are creative, life-long learners, adaptable, fully committed to the Army profession, and capable of exercising mission command.

Develop Cohesive and Effective Teams

Teamwork is the essence of how the Army operates. The Army trains confident and proficient individual Soldiers but employs them as teams that work together to meet every mission requirement and to overcome every obstacle. Whether training as a team of two Soldiers or as a large combined arms team, developing and encouraging teamwork in training sets the foundation for operating when deployed. Commanders instill and encourage teamwork as training is planned, prepared, executed, and assessed.

See chap. 4, Army Team Building.

III. Battle Focus

A battle-focused unit trains selectively. It cannot train to standard on every task at once, whether due to time, or other resource constraints. A unit that attempts to train to proficiency all the tasks it could perform only serves to diffuse its training effort. A unit that simultaneously trains to all its capabilities at once will most likely never achieve a T or T-in all those tasks. Focusing on the tasks to train, based on the higher commander's guidance, and taking into account that time and resources are limited, is battle-focused training.

The battle focus concept involves understanding the responsibility for and the links between the collective METs and the individual tasks that support them. Figure 1-4 depicts the relationships and the proper sequence to derive optimum training benefits from each training opportunity.

The commander and command sergeant major—or first sergeant—coordinate the METs, collective tasks, and individual tasks on which the unit will focus during a given period. The command sergeant major or first sergeant identifies the supporting individual tasks for each collective task. The unit's Combined Arms Training Strategy (CATS) provides a resource for this coordination. The CATS contains a comprehensive listing of all collective tasks cross-referenced to supporting individual tasks by task number and title. Although NCOs have the primary role in training and sustaining individual Soldier skills, officers at every level are responsible for training to established standards during both individual and collective training. Commanders apply a battle focus to training for all capabilities or missions across the range of operations.

A. Mission-Essential Task (MET)

Commanders rarely have enough time or resources to complete all necessary tasks. Each commander has to determine what is essential and then assign responsibility for accomplishment. The concept of METs provides the commander a process to provide the unit its battle focus. *See facing page.*

Standardized Mission-Essential Task List (METL)

For company and larger units with a TOE, the applicable proponent develops the unit METL. This METL is referred to as the unit's standardized METL throughout this publication. It is developed and standardized by the responsible proponent; staffed with the Army commands and Army Service component commands; approved and published by the Headquarters, Department of the Army; and available on ATN. The unit's standardized METL is based on its echelon and design capabilities.

Non-Standardized METL Development

Not all Army units have a standardized METL. For company and larger units without a standardized METL (for example, a unit based on a TDA), the unit commander conducts a mission analysis, develops the unit METs, and has these approved by the next higher commander. The unit then publishes the METs and a METL in the

Mission-Essential Task (MET)

Ref: FM 7-0, Train to Win in a Complex World (Oct '16), pp. 1-8 to 1-9.

Commanders rarely have enough time or resources to complete all necessary tasks. Each commander has to determine what is essential and then assign responsibility for accomplishment. The concept of METs provides the commander a process to provide the unit its battle focus. A mission-essential task is a collective task on which an organization trains to be proficient in its designed capabilities or assigned mission. A mission-essential task list is a tailored group of mission-essential tasks. Each MET aligns with the collective tasks that support it. All company and higher units have a mission-essential task list (METL). Units based on a table of organization and equipment (TOE) have an approved and standardized METL based on the type of unit by echelon. Standardized METLs can be found on the Army Training Network (ATN), Digital Training Management System (DTMS), and CATS. Units that do not have a standardized METL—like a unit based on a table of distribution and allowances (TDA)—develop its METs and METL.

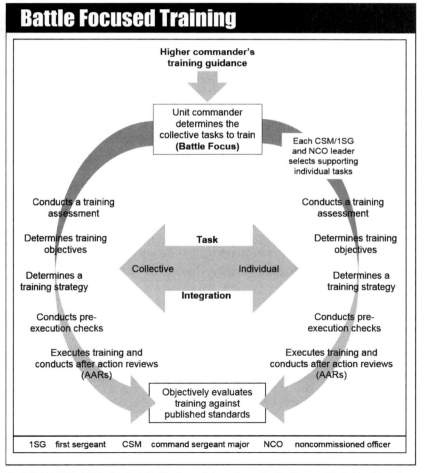

Battle Focused Training

Ref: FM 7-0 (Oct '16), fig. 1-4. Battle focus integration of collective and individual training.

DTMS. When no collective tasks exist for a TDA unit, the unit commander develops the METs and supporting collective tasks, develops the conditions and standards for the task, and has these approved by the next higher commander.

B. Battle Task

A battle task is a collective task on which a platoon or lower echelon trains that supports a company MET. A battle task can include any associated supporting collective tasks. Battle tasks are approved by the company commander. Platoon and lower echelons do not have METs or a METL. Based on the company METs and METL, the platoon leader—with the platoon sergeant—conducts a mission analysis to determine the platoon battle tasks that best support the company METs.

C. Planning Framework

Senior commanders, as stewards of the Army Profession, provide the necessary resources to train, including time, and protect subordinate units from unprogrammed taskings or other training distractions. They publish training guidance (that includes a calendar) to give subordinate commanders adequate time to properly plan and resource training.

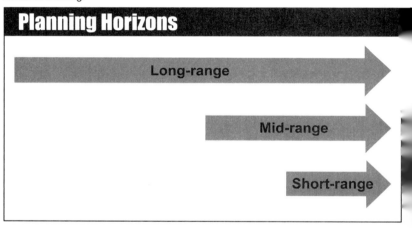

Planning Horizons

Long-range

Mid-range

Short-range

Ref: FM 7-0 (Oct '16), fig. 1-5. Planning horizons for training. See pp. 6-4 to 6-8 for further discussion of planning horizons from ADP 7-0.

IV. Training Environment

Units obtain effective training when they create a realistic and challenging training environment. A training environment is an environment comprised of conditions, supporting resources, and time that enables training tasks to proficiency. An effective training environment enables an individual or a unit to achieve proficiency in the individual and collective tasks trained. The commander sets the conditions of the tasks selected to train with as much realism as possible. Supporting resources provide the tools that enable modifying those conditions to be more challenging and complex for Soldiers and the entire unit. Commanders leverage available resources, to include the mix of live, virtual, and constructive (LVC) training enablers. When used properly, resources create a powerful training multiplier that more closely replicate an actual operational environment. The time available to train is often one aspect of the training environment of which there is never enough. Training within the limits of the planning horizon drives when the unit or individual is expected to be proficient in the tasks selected to train. Careful development of a training environment can produce exceptional results and ultimately increase training readiness.

See pp. 6-28 to 6-29 and 7-4 to 7-6 for discussion on creating realism in training.

III. Training for Battle Rhythm

Ref: FM 7-0, Train to Win in a Complex World (Oct '16), pp. 1-11 to 1-20.

Commanders integrate and synchronize training activities, meetings, briefings, conferences, and reports among their subordinates and with their higher commander. Commanders establish training for a unit's battle rhythm. Battle rhythm is a deliberate cycle of command, staff, and unit activities intended to synchronize current and future operations (FM 6-0). In the context of unit training, establishing a battle rhythm helps sequence the activities, events, and actions that regulate the flow and sharing of information that supports the training process. Effectively training for battle rhythm—

- Facilitates and establishes interactions related to training among the commander, staff, and subordinate units.
- Establishes a routine for staff interactions and coordination.
- Facilitates planning by the staff and decision making by the commander.

Training for a unit's battle rhythm consists of conducting periodic meetings and briefings, meeting report requirements, and experiencing other activities synchronized by time and purpose. These activities and products include, but are not limited to—

- Publishing command training guidance (CTG).
- Training meetings.
- T-Week concept.
- Training briefings.
- Installation training resource synchronization conferences.
- Commanders' dialogues.
- Time management cycles.
- UTP calendars.
- Company training schedules.
- Planning horizons (long, mid, and short).

The unit commander, in conjunction with the higher commander's guidance, establishes and enforces the training for the unit's battle rhythm. These activities are heavily influenced by policy, doctrine, unit standard operating procedures (SOPs), and training priorities established by the higher commander. All unit leaders understand and comply with the activities that comprise the training rhythm.

Training Plans Tied to Resources Needed to Train

Without the right resources, effective training will not occur. Available resources directly affect unit training readiness. Each commander and staff understands the resource coordination and synchronization cycle on the installation on which units conduct training. Commanders and staffs coordinate and synchronize procedures for the normal classes of supply; training aids, devices, simulators, and simulations (TADSS); integrated training environment (ITE) considerations and resources; and available training facilities. At a home station, all training resources are limited and shared with other units on the installation. Commanders and staffs aware of an installation's resource cycle are more likely to secure the right training resources when they are needed to train.

I. Published Training Guidance (CTG/UTP) (Training for Battle Rhythm in Units)

Ref: FM 7-0, Train to Win in a Complex World (Oct '16), pp. 1-11 to 1-14.

So that commanders and units have sufficient time to plan and coordinate long-range training, senior commanders publish CTG. Published guidance communicates their train ing and readiness priorities throughout the command and provides subordinates sufficie time to develop and resource training that supports that guidance. Publication of the CT establishes the unit's training for battle rhythm when it is not deployed on operations.

See p. 6-17 for discussion of CTG.

For the Regular Army and Reserve Component, each successive echelon publishes the nested CTG. For division and higher units, the format of the CTG is at the commander's discretion. For brigade and below units, the format is the UTP operation order (OPORD A published CTG always includes the corresponding training calendar.

See pp. 6-37 to 6-40 for further discussion of UTP operation order (OPORD).

The timelines in table 1-1 provide guidance for when CTG or UTPs are published by echelon for the Regular Army. This separation by echelon ensures that long-range planni and guidance is timely and allows each command to conduct parallel and collaborative planning across the force. It also ensures that crucial training resources needed to train are identified well in advance and are available at the start of training. Table 1-2 shows th same information for the Reserve Component (known as RC). Note that Regular Army ar Reserve Component units' CTG planning horizons significantly differ. For example, a Reg lar Army division commander's long-range planning horizon is two years, whereas a like echelon Reserve Component unit commander's long-range planning horizon is five years

Echelon	Publishes CTG with calendar NLT[1]:	Planning horizon
Corps	12 months prior to training start	2 years
Division	10 months prior to training start	2 years
Installation	10 months prior to training start (calendar only)	1 year
Brigade	8 months prior to training start	1 year
Battalion[2]	6 months prior to training start	1 year

[1] Publication dates also apply to similar command-level TDA organizations or activities. For example, a TRADOC COE normally commanded by a major general follows the same planning cycle as a division commander.

[2] Companies develop and publish their own UTP. The battalion commander, in collaboration with subordinate company commanders and the battalion staff may develop a consolidated battalion UTP.

COE	center of excellence	TDA	table of distribution and allowances
CTG	command training guidance	TRADOC	Training and Doctrine Command
NLT	no later than	UTP	unit training plan

Ref: FM 7-0 (Oct '16), table 1-1. Regular Army long-range planning by echelon.

Echelon	Publishes CTG with calendar NLT[1]:	Planning horizon
Flag officer CMD, separate brigade, regiment or group	18 months prior to training start	5 years
Brigade or separate battalion	10 months prior to training start	5 years
Battalion[2]	6 months prior to training start	2-3 years

1 These actions also apply to similar command-level TDA organizations or activities. For example, a regional support command, commanded by a major general follows the same planning cycle as a division commander.

2 Companies develop and publish their own UTP and calendar. The battalion commander, in collaboration with subordinate company or troop commanders, and the battalion staff may consolidated a battalion UTP.

CMD	command	TDA	table of distribution and allowances
CTG	command training guidance	UTP	unit training plan
NLT	no later than		

Ref: FM 7-0 (Oct '16), table 1-2. Reserve Component long-range planning by echelon.

within a brigade, on receipt of a division CTG, the brigade commander begins mission analysis to determine how best to meet the division commander's guidance. Adhering the concept of collaborative and parallel planning, each subordinate unit also begins the same process to begin formulating how each echelon will support the higher commander's guidance. Effective collaborative planning ensures that each echelon publishes plans well prior to the start of training. Because training relies on units having the right resources available at the right time, collaborative planning begins early enough in the planning cycle so units have the resources to train when they need them.

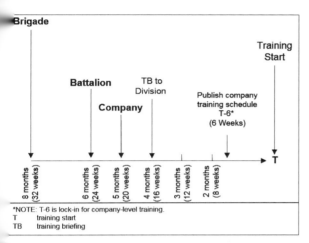

*NOTE: T-6 is lock-in for company-level training.
T   training start
TB   training briefing

Ref: FM 7-0 (Oct '16), fig. 1-6. UTP publication timelines within a notional Regular Army brigade.

In figure 1-6, the timelines are by echelon within a Regular Army notional brigade. Figure 1-7 shows the publication timelines with a notional Reserve Component flag officer command. These timelines allow sufficient planning and publication time for each successive command to issue its UTP. They also allow sufficient time for collaborative planning, parallel planning, and coordination of resources prior to the start of training.

Six weeks from the start of training, the company not only publishes its training schedule, but it also locks in company-level training (for the Reserve Component, this occurs three months or 90 days from the start of training [see figure 1-7]). Any changes to the approved company training are not authorized past this time unless approved by the next higher commander.

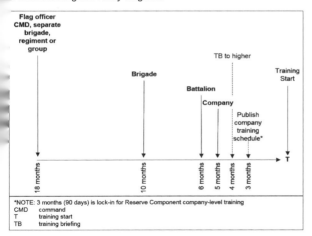

*NOTE: 3 months (90 days) is lock-in for Reserve Component company-level training.
CMD   command
T   training start
TB   training briefing

Ref: FM 7-0 (Oct '16), fig. 1-7. UTP publication timelines within a notional Reserve Component flag officer command.

See pp. 6-49 to 6-72 for discussion of training schedules (T-Week concept).

II. Army Training Management System (ATMS

The Army Training Management System (ATMS) is the Army enterprise program automating management of unit and individual training. ATMS consists of Web-based applications and centralized databases: ATN, CATS, and DTMS. The ATMS suite of applications automates routine command, unit, institution, and individual training and processes.

ATMS enablers directly support ADP 7-0, ADRP 7-0, this publication, and other relevant Army doctrine and policy guidance. The centrally managed enterprise data bases—such as the individual training record—organize, store, and make available data for displays, reports, queries, and data sharing. Though centrally managed, the data collected from the ATMS belong to the commander. See the ATN for details on ATMS.

The ATN provides a single, Web-based portal with links to Army training doctrine, processes, and resources used by Army units. As a collaborative, online resource, the ATN relies on input from units and Soldiers. It is also the primary access point for CATS and DTMS. The ATN is also home to all published standardized METLs. The ATN is accessible at https://atn.army.mil. Users can access the ATN via an Army-issued common access card (known as CAC) and via the defense system log on with the appropriate credentials.

CATS provide training strategies that are—

- Recommended by proponent.
- Based on tasks.
- Driven by events.
- Holistic.
- Focused on the METL (TOE units).

The strategies are based on analysis of the missions, functions, and capabilities as stated in the unit's TOE and the proponent-generated unit task list (known as UTL). CATSs utilize task sets as the primary building blocks of the UTP. Task sets are groups of collective tasks selected to be trained together that are necessary for a unit to achieve proficiency in a given capability or function. Task sets outline numerous training events using a crawl, walk, and run methodology to assist trainers to develop their UTPs. CATSs also provide the task, purpose, outcome, and execution guidance for each recommended training event. Each CATS identifies the types and frequencies of training events at the respective echelon that should be conducted to achieve proficiency. CATSs save planning time by providing descriptive, proponent-approved, and unit-vetted training strategies. Units can easily enter these strategies in DTMS as a training plan and then tailor them as needed. Users can access CATSs from the ATN homepage and DTMS at https://atn.army.mil.

DTMS automates specific training and management processes through its Web-based program. It provides the ability to digitally develop, record, and coordinate training plans within organizations as well as record training assessments, training completion, and training readiness. Users can access DTMS through ATN at https://atn.army.mil. DTMS enables leaders to perform some of the following functions:

- Review the higher commander's training guidance and disseminate other training documents.
- View and review unit METLs.
- Manage the UTP calendar.
- Manage mandatory, individual, collective, and deployment training tasks and requirements.
- Assess and record individual training records (known as ITRs) for Soldiers.
- View and update the digital job book.

III. Multiechelon Training

Ref: FM 7-0, Train to Win in a Complex World (Oct '16), pp. 1-14 to 1-15.

Multiechelon training is a training technique that allows for the simultaneous training of more than one echelon on different or complementary tasks (ADRP 7-0). As each echelon conducts its mission analysis to determine the tasks to train, it provides a logic trail from individual Soldier tasks to brigade-level METs. An effective logic trail clearly nests from one echelon to the next and effectively crosswalks the tasks up the echelons and down the echelons. Although not an integral part of planning, this task crosswalk enables leaders to visualize how the top-down training guidance directly supports the bottom-up alignment of individual and collective tasks that support the higher unit.

To illustrate this concept, see figure 1-8. In this example, an infantry brigade combat team (known as IBCT) commander focuses training on offensive operations—specifically conduct a movement to contact— and states this in the training guidance. Through mission analysis, the subordinate artillery battalion commander determines that to support a brigade movement to contact, the battalion needs to focus training on the task, Conduct Battalion Fire Missions. Likewise, other subordinate commanders do their mission analyses to determine the collective tasks on which they must focus training to support the brigade commander's guidance.

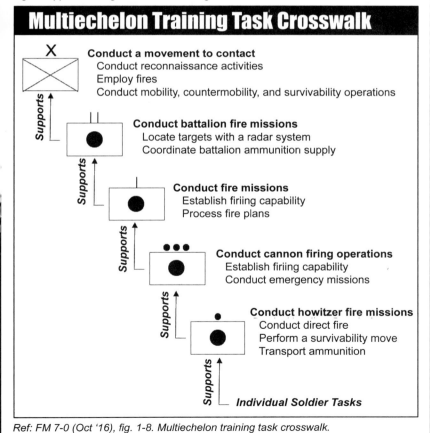

Multiechelon Training Task Crosswalk

X

Conduct a movement to contact
Conduct reconnaissance activities
Employ fires
Conduct mobility, countermobility, and survivability operations

Conduct battalion fire missions
Locate targets with a radar system
Coordinate battalion ammunition supply

Conduct fire missions
Establish firiing capability
Process fire plans

Conduct cannon firing operations
Establish firiing capability
Conduct emergency missions

Conduct howitzer fire missions
Conduct direct fire
Perform a survivability move
Transport ammunition

Individual Soldier Tasks

Ref: FM 7-0 (Oct '16), fig. 1-8. Multiechelon training task crosswalk.

Army Training

- View and update the digital small-unit leader dashboard.
- Manage the Army's electronic individual training record.
- Use the common access card (known as CAC) to sign in to large-group traini sessions.
- Enable bulk data uploads to allow units to record training completion.
- Use the Survey Tool to collect customer and user information.
- Use the Unit Individual Training Management (known as UITM) module to sup port central management of distributed individual training.

Other Supporting Training Resources

In addition to the Web-based resources available within ATMS, other additional resources provide information and access to data and knowledge to assist trainers. These include, but are not limited to the Central Army Registry (CAR) and Center fc Army Lessons Learned (known as CALL).

The CAR is a Web-based digital catalog and repository that serves as the warfight-ers' one-stop source for training-related products such as doctrine, published tasks, training circulars, training support packages, and graphic training aids. Users can first search for training products in the CAR by identification, title, and keywords, an then browse the CAR catalog by product type and proponent. The CAR is available on ATN under the Unit Training Management or myTraining tabs. Users can directly access the CAR at https://atiam.train.army.mil/catalog/dashboard.

The Center for Army Lessons Learned is the Army's source for adaptive learning based on lessons and best practices from the Army. It provides timely and relevant knowledge by using integrated systems and interactive technology. Users can ac-cess the Center for Army Lessons Learned at http://usacac.army.mil/organizations/mccoe/call.

IV. Training Resource Synchronization Conferences

The senior commander on an installation hosts periodic installation-level resource synchronization conferences. Ideally, the senior commander schedules these train-ing resource conferences every quarter (see figure 1-9). These conferences provide leaders two types of information. First, it identifies installation training resources. These resources may include training areas, ranges, ITE facilities and resources, and TADSS availability. Second, the conference shows the availability of any un-scheduled resources.

As echelons develop UTP calendars, they coordinate and requisition training re-sources. The installation-level resource synchronization conferences verify that the senior commander acknowledges and validates that units require training resources to execute training. This validation is the senior commander's endorsement that the resources will be available when needed. Effective leaders—especially at the brigade and battalion levels—must attend these conferences to prepare their training plans. At these conferences, leaders learn of locally available installation training support resources and the method to schedule for their units' training cycle. Once training requirements are identified at the company level, brigade and battalion com-manders and staff work diligently to properly resource company-level training.

The senior commander on the installation is responsible for prioritizing installation training resources (see AR 350-1). The higher commander determines the priority of units to training readiness and resources. Units with a higher priority often affect the availability of critical training resources for units with a lower priority. For example, a unit within six months of deploying has a higher priority for using ranges and training areas than a unit that is not scheduled for deployment. Knowledgeable commanders know when these conferences and meetings occur, and they ensure their unit is represented by the right leader who can make decisions on behalf of the commander.

Training Resource Synchronization (Notional)

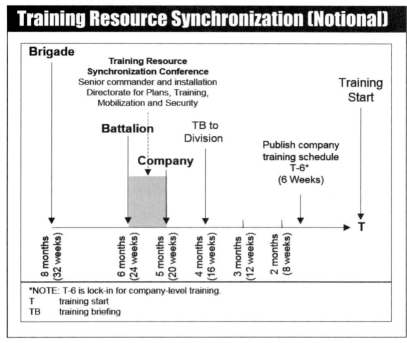

Ref: FM 7-0 (Oct '16), fig. 1-9. Notional training resource synchronization conference for a Regular Army brigade.

Note. In figure 1-9, the installation training resource synchronization conference occurs within a planning and publication window that allows for validation of training resources no later than 5 months from the start of training and prior to the training briefing. For Reserve Component units, the coordination and synchronization of training resources require an understanding and visibility of training resource conferences all installations. This is key when Regular Army and Reserve Component installations and facilities provide training resources to support UTPs.

V. Reserve Component Training Considerations

Ref: FM 7-0, Train to Win in a Complex World (Oct '16), pp. 1-18 to 1-20.

When deployed for operations, the Army executes missions as one force in conjunction with joint forces, multinational forces, and interagency organizations. Both the Regular Army and Reserve Component share the same training doctrine and procedures and train to the same standard. However, in the training environment, the planning horizons differ somewhat for Reserve Component units as does the time available to train. Geographic dispersion of units also impacts Reserve Component training. An average reserve battalion can be spread over hundreds of miles increasing the complexity for these units to accomplish training. Additionally, many reserve units must travel many miles to the nearest training area, and individual Soldiers often travel extended miles to get to their training sites.

Primary differences between Regular Army and Reserve Component training planning and activities are most evident in—

Planning Horizons

The long-, mid-, and short-range planning horizons generally have a longer duration for Reserve Component units and typically span years. For example, the long-range planning horizon (and subsequent UTP) for a Reserve Component brigade may span up to years.

For a Regular Army brigade, this would typically be 1 year (see tables 1-1 and 1-2 on p. 5-20).

Resource Coordination

Ensuring the right training resources are available at the start of training can often be problematic for Reserve Component units. These units coordinate with their own as well as Regular Army installations for training resources, facilities, and support. Additionally, Reserve Component units also coordinate training plans with other Reserve Component units and Regular Army units. Understanding the training resource cycles and conferences that occur for Reserve Component and supporting Regular Army installations requires a knowledge of—and liaison with—multiple facilities and training areas.

See fig. 1-9 on p. 5-25 and corresponding note pertaining to Reserve Component units.

Yearly Training Briefing (YTB)

To ensure that the UTP remains on track through the long-range planning horizon, Reserve Component units conduct yearly training briefings (YTBs) rather than quarterly training briefings (QTBs) conducted by Regular Army units.

For briefings pertaining to Reserve Component units, see table 1-2 on p. 5-20 and pp. 6-73 to 6-76.

T-Week Concept

For Regular Army units, T-Week activities conform to a weekly schedule. Reserve Component units typically modify this construct and follow a monthly break out of specific company-level activities. Since units can tailor these timelines and activities to its needs, many Reserve Component units establish a T-month concept using the same methodology and procedures employed by Regular Army units, but on a monthly schedule.

To illustrate how available training time affects Reserve Component units and the associated activities affect planning, preparing, executing, and assessing training, see figure 1-10 on the facing page.

See pp. 6-49 to 6-72 for discussion of the T-Week concept.

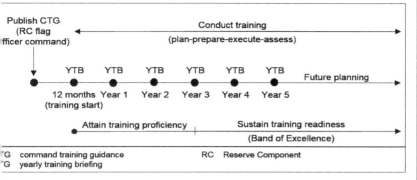

Ref: FM 7-0 (Oct '16), fig. 1-10. Notional Reserve Component unit training long-range planning horizons .

Premobilization and Postmobilization Training

Mobilization is not the starting point for planning battle focused training. Reserve Component units have premobilization readiness and postmobilization training requirements. Units must develop premobilization training plans and receive approval for the current fiscal and training year. Units integrate postmobilization training plans with the premobilization training plans and then update and receive approval for each training year as well.

Premobilization training directly links to postmobilization training. A critical objective is to identify achievable, sustainable training requirements, which provide the focus for effective premobilization unit training. Reserve Component commanders train their units to standard on established premobilization tasks.

Postmobilization expands organizational training, raises the echelon trained, and increases the amount of multiechelon and combined arms training accordingly. Units create postmobilization plans at the same time as premobilization plans. Units update postmobilization plans regularly as premobilization training and revised commanders training assessments are completed.

Premobilization Training Plans

Premobilization training focuses on company-level individual and collective tasks. Premobilization training plans identify training requirements, training events, equipment, and training support packages to attain and sustain task proficiency. The Reserve Component challenge in premobilization is to generate sufficient readiness to ensure as short a postmobilization period as possible. Sufficient readiness requires a clear linkage of tasks and time than the Regular Army. Proficiency in these tasks enables training to full METL proficiency when the unit is mobilized. The UTP includes focusing on METL tasks, to include preparation for and execution of annual training.

Postmobilization Training Plans

Postmobilization training focuses on company-level and above collective tasks. These plans identify training requirements, training events, equipment, and training support packages needed to train the unit to METL proficiency upon mobilization. Postmobilization plans are updated annually and reflect input from the execution of the premobilization plan. The commander approving the unit's METL and UTP also approves the postmobilization plan. The plan is then provided to the mobilization station commander where the postmobilization training will occur.

Installation commanders are responsible for supporting the execution of postmobilization training activities. They determine resource requirements and develop plans to support the unit reach its deployment training requirements. Reserve Component commanders conduct periodic visits with the supporting installation commander to inspect training areas and facilities, identify and resolve support challenges, and clarify and refine training support requirements.

VI. Commanders' Dialogues

Units that train the way they fight establish and maintain planning horizons. When planning horizons are sound, units can deliver quality training and achieve training readiness. Commanders who train consistently and effectively conduct training meetings routinely from company to brigade levels. These commanders also conduct commanders' dialogues to maintain battle focus and keep training on schedule. The continuous process of planning, preparing, executing, and assessing each training event of the UTP requires commanders to lead and manage the frequent and recurring series of meetings.

Discussions and dialogues between the unit and higher commander occur throughout the training process. These recurring dialogues help ensure both commanders agree with the direction and scope of unit training. The dialogues also enable the higher commander to approve the training and to ensure the necessary resources are coordinated and available when training occurs.

Commanders' dialogues are truly dialogues and intended as points of discussion between the two commanders. These dialogues provide critical decision points for both commanders while planning, preparing, executing and assessing training. Commanders can adjust training plans at these decision points, if necessary, and verify that units have critical resources when and where they are needed to train. Table illustrates when commanders' dialogues should occur.

Commanders' dialogues take place...	At this critical point...
When mission-essential tasks are discussed	Mission analysis backbrief.
When the unit training plan is briefed to the commander two levels up	Training briefing.
During training meetings	Weekly training meeting at company and battalion; monthly at brigade.
During cyclical training briefings	Quarterly training briefing (Regular Army); yearly training briefing (Reserve Component).
During external evaluations	Before, during, and after external evaluations.

Ref: FM 7-0 (Oct '16), table 1-3. Commanders' dialogue at critical points in the training process.

Planning Training (Unit Training Mgmt)

Ref: ADP 7-0, Training (Jul '19), chap. 4 and FM 7-0, Train to Win in a Complex World (Oct '16), chap 2.

. The Army Operations Process
as Framework for Unit Training)

The operations process of **plan, prepare, execute, and assess** is the framework for unit training. Units that train using the operations process as they train—as well as its terminologies, processes, and procedures—make the transition to actual operations more seamless and effective.

The Operations Process

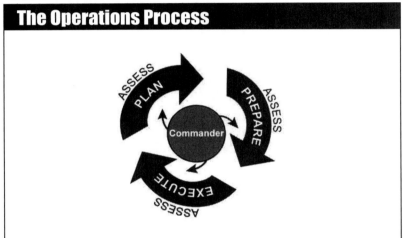

Ref: ADP 7-0 (Jul '19), fig. 4-1. The Army operations process.

The unit commander is central to unit training in the same way a commander is central to the operations process. Planning, preparing, executing, and assessing unit training does not significantly differ from conducting an operation. Each unit begins a training cycle based on training guidance from the next higher commander. The unit then develops a **long-range plan known as the Unit Training Plan (UTP)** to progressively develop and sustain training proficiencies. Before a training event begins, leaders and staff complete much work well in advance of training. Leaders prepare detailed plans, develop training objectives, and most importantly coordinate the resources necessary to train. Additionally, leaders determine who will observe the training and determine the criteria observers will use for evaluating performance. Observed training is recorded by leaders and evaluators. These recorded evaluations provide commanders an essential part of the training feedback mechanism necessary to make accurate and objective assessments of proficiency. Commanders continually assess training proficiency to ensure the unit and individual Soldiers meet task and weapon standards. Each training event involves planning for, preparing for, executing, and assessing training.

See overview on p. 6-8 for further discussion of the operations process and training. The process for developing the UTP is discussed in the remainder of this chapter.

Unit Training Management (UTM) Overview

Ref: Unit Training Management (Guide), Combined Arms Center - Training (Aug '12).

Unit Training Management (UTM) provides the how-to details of the US Army's training processes as described in Army Doctrine Publication (ADP) (Training Units and Developing Leaders, dated August 2012) and Army Doctrine Reference Publication (ADRP) 7- (Training Units and Developing Leaders, dated August 2012). UTM provides the key how-to details that bridge the doctrine and the dynamic tools (ATN/CATS/DTMS/HQ D, Standardized METL) that make planning, preparing, executing and assessing unit training possible.

The content of UTM is delivered in several ways for Soldiers to use. The primary portal to UTM is through the **Army Training Network (ATN)**. From ATN, users have access t view UTM and navigate to any part of it. There are also downloadable modules that ca be used as is, or can be unit -modified for additional instructional purposes. And finally, UTM is delivered in a book format to download, or print as needed.

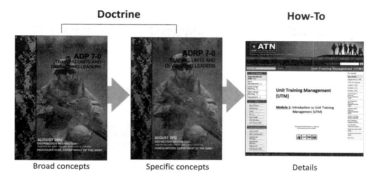

Doctrine		How-To
Broad concepts	Specific concepts	Details

UTM Resources Page

All supporting UTM resources (tutorials and examples) as well as links found in each module are available from a single source on ATN. The UTM Resources Page on ATN allows users to access all supporting UTM products without having to search within each UTM module. All UTM modules and associated products can be easily downloaded for Soldier, or unit use as needed.

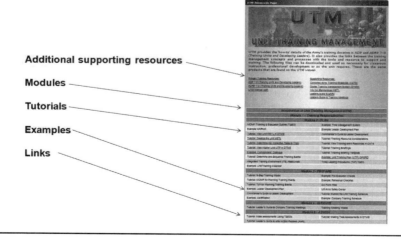

Additional supporting resources

Modules

Tutorials

Examples

Links

UTM content provides the links between the doctrine, the how-to and the web-based tools (DTMS, ATN, CATS, DTMS and HQ DA Standardized METL) that help you plan-prepare-execute and assess unit training and leader development

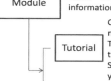

Module	Builds from ADRP concepts – more discussion, detail and information. Processes are not echelon dependent.

Tutorial	Continues the concept thread from the module with much more detail and specifics of 'how do I do this'. Tutorials are ppt and are positioned in the module where the discussion fits. Links to ATN, CATS, DTMS and HQ DA Standardized METL take you *where* you need to go – *when* you need to go there.

Example	Examples of training management products – like OPORDs, briefs, etc. Shows 'what right looks like'

Enablers

Enablers are those training resources that help commanders, leaders and training managers do the job of training units. Enablers are based on the training doctrine of ADRP 7-0 and the processes and concepts found in Unit Training Management (UTM).

As you navigate through the training processes of UTM, at the right point in any particular process, there will be links to an explanation of how these enablers help users perform a particular function, as well as a link to take the user to that resource. The 'Enablers' tab on the main navigation bar on ATN is available at anytime to go to any of the primary enablers mentioned here – as well as others that provide valuable training support.

Army Training Network (ATN)

The Army Training Network (ATN) provides a single, web-based portal to the doctrine, processes and resources for training Army units. It is a collaborative, online resource that relies on input from Soldiers and units around the world. ATN is accessible at https://atn.army.mil

Digital Training Management System (DTMS)

The Digital Training Management System (DTMS) is a web based program that provides users the ability to digitally develop, record and coordinate training plans, coordinate training plans within the organization, and assess training completion/readiness. DTMS is accessible at: https://dtms.army.mil

Combined Arms Training Strategies (CATS)

The Combined Arms Training Strategies (CATS) provide proponent recommended training strategies to align collective tasks to events and resources to help maximize effective training in the time available. CATS is accessible through ATN under the 'Enablers' tab, or at: https://atn.army.mil/dsp_CATSviewer01.aspx

HQ, Department of the Army (DA) Standardized METL Viewer

The HQ, Department of the Army (DA) Standardized METL Viewer provides an easy to navigate way to view brigade and higher level HQDA Standardized Mission Essential Task Lists (METL). In addition to viewing these METLs, user can also view the associated Task Groups (TG), as well as related collective tasks and their Training & Evaluation Outlines (T&EO). The FSO METL Viewer is available on ATN under the 'Enablers' tab, or by going to: https://atn.army.mil/fso/default.aspx

II. Planning Horizons for Training

Planning horizons for training mirror those described in ADP 5-0. The long-, mid-, and short-range planning horizons help commanders place the execution of the U in the time frames necessary to develop and sustain unit training proficiencies. Th planning horizons also assist commanders in understanding the activities, coordir tion, and planning necessary to ensure they have resources available when traini begins.

Planning for unit training follows the military decision-making process (known as t MDMP) or troop leading procedures (known as TLP). Commanders with a coordir ing staff use the military decision-making process when developing a plan; commanders of company-level and smaller units use troop leading procedures when planning training events. Planning for unit training supports the training principle: train as you fight. Leaders trained in—and proficient in—the Army's planning processes adapt more easily to planning and executing operations when deployed.

See pp. 6-11 to 6-32 for further discussion of planning for unit training using the MDMP or TLP from FM 7-0.

A. Long-Range Planning

Army units develop long-range training plans focused on developing and sustainin training proficiencies. The UTP is the unit's long-range training plan that identifies the methodology and progressive training events that build and sustain proficiency Units develop their UTP by using the Army operations process and by following tra ing guidance.

The long-range planning horizon covers a unit's training strategy spanning many months and often years (see FM 7-0 for recommended long-range planning horizo by echelon). This planning synchronizes unit efforts and supporting installation agencies so that training events can be fully resourced and executed. The long-range planning horizon is described by training guidance and graphically depicted on the unit's long-range training calendar as a primary component of the UTP. The mid-range planning horizon further refines the long-range planning horizon by detai ing the activities and coordination required for each training event. The short-range planning horizon defines the specific final actions weeks prior to and at the point of training event execution.

Training Guidance

Issuing training guidance is every commander's responsibility. It begins the process for subordinate commanders to understand and determine what tasks and weapons to train in order to support the higher command's training focus. Once guidance is received from the next higher commander, the process of mission analysis helps the unit commander determine how best to support the next higher unit and determine the collective tasks and weapons proficiencies necessary to ensure mission success. The unit commander then issues training guidance to subordinates; the guidance communicates the commander's training expectations. This communication ensures that training plans and activities are nested from one echelon to the next. Commanders issue training guidance early enough in the process to ensure subordi nates have sufficient time to plan and resource their own training effectively.

See p. 6-13 for discussion of commander's training guidance from FM 7-0.

Mission Analysis

When conducting a mission analysis, in addition to the next higher commander's training guidance, the unit commander gathers and analyzes all available information to assess the current condition of the unit's training proficiencies. Once the unit commander has identified and assessed the collective tasks and weapon qualification standards on which to train, the unit commander backbriefs the next higher commander the results of the analysis. During this dialogue, the two commanders confirm that the unit commander understands the next higher training guidance, focusing on the tasks that will be trained.

After the backbrief, the unit commander begins to develop the UTP covering the long-range planning horizon. The UTP with its associated long-range training calendar identifies the progressive training events (crawl-walk-run) for the unit to train. Subordinate commanders and leaders continue parallel and collaborative planning throughout this process as they conduct their own mission analysis and develop their UTPs to support the higher unit's capabilities or mission.

Course of Action Development

Commanders develop training courses of action by taking the results of the mission analysis and dialogue between the two commanders to formulate the best plan to train the unit. Typically, given the constraints of mission, time, and resources, a commander develops a single course of action (COA) rather than multiple COAs. COA development focuses on determining and sequencing the progressive multiechelon training events that train the selected METs and unit weapons.

Commanders and other leaders closely review known information as they develop the COAs. For organizations based on a table of organization and equipment, the combined arms training strategy (CATS) provides a starting point to begin development of a training COA. At the company level, the CATS reflects a proponent-recommended crawl-walk-run progression of training events given the METs selected to train. Additionally, each strategy provides recommendations on who, what, and how often to train. The CATS also provides fundamental planning and event information to include training aids, devices, simulators, and simulations (known as TADSS); training gates; multiechelon training events; major resources; and a purpose, outcome, and recommended execution guidance.

Planning Considerations for each Course of Action

As the commander and staff develop training COAs, they—

- Prepare the long-range calendar.
- Apply the command or installation time management cycle.
- Post the next higher unit (multiechelon) training events.
- Determine own unit training events.
- Identify training objectives for each training event.
- Use a backward planning approach using a crawl-walk-run progression of training.
- Consider the training environment for each event.
- Ensure time is programmed for subordinate units to train.

Unit Training Plan Briefing

Once the UTP is briefed to the next higher commander (company to battalion; battalion to brigade), the plan is briefed by brigade-level commanders to the division-level commander for final approval. The briefing covers the long-range planning horizon of the UTP. It normally spans years for both Regular Army and Reserve Component units. Units conduct follow-on periodic training briefings describing progression in training proficiencies on a quarterly basis in the Regular Army and annually in the Reserve Component. These quarterly or annual briefings provide commanders opportunities to describe and discuss planned training and discuss changes to the UTP if necessary

Publish the Unit Training Plan

Once the division-level commander approves the brigade level UTP, it is then published to battalions; battalions publish their UTP to companies; and companies publish their UTP to platoons. There is no UTP below company level, but platoons and below nest what they train and how they train to support company UTPs. At brigade level and below, commanders publish the UTP in the operation order form with the associated long-range training calendar.

See pp. 6-33 to 6-36 for a sample unit training plan (UTP) format.

B. Mid-Range Planning

The mid-range planning horizon focuses on preexecution planning for each training event identified in the UTP. The mid-range planning horizon is applied to each training event depending on the date training is to occur. In most cases, this is months in advance of training event execution. Training events provide the venue which individual tasks, collective tasks, and weapon systems are trained, observed and evaluated, but by themselves are not a measure of unit training proficiency. Training objectives selected for tasks trained during each training event identify the tasks trained and the desired outcome of each in terms of the task proficiencies to achieve. Effective commanders continually evaluate and assess task and leader proficiency as units execute training events. All training events are planned and executed following the Army operations process (plan, prepare, execute, and assess). Additionally, the effectiveness of training events to achieve task proficiency is evaluated and assessed after the fact to make future events better. Advance resource planning and coordination are essential to the successful execution of training events. Without the right resources available at the right point in time, meaningful and effective training will not occur and valuable training time lost.

During the mid-range planning horizon, training meetings and quarterly or yearly training briefings provide venues for the commander and unit leaders to meet periodically to ensure training event planning, resourcing, and coordination stay on track. Brigades conduct training meetings monthly whereas battalions and companies conduct them weekly. At battalion and brigade levels, training meetings focus primarily on overall training plan progress and ensure that resources for subordinate units are coordinated within the command and at the installation level. Company-level training meetings focus on the commander's assessment of the most recent training; they ensure that resources for future training is coordinated and locked-in. Training meetings also enable the commander to track and assess the progress of the UTP and to modify the plan as needed.

Quarterly / Yearly Training Briefings

Quarterly or yearly training briefings conducted during the mid-range planning horizon provide division-level commanders visibility of the progression of brigade UTPs They also provide senior commanders the opportunity to provide interim training guidance and to make training plan course corrections as necessary.

See pp. 6-73 to 6-76 for discussion of quarterly/yearly training briefings from FM 7-0

C. Short-Range Planning

As the date of training execution approaches, planners and leaders continue to monitor and coordinate actions and activities to ensure success of each training event. These final preparations ensure that proper coordination and resourcing has been conducted and also ensures that units are prepared to conduct training as planned. For Regular Army units the short-range planning horizon is six weeks prior to training execution. For Reserve Component units, this is ninety days from training execution.

In preparation for training event execution, preexecution checks are essential to ensure that all actions and activities prior to execution are completed. For example, in planning a range, the unit identifies when ammunition requisitions must be submitted. Another example would be the weeks before the event that Class I must be ordered. These weeks just before the training event occurs are organized in 'T-weeks'—a backward planning technique that identifies specific activities units conduct prior to training to ensure coordination is done in time and resources are available when needed.

See p. 6-48 and 6-56 for discussion of preexecution checks and pp. 6-49 to 6-72 for T-week activities from FM 7-0.

Lock-In and Protect Training

As a key part of final training event preparations, commanders aggressively protect approved and scheduled training from subsequent changes and unprogrammed training distracters. Failure to protect training can easily derail the unit's ability to execute effective and meaningful training. It also creates an atmosphere in which leaders and Soldiers lose confidence in the unit's leadership. When the chain of command fails to lock in and protect training, Soldiers perceive that training is not a priority. When the chain of command locks in training, commanders publish training schedules at the company level and aggressively protect it. When this high degree of training discipline is maintained, Soldiers and their leaders can confidently predict that training will occur as planned.

Publish Training Schedules

Company training schedules are published weekly during the short-range training horizon. Training schedules provide the primary means of communicating unit training to Soldiers. At a minimum, training schedules include the following information:

- The dates and times when the training will occur.
- The attendees (such as 1st platoon, Company A).
- The tasks to be trained (task title and number).
- The trainers (primary and alternate).
- Uniform and equipment requirements.
- The location of training (such as training area or simulations facility).
- References (such as technical manuals, field manuals, and Soldier training publications).
- Submitting authority and signature (company-level commander).
- Approving authority and signature (battalion-level commander).

Training schedules are written orders and provide predictability by locking in approved training weeks (and months for Reserve Component units) before training begins. Training schedules are usually organized by—or coincide with—training weeks and cover a full week or more. Adhering to published training schedules maintains stability and discipline since these are a Soldiers' primary source of knowing daily training requirements.

See pp. 6-62 to 6-64 for discussion of training schedules from FM 7-0.

Planning
Training

The Operations Process (as the Framework for Unit Training)

Ref: ADP 7-0, Training (Jul '19), chap. 4.

The operations process of **plan, prepare, execute, and assess** is the framework for unit training. Units that train using the operations process as they train—as well as its terminologies, processes, and procedures—make the transition to actual operations more seamless and effective.

The unit commander is central to unit training in the same way a commander is central to the operations process. Planning, preparing, executing, and assessing unit training does not significantly differ from conducting an operation. Each unit begins a training cycle based on training guidance from the next higher commander. The unit then develops a long-range plan (known as the UTP) to progressively develop and sustain training proficiencies. Before a training event begins, leaders and staff complete much work well in advance of training. Leaders prepare detailed plans, develop training objectives, and most importantly coordinate the resources necessary to train. Additionally, leaders determine who will observe the training and determine the criteria observers will use for evaluating performance. Observed training is recorded by leaders and evaluators. These recorded evaluations provide commanders an essential part of the training feedback mechanism necessary to make accurate and objective assessments of proficiency. Commanders continually assess training proficiency to ensure the unit and individual Soldiers meet task and weapon standards. Each training event involves planning for, preparing for, executing, and assessing training.

PLAN Training

Planning for unit training follows the military decision-making process (known as the MDMP) or troop leading procedures (known as TLP). Commanders with a coordinating staff use the military decision-making process when developing a plan; commanders of company-level and smaller units use troop leading procedures when planning training events. Planning for unit training supports the training principle: train as you fight. Leaders trained in—and proficient in—the Army's planning processes adapt more easily to planning and executing operations when deployed.

See chap. 6, Planning Training. See also pp. 7-9 to 7-12.

PREPARE Training

Preparing for training involves those activities performed prior to training to improve the unit's abilities to train effectively.

See pp. 7-13 to 7-16 for further discussion from FM 7-0.

EXECUTE Training

Effective training occurs following detailed and coordinated planning and preparation. Each training event aims to ensure that—in a building block manner—training objectives and training proficiencies are met. Training also allows tactics, techniques, and procedures (known as TTP) to be identified, developed, tested, and implemented.

See chap. 7, Conducting Training.

ASSESS Training

Assessing unit training is a two-step process of objectively evaluating performance and assessing the results of evaluations. Following observed and evaluated training, commanders assess the unit's ability to execute tasks to standard. In addition to evaluations, commanders consider after action reviews, the commander's own personal observations, and other sources of feedback before making objective, holistic assessments of tasks, weapons, and overall unit training proficiency.

See chap. 8, Assessing Training.

Ia. Unit Training Plan (UTP) Overview

Ref: ADRP 7-0, Training Units & Developing Leaders (Aug '12), chap. 3.

Training readiness stems from attaining proficiency in individual and collective tasks. To do that, unit commanders develop their **unit training plan (UTP)**, focusing on the tasks to train, based on the higher commander's guidance. This is battle-focused training. Following the general framework of the military decisionmaking process (MDMP) (or troop leading procedures [TLP] for company and below), unit commanders begin the process to determine the METs—what to train. Training readiness is at the core of this determination—whether it is training to maintain and sustain certain capabilities or training to meet the requirements of an assigned mission.

Each unit begins a training cycle based on training guidance from the next higher commander. The unit then develops a **long-range plan known as the Unit Training Plan (UTP)** to progressively develop and sustain training proficiencies. Before a training event begins, leaders and staff complete much work well in advance of training. Leaders prepare detailed plans, develop training objectives, and most importantly coordinate the resources necessary to train. Additionally, leaders determine who will observe the training and determine the criteria observers will use for evaluating performance. Observed training is recorded by leaders and evaluators. These recorded evaluations provide commanders an essential part of the training feedback mechanism necessary to make accurate and objective assessments of proficiency. Commanders continually assess training proficiency to ensure the unit and individual Soldiers meet task and weapon standards. Each training event involves planning for, preparing for, executing, and assessing training. (ADP 7-0)

Development of a Unit Training Plan

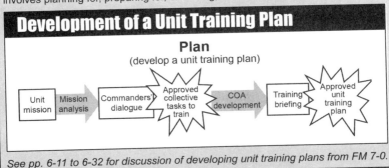

Plan
(develop a unit training plan)

Unit mission → Mission analysis → Commanders' dialogue → Approved collective tasks to train → COA development → Training briefing → Approved unit training plan

See pp. 6-11 to 6-32 for discussion of developing unit training plans from FM 7-0.

The commander is central to determining the few tasks on which the unit must train. Commanders, with the assistance of unit leadership, follow the operations process. Commanders first plan for training. They identify the collective tasks on which to train, identify, and sequence training events; identify resources required; and provide the guidance necessary to achieve mission readiness. While commanders plan, they exercise mission command to enable their subordinates to determine how they will achieve their training objectives. Thorough preparation ensures that training conditions reflect the expected mission and that commanders have the resources and enablers necessary to train. Commanders then execute the training. Lastly, they assess the training. Assessments help commanders determine if units need to retrain tasks and if the training plan requires modification. The process of determining essential tasks begins with receipt of guidance from the higher commander.

Each unit commander begins the training cycle with top-down training guidance from the higher commander. The receipt of guidance begins a process of determining the correct collective tasks on which to train. The commander then develops a UTP to conduct that training in the time allotted. Planning for training follows the MDMP for battalion and above or TLP for company and below.

Command Training Guidance (CTG)

Guidance from the higher commander to the subordinate unit commanders begins the training planning process. This top-down CTG communicates the higher commander's training priorities and helps provide a battle focus for the entire unit. Effective communication at each echelon ensures that subordinates understand the higher commander's guidance for training, that UTPs fully support the higher unit capability or mission, and that UTPs nest at each succeeding echelon.

In the CTG, the higher commander identifies—

- The unit's training focus, including its capabilities and mission.
- The desired readiness level down to brigade.
- The long-range planning horizon.
- The installation or command time management cycle.
- Brigade-level external evaluation (EXEVAL) dates and responsibilities by unit.
- Combat training center (known as CTC) rotation dates (by unit).
- Training environments in which to train.
- Other training guidance as necessary.

Division and higher commanders determine the desired readiness levels down to brigade. (Refer to AR 220-1 for a description of readiness levels.) Due to the classification level of this information, the written CTG to subordinates does not include the desired readiness levels. Instead, the two commanders discuss and determine the desired readiness levels. This determination affects the installation-level resources priorities made by the senior commander as well as the installation time management cycle.

At division level and higher, the format of CTG is at the discretion of the commander. Many commanders use the memorandum format, while others use an OPORD format. At brigade to company level, a five-paragraph OPORD is used. Its training guidance is communicated in the UTP.

See p. 6-13 for further discussion.

The resulting plan consists of training events that progressively develop task proficiency. Each training event follows a plan, prepare, execute, and assess cycle. Prior to the start of training, leaders verify availability of and coordinate for resources. Units execute training to standard, and leaders evaluate that training and determine if the unit meets proficiency standards. Leaders report to commanders on the unit's success for achieving proficiency. This bottom-up feedback provides commanders with complete information and data to accurately assess the unit and adjust training plans as necessary.

See pp. 6-11 to 6-32 for discussion of developing unit training plans from FM 7-0.

Ib. Developing the Unit Training Plan (UTP)

Ref: FM 7-0, Train to Win in a Complex World (Oct '16), chapter 2.

When the mission analysis backbrief is complete, the unit commander begins developing the **unit training plan (UTP).** This process begins with the development of training courses of action (COAs). Given the selected METs to train, the long-range planning horizon, training environments, and the higher commander's training guidance, planning can begin. Leaders first gather the information they know. Steps 3 through 6 of the MDMP provide a sequential and logical framework to develop a training COA. The resulting COA is approved by the next higher commander and becomes the UTP with a calendar.

See p. 6-5 for discussion of development of training courses of action.

Developing the Unit Training Plan

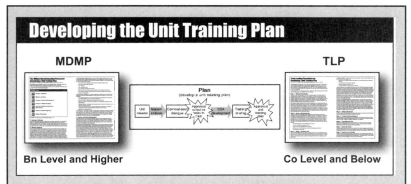

MDMP   TLP

Bn Level and Higher   **Co Level and Below**

MDMP - Battalion Level and Higher

At battalion level and higher (units with a coordinating staff), commanders follow the steps of the military decision making process (MDMP) to plan unit training. Some steps of the MDMP for operations translate differently for training and are addressed in this chapter.

TLP - Company Level and Below

At the Company level and below (units without a coordinating staff), the troop leading procedures (TLP) are used. The UTP development at company level follows the same concepts employed at battalion and higher echelons. Companies use the troop leading procedures that follow steps similar to the military decisionmaking process (MDMP) —used at battalion and higher with units with a coordinating staff. At the discretion of the battalion commander, company commanders— collaborating with the battalion staff (primarily the S-3 and S-4)—may develop an overarching battalion UTP rather than individual companies developing separate UTPs. In this instance, the battalion staff ensures that the COA development includes company training events integrated into the battalion UTP. The battalion staff ensures that time is available for individual company training events, company training objectives are identified, and company-level training resources are programmed and coordinated for as part of the battalion UTP.

Refer to BSS6: The Battle Staff SMARTbook, 6th Ed. for discussion of MDMP & TLP.

Step 1. Receipt of Training Guidance

Training readiness stems from attaining proficiency in individual and collective tas[...]
To do that, unit commanders develop their UTP, focusing on the tasks to train, bas[...]
on the higher commander's guidance. This is battle-focused training. Following th[...]
general framework of the military decisionmaking process (MDMP) (or troop leadi[...]
procedures [TLP] for company and below), unit commanders begin the process to[...]
determine the METs—what to train. Training readiness is at the core of this determ[...]
nation—whether it is training to maintain and sustain certain capabilities or training
to meet the requirements of an assigned mission.

The process of determining essential tasks begins with receipt of guidance from th[...]
higher commander.

Step 1: Receipt of Training Guidance

MDMP Steps

Step 1
Receipt of Mission

Receipt of training guidance from the higher commander begins the mission analysis process.

Step 2
Mission Analysis

Step 3
Course of Action
(COA) Development

Step 4
COA Analysis
(War Game)

Step 5
COA Comparison

Step 6
COA Approval

Step 7
Orders Production,
Dissemination, and
Transition

Ref: FM 7-0 (Oct '16), fig. 2-1. Receipt of training guidance begins the planning process.

raining Guidance

ef: FM 7-0, Train to Win in a Complex World (Oct '16), pp. 2-1 to 2-2.

he Army uses the operations process of plan, prepare, execute, and assess as its aining framework. Using this framework, the unit commander remains central to the aining process in the same way the commander is central to the operations process. anning, preparing, executing and assessing unit training does not significantly ffer from performing these activities for an operation. Each unit commander begins e training cycle with top-down training guidance from the higher commander. The ceipt of guidance begins a process of determining the correct collective tasks on hich to train. The commander then develops a UTP to conduct that training in the ne allotted.

he resulting plan consists of training events that progressively develop task profi- ency. Each training event follows a plan, prepare, execute, and assess cycle. Prior the start of training, leaders verify availability of and coordinate for resources. Units kecute training to standard, and leaders evaluate that training and determine if the it meets proficiency standards. Leaders report to commanders on the unit's suc- ss for achieving proficiency. This bottom-up feedback provides commanders with mplete information and data to accurately assess the unit and adjust training plans necessary.

command Training Guidance (CTG)

uidance from the higher commander to the subordinate unit commanders begins e training planning process. This top-down CTG communicates the higher com- ander's training priorities and helps provide a battle focus for the entire unit. Effec- e communication at each echelon ensures that subordinates understand the higher mmander's guidance for training, that UTPs fully support the higher unit capability mission, and that UTPs nest at each succeeding echelon.

the CTG, the higher commander identifies—

- The unit's training focus, including its capabilities and mission.
- The desired readiness level down to brigade.
- The long-range planning horizon.
- The installation or command time management cycle.
- Brigade-level external evaluation (EXEVAL) dates and responsibilities by unit.
- Combat training center (known as CTC) rotation dates (by unit).
- Training environments in which to train.
- Other training guidance as necessary.

vision and higher commanders determine the desired readiness levels down to igade. *(Refer to AR 220-1 for a description of readiness levels.)* Due to the classifi- tion level of this information, the written CTG to subordinates does not include the esired readiness levels. Instead, the two commanders discuss and determine the esired readiness levels. This determination affects the installation-level resources iorities made by the senior commander as well as the installation time management cle.

division level and higher, the format of CTG is at the discretion of the commander. any commanders use the memorandum format, while others use an OPORD rmat. At brigade to company level, a five-paragraph OPORD is used. Its training uidance is communicated in the UTP.

e pp. 6-33 to 6-36 for a sample UTP and pp. 5-20 to 5-21 for discussion of blished training guidance (CTG/UTP) battle rhythm.

Planning
Training

Step 2. Mission Analysis

On receipt of training guidance from the higher commander, the unit commander always conducts a mission analysis to understand the guidance given by the high commander and to determine how the unit can best support that guidance. Missic analysis also starts the parallel and collaborative planning process within the com mand. Before beginning mission analysis, the unit commander gathers supportin references. These references provide the most current sources of information su as doctrine, technical manuals, unit SOPs, and on-line resources. Additionally, the unit commander gathers information on installation-level training resources to detern what they are, their availability, their location, and the requirements to secure them.

In conducting a mission analysis, the unit commander will—

- Identify and understand potential operational environments.
- Determine the METs to train.
- Assess the METs to train.
- Identify the long-range planning horizon.
- Identify training readiness issues.

Mission analysis provides the collective tasks on which the unit will focus its traini

Step 2: Mission Analysis

MDMP Steps

Step 1
Receipt of Mission

Step 2
Mission Analysis

Mission analysis provides the collective tasks to focus unit training.

Step 3
Course of Action
(COA) Development

Step 4
COA Analysis
(War Game)

Step 5
COA Comparison

Step 6
COA Approval

Step 7
Orders Production,
Dissemination, and
Transition

Ref: FM 7-0 (Oct '16), fig. 2-3. Mission analysis helps determine battle focus.

Planning
Training

Identify and Understand an Operational Environment

A major consideration in determining tasks to train, as well as building the necessary rigor into training, is identifying and understanding an operational environment. An operational environment is a composite of the conditions, circumstances, and influences that affect the employment of capabilities and bear on the decisions of the commander (JP 3-0). An operational environment is addressed in the higher commander's training guidance. An analysis and understanding of an operational environment will help determine not only tasks that the unit may need to train but also the correct conditions to replicate in training to ensure that units train the way they expect to fight. An effective training environment replicates an operational environment.

Determine Mission Essential Tasks (METs) to Train

The higher commander's training guidance provides the unit commander with capabilities or a mission to train. This is given as specific capabilities on which to train or as an assigned mission (who, what, when, where, and why) on which to train. In either case, the unit commander performs a mission analysis to determine the METs that best support the higher commander's guidance. Whether the unit trains directly against tasks from its METL or develops METs for an assigned mission, commanders with a standardized METL always report training readiness against that standardized METL.

Refer to AR 220-1 and DA Pam 220-1 for more information on reporting training readiness.

Train to Specific Capabilities

When the unit is not assigned a mission to train, the unit may be directed to train to specific capabilities. In this case, the commander prioritizes the METs on which to train. Commanders consider the following when determining the priorities:

- The higher commander's guidance.
- The tasks most likely to be assigned.
- The task most likely to have the lowest current assessment proficiency rating—untrained (U), marginally practiced (P-), practiced (P), and trained (T-).
- Most likely operational environments for which to train.
- The long-range planning horizon (the time it will take to train).

For TOE units, commanders use the standardized METL as the primary source for selecting the priority of the METs to train. Figure 2-4 illustrates an example of how the priorities shift after a commander conducts a mission analysis. The unit's METL does not indicate which of these METs should be trained in priority. Following mission analyses, and based on current and projected task assessments and unit requirements, the commander determines the priority in which to train these tasks. In figure 2-4, the task "Conduct an Area Defense" is trained as the unit's first training priority.

METL		**METL (training priority)**
• Conduct an attack		• Conduct an area defense
• Conduct an area defense	**Mission**	• Conduct area security
• Conduct area security	**Analysis**	• Conduct pre-deployment
• Conduct pre-deployment		• Conduct an attack
METL mission-essential task list		

Ref: FM 7-0 (Oct '16), fig. 2-4. Notional mission analysis when prioritizing capabilities to train.

Train to an Assigned Mission

When directed to train to an assigned mission, the unit commander identifies speci fied and implied tasks from the higher commander's CTG. From these tasks, the commander identifies unit essential tasks. The essential tasks then become the unit METs that focus training. A specified task is a specifically assigned to a unit by its higher headquarters (FM 6-0). The training guidance states specified tasks. An implied task is a that must be performed to accomplish a specified task or mission but is not stated in the higher headquarters' order (FM 6-0). A major consideration i determining implied tasks is identifying and understanding an operational environ- ment on which to train. This understanding, along with an analysis of an operationa. environment may help determine additional implied tasks on which the unit may need to focus training. An essential task is a specified or implied task that must be executed to accomplish the mission (FM 6-0). In training, essential tasks for an as- signed mission become METs.

Each identified essential task becomes a MET. The resulting list of tasks become th collective tasks on which the unit trains. (See figure 2-5) Commanders ensure that the assigned METL is not too broad in scope and that the METs are limited to those collective tasks that must be executed to accomplish the mission. An assigned MET based on an assigned mission that has an excessive number of METs only serves t diffuse the unit's battle focus.

Development of a METL (Assigned Mission)

Higher Commander's
Training Guidance
(for an assigned mission)

Mission Analysis

Determine the METs that focus training

METL for an
Assigned Mission

MET - Mission-Essential Task
See p. 5-9.

METL - Mission-Essential Task List
See p. 6-6.

Ref: FM 7-0 (Oct '16), fig. 2-5. Development of a METL for an assigned mission.

The higher commander may assign a mission different from the subordinate unit's designed capabilities. In this instance, figure 2-5 depicts that the METs on which the unit trains are determined through mission analysis in support of the assigned mis- sion. To assist in that analysis, the unit commander refers to the METs and collective tasks of the type unit that does have the capabilities called for. Commanders also refer to the function CATS feature for useful information to help determine the correct collective tasks to train. Figure 2-6 illustrates this process. In this scenario, an artil- lery unit receives an assigned mission focused on providing transportation support rather than providing fire support. Following mission analysis, METs are derived to support a transportation focus for the unit to train.

Mission: Provide transportation support . . .

METL
- Control field artillery fire missions
- Synchronize fire support
- Employ fires

Mission Analysis

METL for an assigned mission
- Plan brigade transportation support
- Manage transportation operations
- Direct seaport of debarkation support

METL   mission-essential task list

Ref: FM 7-0 (Oct '16), fig. 2-6. Development of a METL for an assigned METL with other capabilities.

Assess Mission-Essential Tasks

Ref: FM 7-0, Train to Win in a Complex World (Oct '16), pp. 2-6 to 2-7.

After identifying the METs on which to focus training, the commander assesses the current task proficiency and the projected task proficiency. This initial assessment represents a current snapshot of the unit's training readiness. An early baseline assessment of METs enables the commander to begin considering the future scope of training. This assessment may provide useful information for the mission analysis backbrief between the two commanders at the conclusion of the mission analysis process. Using the proficiency ratings discussed in the discussion beginning in paragraph 1-6, the commander assesses each MET. The proficiency ratings are untrained (U), marginally practiced (P-), practiced (P), trained (T-), and fully trained (T). The commander enters these ratings in the DTMS.

Assessment of METs (Example)

METs	Current	Projected
Conduct an attack	T-	P
Conduct stability operations	U	P-

MET	mission-essential task	T-	trained
P	practiced	U	untrained
P-	marginally practiced		

Ref: FM 7-0 (Oct '16), fig. 2-7. Initial and projected start-of-training MET assessments.

The commander also considers the assessments of the METs at the start of training. If given sufficient lead time between the beginning of training planning and execution, the assessments taken at the beginning of planning may significantly differ from the execution of training. The commander considers factors that might impact the unit's training proficiency when training starts such as personnel turnover, skill atrophy over time, and crew certification. Ideally, planning begins months before training begins. This means that some proposed METs may rate higher in proficiency at the start of training and others may atrophy to a lower proficiency rating during this period.

For the commander to make an informed and accurate start-of-training assessment, subordinates provide bottom-up feedback. The commander uses this feedback in the assessment. The best assessment of the unit's proficiency requires the commanders to be as objective as possible. An objective assessment helps inform the commander in the development of the UTP.

Planning
Training

Identify the Long-Range Planning Horizon

The long-range planning horizon is provided in the higher commander's CTG. This horizon represents the time allocated for the unit to achieve and sustain training proficiency. Having a clear understanding of the time the unit has to train is essenti to developing a successful training plan.

Identify Training Readiness Issues

During the mission analysis process, the commander may identify other training readiness issues. Some issues may necessitate a discussion between the unit com mander and higher commander during the mission analysis backbrief. These issue range from the time available to train, resources available to train, or other concern that the unit commander may want to discuss with the higher commander.

Conducts Mission Analysis Backbrief

The unit commander completes the mission analysis, selects the METs to train, ar backbriefs the higher commander on the results of the analysis. This backbrief is part of the commanders' dialogue process. The unit commander restates and verifi an understanding of the higher commander's training guidance.

During the mission analysis backbrief, the unit commander discusses proposed ur METs on which to train that support the higher commander's training guidance. Th discuss the long-range planning horizon and training environments. They also dis cuss any other training issues related to the unit's ability to attain training proficien in the time required. The higher commander approves or modifies the unit METs fc training. The unit commander then begins to develop a UTP to train the unit on the selected METs.

Mission Analysis Backbrief

At the conclusion of mission analysis, a backbrief by the unit commander helps ensure both are in concurrence with the higher commander's guidance and the mission-essential tasks selected to train.

Ref: FM 7-0 (Oct '16), fig. 2-8. Mission analysis backbrief.

Following the backbrief, the commander notifies subordinates of the results. At brigade and below, commanders use a warning order (WARNORD) format to com municate results. This order prompts subordinate commanders and leaders to beg their own mission analysis as well as to conduct parallel and collaborative plannin If the higher commander's training guidance included an assigned mission, the un commander includes the unit's restated mission. In this mission of who, what, whe where, and why, the what covers the selected METs. If the training guidance did r include an assigned mission, the what becomes the prioritized METL tasks approv by the next higher commander.

Units based on a TDA—and other units without a standardized METL—perform a mission analysis to develop their METs and METL. TDA units are typically not de ployable and perform their as-designed functions every day. Since TDA units do n have a standardized METL, their unit commanders develop many of the individual and collective tasks on which they train. Many of the tasks these units routinely perform are already established and published in the Army's training development capability database and accessible through ATN. Other tasks that are specific to th functions performed by the unit may need to be developed by the unit commander and approved by the higher commander. Table 2-1 illustrates sample tasks TDA commanders might consider as part of their mission analysis.

Sample TDA Collective Tasks

- Provide installation resiliency services.
- Conduct training in general subjects (basic skills).
- Administer cadre training programs:
- Certifications.
- Professional development (faculty development programs).
- Mandatory training (installation and local command requirements).
- Conduct administrative, logistic, and training in support of base operations.
- Provide installation predeployment and deployment services and operations.
- Provide installation railhead support.
- Train, support, and evaluate United States Army Reserve training units.
- Conduct installation and command physical fitness training and testing.

Ref: FM 7-0 (Oct '16), table 2-1. Sample TDA collective tasks.

At the conclusion of mission analysis, the TDA commander determines which tasks are essential to the success of the unit. Following mission analysis—just as in a TOE-based unit—the unit commander backbriefs the higher commander to obtain approval of the TDA METL.

Following the mission analysis backbrief, the unit commander can begin formulating a UTP that supports the higher commander's guidance and supports training the unit on the selected METs. The mission analysis step is crucial to the entire process because it relies on an accurate determination and assessment of the METs selected to train. The conclusion of the mission analysis backbrief directly affects developing the training plan for the unit and ultimately affects unit training readiness over the long-range planning horizon.

Step 3. Course of Action (COA) Development

Leaders first gather the information they know. Steps 3-6 of the MDMP provide a sequential and logical framework to develop a training COA. (See figure 2-10.) The resulting COA is approved by the next higher commander and becomes the UTP (which includes the UTP calendar).

When creating COAs, the primary goal is to develop a UTP that progressively develops MET proficiencies to an end state (when the unit is proficient) and beyond. This end state corresponds to the commander's visualized end state for training and directly supports the capability or mission on which to train. Developing training COAs accounts for the unit's current training proficiencies, the home station training environment, installation resource availability, and leadership knowledge and experience.

Whether planning within the framework of the MDMP or TLP, planners consider:

- Prepare the UTP calendar.
- Apply the command or installation time management cycle.
- Post the higher unit (multiechelon) training events.
- Determine unit training events.
- Identify training objectives for each training event.
- Use a backward planning approach using a crawl-walk-run methodology.
- Consider the training environment.
- Ensure time is programmed for subordinate units to train.

See p. 6-21 for overview chart and further discussion.

Prepare the Unit Training Plan Calendar

The UTP calendar is extremely important since it visually defines the time available to train. Once planners begin to apply the actual days available to train a COA, they will note that time is the greatest restricting factor to planning unit training. Planner have to contend with installation or command time management cycles, resources and facilities constraints, and limited classes of supply. Additionally, the unit competes with other units on the installation for the same limited resources. A simple calendar format depicting the planning horizon provides an excellent starting point for planners. The CATS planning tool in DTMS helps planners visualize the long-range planning horizon, too.

Apply the Command or Installation Time Management Cycle

Time management cycles create prime time training periods for subordinate organizations to achieve battle focus in training. At the installation level, the senior Army commander establishes a time management cycle to protect and prioritize training time and resources for installation units. Time management cycles help subordinate units identify, focus, and protect training periods and resources needed to support unit training. This cycle ensures that subordinate organizations can concentrate on executing their UTP. Subordinate units can publish additional time management cycles, but they must synchronize these additional cycles to support the command or installation cycle UTPs and their supporting calendars identify time management cycles.

No matter the time management cycle that the senior commander establishes, all unit commanders must enforce it. Senior commanders must ensure that the planning and execution is highly disciplined and that all members of the command support and comply with training at designated times. Without the support and oversight of senior commanders, battalions, companies, platoons, and Soldiers will not be able to train to proficiency. Since specific activities vary among installations according to the local situations and requirements, the senior commander, in coordination with the installation staff, coordinates the unit's training requirements to protect unit training times.

One time management cycle used throughout the Army is the Green-Amber-Red cycle. Many units and installations employ this time management cycle or some variation of it. The commander employs the best method of a time management cycle based on the installation's readiness requirements, unit's readiness requirements, and resource allocations.

See p. 6-27 for discussion of a sample time management cycle (Green-Amber-Red cycle).

Post the Higher Unit (Multiechelon) Training Events

Planners start by placing all multiechelon training events directed by their higher headquarters on the UTP calendar. Such training events include the higher unit's EXEVAL (such as a combat training center rotation and brigade field training exercise [FTX]).

COA development not only focuses on the METs selected to train, but is also developed around multiechelon training. Training more than one echelon deep (such as a company with platoons or a battalion with companies) provides a degree of realism not possible when training independent echelons. Training with other support elements—like medical support, engineer support, or military intelligence support—drives a more realistic training environment that replicates how the unit will actually operate. Each COA development is about training the entire organization to MET proficiency over the long-range planning horizon. COA development focuses on depicting only those training events in which subordinate units must participate.

COA Development

Ref: FM 7-0, Train to Win in a Complex World (Oct '16), p. 2-10.

Step 3: COA Development

MDMP Steps

Step 1
Receipt of Mission

Step 2
Mission Analysis

Step 3
Course of Action
(COA) Development

Following the misson analysis backbrief, the unit commander leads the effort to develop potential training courses of action.

Step 4
COA Analysis
(War Game)

Step 5
COA Comparison

Step 6
COA Approval

Step 7
Orders Production,
Dissemination, and
Transition

Ref: FM 7-0 (Oct '16), fig. 2-10. Steps 3-6 of the MDMP as it relates to unit training.

From company to brigade levels, developing the UTP calendar is fundamental to graphically developing training of COAs. (See ADRP 5-0 for developing COAs.) Often several possible best ways exist to train the unit. The development of several unit calendars allows the commander to choose the most viable ways to train the unit. The calendar graphically represents the unit's plan to train. Planners viewing the calendar framework generate options for analysis and comparison that satisfy the commander's guidance for training. As planners develop different COA options, they ensure each COA is—

- **Feasible**—doable.
- **Acceptable**—benefit is worth the cost.
- **Suitable**—appropriate.
- **Distinguishable**—not similar to another COA.
- **Complete**—no clear gaps.

HEADQUARTERS
1st Brigade, 52nd Infantry Division

	JULY	AUGUST	SEPTEMBER	OCTOBER	NOVEMBER	DECEMBER
Time management cycle →	RED		GREEN			AMBER
1st Brigade	QTB	Brigade Gunnery	STAFFEX		CPX	QTB
2-77 Field Artillery	QTB	Brigade Gunnery	STAFFEX	FTX		QTB
Company A	QTB	Brigade Gunnery		FTX		QTB

CPX	command post exercise	QTB	quarterly training briefing
FTX	field training exercise	STAFFEX	staff training exercise

Ref: FM 7-0 (Oct '16), fig. 2-11. Multiechelon training events demonstrated in a notional UTP calendar.

Figure 2-11 demonstrates the building of multiechelon events from the top echelon to the bottom. Each headquarters develops the multiechelon training events that focus on attaining MET proficiency while preserving sufficient time on the UTP calendar for subordinates to plan and execute their own training.

Higher headquarter events affect subordinate unit planning as each unit develops COAs. A brigade that plans a minimum of brigade-level multiechelon events leaves time for the battalions to train. A brigade that plans too many brigade-level multiechelon events leaves less time for the battalions to train and even less time for companies and platoons to plan and execute their training in support of the brigade.

Following approval of the COA, other training activities—such as mandatory training, predeployment training, and installation support—can and should be included on the UTP calendar. This calendar provides the unit with a complete view of all training scheduled. When creating potential COAs and the UTP calendar, planners account for how the unit will achieve training proficiency.

Determine Unit Training Events

Commanders link training strategies to training plans by identifying and planning training events. Training events are the building blocks that are the foundation of a COA. During COA development, commanders and staffs broadly assess the number, type, and duration of training events that a unit may require to train the METs to proficiency.

Effective and realistic training events require commanders to analyze the tasks to be trained, the opposing force's (OPFOR's) counter tasks, and variables represented in a training scenario. Well-developed events incorporate conditions replicating an anticipated operational environment as much as possible. They place Soldiers and leaders in complex, ambiguous, challenging (morally and ethically), and rapidly changing conditions. Effective training includes events that require units and leaders to transition quickly between METs to develop adaptive and innovative leaders with decision-making agility.

METs are not trained in isolation. They are trained with their associated supporting collective and individual tasks during training events. Knowing what training events to train is an important first step in COA development. Ideally, the right series of training events will train multiple METs. Determining the right mix and sequence of training events ensures that units maximize valuable training time and resources and do not waste training time.

Green-Amber-Red Cycle

Ref: FM 7-0, Train to Win in a Complex World (Oct '16), pp. 2-11 to 2-13, figure 2-11.
Multiechelon training events demonstrated in a notional UTP calendar

One time management cycle used throughout the Army is the Green-Amber-Red cycle.
Many units and installations employ this time management cycle or some variation of it.

HEADQUARTERS
1st Brigade, 52nd Infantry Division

	JULY	AUGUST	SEPTEMBER	OCTOBER	NOVEMBER	DECEMBER
Time management cycle →	RED		GREEN			AMBER
1st Brigade	QTB	Brigade Gunnery	STAFFEX		CPX	QTB
2-77 Field Artillery	QTB	Brigade Gunnery	STAFFEX	FTX		QTB
Company A	QTB	Brigade Gunnery		FTX		QTB

CPX command post exercise	QTB quarterly training briefing
FTX field training exercise	STAFFEX staff training exercise

Green

Training is focused on multiechelon, unit collective tasks and on MET proficiency.
Training is planned and synchronized with the availability of major training resources
and key training facilities. Senior commanders ensure that subordinate organizations
conduct training without distraction or unprogrammed external taskings.

- Requires maximum Soldier attendance at mission-essential training.
- Eliminates administrative and support requirements that prevent personnel from participating in training to the maximum extent possible.
- Limits leaves and passes.

Amber

Training is focused at the individual, leader, crew, and squad levels. Individuals maximize
their own self-development by using installation education centers and distributed learning
resources. Organizations are assigned support taskings beyond the capability of those
units in the red cycle, but commanders strive for minimal disruptions to units in this cycle.

- Provides time for Soldiers to attend education and training courses.
- Enables some sub-organizations to schedule collective training.
- Diverts selected personnel to support requirements when all available personnel in organizations in the red period are completely committed to support requirements.
- Enables scheduling for periodic maintenance services.

Red

Training is focused to maximize self-development and individual task proficiency. Units in
this cycle perform unit-level administrative requirements and allow the maximum number of
Soldiers to take leave. More often, post support requirements take priority. During this cycle,
leaders expand on providing additional mentoring, coaching, counselling to subordinates.

- Maximizes leaves and passes. When appropriate, unit schedules block leave.
- Coordinated and scheduled routine medical, dental, and administrative appointments with installation support facilities.

For TOE units, planners identify the training events by using the CATS. This strateg enables planners to develop training since it provides a proponent-recommended strategy. For TDA units and for units assigned to perform a functional mission, the CATS provides a wealth of information concerning tasks and training events. Planners consider carefully before modifying a CATS since it affects TDA and unit UTP development. The CATS shows recommended multiechelon events and identifies EXEVAL criteria. Effective planners start a unit UTP development by overlaying a CATS solution over known, actual calendar requirements.

All training events require training areas, facilities, and resources. Some events may require OPFORs, observer-controllers/trainers (OC/Ts), and role players. Othe events may need training support system products and services, such as instrumen tation and TADSS. Finally, a training event itself is only a tool to meet and sustain MET proficiency. Selected individuals evaluate all training events for their contribution to training readiness.

Identify Training Objectives

A training objective is a statement that describes the desired outcome of a training activity in the unit. Training objectives represent what the commander wants to achieve at the conclusion of each training event. Training objectives help chart the course for how training events contribute to MET proficiency. A training objective consists of the following:

- Task
- Condition
- Standard
- Training proficiency

See facing page for further discussion.

Use a Backward Planning Approach

Backward planning is a simple technique that begins at the commander's visualized training end state. This end state is the point at which the unit expects to be trained to standard in the selected METs. The unit EXEVAL is the training event tha normally culminates the end state on the UTP calendar. The unit commander two levels up designs the EXEVAL to evaluate the unit METL and resources the EXEVA so the unit commander has an opportunity to assess the unit. All units in the Army undergo an EXEVAL to validate a rating proficiency of trained or fully trained.

HEADQUARTERS **2d Brigade, 52nd Infantry Division**						
	JULY	AUGUST	SEPTEMBER	OCTOBER	NOVEMBER	DECEMBER
Time management cycle →	AMBER			GREEN		RED
2d Brigade	QTB	COMMEX	FTX	EXEVAL		QTB
1-5 Infantry	QTB		FTX	EXEVAL		QTB
Company A	QTB		FTX	EXEVAL		QTB
COMMEX communications exercise EXEVAL external evaluation				FTX field training exercise QTB quarterly training briefing		

Ref: FM 7-0 (Oct '16), fig. 2-13. Example EXEVAL posted on a notional brigade U calendar.

Training Objectives

Ref: FM 7-0, Train to Win in a Complex World (Oct '16), pp. 2-15 to 2-16.

A training objective is a statement that describes the desired outcome of a training activity in the unit. Training objectives represent what the commander wants to achieve at the conclusion of each training event. Training objectives help chart the course for how training events contribute to MET proficiency. A training objective consists of the following:

- **Task**. A clearly defined and measurable activity accomplished by organizations and individuals.
- **Condition**. The circumstances and environment in which a unit is to perform a task.
- **Standard**. The minimum acceptable proficiency required in the performance of a particular training task.
- **Training proficiency.** This is the task proficiency rating that the commander expects the unit to meet at the conclusion of the event.

Training objectives are similar to tactical objectives in that they focus on the effects the commander wants to achieve. In this case, the effects focus on progressively (crawl-walk-run) mastering the METs. Training objectives help the unit focus on what it needs to accomplish during each event and how the event contributes to the overall attainment of the commander's visualized end state. A training objective can be a simple statement of goals for the event or as complex as aligning the METs being trained with the anticipated final assessment at the end of the event. Planners identify training objectives for each multiechelon training event that comprises COAs. Planners also develop and publish training objectives for each training event internal to the unit.

Sample Brigade Training Objective

Task: Conduct an Attack, #07-6-1092

Conditions: The brigade is conducting operations independently and has received an operation order or fragmentary order to conduct an attack at the location and time specified. Coalition forces and noncombatants may be present in the training environment.

Standards:
1. Brigade leaders gain and or maintain situational awareness. Brigade commander and staff receive an order or anticipate a new mission and begin the military decisionmaking process. Brigade task-organizes forces within the brigade.
2. Staff obtains guidance from the commander. The staff plans, coordinates, and achieves the desired effects utilizing organic and attached assets.
3. Staff plans mobility, countermobility, and survivability; chemical, biological, radiological, and nuclear support; air defense support; and sustainment supporting operations.
4. Brigade commander and staff conduct risk management.
5. Brigade commander and staff conduct backbriefs and rehearsals to ensure that subordinates understand commander's intent and concept.
6. Brigade executes the attack and masses available combat power to destroy enemy in accordance with the commander's intent.
7. Brigade consolidates and reorganizes as necessary.
8. Brigade continues operations as necessary.

Training proficiency: The brigade is a 'T-' (trained) assessment for the task Conduct an Attack, task #07-6-1092.

Ref: FM 7-0 (Oct '16), fig. 2-12. Sample brigade training objective.

Planning
Training

Use the Crawl-Walk-Run Methodology

Sequencing training events from simple to increasingly more complex events provides Soldiers, leaders, and the unit with the ability to build individual and collective task proficiencies as the UTP progresses. This approach ensures that task proficiencies progressively build on each other, laying a solid foundation before moving on to more complex tasks and events.

See facing page for further discussion.

Consider the Training Environment

The ability of a unit to conduct all training events in a live environment is impractical. The realities of limited training time and resources dictate that commanders, as stewards of the Army Profession, use creative and innovative means to conduct training in other-than-live training environments. Effective commanders and subordinate leaders plan and execute multiechelon training that combines required, needed and optional training on several METs whenever possible. How units execute training events is an important consideration as COAs are developed. Ideally, with unlimited time and resources, all unit training is best executed when done in a live environment. However, this is not feasible due to limited time, resources, and safety considerations. Commanders leverage all the training support enablers available to get the best results possible.

See pp. 6-28 to 6-29 (LVC) for discussion of the training environment.

Ensure Time is Scheduled for Subordinate Units to Train

Each headquarters ensures that it leaves available training time in its plan. Time must be allocated for subordinate units to determine and schedule their own training events. On the UTP calendar, this time is referred to as white space. White space is the open time on the training calendar for each subordinate unit to develop its own level of crawl-walk-run events. If each succeeding headquarters fills all the available training time, subordinate units will have no time available to plan training. For example, if a battalion accounts for all available training time in its UTP calendar, then its companies will have no time to develop and schedule the training they may need to plan and execute at their level.

Step 4. Course of Action Analysis (War Game)

Once multiple COAs are developed based on the higher commanders' training guidance, planners analyze them to identify difficulties, coordination issues, or resource issues as well as potential risks of potential planned events. Identification of major resources that may require immediate coordination and/or help from higher headquarters is important to prevent future training shortfalls. These adjustments may require decision points for the commander or adjustments to the events and their sequencing *(refer to FM 6-0)*.

Planners consider the following major resources:

- Land, facilities, and ranges.
- Ammunition and TADSS.
- Blended training environments and ITEs.
- Classes of supply (to include unit Class V allocations).
- OPFORs, role players, and master scenario events lists (MSELs).
- Resources not readily available at home station.
- Unit availability (Green-Amber-Red).

Commanders and staffs also use the CATS to better understand each training events requirements to include major classes of supply, TADSS, and other important planning factors.

Crawl-Walk-Run Methodology

Ref: FM 7-0, Train to Win in a Complex World (Oct '16), pp. 2-15 to 2-16.

Sequencing training events from simple to increasingly more complex events provides Soldiers, leaders, and the unit with the ability to build individual and collective task proficiencies as the UTP progresses (see figure 2-14). This approach ensures that task proficiencies progressively build on each other, laying a solid foundation before moving on to more complex tasks and events.

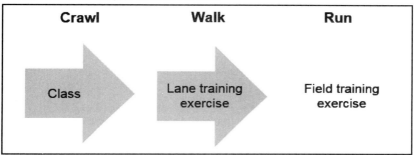

Ref: FM 7-0 (Oct '16), fig. 2-14. Sample of crawl-walk-run training events/

CATSs indicate whether a training event is a crawl, walk, or run level event. In the crawl stage, the unit trains to first understand task requirements and standards (in figure 2-15 on page 2-16, the class scheduled for company A in August). In the walk stage, the unit trains the task with added realism by encountering changing conditions. Soldiers also begin to understand that tasks are not executed in or by themselves and to understand the linkages to other associated tasks (in figure 2-15 on page 2-16, the platoon situational training exercise scheduled in September). Soldiers also begin to work mutually as crews, teams, and small units. At the run stage, Soldiers train collectively to achieve task proficiencies under increasingly realistic conditions and to work mutually as effective and efficient teams (in figure 2-15, the company gunnery in October followed by the company FTX in November). This crawl-walk-run approach to planning and sequencing training events develops Soldiers, leaders, and units able to meet individual and collective task proficiencies in a reliable and predictable way.

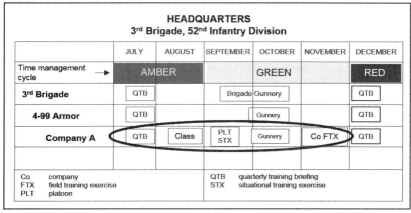

Ref: FM 7-0 (Oct '16), fig. 2-15. Company crawl-walk-run training events on the UTP calendar.

Live, Virtual, and Constructive (LVC) Training Environments

Ref: FM 7-0, Train to Win in a Complex World (Oct '16), pp. 2-16 to 2-18.

The Army relies on a creative mix of LVC training environments to provide realistic training. Live training is training executed in field conditions using tactical equipment. It involves real people operating real systems. Live training may be enhanced by TADSS. Field training exercises, live fire exercises, deployment exercises, and battle drills under live conditions replicate an actual operational environment as closely as possible. Virtual training is executed using computer-generated battlefields in simulators with the approximate characteristics of tactical weapon systems and vehicles. Units use virtual training to exercise motor control, decision-making, and communication skills. Sometimes called human-in-the-loop training, it involves real people operating simulated systems. People being trained practice the skills needed to operate actual equipment, for example, flying an aircraft. Gaming is a subset of the virtual training environment. The military uses gaming technologies to create capabilities to help train individuals and organizations. Games support the development of individual-level tasks and skills and facilitate the assessments of small-unit or team collective task training. Gaming can operate in a stand-alone environment or be integrated with live, virtual, or constructive environments. Constructive training uses computer models and simulations to exercise command and staff functions. It involves simulated people operating simulated systems. Constructive training can be conducted by units from platoon through echelons above corps. LVC training is a broad taxonomy that covers the degree to which a training event uses simulations.

Units use virtual and constructive training environments to supplement, enhance, and complement live training. Virtual and constructive training environments help raise the entry level of proficiency for live training and reduce the time needed to prepare training. These environments also provide a variety of training environments, allowing training units to replicate multiple scenarios under different conditions. Based on training objectives and available resources—such as time, ammunition, simulations, and range availability—commanders determine the right mix and frequency of LVC training to ensure organizations use resources efficiently.

Commanders employ each training environment independently or combine two or more environments to meet the training objective. Employing a training environment independently is the easiest to plan and prepare. If using more than one training environment, leaders may use either a blended training environment (BTE) or ITE. An installation creates a fielding schedule for units to use an ITE.

Blended Training Environment

Blended training is unit training conducted concurrently within two or more training environments (live, virtual, or constructive simulation). Blended training lacks the sophisticated integrating technologies that allow the different environments to interact. When properly planned and resourced, blended training can include information systems that enable the unit commander and other leaders to receive a common operational picture or that enable the activity in one training environment to be used to stimulate reaction in the other. For example, if a company only has maneuver space for one live platoon, but wants to train the company headquarters and leadership in mission command tasks, then it can train two platoons in a tactical simulation or virtual environment and train the third platoon in a live training environment. In this example, the company leaders have the tactical challenge of commanding all three platoons and providing a more realistic training event than if only the live platoon were training. In contrast, the ITE is enabled by a sophisticated integrated architecture that allows full interaction between virtual and constructive environments, to include information systems. This architecture also allows limited interaction between live forces and virtual or simulated environments (for example, virtual d simulated artillery can cause casualties in live forces, if enabled, and support 'live' fire arkers). The limitation of the ITE is its limited availability. A unit can plan, prepare, and ecute blended training using ordinary computers with Internet access and using limited aining space for concurrent live training. The disadvantage of blended training is that all anning and preparation are the unit's responsibility whereas integrated training requires ly limited input from the unit (the tasks and training environment for which they want to ain) and select system training for operators to enable effective, integrated training.

ntegrated Training Environment (ITE)

n ITE uses consistent (common TADSS enablers across installations) and continuous /C training environments to stimulate information systems. An ITE uses correlated terrain atabases in the TADSS and the Live, Virtual, Constructive—Integrating Architecture. This rchitecture—including standards, protocols, hardware, and software—enables seamless, ynchronized integration among information systems and the simulations or simulators.

ll training requires some form of training support—such as TADSS, facilities, services, anges, and maneuver space. Planning and preparing a BTE and ITE is more complex than onducting simple maneuver or movement training. A BTE and ITE enable units to increase aining opportunities with fewer resources. These environments enable units to customize e complexity of training conditions to make the training more challenging. Additionally, ese environments enable units to assess and retrain quickly with a relatively low cost.

raining events that involve CATS often provide various live, virtual, or constructive ptions. For example, training often includes a walk-level (such as a situational training xercise) virtual event and a similar situational training exercise live event for the unit's crawl-walk-run level training.

ust as leaders must understand an operational environment in combat, a leader must nderstand the training environment at home station. Competent leaders understand the raining environment early in the process whether at home station or elsewhere. Specifically, leaders take initiative, quickly develop partnerships with the right personnel (for example staff from the Directorate of Plans, Training, Mobilization and Security; range control; or mission training complex), and familiarize themselves with training capabilities. Subsequently, unit leaders take subordinate leaders on a terrain walk of those capabilities.

Figure 2-16 below depicts different training environments and their mixtures at different echelons in relation to the event level of training. There are several LVC options available; commanders determine the mix. For more information on the BTE and ITE, go to the ITE page on ATN.

Several Options: Commanders Determine the Mix								
	Leaders			**Staffs**			**Units**		
	Crawl	*Walk*	*Run*	*Crawl*	*Walk*	*Run*	*Crawl*	*Walk*	*Run*
Brigade	L/V/C	L/V/C	L/V/C	L/C	L/C	L/V/C		L/V/C	L/V/C
Battalion	L/V/C	L/V/C	L/V/C	L/C	L/C	L/V/C		L/V/C	L/V/C
Company	L/V	L/V	L				L/V	L/V	L
Platoon	L/V/C	L/V	L				L/V	L/V	L
Crew/Squad	L/V/C	L/V	L				L/V	L/V	L
Individual	L/V/C	L/V/C	L	L/V	L/V	L	L/V	L/V	L
C constructive			L live			V virtual			

Step 5. Course of Action Comparison

COA comparison is an objective process to evaluate COAs independently and against set evaluation criteria approved by the commander and staff. The commander and staff aim to identify the strengths and weaknesses of each COA, enable selecting a COA with the highest probability of success, and further develop that COA in an OPORD (UTP).

Compare Courses of Action

Comparison of the COAs is critical. The staff uses any technique that helps develop accurate and informed recommendations and assists the commander to make the best decision. A common technique is the decision matrix. This matrix uses evaluation criteria developed during mission analysis and refined during COA development to help assess the effectiveness and efficiency of each COA.

The decision matrix is a tool to compare and evaluate COAs thoroughly and logically. However, the decision matrix is also based on subjective judgments that may change during the evaluation. Values reflect the relative advantages or disadvantages of each criterion for each COA as initially estimated by a chief of staff or executive officer during mission analysis. At the same time, the chief of staff or executive officer determines weights for each criterion based on a subjective determination of their relative value. The lower values signify a more favorable advantage.

The decision matrix provides a very structured and effective method to compare COAs against criteria that, when met, suggest a likelihood of producing success. Staffs give specific broad categories of COA characteristics a basic numerical value based on evaluation criteria. They subjectively assign weights regarding their relative importance to existing circumstances. Then staffs multiply basic values by the weight to yield a given criterion's final score. A staff member then totals all scores to compare COAs.

The staff compares feasible COAs to identify the one with the highest probability of success (MET attainment within the planning horizon). After completing the analysis and comparison, the staff identifies a preferred COA and makes a recommendation to the commander. If the staff cannot reach a decision, the chief of staff or executive officer decides which COA to recommend. (See ADRP 5-0 and FM 6-0 for discussions of COA comparison.)

Course of Action Decision Briefing

Once the staff chooses a training COA for execution, the staff then delivers a decision briefing to the commander. The chief of staff or executive officer highlights any changes to each COA resulting from war¬gaming. The decision briefing includes—

- The commander's training guidance of the higher and next higher commanders.
- The training status of the entire unit (all subordinates).
- The current and projected proficiency rating of the METs—untrained (U), marginally practiced (P-), practiced (P), trained (T-), and fully trained (T).
- The COAs considered, including—
  - Assumptions used.
  - Results of training estimates (as applicable).
- A summary of the war game for each COA, including critical events (such as long-range planning horizon, decision points, and availability of important training facilities and resources), modifications to any COA, and war-game results.
- Advantages and disadvantages (including risks) of each COA.
- The recommended COA. If a significant disagreement exists, then the staff should inform the commander and, if necessary, discuss the disagreement.

tep 6. Course of Action Approval

At the conclusion of the decision briefing, the unit commander—with the advice of the staff, chief of staff or executive officer, and command sergeant major or first sergeant—determines which COA best supports unit training. The selected COA is briefed to the next higher commander for approval.

Step 6: COA Approval

MDMP Steps

Step 1
Receipt of Mission

Step 2
Mission Analysis

Step 3
Course of Action
(COA) Development

Step 4
COA Analysis
(War Game)

Step 5
COA Comparison

Step 6 **COA Approval**	*The next higher commander approves the best course of action that trains the unit.*

Step 7
Orders Production,
Dissemination, and
Transition

Ref: FM 7-0 (Oct '16), fig. 2-17. COA approval.

Step 7. Publish the Unit Training Plan (UTP)

Once the higher commander approves the COA, it ultimately becomes the UTP. The staff organizes the COA, the guidance given by the higher commander, and all additional clarifying information into a five-paragraph field order (brigade and below).

When completed, the staff publishes the unit training plan (UTP) in accordance with the training guidance publication timelines found in tables 1-1 and 1-2 (see pp. 5-20 to 5-21) to subordinate and higher units as appropriate and posts it to DTMS.

See pp. 6-33 to 6-36 an example of a UTP format and general content.

While executing the UTP, the commander may direct changes to the base plan. At brigade and below, the commander communicates these changes to subordinates using fragmentary orders (FRAGORDs) that refer to the base UTP OPORD.

Subordinates receive the FRAGORDs and then begin to develop each of the UTP training events further. The subordinates employ the Army training model by planning for, preparing for, executing, and assessing each training event. They aim for the unit to train the METs to standard. In the development of the UTP and UTP calendar, the staff accounts for how the unit will achieve training proficiency to meet mission requirements.

After developing the training events, the staff publishes the UTP and UTP calendar. An effective UTP calendar includes internal training events such as mandatory training, predeployment training, and installation support. These details provide the unit a complete view of all training requirements during the planning horizons.

As the UTP is executed, unit commanders have a responsibility to minimize training distracters. A major training distracter occurs when the higher headquarters levies tasking requirements to subordinate units after training plans are approved and published. Taskings issued outside tasking policy timelines (refer to AR 350-1) contribute to training planned, but not conducted.

See facing page (p. 6-33) for overview and further discussion of Step 7: Orders Production, Dissemination and Transition.

Training Briefing (TB)

To ensure the division-level commander has visibility of, and concurs with the approved UTPs, the brigade commander conducts a training briefing (TB) with the division-level commander. The TB is a backbrief to the division commander of the overall unit long-range training strategy as described by the UTP.

Periodic reviews and updates of UTP execution briefed during the TB are conducted during QTBs (for Regular Army units) or YTBs (for Reserve Component units).

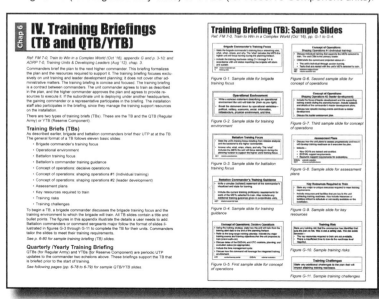

See pp. 6-73 to 6-76 for discussion of training briefings.

Ic. Unit Training Plan Format (OPLAN/OPORD)

Ref: ADRP 7-0, Training Units & Developing Leaders (Aug '12), chap. 3.

Once the higher commander approves the COA at the TB, the plan is developed as the UTP. The commander—supported by the staff at battalion and higher—begins to organize the COA, the guidance given by the higher commander, and all additional clarifying information into a five-paragraph field order. When completed, the commander disseminates it to subordinate and higher units as appropriate and posts it to the DTMS.

Step 7. Orders Production, Dissemination, and Transition

Figure F-1 below illustrates the seven steps of the MDMP. Figure F-2, on the following pages, illustrates a sample UTP OPORD for brigade, battalion, and company levels.

Step 7: Orders Production

MDMP Steps

Step 1
Receipt of Mission

Step 2
Mission Analysis

Step 3
Course of Action
(COA) Development

Step 4
COA Analysis
(War Game)

Step 5
COA Comparison

Step 6
COA Approval

Step 7
Orders Production,
Dissemination, and
Transition

Once the training course of action is approved, the unit training plan is disseminated via the Digital Training Management System.

Ref: FM 7-0 (Oct '16), fig. F-1. Production and dissemination of the UTP. See BSS5: The Battle Staff SMARTbook, 5th Ed. for a complete discussion on preparing an OPORD.

Planning Training

Annotated OPLAN/OPORD Format

Ref: *FM 7-0, Train to Win in a Complex World (Oct '16), app. F.*

[CLASSIFICATION]

Place the classification at the top and bottom of every page of the OPLAN or OPORD. Place the classification marking at the front of each paragraph and subparagraph in parentheses. Refer to AR 380-5 for classification and release marking instructions.

Copy ## of ## copies
Issuing headquarters
Place of issue
Date-time group of signature
Message reference number

The first line of the heading is the copy number assigned by the issuing headquarters. A log is maintained of specific copies issued to addressees. The second line is the official designation of the issuing headquarters (for example, 1st Infantry Division). The third line is the place of issue. It may be a code name, postal designation, or geographic location. The fourth line is the date or date-time group that the plan or order was signed or issued and becomes effective unless specified otherwise in the coordinating instructions. The fifth line is a headquarters internal control number assigned to all plans and orders in accordance with unit standing operating procedures (SOPs).

OPERATION PLAN/ORDER [number] [(code name)] [(classification of title)]
Example: **OPORD 3411 (OPERATION DESERT DRAGON) (UNCLASSIFIED)**

Number plans and orders consecutively by calendar year. Include code name, if any.

(U) References: *List documents essential to understanding the operation plan (OPLAN) or operation order (OPORD). For example, higher headquarters training guidance, higher headquarters directives, OPORDs, ADP 7-0, ADRP 7-0, FM 7-0, Combined Arms Training Strategies (CATSs), Army Training Network (ATN), Digital Training Management System (DTMS), and decisive action standardized mission-essential task list (METL).*

(U) Time Zone Used Throughout the OPLAN/OPORD: *State the time zone used in the training environment during execution. (Optional)*

(U) Task Organization: *Describe the organization of forces available to the issuing headquarters and their command and support relationships. Refer to Annex A (Task Organization) if long or complicated.*

1. **(U)** <u>Situation</u>. Describe the conditions and circumstances of an operational environment for which the unit must train in the following subparagraphs:

    a. (U) <u>Training Environment</u>. Use the operational variables to describe the environment at battalion and above and use the mission variables for company and below (a useful resource for the variables is ADRP 3-0, Operations).

    b. (U) <u>Friendly Forces</u>. Briefly identify the missions of friendly forces and the objectives, goals, and missions of civilian organizations that impact the issuing headquarters.

    c. (U) <u>Training Risk, Challenges and Resources</u>. List any significant training risks (such as insufficient time or resources) and challenges (such as difficulty obtaining resources or assets required to execute training) identified during planning. Describe any approved mitigating measures. This is not personnel safety risk.

[page number]
[CLASSIFICATION]

PLAN/OPORD [number] [(code name)]—[issuing headquarters] [(classification of title)]
*ace the classification and title of the OPLAN/OPORD and the issuing headquarters at
the top of the second and any subsequent pages of the base plan or order.*

d. (U) <u>Attachments and Detachments</u>. List units attached or detached for training
m the issuing headquarters. State when attachment or detachment is effective if dif-
ent from the effective time of the OPORD. Do not repeat information already listed in
nex A (Task Organization).

e. (U) <u>Assumptions</u>. List assumptions used for unit training plan (UTP) development,
example key challenges to training readiness, scarce or unique resources required to
in, and estimated training time to achieve task proficiency.

(U) Mission. State the unit's mission—a short description of the who, what (task),
en, where, and why (purpose) that clearly indicates the action to be taken and the
son for doing so. (Always include the mission-essential tasks [METs] and collective
ks in the mission statement, as they are the essential tasks to be trained as a result
mission analysis.)

(U) Execution. Describe how the commander trains the unit to proficiency in terms of
mmander's guidance, an overarching concept of operations, task assessment, speci-
d tasks to subordinate units, and key coordinating instructions in the subparagraphs
low.

a. (U) <u>Commander's Training Guidance</u>. Provide commander's training guidance
a brief statement to include unit METs or collective tasks. The commander's training
idance is a clear and concise statement of the tasks' proficiency and leader traits and
lls that the unit must achieve to successfully conduct operations in an anticipated
erational environment. It succinctly describes what constitutes the success of the
ining plan and provides the purpose and conditions that define that desired end state.

b. (U) <u>Concept of Operations</u>. The concept of operations is a statement that directs
manner in which subordinate units cooperate to obtaining MET or collective task pro-
ency and leader development. The concept establishes the sequence of actions and
ining events that the force will use to achieve the commander's training end state. It
normally expressed in terms of decisive, shaping, and sustaining operations. The UTP
endar helps portray the concept of operations and is located in Annex C (Collective
aining Plan).

(1) (U) <u>Decisive Operations (Collective Training)</u>. Describe the collective training
n that units will use to achieve MET or collective task proficiency. Refer to Annex C
ollective Training Plan) for the training focus for each training event on the calendar.

(2) (U) <u>Shaping Operation #1 (Individual Training)</u>. Describe the individual
ining plan and how it supports the achievement of MET or collective task proficiency.
fer to Annex D (Individual Training Plan) for specific tasks.

(3) (U) <u>Shaping Operation #2 (Leader Development)</u>. Describe the unit's leader
velopment plan. Include leader certification, skills required to support the unit MET or
lective task, officer professional development programs, and noncommissioned of-
er professional development programs. Refer to Annex E (Leader Development Plan)
specific tasks.

c. (U) <u>Assessment</u>. Describe how the commander plans to assess training, MET
collective task proficiency, and leader development (may also require an annex or
pendix).

Continued on next page
Continued on next page

Planning Training

d. (U) <u>Tasks to Subordinate Units</u>. State the task assigned to each unit that reports directly to the headquarters issuing the order.

e. (U) <u>Coordinating Instructions</u>. List instruction and tasks applicable to two or more units not covered in the unit's training SOPs.

(1) (U) <u>Timing</u>. State the time or condition when the OPORD becomes effective and list the operational timeline.

(2) (U) <u>Training Friendly Force Information Requirements</u>. List the commander's plan to address key challenges to training.

(3) (U) <u>Other Coordinating Instructions</u>. List additional coordinating instructions and tasks that apply to two or more units.

4. (U) Sustainment. Describe the concept of sustainment, including priorities of sustainment by unit. Include installation requirements not included in SOPs. Include the projected dates of installation training resource conferences.

5. (U) Command and Signal. Include any changes from steady state (garrison) operations or state "no change."

ACKNOWLEDGE: *Provide instructions for how the addressees acknowledge receipt of the OPLAN or OPORD. The word "acknowledge" may suffice. Refer to the message reference number if necessary. Acknowledgement of an OPLAN or OPORD means that it has been received and understood.*

[Commander's last name]

Commander's rank]

The commander or authorized representative signs the original copy. If the representative signs the original, add the phrase "For the Commander." The signed copy is the historical copy and remains in the headquarters' files.

OFFICIAL:

[Authenticator's name]

[Authenticator's position]

Use only if the commander does not sign the original order. If the commander signs the original, no further authentication is required. If the commander does not sign, the signature of the preparing staff officer requires authentication and only the last name and rank of the commander appear in the signature block.

ANNEXES: *List annexes by letter and title. Army and joint OPLANs or OPORDs do not use Annexes I and O as attachments and in Army orders label these annexes "Not Used." Annexes T, X, and Y are available for use in Army OPLANs or OPORDs and are labeled as "Spare." When an attachment required by doctrine or an SOP is unnecessary, label it "Omitted."*

Annex A–Task Organization Annex B– Training Environment Annex C– Collective Training Plan

Appendix 1 – METL with projected assessment for start of training and end of training

Appendix 2 – Calendar

Appendix 3 – Collective Training Event Objectives Annex D– Individual Training Plan Annex E– Leader Development Plan

DISTRIBUTION: A (example only)

[page number]
[CLASSIFICATION]

II. Unit Training Meetings

Ref: ADRP 7-0, Training Units & Developing Leaders (Aug '12), pp. 3-11 and FM 7-0, Train to Win in a Complex World (Oct '16), pp. 3-8 to 3-14.

Training meetings provide an integrating function to allow the commander, staff, subordinate commanders, and other leaders to manage current and future training events that support the UTP. Training meetings provide commanders with continuous bottom-up feedback on requirements, task proficiency, task performance, and the quality of the training conducted. They give the commander an opportunity to provide feedback to the unit on its unit training and leader development. The meetings allow the commander to allocate resources to ensure subordinates have what they need to achieve their objectives.

Unit Training Meetings

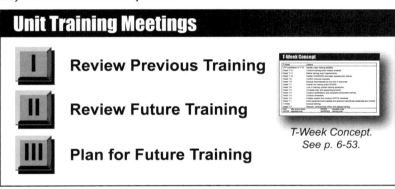

I Review Previous Training

II Review Future Training

III Plan for Future Training

T-Week Concept. See p. 6-53.

The T-Week concept provides the general framework and guide for planning and coordination of training events during training meetings. See pp. 6-53 to 6-76.

Training meetings are the single most important meeting for managing training in brigades, battalions, and companies. Normally, platoons, companies, and battalions meet weekly. At company and platoon level, training meetings focus on the specifics of assessing previous training events, training preparation, pre-execution checks, and execution. Companies must become proficient in individual skills and small-unit collective tasks to support battalion and brigade collective task proficiency. At battalion level and above, training meetings primarily cover training management—especially resourcing issues—as well as staff training proficiencies. Meeting frequency is a function of command preference, but occurs often enough to ensure subordinate units have what they require to execute training.

Training meetings are non-negotiable-they are key to near-term planning. Training meetings create the bottom-up flow of information regarding specific training proficiency needs of the small unit, staff, and individual soldier. Training meetings are planned and appear on the training schedule.

At training meetings, each echelon reviews recently conducted training. They also refine and plan training for the next 6 to 8 weeks. Training meetings provide guidance to ensure the quality of training. Well-structured, organized, and recurring training meetings impact directly on the unit's mission. Training meetings should last no more than 1 hour and should focus on training (leaders should not discuss readiness status issues, nor treat the meeting as a command and staff meeting, etc.).

I. Unit Training Meetings [Overview]

Ref: FM 7-0, Train to Win in a Complex World (Oct '16), pp. 3-8 to 3-10.

Training meetings provide the commander and unit leaders a forum to meet periodically to assess past, current, and future training. Training meetings are among the most important meetings a unit conducts. Brigades conduct training meetings monthly whereas battalions and companies conduct them weekly. At company training meetings the commander assesses training just conducted based on the bottom-up feedback provided by evaluators. At brigade and battalion levels, training meetings focus on overall long-and mid-range planning progress and ensuring that training resources for subordinate units are coordinated for within the command and at the installation level. Training meetings also provide a forum for the command to track and assess UTP progress and direct modifications to the plan, as needed.

Note. Although this discussion focuses on the company level, training meetings held at battalion and brigade are no less important and are equally vital to ensuring unit training proficiency. Training meetings at all echelons apply the basic ideas discussed in this section.

Battalion and Brigade Training Meetings

In support of company-level training, battalions and brigades also conduct training meetings. These focus on overall UTP progress and more critically, on ensuring that training resources for subordinate companies are coordinated for and available when training begins. The brigade is responsible for interfacing with agencies in the installation training support system (typically, the installation Directorate of Plans, Training, Mobilization and Security). Training meetings occur weekly at the battalion level and monthly at brigade level. At battalion and brigade levels, attendees include—

- Commander.
- Deputy commander (at brigade-level).
- Executive officer.
- Command sergeant major.
- Battalion commanders and command sergeants major (at brigade-level); company commanders and first sergeants (at battalion level).
- All primary coordinating staff (such as the S-1, S-2, and S-3).
- Key staff officers and NCOs.
- Supporting and supported unit representatives.

The agenda topics covered at brigade and battalion training meetings include—

- Training just completed (last month). This is the forum for the commander, based on bottom-up feedback (such as AARs and T&EOs) to assess the METs trained in this period.
- Training scheduled but not conducted (and why).
- Training highlights (to include event training objectives for the next 45 days down to company level).
- Installation training resource synchronization conferences scheduled for the next 6 to 90 days and the status of unit training resource requests.

Company Training Meetings

At company training meetings, the T-Week concept (see appendix H) drives the discussion for the detailed planning of each training event. Also at the company level, bottom-up feedback from subordinate leaders and evaluators provide the necessary input to objectively assess training conducted.

See facing page for a hypothetical company training meeting (fig. 3-6).

Notional Company Training Meeting Vignette

On Tuesday at 1300, B Company conducts its recurring training meeting. In attendance is the company commander, first sergeant, executive officer, supply sergeant, and platoon leaders and platoon sergeants. The company commander, CPT Angela Hawkins, begins the meeting on time following a set agenda. She and the executive officer also keep the meeting from straying to other tangents and focus

Last week, the company conducted a FTX. During this event, the company focused one of its training objectives on the collective task 'Occupy an Assembly Area.' CPT Hawkins indicated that this task was previously assessed as a P-rating. The commander wanted to use the FTX to improve this assessment to a T-rating. During the training meeting, the commander reviews the bottom-up feedback from the platoon leaders, the T&EOs provided by observers from company A, and her own observations. Based on this feedback, she assesses the company as a T-rating for this task. The executive officer updates the task 'Occupy an Assembly Area' from a

Platoon leaders and sergeants stated that they conducted hip-pocket training during the FTX. They acknowledge the unit still needs to use available down time to work on Warrior tasks and battle drills identified by the commander and first sergeant. CPT Hawkins emphasizes that leaders need to take every available opportunity to train Soldiers to improve individual skills. She states that with limited training time, company leaders need to take advantage of available time to improve on these

Attention now turns to the coordination for upcoming events within the next six weeks. The executive officer pulls up the UTP calendar from the DTMS to review these future events. The commander sees that the company is at T-Week 5 for an M4 qualifying range. She asks the executive officer if the DA Form 581 (Request for Issue and Turn-In of Ammunition) request for ammunition is approved and if convoy clearances and driver certifications for the pick-up at the ammunition holding area are on track. The executive officer indicated that approvals, clearances, and certifications are in and that 1LT Johnson and SSG Rolf are the range officer and NCO in charge of the range. The commander asks them both for an update on range safety and the plan to run each platoon through a virtual weapons trainer prior to the range.

Looking beyond 6 weeks at the mid-range planning horizon, the commander reviews the training objectives for each major training event to make sure that the company stays on track with the UTP. She provides additional planning guidance at this time and emphasizes to the platoon leaders that resource planning is vitally important at every step in the T-weeks leading up to any event.

At 1430 hours, the commander concludes the company training meeting.

Quarterly and Yearly Training Briefing (QTB/YTB)

QTBs (for Regular Army) and YTBs (for Reserve Component) are periodic UTP updates the commander two echelons above. These briefings support the TB that is briefed or to the start of training. Similar to the TB, the brigade commander provides the brigade training overview, and battalion commanders and command sergeants major of the current status of UTP progress. Battalion commanders in separate brigades and regiments present the QTB to corps major subordinate commanders. The YTB for Reserve Component units is normally presented to the next higher commander. The YTB conducted prior to the start of the fiscal year in Reserve Component units.

See pp. 6-73 to 6-76 for further discussion.

II. Training Meetings

Ref: FM 7-0, Train to Win in a Complex World (Oct '16), app. C.

Training meetings provide the commander and unit leaders with visibility of the current state of unit training readiness and are the key to keeping the UTP on course. Accordingly, they are a recurring entry on the company's weekly training schedule. Training meetings also facilitate the top-down/bottom-up flow of training information and coordination.

The T-Week concept provides the general framework and guide for planning and coordination of training events during training meetings. See pp. 6-53 to 6-76.

Note. Although the following discussion focuses on the company level, training meetings held at battalion and brigade are no less important and are equally vital to ensuring unit training proficiency. Training meetings at all echelons apply the basic ideas discussed in this section.

Feedback is an important aspect of training meetings and is used to refine the UTP as it progresses. Feedback takes many forms including personal observation, AAR and informal evaluations. Subordinates provide their bottom-up feedback when they assess the training proficiency needs of the unit and individual Soldiers. Leaders provide top-down feedback when they conduct training meetings. The agenda of a training meeting includes reviewing past training, identifying and planning necessary retraining, planning and preparing future training, and exchanging timely training information between leaders. A training meeting is a forum for discussing training assessments and unit, leader, and task proficiencies.

Training meetings are not a forum for discussion of administrative operations or activities not related to training. Training is the sole topic. Training meetings have three goals:

- **Review past training** (previous week) to include—
  - Training scheduled but not conducted and the reason why it was not conducted.
  - The commander's review of bottom-up feedback and assessment of tasks trained. After the assessment, commanders record them in DTMS.
- **Review future training events** (to T-Week 5) to include—
  - Re-confirming the training focus and training objectives for future events. Validate tasks (collective and individual) to train focusing on the METs.
  - Ensuring training resources are coordinated and locked in for each event as well as resolving resource discrepancies.
- **Ensure that face-to-face cross-communication between leaders occurs** and that they discuss and resolve training issues. Subordinate leaders provide assessments of proficiencies as well as ensure tasks trained at platoon, squad and individual levels are executed and assessed to standard and support the tasks the company must train.

Successful training meetings—

- Validate the tasks (collective and individual) to train for upcoming events, focusing on the METs.
- Synchronize unit METs with training events.
- Delegate and confirm responsibilities critical to executing events.
- Review and confirm resource requirements and statuses.
- Ensure communication between leaders.
- Refine the training focus—METs and training objectives—for upcoming events

Leaders alternate training events with training meetings. After a unit executes tasks during a training event, the leader assesses the unit's performance of the training event. The unit continues to retrain the MET to standard until it attains proficiency. When an external trainer makes an assessment, the commander records the unit proficiency in the DTMS.

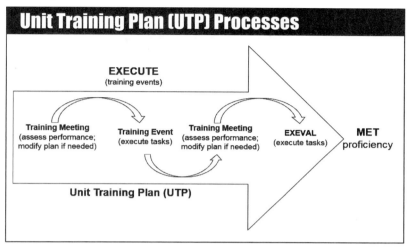

Unit Training Plan (UTP) Processes

EXECUTE
(training events)

Training Meeting
(assess performance;
modify plan if needed)

Training Event
(execute tasks)

Training Meeting
(assess performance;
modify plan if needed)

EXEVAL
(execute tasks)

MET
proficiency

Unit Training Plan (UTP)

Ref: FM 7-0 (Oct '16), fig. C-1. UTP processes from execution to MET proficiency.

Commanders individually manage and coordinate each training event to ensure the UTP is executed as designed. If the staff needs to modify the UTP based on the unit achieving (or not achieving) specific, published training objectives, then the staff uses the commander's guidance given during training meetings. This guidance drives future training event planning, and ultimately, the UTP.

Training Meeting Recurrence Time

Company training meetings have set routines. They occur at a regular time and place while following a set agenda. Company training meetings include updating company METs and coordinating for training. Lastly, training meetings include a review of preexecution checks as well as a plan for future training.

Generally, leaders conduct training meetings on the same day and time each week. This regularity provides a degree of battle rhythm in training, consistency, and predictability. Leaders can conduct training meetings using collaborative electronic means, like a video teleconference (commonly known as VTC), or a teleconference as necessary.

Leaders consider several factors before selecting a time to conduct training meetings. Main considerations include—

- Enabling leaders to attend.
- Minimizing training disruptions.
- Allowing subordinate leaders time to prepare.
- Local policy.

Reserve Component company commanders encounter more challenges when scheduling training meetings. They have three alternatives:

- Conduct the meeting during a regularly scheduled drill period.
- Conduct the meeting during an additional training assembly.
- Conduct the training meeting during a "for points only" or non-paid assembly.

A. Training Meeting Participants

Ref: FM 7-0, Train to Win in a Complex World (Oct '16), pp. C-2 to C-4.

Leader participation is essential for a successful company training meeting. The commander determines the participants to attend. The following lists suggested participants to attend company training meetings and their responsibilities.

Training Meeting Participants

- Company Commander
- Executive Officer
- First Sergeant issloned Officers (NCOs)
- Platoon Leaders
- Platoon Sergeants
- Key Staff Noncommissioned Officers
- Supporting Maintenance Personnel
- Supply Sergeants
- Master Gunners
- Attached and Other Support Leaders

Company Commander

The commander (known as CO) runs the training meeting and is responsible for following the agenda. Prior to the meeting, the commander updates the training estimate of the company's proficiency to meet UTP training objectives. The commander reviews the assessment of the collective tasks to train, the UTP calendar, upcoming training schedules, and upcoming training event OPORDs. The commander then provides guidance for upcoming events and adjusts the focus for future training events' based on this review. Next, the commander confirms the status of resource requests and their requirements. The commander updates the training estimate—to include collective task assessment, training risk status of external resources, and status of trainers—and specifies the individual Soldier tasks for hip-pocket training with advice from a company first sergeant.

Executive Officer

The executive officer (known as XO) runs the training meeting in the commander's absence and coordinates training for all the Soldiers in sections or attachments without platoon leaders or platoon sergeants. The executive officer reviews the current assessment for METs and supporting collective tasks. The executive officer provides the status of resources to support upcoming events and identifies resource issues affecting upcoming training. Additionally, the executive officer identifies and consolidates new resource requirements based on an adjustment of tasks to train for upcoming events.

First Sergeant

The first sergeant (known as 1SG) is the senior enlisted advisor to the commander on all issues that affect not only individual training in the unit but also collective training. The first sergeant provides an assessment of individual and collective tasks as well as on training of key warrior tasks and battle drills that support the company's collective tasks to train. The first sergeant provides guidance and advice on training plans and reviews preexecution checks discussed during the training meeting. Additionally, the first sergeant helps in the leader development of officers and NCOs by actively participating forming effective training plans for platoons (tasks to train and identification of resource requirements). The first sergeant advises the commander on the selection of individual soldier tasks for hip-pocket training.

Platoon Leaders

Based on training conducted, platoon leaders brief on their assessments of collective tasks and on training of key leader tasks, warrior tasks, and battle drill proficiency of their platoon. Platoon leaders recommend adjusting training focus (tasks to train) for upcoming events based on their assessments. Additionally, they confirm previously submitted resource requirements for upcoming events, or they identify new resource requests based on a change to the training focus for an upcoming event.

Platoon Sergeants

Platoon sergeants provide their assessment of section-or crew-level and individual tasks based on training conducted. They observe and receive feedback from squad leaders on the status of individual training conducted and support the company's collective tasks. Platoon sergeants brief the status of specific essential preexecution checks—including the status of trainer, resources, tasks to train, or site reconnaissance—for upcoming events. Additionally, platoon sergeants provide input to any changes—such as collective tasks, warrior tasks, battle drills to train, and resource requirements—to upcoming events.

Key Staff Noncommissioned Officers

Master gunners and other key staff NCOs attend training meetings and advise the commander on the status of specialized training. For example, the master gunner works with the first sergeant to track individual and crew-served weapons qualifications and helps leaders with gunnery training assessments. Other key NCOs identify and advise leaders on opportunities to integrate specialized training into upcoming events. Additionally, they advise leaders on specialized resource requirements for upcoming events.

Supporting Maintenance Personnel

Supporting maintenance personnel coordinate the maintenance efforts of the company and work with the commander and executive officer to ensure timely support is provided. Supporting maintenance personnel provide input on the status of maintenance training in the company, recommend maintenance-related training, and inform the commander of scheduled services and inspections that will impact training. These personnel identify any issues that will impact upcoming training events. Additionally, they may advise the commander on maintenance training requirements based on an assessment of training previously conducted.

Supply Sergeants

Supply sergeants provide input to the commander on supply-related issues, inspections, and inventories. Supply sergeants also work with the executive officer and first sergeant to coordinate necessary support from outside sources. They assist the executive officer and first sergeant in identifying, coordinating, and resourcing logistic support requirements—internal and external—for future training events.

Master Gunners

Unit master gunners (if applicable) provide the status of training and requirements for gunnery for the entire unit. They continually coordinate and update this information with the company executive officer and first sergeant prior to the training meeting.

Attached and Other Support Leaders

Other leaders attend training meetings to coordinate their training efforts with those of the company. For example, a commander for an artillery battery with an attached target acquisition radar section may attend the meeting. These leaders provide their assessment of tasks and battle drills previously trained. They confirm the tasks to train and the status of resource requirements for upcoming events.

B. Training Meeting Agenda

Ref: FM 7-0, Train to Win in a Complex World (Oct '16), pp. C-4 to C-9.

The agenda is keyed to the T-Week concept. There are three phases to company training meetings. The first is used to assess previous training (T-Week +1). The second phase is used to coordinate upcoming events (T-Week 5 through T-Week 1). The final phase is used to plan training for future training events (T-Week 7 and T-Week 6). The agenda maintains a focus for all to see, understand, and follow. Staffs post the agenda prior to the meeting.

See pp. 6-49 to 6-72 for a detailed discussion of the T-Week Concept.

Training Meeting Phases

 Review Previous Training

 Review Future Training

*T-Week Concept.
See p. 6-49.*

 Plan for Future Training

Agenda Items

In the first phase of the training meeting agenda, the commander reviews the previous week's training:

- Update the platoon or subordinate element assessments, to include collective and individual tasks, warrior tasks, and battle drill training (T-Week +1).
- Identify training not conducted.
- Update company assessments (METs).
- Identify retraining required.
- Identify DTMS database update requirements and responsibilities.

In the second phase of the training meeting agenda, the commander coordinates by—

- Reviewing FRAGORDs that include new or updated command guidance.
- Conducting preexecution checks T-Week 5 through T-Week 1.
- Identifying any changes to upcoming events (tasks to train).

In the third phase of the training meeting, the commander discusses future planning:

- Review battalion and company UTP calendar for adjustment as needed.
- Provide commander's updated planning guidance for events (adjust training focus of events).
- Demonstrate how platoon tasks support the company METLs (from the company UTP).
- Review the draft training schedule for T-Week 6 and T-Week 7.
- Review the major T-Week milestones for T-Week 8 through UTP publication, assign responsibility for the tasks, and receive updates.
- Confirm and identify additional resource requirements.

me Requirements

aining meetings should not last more than an hour and a half if well organized. The
ent is for the commander to achieve the meeting objectives as quickly and efficiently
possible.

Action	Time
Review of previous week's training	30 Minutes
Preparation for T-5 through T-1 training	30 Minutes
Future planning (T-7 and T-6), including a review of major milestones (T-8 through UTP publication)	30 Minutes
T training week UTP unit training plan	

ef: FM 7-0 (Oct '16), table C-1. Approximate times for each phase of a training meeting.

hase I: Review Previous Training

eview Last Week's Training

ommanders begin the meeting by discussing the training just completed. The bottom-
p input by the platoon leaders and platoon sergeants is critical to assessing collective,
ader, and individual training proficiency of the unit. Company leaders discuss the
genda items listed below and then record the assessments in DTMS.

latoon Assessment

latoon leaders and platoon sergeants assess collective and battle task proficiency rat-
ngs and Soldier proficiency ratings since the last training meeting. The sources of the
latoon assessment may be formal or informal and based on the task T&EO. A platoon
ssessment includes—

- Collective tasks, battle tasks, leader tasks, Soldier tasks, warrior tasks, battle drills.

- The proficiency rating—fully trained (T), trained (T-), practiced (P), marginally practiced (P-), and untrained (U)—of all training conducted by the platoon assessments
  from T&EOs (also GO and NO-GO results from the performance steps, as necessary).

raining Shortfalls

As each platoon completes the training assessment, leaders address training shortfalls.
A training shortfall occurs when a unit plans training but does conduct it. Platoon leaders
nust explain to the commander the reasons for not executing training and the plans to
eschedule the missed training. A training shortfall also occurs when a unit fails to meet
training objectives. If a unit fails to meet objectives, it must retrain on those tasks until
t earns a fully trained (T) or trained (T-) proficiency rating score. Commanders record
training shortfalls that include—

- Training planned but not conducted (include discussion of tasks not trained).
- The reason for not executing training.
- A retraining plan, if needed.

Assessment of completed training may reveal training that is incomplete or not conducted to the Army standard. Leaders conduct retraining at the first opportunity, ideally during
the same training period. However, when this cannot happen, leaders may need to adjust
subsequent training events (adding or subtracting tasks to train) to retrain on those tasks
that the unit failed to train to standard. Staff then adjust the UTP for future events.

In reviewing retraining requirements, company leaders consider several factors:

- The number of Soldiers or elements involved.
- The sequential order of retraining with other planned training. Leaders determine if
  one task needs to be trained before proceeding to a future task.
- Resource availability (such as ranges, instructors, and logistics).
- Original planning and modification for the task, as necessary.

Continued on next page

Planning
Training

Training Meeting Agenda (Cont.)

Ref: FM 7-0, Train to Win in a Complex World (Oct '16), pp. C-4 to C-9.

- The time and place to conduct rescheduled training at the first available opportunit
- The resources available, in particular the resources needed to retrain a task. Retraining takes priority over training new tasks.

Updated Company Mission-Essential Task Assessments

Once subordinates have provided their assessments, the commander and first sergean provide their input to training conducted and identify any training shortfalls. This proces not only ensures a common understanding of the commander's training end state (bas on the unit mission and guidance) for the unit but also develops subordinate leaders. Through this open dialogue, commanders hold their subordinate leaders responsible for training their respective organizations. This is a critical aspect of the process as it is imperative that leaders develop subordinates.

After all platoons complete their training assessments and discuss any training shortfall the commander—with input from the first sergeant, platoon leaders, and executive officer—ensures that company MET assessments are updated in DTMS.

Phase II: Review Future Training Events

Coordination For Short-Range Training

Coordination for training (T-Week 5 through T-Week 1) requires a review of command guidance and preexecution checks.

Review of Command Guidance. During a review of command guidance, the unit reviews FRAGORDs or any other new or updated command guidance that will impact training (T-Week 5 through T-Week 1). The guidance could be either externally directed or based on the commander's assessment of the unit. Commanders convey the purpose of the training and the desired end state, but exercising mission command, they leave the how to achieve the results to subordinates. This latitude allows subordinates to use their critical and creative thinking to support the commander's guidance and vision. Additionally, leaders understand and assess the impact of this command guidance on the current training plan, discussing this impact and its associated risks.

Leaders identify training events that the staff will modify to incorporate the tasks previously identified during the assessment of last week's training. Again, leaders discuss the adjustments to the current training plan to understand clearly their impact on the commander's end state for upcoming training. Once leaders understand the training focus for the upcoming events, the company leadership reviews key aspects of the preexecution checks for these events.

Preexecution Checks

Preexecution checks are procedures, usually using checklists, employed to ensure all planning and prerequisite training (collective, Soldier, and leader) has been conducted prior to the execution of training. These are not precombat checks. A critical part of the training meeting is the discussion of preexecution checks. Preexecution checks are developed by the chain of command, and responsibility for their execution is fixed to ensure training is resourced and conducted properly. As units develop training schedules more fully, these checks become increasingly detailed. Preexecution checks provide the attention to detail that units need to use time and other resources efficiently.

Units modify and refine their lists based on their specific organization and mission. See facing page for sample questions for the preexecution checks. Units strive to answer each question with a yes. If a unit fails to answer in the affirmative, then it has failed to meet that requirement.

eviewing preexecution checks, the commander ensures training events are fully
ined and coordinated with all elements of the company. The time for the company
omplete the checks depends on unit and organization SOPs. It is imperative the
pany commander understands the resource timeline requirements. Regular Army
manders plan one to six weeks out (or even further based on requesting timelines for
urces) when reviewing preexecution checks. Reserve Component commanders plan
hree months. Within these training windows, commanders review preexecution checks
everse order. Commanders start at the last week (for Regular Army) or last month (for
erve Component) and work down until the next training period is covered in detail.
execution checks should be a part of the unit's SOP for training.

following page for list of possible preexecution checks.

ase III: Plan for Future Training

n For Future Training

e third phase of the training meeting, the commander discusses future planning.
nda items for this phase include the following:

- Review battalion and company UTP including its calendar for adjustments.

- Provide the commander's updated planning guidance for events (training objectives).

- Demonstrate how platoon tasks support company METs.

- Review draft training schedule for T-Week 7 and T-Week 6.

- Confirm and identify additional resource requirements.

- Identify individual tasks for hip-pocket training.

company commander must check the battalion UTP. Events indicated on the battalion
calendar or found in the UTP are put on the company training schedule first. After
e events are posted, the commander issues guidance (company tasks to train and the
state of training) for these future events. These tasks support the company's METs
the UTP and the battalion's training focus for the event. The commander's guidance
ts the planning process to support the company's training focus, identify tasks, and
elop preexecution checks to fix responsibilities.

-Pocket Training

pocket training usually consists of individual tasks on which the unit can train when
periences inactive periods during scheduled training. Ideally, leaders train these
cted tasks in 15 to 30 minutes since more time may not be available. It is another
nique for managing sustainment training. Normally, the company commander selects
s for this type of training. Commanders can use training meetings to obtain input from
ordinates on what training needs to be sustained. Hip-pocket training gives leaders
fidence in their abilities to train and results in more efficient use of Soldiers' time. Initial
ning or collective task training ordinarily requires more time and resources than will be
lable for short notice, unscheduled training.

toon Leader And Platoon Sergeant Input

ed on their training assessments, platoon leaders and platoon sergeants review cur-
events identified in the company UTP and validate tasks to train to improve training
iciency. Additionally, these leaders discuss resource requirements. Platoon leaders
platoon sergeants brief the resulting plans (adjusted training focus for future events)
e commander during the training meeting.

ining Schedule Development

nmanders receive input from all platoons and other elements of the company before
ulating the draft training schedule. Because of support limitations or other conflicts,
commander may have to disapprove a training event that a platoon requested or move
another week (Regular Army) or month (Reserve Component).

Possible Training Preexecution Checks

Ref: FM 7-0, Train to Win in a Complex World (Oct '16), fig. C-2, p. 4-21.

The primary trainer indicated on the training schedule briefs preexecution checks. If the primary trainer is the platoon sergeant, then the platoon sergeant briefs the preexecution checks during the training meeting. For almost every training event for platoon and below, the platoon sergeant is the key coordinator. The platoon sergeant coordinates the efforts of other NCOs in the platoon and ensures that training is thoroughly prepared.

- Has unit integrated the lessons learned since the last time they conducted training?
- Is the opposing force equipped and trained (if applicable)?
- Has unit integrated attached elements into planning and execution of training?
- Has unit completed a DD Form 2977 (Deliberate Risk Assessment Worksheet)?
- Do the trainers have the list of tasks to be trained?
- Have leaders identified prerequisite tasks for the training event? Are Soldiers trained on prerequisite tasks prior to the event?
- Does unit have leaders certified to conduct range operations?
- Are trainers identified and available for training?
- Do trainers have training and evaluation outlines for all tasks to be trained?
- Do trainers have a copy of the operation order?
- Has unit programmed rehearsal time for trainers?
- Has unit requested training ranges, facilities, and training areas?
- Has unit conducted a reconnaissance?
- Does unit have range or maneuver books on hand?
- Has unit submitted and received approval for convoy clearances?
- Has unit identified, requested, and approved training aids, devices, simulators, and simulations (TADSS)?
- Can trainers properly operate all TADSS?
- Has unit requested Class I (food)?
- Has unit requested and picked up Class II (fuel)?
- Has unit requested and picked up Class V (ammunition)?
- Has unit requested transportation?
- Does unit have sufficient expendable supplies on hand?
- Has unit deconflicted external taskings and appointments?
- Has unit scheduled time for retraining as necessary?
- Has unit specified the recovery plan in the operation order?
- Has unit scheduled time for an after action review?
- Has unit coordinated the backbrief for the chain of command?

See also p. 6-56.

III. T-Week Concept (Training Schedules)

Ref: FM 7-0, Train to Win in a Complex World (Oct '16), app. H.

The T-Week concept provides a detailed, backward-planning approach when planning training events. This concept also provides important considerations and specific activities for training event planning and coordination. Depending on the scope and complexity of the event, effective planners adjust activities that occur in each T-Week to fit resourcing and coordination requirements. When followed, planners ensure that they complete all actions to identify and coordinate leader and resource requirements prior to training. Each week previous to the execution of training requires planners to carefully coordinate all necessary training resources. These may include training areas, Class V requisitions, convoy clearances, and personnel certifications.

T-Week Concept

T-Week	Actions
UTP publication to T-13	Identify major training facilities
Week T-12	Conduct training event mission analysis
Week T-11	Refine training event requirements
Week T-10	Publish WARNORD and begin preexecution checks
Week T-9	Confirm resource requests
Week T-8	Execute reconnaissance and lock in resources
Week T-7	Publish the training event OPORD
Week T-6	Lock in training; publish training schedules
Week T-5	Complete plan and supporting products
Week T-4	Conduct certifications and complete prerequisite training
Week T-3	Conduct rehearsals
Week T-2	Finalize support and conduct OPFOR rehearsal
Week T-1	Draw equipment and supplies and execute subordinate rehearsals and checks
T-Week	Execute training
Week T+1	Recover, conduct final AARs, and assess training

AAR	after action review	OPORD	operation order
OPFOR	opposing force	WARNORD	warning order

Ref: FM 7-0 (Oct '16), table H-1. Illustrative T-Week concept. Note: Reserve Component units should aggregate activities based on their monthly (rather than a weekly) schedule and published UTP.

The degree of difficulty in planning training events varies. For example, preparations for conducting a class are significantly simpler than planning a FTX. More complex training events require more time to plan and coordinate.

Planners use the T-Week concept as a guide to assist in planning training activities that should occur in anticipation of each event. Each T-Week has an associated series of training activities that help guide planners and advise the commander of the actions the unit must accomplish to execute an effective training event.

The anchor point for the T-Week concept is the week training is executed. This is designated as T-Week. A minus sign (-) indicates the number of weeks prior to a particular training event execution. For example, T-5 is five weeks before the training event occurs. A plus sign (+) indicates the number of weeks following the event, for example, T+1 is one week after the training event. Units modify the T-Week concept to mirror their own local and command training requirements.

Planning Training

The rest of this appendix breaks down major T-Week activities. Units can use this appendix as a guide for developing their own training activities and training event Although this appendix contains extensive descriptions, they do not account for a individual unit or installation's particular resource requirements for planning and c ordination. Additionally, each major training event falls into its own T-week constru as various points on the long-range, mid-range, and short-range planning horizon

UTP Publication to T-13: Identify Major Training Facilities

Even before the UTP is published during the planning process, trainers begin to identify the major training resources and facilities that a training event will require. soon as leaders identify the need for certain training resources and facilities, traine actively begin to secure these for training. Successful planners and trainers requir extensive knowledge of the facilities available on the installation. The installation Directorate of Plans, Training, Mobilization and Security is the primary source for t commander and trainers. This directorate documents and manages locally availab training resources and the manner to schedule their use. These resources fall und the Army training support system. *(Refer to AR 350-2.)*

Training Support Center Resources

An installation training support center is an organization that supplies training aids, devices, and facilities. Different installations offer different resources. A training sup port center may have the following resources available:

- Training land and training areas.
- Indirect firing points.
- Range facilities (to include multipurpose range complex, if available). Such facilities include range control facilities, processes, and may have certification requirements.
- Classroom facilities.
- LVC facilities.
- TADSS and TADSS warehouse.
- Medical Simulation Training Center.
- Flight simulators.
- Multiple Integrated Laser Engagement System (known as MILES) sets.
- Engagement Skills Training (known as EST) 2000.
- Improvised mock explosive training devices.
- Call for Fire Trainer (known as CFFT).

Early planning enables planners to schedule and lock in training facilities and resources for a unit. Depending on the installation, certain facilities are more heavily used than other facilities. Effective planners understand when and how to schedule such vital facilities. Once they schedule and reserve a facility for a unit, the com- mander ensures the unit occupies and uses the facility on the date and at the time scheduled. If planners or leaders cancel a training event, they do it as far in advance as possible so other units can schedule and use the facility.

Installation Planning and Forecasting Tools

Most installations publish a local supplement to provide training support requests for local procedures, tools, and timelines. Some supplements provide links to common forecasting tools, requesting tools, and unique training resources, such as—

- Total Ammunition Management Information System (known as TAMIS).
- Range Facility Management Support System (known as RFMSS).

- Integrated Training Area Management (known as ITAM).
- Mission training complexes.
- Training support centers.
- Medical evacuation (known as MEDEVAC) procedures and frequencies.

G-4s also publish procedures for all other classes of supply and services, food service, maintenance and transportation support, and nonstandard support items such as chemical latrines.

As the unit refines the plan, planners may need to cancel or modify training activities (planners do not cancel or modify activities when the unit is less than 6 weeks from that training). When planners identify that the unit will not need facilities and ranges early enough in the planning cycle, then other units can use the facilities. Installations usually conduct installation-level resource synchronization conferences to schedule and lock in major facilities (see paragraph 1-68 for a discussion on resource synchronization conferences). These conferences may be quarterly, semi-annual, or annual. They provide all units on the installation visibility of facility usage and availability for unit scheduling. Such facilities can include ranges, railhead training facilities, and simulation centers.

-12: Conduct Training Event Mission nalysis

In week T-12, planners conduct training event mission analysis. Gathering the information required to conduct training event planning is critical to developing successful events. Planners use historical information to begin mission analysis. Examples include AARs, inspection results, OPORDs, and troop lists. Historical information provides planners with the start point to shape future planning and for training assessment analysis.

Commanders refer to the approved UTP to re-confirm the METs and training objectives selected to train for each particular training event. Each training event requires a high degree of planning and coordination weeks in advance of execution. The resulting mission analysis ensures that planners account for the training event and the correct METs aligned in the UTP as they begin planning for the training event.

Prerequisite Training

Prerequisite training is any training that a unit must complete or master before the planned training event. Prerequisite events can be any level event—such as classroom instruction, STXs, FTXs, and command post exercises—and are usually required at each progressive level of training difficulty. Commanders determine which events are prerequisites and ensure units perform the tasks to standard prior to beginning the next training event in the UTP. The CATS is the primary resource to view the proponent recommended prerequisite training. In the end, the commander decides whether to perform the CATS's recommended prerequisites, reduce or increase the CATS recommended frequencies, or choose a different prerequisite event based on the commander's experience.

Note. The Combined Report in CATS uses the term training gates to describe the recommended prerequisite events as well as the sequence (crawl-walk-run) for the events. See p. 6-27 for discussion of crawl-walk-run.

Sergeant's Time Training (STT)

As a subset of prerequisite training, commanders, sergeants major, first sergeants, and leaders at every level should always protect, support, incorporate, and maximize the importance of sergeant's time training (STT). STT is standards-based, performance-oriented, and mission-focused training. Commanders emphasize individual Soldier training in support of METs by allocating dedicated training time for NCOs using STT. STT recognizes the NCO's primary role in conducting individual, crew, and small-team training. If individual Soldiers and leaders cannot perform their basic tasks, the unit will never successfully accomplish or gain proficiency in its METs.

Units conduct this beneficial and effective training every week. Many installations serve 3 or 4 hours each week for STT. The day or time of the week is not important. Units plan for, resource, rehearse, and execute STT with no external distracters.

STT builds cohesive teams. Based on their training assessment and platoon leader guidance, NCOs select specific individual, warrior, crew, and small-team tasks that support the unit's METs. Once these tasks are approved, NCOs plan for, prepare, rehearse, execute, and assess the training. Training the team to standard, not to time, is the bottom line; if additional time is needed or tasks must be retrained, the first line leaders must communicate these needs up the chain of command. Units can also use this time to train and educate Soldiers on the essential characteristic of the Army Profession.

STT develops junior leaders. Commanders demonstrate to junior leaders how to approve the selected tasks, provide the necessary resources, allocate time to prepare and monitor the training. When subordinates demonstrate initiative, commanders exercise mission command to engage junior leaders. Command sergeants major or first sergeants supervise the training, and they coach, teach, and mentor junior NCOs.

T-11: Refine Training Event Requirements

In week T-11, planners refine training event requirements. As the unit works through planning for the training event, planners require key pieces of information. An approved UTP contains initial training objectives for each training event, additional guidance, and MET or collective task proficiency requirements. Commanders and staffs review training objectives and refine them as necessary as well as identify additional tasks to train during the event. After refining objectives and tasks, commanders and staff refine the associated requirements for the objectives and tasks. These requirements can include facilities, resources, or materiel. Commanders and staffs refine these objectives and tasks as they execute the UTP and plan, prepare, execute, and assess each training event. Because every plan must be fluid and account for adjustments, commanders and staffs adjust the training objectives for each event during planning to reflect proficiencies mastered or required retraining after each event. See figure H-1 for a sample training objectives for a FTX.

---

17 – 21 February 2017
FTX Armor Company, Training Objectives

Task(s) Focus:
Conduct an Attack (07-2-9001)
Conduct Area Security (07-2-1324)
Breach an Obstacle (17-2-3070)

Conditions: In a complex, live environment, facing an enemy platoon in a prepared defense, occupying a village conduct continuous operations, in both day and night and in various MOPP levels.

Standard: The company conducts operations in accordance with the SOP, the order, and higher guidance.

Training Proficiency: Achieve a T- proficiency rating in the collective tasks Conduct an Attack (07-2-9001), Conduct Area Security (07-2-1324), and Breach an Obstacle (17-2-3070).

FTX	field training exercise	SOP	standard operating procedure
MOPP	mission-oriented protective posture	T-	trained

Ref: FM 7-0 (Oct '16), fig. H-1. Sample training objectives.

The UTP states a broad end state for each training event expressed as a training objective. Based on the commander's current assessment of unit training made during training meetings, training objectives may require refinement. This refinement ensures that the unit continues to progress at the training levels required to attain

MET or collective task proficiency on time. An event end state clearly defines the task proficiency rating required at the end of the event. The end state focuses on the selected METs or collective tasks as well as on leader and individual Soldier training objectives.

After the training objectives for the event are refined, commanders and trainers refer to each task's T&EOs. This reference ensures the unit and OC/Ts can identify the standards for the tasks. OC/Ts also evaluate the training. A unit TDA—for units without proponent-published T&EOs for their tasks—may lack established standards. When no standard exists, the commander determines the conditions and standards, and the next higher commander approves the task. See appendix B for a discussion on T&EOs.

T&EOs are accessed via the "Task Search" on the ATN homepage. Users can also access T&EOs via the CATS Viewer and via DTMS on ATN, if the user has these privileges. T&EOs are also available on the CAR. Planners publish the applicable task T&EOs by task number and title in the OPORD and in separate packets to evaluating personnel. This ensures that commanders, planners, OC/Ts, and leaders at every level can reference and refer to published task standards prior to the commencement of the training event.

The UTP has an initial end state for the event expressed as a training objective. Based on the commander's assessment of training during training meetings leading up to the event, the training objective may also need to be refined or restated. This refinement ensures that the unit continues to progress at the training levels required to attain MET proficiency on time. The event end state should clearly define the performance proficiency level required at the end of the event. The end state focuses on METs as well as on leader and individual training objectives. Any refinement to the training objective includes refining requirements needed to complete the new objectives. For example, planners may need to schedule a range training event.

In refining training event training objectives, CATSs provide additional recommended training event details to consider. For example, commanders consider the integration of combat multipliers while conducting multiechelon training whenever possible. This integration optimizes the time available and ensures the unit trains as it will fight. The CATS also recommends the training audience to optimize the number of individual Soldiers trained during each event.

Training Event Planning Guidance

Commanders provide preexecution guidance to subordinate units early in the planning process. This ensures they meet the commander's guidance throughout the planning process. This guidance helps keep subordinate leaders and planners in synch with the commander's vision for the event. Preexecution guidance can include the following:

- Review AARs from previous events.
- Review training objectives for the event.
- Review applicable T&EOs for each MET trained.
- Review major resource requirements from the UTP.
- Train during normal duty hours unless requested otherwise.
- Identify and assess prerequisite training.
- Update during unit training meetings.

Refer to TC 7-101 for designing exercises. During T-11, planners review the preexecution guidance and refine the requirements as necessary.

Trainer, Evaluator, Observer-Controller/Trainer, and Opposing Force's Duties

Based on the event training objectives, commanders determine the duties for trainers, evaluators, OC/Ts, and OPFORs. Successful planners clearly identify each p of the event to include the requirements and purpose. Planners also identify, qual and later refine supporting individuals (internal or external resource requirements for an event. These personnel should be disinterested persons with regard to the outcome of the training event—typically personnel from outside the evaluated unit In support of OC/T and OPFOR personnel duties, units often provide standardized evaluator packets based on their SOPs, so evaluators understand how the unit op ates tactically.

T-10: Publish Warning Order and Begin Preexecution Checks

In week T-10, commanders publish the WARNORD and begin preexecution check Commanders conduct an initial countertask analysis. This analysis identifies requi ments to train the tasks selected for the event, such as OPFOR actions required t stimulate the collective tasks. These tasks correlate directly to the training environ ment identified in the higher unit training WARNORD. Additional resources are available through the TRADOC Intelligence Support Activity (known as TRISA), Contemporary Operational Environment and Threat Integration Division (known as CTID) site, and the Training Brain Operations Center.

AR 350-2 discusses the roles, responsibilities, and details on the training environment and OPFOR resources.

As part of the training event WARNORD, individual Soldier training objectives—the individual tasks trained by Soldiers during the event—are developed and published in the WARNORD. These training objectives should include individual-focused task and battle drills. These objectives directly correlate to the training environment iden fied in the training WARNORD. These are usually either to be trained during the event, or included with all prerequisite training to be accomplished no later than T-4 Individual supporting tasks and battle drills are found in CATS listed under each of the collective tasks. The training gates are located in the CATS Combined Report and listed under the type of event (such as a FTX).

Training Support

Training support includes selecting training environments, developing a base tactica scenario, and publishing a WARNORD. Once the tasks and the training environmen are determined for an event, the training support enablers must be selected. Trainin support consists of TADSS; facilities (mission training complexes and ranges), and services (personnel running the ranges).

See facing page for discussion of training support to include publishing the warning order.

Preexecution Checks

Preexecution checks are informal checks that units complete to coordinate prior to conducting training events; these are not precombat checks. The chain of command develops these checks to prepare participants systematically and to ensure that units resource and properly conduct training. As units develop training schedules, the checks become increasingly detailed. Preexecution checks provide the attention to detail needed to use resources efficiently.

See following page (p. 6-56) for discussion of prexecution checks.

Training Support (T-10)

Ref: FM 7-0, Train to Win in a Complex World (Oct '16), pp. H-7 to H-8.

Training support includes selecting training environments, developing a base tactical scenario, and publishing a WARNORD. Once the tasks and the training environment are determined for an event, the training support enablers must be selected. Training support consists of TADSS; facilities (mission training complexes and ranges), and services (personnel running the ranges).

1. Select Training Environments

Collective training events take place in three types of training environments: LVC. Planners consider employing each environment independently (the easiest to plan and prepare) or a combination of two or more environments to meet the objective. If using more than one training environment, then leaders use either a BTE or an ITE. Planners choose the environment based on the installation's openings in the fielding schedule and the environment that best enables the unit to accomplish its training objectives in the time allotted.

Just as a leader must understand an operational environment in combat, a leader must understand the training environment for a training event. Leaders and trainers take the initiative, quickly develop partnerships with the right people—personnel at the Directorate of Plans, Training, Mobilization and Security; range control, and the mission training complex—and familiarize themselves with training capabilities. Subsequently, they take subordinate leaders on a terrain walk of those facilities and capabilities.

See pp. 6-28 to 6-29 (LVC) and pp. 7-4 to 7-7 (realistic training) for further discussion

2. Develop a Base Tactical Scenario

A primary driver to the training event is the development of a tactical scenario. The tactical scenario provides a realistic backdrop to training when it properly replicates an operational environment. Focused on the training objectives to achieve during the event, a tactical scenario simulates the situations that cause the unit and Soldiers to act and react to specific situations, whereby the training objectives (collective tasks) can be evaluated and assessed. After determining the OPFOR requirements, a determination of the initial requirements for scripting and role-playing as well as complete the MSEL. All the information gathered and developed during weeks T-11 and T-10 inform the commander of the personnel, logistics, and other resource requirements to support the performance of the training event.

3. Publish WARNORD

Once planners compile the information gathered and developed during weeks T-11 and T-10, the commander issues a WARNORD tasking subordinates and requiring coordination to support the event. The staff distributes the WARNORD at the end of mission analysis to facilitate parallel planning at the subordinate unit level. At a minimum, the WARNORD contains the training audience, training objectives, location, date, resources, and personnel support requirements and training environment guidance.

Planning Training

Preexecution Checks (T-10)

Ref: FM 7-0, Train to Win in a Complex World (Oct '16), pp. H-8 to H-9.

Preexecution checks are informal checks that units complete to coordinate prior to conducting training events; these are not precombat checks. The chain of command develops these checks to prepare participants systematically and to ensure that units resource and properly conduct training. As units develop training schedules, the checks become increasingly detailed. Preexecution checks provide the attention to detail needed to use resources efficiently.

Preexecution checks are an important component of preparation for training events. A unit goes through the checks intending to have a YES for every response. Checks with a NO response require the unit to make corrections. Sample questions for a preexecution checklist can include the following:

- Is the current level of collective or individual task proficiency rating a trained or fully trained?
- Have the lessons learned from the last time training been applied?
- Has the OPFOR been equipped and trained (if applicable)?
- Are combat multipliers integrated into planning and execution of training?
- Has a risk assessment been completed? Have safety considerations been completed?
- Are Soldiers trained on prerequisite tasks?
- Has the appropriate training support been requested?
- Has reconnaissance of the training site been conducted?
- Are ranges and maneuver books on hand?
- Are leaders certified to conduct range operations?
- Are leaders briefed on environmental considerations?
- Have convoy clearances been submitted and approved?
- Have TADSS been identified, requested, and approved?
- Can trainers properly operate all TADSS?
- Has Class I been requested?
- Has Class III been requested and picked up?
- Has Class V been requested per ammunition supply point requirements and picked up?
- Has transportation been requested?
- Are sufficient expendable supplies on hand?
- Is a rehearsal time programmed for trainers?
- Has a backbrief for the chain of command been coordinated?
- Are times scheduled for AARs at the end and throughout the exercise?

See also p. 6-48.

Individual Tasks

Individual training task focus (weeks T-9 to T-7) in preparation for the company FTX:

- Move Under Direct Fire (071-COM-0502)
- Direct Main Gun Engagements on M1-Series Tank (171-126-1322)
- Direct Machine Gun Engagements on M1-Series Tank (171-126-1262)
- Communicate in a Radio Net (113-571-1003)
- Engage Targets with M16 / M4 Series Carbine (071-COM-0030)

Battle Drills

Battle drill focus training (weeks T-6 to T-4) in preparation for the company FTX:

- React to an IED Attack While Mounted (05-3-D0017)
- React to Direct Fire Contact (07-3-D9501)
- React to Indirect Fire (07-3-D9504)
- React to CBRN Attack (17-3-D8006)
- Breach of a Mined Wired Obstacle (07-3-D9412)

Training Gates

Individual tasks and battle drills nested with training gates (from CATS) for an armor company FTX:

- STX Attack
- STX Defend
- STX Breaching Operations

CATS	Combined Arms Training Strategy	IED	improvised explosive device
CBRN	chemical, biological, radiological, and nuclear	STX	situational training exercise
FTX	field training exercise		

Ref: FM 7-0 (Oct '16), fig. H-2 illustrates individual training objectives provided to a company by a platoon.

Training Environment

As part of the training environment identified in the WARNORD, the staff analyzes potential operational environments to provide the requisite amount of realism to the training. A training environment that properly replicates a potential operational environment provides a higher degree of fidelity to the training scenarios developed in support of the event. Ultimately, it makes the training more challenging and realistic for the unit and at the Soldier level. When published in the WARNORD, information regarding the training environment helps subordinate units identify the necessary training resources to coordinate prior to the event.

Defining the training environment involves determining the tasks to be trained, the necessary OPFOR countertasks, and variables that provide the necessary physical, mental, and ethical stressors. The training environment provides a generalized representation of potential enemies and projected operational environment conditions that challenge unit task execution. For example, when this information is published in a WARNORD for a mission rehearsal exercise where an operational environment is known, trainers apply known information from the theater of operations to make training more realistic.

See pp. 6-28 to 6-29 (LVC) for further discussion.

T-9: Confirm Resource Requests

In T-9, commanders confirm resource requests. When the UTP is published to T-13, the UTP identifies major resource requirements and the planners requisition and schedule all supporting resources with the local installation. In T-9, commanders and staff confirm resources requisitioned before T-13 to ensure their availability when and where needed during T-Week. The unit also continues to review and refine requirements for every class of supply to support both the administrative and tactical executions of the training event. Planners can access general resource requirements (Classes V and IX) and other information in the CATS. The commander modifies these general requirements based on the desired end state of training or the local training environment. Planners draw and confirm resource estimates from three main sources: CATS, tactical logistic planning tools, and request support.

Security classification of a training event and its associated measures can impact administrative resource requirements. The higher the classification of an event, the more limiting the resources. For example, a training event with a higher classification may require more guards, protocols, and destruction capabilities.

Combined Arms Training Strategy (CATS)

The CATS provides proponent-recommended resources necessary to conduct training. It provides units with a good starting point to begin determining their requirements. Successful planners review historic documentation from previous training events and gather experience from the commander and staff. Planners then refine and improve data gathered from the CATS and forecast their unit needs. The more resource-constrained the training environment, the more likely leaders will use virtual, constructive, or combined capabilities to support training.

After determining OPFOR requirements and the tactical scenario, commanders make a more informed estimate of the TADSS required to support the training event. The CATS contains general TADSS recommendations for each training event. The commander modifies the recommended TADSS based on the desired end state of training and the local training environment. Commanders and planners use the TADSS to refine or research their requirements. The CATS provides TADSS's descriptions, contacts for every installation, and a list of resources and supporting materials. Successful trainers check in with their local installation-level TADSS office first to determine locally available resources and to coordinate off-installation support when needed.

Tactical Logistic Planning Tools

Commanders and planners use installation planning tools to confirm resource requests. Various planning tools such as the operational logistic planner are available for planning every class of supply. The operational logistic planner is the official U.S. Army tool for planning tactical logistic requirements, but others planners are readily available.

Request Support

Almost every resource and class of supply has different systems, Web sites, procedures, and timelines for forecasting and requesting. Effective training requests require commanders and planners to verify that the installation or approval authority processes their requests promptly. Requests should be processed as soon as possible and in accordance with the required timelines set by higher.

T-8: Execute Reconnaissance and Lock In Resources

In week T-8, commanders execute reconnaissance and lock in resources. After determining the training environment and required training support resources, commanders conduct an initial reconnaissance of the training sites and facilities. A thorough and detailed reconnaissance ensures that the training environment provides the necessary conditions to facilitate the training of the collective tasks to the level of fidelity needed. This reconnaissance enables commanders to identify details to complete the plan, specifically the simulations architecture possibilities and limitations. This reconnaissance also helps commanders identify any previously overlooked resources and other issues including security issues, traffic control, and possible route concerns. A reconnaissance requires the following minimum personnel: leaders, evaluators, trainers, OC/Ts, and OPFOR.

Training Area Reconnaissance Questions

A unit strives to have a YES or clarification for every response. Questions with a NO or vague response require the unit to make corrections.

See facing page for further discussion.

Training Area Reconnaissance (T-8)

Ref: FM 7-0, Train to Win in a Complex World (Oct '16), pp. H-10 to H-11.

A unit strives to have a YES or clarification for every response. Questions with a NO or vague response require the unit to make corrections. During the initial reconnaissance, commander and planners answer the following administrative questions:

- Are reconnaissance personnel familiar with the training event OPORD and commander's guidance?
- Are there safety-related environmental factors (flash flood area, electric hazards, or wildlife)?
- Does the terrain support administrative employment of equipment and personnel? How?
- Are sleep areas located in acceptable area?
- Is the maintenance area acceptable?
- Is the distance from garrison less than one mile?
- Is the amount of fuel required acceptable and sustainable? Confirm.
- Is heavy equipment transport an option?
- Are maps available?
- Is satellite imagery updated?
- Is the resupply point located in acceptable area? Confirm.
- Can roads and bridges support heavy vehicle crossing? Confirm.
- Is the road network in the area of operations sufficient to support the operation?
- Does the traffic flow inside the area of operations need to be marked?
- Is there an area sufficient for aerial medical evacuation?
- Are civilians cleared from the area? Confirm.
- Does logistic support exist on site? Does it include water, electric, and sewer?
- Does fixed site support exist on site? What type is it? Will it support the commander's objective?
- Is the access control point located in acceptable area?

During the initial reconnaissance, commander and planners answer the following tactical questions:

- Can the terrain support the commander's objectives?
- Is the area large enough to support the required unit-level maneuver?
- Does the terrain support tactical employment of equipment and personnel? How?
- Is the fuel point located at acceptable distance? Confirm.
- Is the ammunition distribution point located at acceptable distance? What is the blast area?
- Is the network available (for example cell phone, or satellite)?
- Are the command post and alternate command post located in acceptable areas?
- Is the amount of Class IV required acceptable and sustainable? Confirm.
- Is the prisoner exchange point acceptable and sustainable?
- Are enemy avenues of approach located? Identify locations.
- Are fields of fire identified? Identify areas.
- Is the safety danger zone identified? Identify area.
- Are the observations post located in acceptable locations? Identify locations.
- Are alternate and secondary positions in acceptable locations? Identify locations.
- Does terrain facilitate traffic management?

Lock In Resources

H-46. Following initial reconnaissance, commanders and planners re-confirm that all resources are locked-in (request receipts verified and recorded in memo format) to ensure all equipment, facilities, and supplies are available for training. Effective commanders and planners check the local installation requirements for locking in resources. They often manage training resources via annual, quarterly, and weekly conferences or meetings. Common examples of such meetings include but are not limited to—

* A monthly training resource integration conference.
* A weekly range and training area scheduling conference.

T-7: Publish the Training Event Operation Order

In week T-7, commanders publish the training event OPORD. After the commander has approved the plan, the OPORD is published on DTMS. Planners use the standard five-paragraph OPORD format with required modifications to the annexes to reflect training-specific requirements.

The base OPORD for the training event coordinates the actions necessary to manage the execution of the event. This does not include the plan and MSEL. The OPORD identifies the collective and individual tasks to be trained and the desired levels of task proficiency expected to be reached by the conclusion of training. The OPORD also addresses the actions to be taken to retrain the collective and individual tasks during the event if the desired end state is not achieved.

See pp. 6-34 to 6-36 for a sample training event OPORD. The staff can publish annexes later as a follow up.

Planners add the friendly force (training audience) and the OPFOR troop list to the published OPORD. The OPORD identifies trainers, evaluators, and OC/Ts. At several weeks out, specific names may not yet be available; however, the OPORD identifies the grade and background necessary to fill the positions. These details help a subordinate or coordinating unit fill the tasking for support through higher headquarters. If planners know the names of individuals, this information is included in the OPORD.

Leader Development Plan

The execution paragraph of the OPORD identifies the leader development plan. This plan addresses prerequisite training leading up to the event, the event itself, and the follow-on post event reviews. Effective training for leaders grows increasingly difficult and complex to train adaptable and agile leaders.

Figure H-3 on the facing page illustrates a leader development plan for a company-level training event.

17 – 21 February 2017
FTX Armor Company, Leader Development

METs or tasks to train:
Conduct an Attack (07-2-9001)
Conduct a Defense (07-2-9003)
Conduct Area Security (07-2-1324)
Breach an Obstacle (17-2-3070)

Leader Objective: Demonstrated ability to make sound tactical decisions enabling unit battlefield success.

Leader Training:
Crawl:
Conduct professional development classes – Attack (T-8); Deliberate Breach (T-7); Defend (T-6); and Area Security (T-5)
Review unit SOPs, collective task T&EO, and TTP (check on learning during rehearsal)
Develop individual training objectives at all echelons (T-10)
Conduct leader certification training as necessary (training area, driver training, and more)

Walk:
Squad Rehearsal (T-3); Platoon Rehearsal (T-2); and Company Rehearsal (T-1)
Conduct Pre-Execution Checks (T-10 – T-1)
Conduct Pre-Combat Checks (T-Week)

Run:
Conduct informal after action reviews at all echelons (T-Week)
Conduct leader performance feedback at all echelons
All leaders facilitate a positive learning environment (T-Week)

FTX	field training exercise	T&EO	training and evaluation outline
MET	mission-essential task	T-	training week
SOP	standard operating procedure	TTP	tactics, techniques, and procedures

Ref: FM 7-0 (Oct '16), fig. H-3. Sample leader development plan for an armor company.

Logistics Plan

The logistic plan to support the training event is the last critical piece of the OPORD. This plan addresses the resources requested at T-9. The logistic plan also lays out the coordination requirements for attached support, such as medical, maintenance, chemical, engineer, and military police support. Figure H-4 depicts an example of a logistic support plan for a company-level training event.

17 – 21 February 2017
FTX Armor Company, Logistic Support Plan

Logistic Support Objective: Provide continuous logistic support to the company, OPFOR and attachments during the FTX.

Class I: Ration cycle M-M-A, Battalion logistics operations 1500 daily at designated resupply point. Estimated headcount – 96; OPFOR headcount – 32. Two days of supply on hand basic load.

Class III: Resupply daily; estimated fuel consumption – 430 gal per day; OPFOR – 300 gal per day. Oil as required.

Class IV: Located at the designated Class IV point; issue on order.

Class V: L602 – 504; OPFOR 288
    K866 – 6; OPFOR 2
    A080– 4,080; OPFOR 2,040
    G950 – 8; OPFOR 4; OC/T 2
    L709– OC/T 30
    LG936 – OC 8

Resupply from ammunition holding area to ammunition supply point on T-Day 1. Distribution on order.

Class VIII: Combat lifesaver bags fully supplied (1 per vehicle); Medical attachment with basic load.

Class IX: Prescriber load list items available on request.

Medical: Medical team attached to the company; combat lifesavers trained – one per vehicle.

Maintenance: Company maintenance and recovery team attached.

FTX	field training exercise	OC/T	observer-controller/trainer	OPFOR	opposing force

Ref: FM 7-0 (Oct '16), fig. H-4. Sample logistic support plan for an armor company.

After commanders identify and request TADSS requirements, commanders schedule the training necessary to ensure trainers and operators are trained and certified prior to the event.

T-6: Lock In Training and Publish Training Schedules

At week T-6, commanders lock in training and publish training schedules. Failure lock in training and adhere to published training schedules can ruin the unit's abili to execute effective training. The act of locking in training creates an atmosphere which leaders and Soldiers at all levels build confidence in the unit's leaders to ens training is predictable, protected, and supported by the chain of command. The mes sage sent by such discipline is that training and leader development are unit prioriti

Training schedules are focused and published at the company level. Unit comman ers issue training schedules as a written order and use them as the primary mean to communicate the scheduled training to Soldiers. Training schedules cite the col lective or individual tasks to be trained. Training schedules are usually organized k or coincide with training weeks and cover a full week or more. Units publish trainin schedules T-6 week from training. Training schedules are signed by the unit com-mander and approved by the next higher commander (see figure H-5). For examp a company training schedule is signed by the company commander and approved by the battalion commander. The commander ensures that training schedules are conspicuously posted in the company area and electronically provides them direct to unit personnel as necessary.

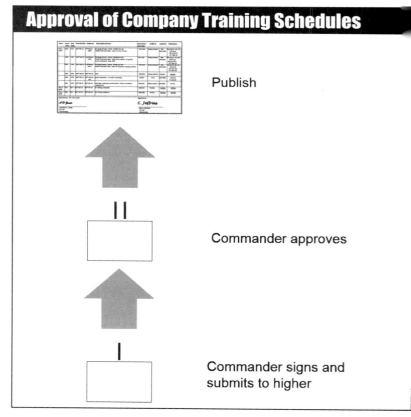

Ref: FM 7-0 (Oct '16), fig. H-5. Approval of company training schedules.

Changes to Published Training Schedules

Changes to training are sometime unavoidable, but to the greatest extent, effective leaders keep changes to an absolute minimum. Higher commanders protect subordinate units from needless, unprogrammed taskings and other training distracters. One protection technique is to establish an approving authority for changes to company-level training schedules once published. For example, if a change occurs to a company training schedule, then the brigade commander must approve the change. This helps keep changes to an absolute minimum and makes training more predictable for Soldiers and trainers. See figure H-6.

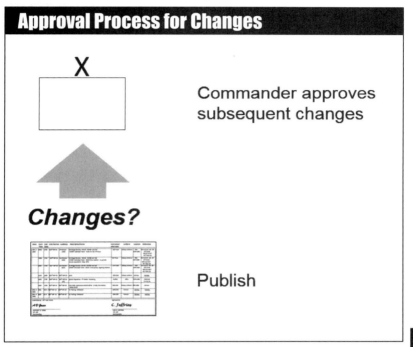

Ref: FM 7-0 (Oct '16), fig. H-6. Recommended approval process for changes.

A training schedule specifies the tasks for a Soldier to train, the location to train, the time to train, the uniform to wear, and the equipment to bring. It also tells a Soldier any additional information, to include the references to read regarding the particular training task, event, or operation. A training schedule also identifies the instructors or trainers.

Published Training Schedules in DTMS

At T-6, the staff locks in and publishes the training schedules and calendars in DTMS upon approval in the unit training meeting. The company and battalion commanders approve and digitally sign the training schedule in DTMS. Once published, Soldiers can view their company's training schedules in their MyTraining Tab on ATN. This access facilitates Soldier knowledge of UTPs and maximizes the Soldiers time to prepare in advance.

See figure H-7, following page.

		WHEN		WHO		WHAT (Tasks)	TRAINERS	UNIFORM/ EQUIPMENT		REFERENCES
						563rd MP CO			WHERE	
						Training Schedule for Period: 3 DEC – 5 DEC 2017				
Date	Start Time	End Time	Unit/Section	Audience	Description/Notes		Instructor/ Alternate	Uniform	Location	Reference
3DEC 20XX	0930	1700	563rd MP CO	1st Platoon (G35)	BN Range Density: MK-19, M240B and M2 CCMRF Individual Tasks: Rules for Use of Force		SGT Rock	Duty Uniform	TBD COF=1980	FM 3-22.27, .65 STP 21-24 MP CS & BCT PLT Task List
	0930	1700	563rd MP CO	2nd Platoon (G35)	BN Range Density: MK-19, M240B and M2 CCMRF Individual Tasks: Determine Location on ground terrain association Map, GPS)		Rock	Duty Uniform	TBD COF=1980	FM 3-22.27, .65 STP 21-24 MP CS & BCT PLT Task List
	0930	1700	563rd MP CO	3rd Platoon (G37)	BN Range Density: MK-19, M240B and M2 CCMRF Individual Tasks: Select a T...ght ...osition		Rock	Duty Uniform	TBD COF=1980	FM 3-22.27, .65 STP 21-24 MP CS & BCT PLT Task List
	1130	1300	563rd MP CO	563rd MP CO	Lunch		CDR/1SG	Duty Uniform	Various	Various
	1600	1700	563rd MP CO	563rd MP CO (22)	Special Pop... Sol... Co...ling		PL/PSG	APFU	COF=1980	FM21-20 TC 3-22.20
	1645	1700	563rd MP CO	...aa Up/A...uncements/End of Day Formation/ ...ety R...			CDR/1SG	Duty Uniform	COF=1980	Various
4DEC 20XX	0001	2359	563rd MP CO	13rd MP CO	...ning ...heduled		CDR/1SG	Various	Various	Various
5DEC 20XX	0001	235 9	563rd MP CO	563rd MP ...	N... Training Scheduled		CDR/1SG	Various	Various	Various

Submitted by:

_____
ANTHONY D. JONES
CPT, MP
Commanding

Approved by:

_____
CARL K. JEFFRIES
LTC, MP
Commanding

Unit commander signs   *For Illustration Only*   Next higher commander signs (approval)

Ref: FM 7-0 (Oct '16), fig. H-7. Example company training schedule.

Deliberate Risk Assessments

The unit staff completes and submits a DD Form 2977 (Deliberate Risk Assessme... Worksheet) to the higher commander for review and approval. More important tha... completing the form is the mental process used by the commander to identify and mitigate safety risks. Often, identifying the right leader positioned at the most dangerous place or time for the unit is the best mitigating control measure.

Refer to ATP 5-19 and the U.S. Army Combat Readiness Center's Risk Managem... courses for mitigating risk.

T-5: Complete Plan and Provide Supporting Products

At T-5, commanders complete the plan and provide supporting products. After pub... lishing the OPORD, locking in the resources, and publishing the training schedule, the staff can begin to complete the rest of the plan.

Completed Plan

The plan covers both the friendly force and OPFOR. The plan drives the training to meet the training objectives. The T-5 plan identifies both the training audience and the OPFOR to ensure all training aids are synchronized and focused. If trainin... involves multiple training support enablers, then identification of the audience and participants is important. Units will require assistance from a local mission training complex to ensure data are uploaded into the simulation.

Completed Master Scenario Events List (MSEL)

Units develop a MSEL at T-10 to develop the training scenario and set the conditions for the unit to display proficiency in the tasks evaluated during the training. The MSEL drives OPFOR actions that stimulate a friendly force reaction. A MSEL scenario is developed chronologically to stimulate friendly force actions from the beginning of the exercise to the end. The MSEL also provides the stimulus for eva... ators to observe and evaluate the selected training objectives.

Exercise Control Plan

Developing an exercise control plan helps synchronize and manage the training event. For a small-unit training event, this can be a simple graphic with timelines and control measures. For a large-scale event, the plan may include a complex scenario, white cell personnel and equipment, OC/Ts, and rules of engagement. In addition to the scenario, a higher headquarters develops an OPORD to drive the training event.

Observer-Controller/Trainer (OC/T) Plan

The OC/T plan addresses who (by name) the OC/Ts are and the assessment plan. It outlines how the OC/Ts (by name) are supported with supplies (and from whom) and details the OC/Ts' duties. The OC/T plan itemizes the OC/T packet contents. For example, the OC/T packet might contain unit SOPs, T&EOs, doctrine, pyrotechnics (Class V) on hand, and a Multiple Integrated Laser Engagement System (known as MILES) sets. OC/Ts read and make themselves familiar with both the friendly forces and OPFOR plans as well as attend key unit events (such as backbriefs, rehearsals, and precombat checks).

OC/Ts ensure all systems work properly prior to the training event to ensure accurate outcomes. OC/Ts familiarize themselves with the training support systems used for the event. Effective OC/Ts conduct work-arounds if live or simulated conditions cannot portray the realism necessary to achieve the training objectives. As with the leaders, OC/Ts ensure the unit conducts the training event safely. They address unsafe acts immediately.

Evaluation Plan

The evaluators may be internal or external to a unit. Evaluators must have a copy of the collective and individual tasks' T&EOs and be familiar with the scenario to ensure proper evaluation. Evaluators can be separate from the OC/Ts, allowing OC/Ts to be strictly trainers and facilitate AARs. OC/Ts can also be evaluators, depending on the commander's guidance and type of exercise. Upon completion, evaluators give evaluation packets to the commander for the commander's assessment.

4: Conduct Certifications and Complete Prerequisite Training

At T-4, commanders conduct certifications and complete requisite training. Evaluators report to the commander. They must understand the collective tasks they are evaluating, the scenario, and the training environment. Commanders ensure the evaluators are prepared. The plan must have all link-up times and list items evaluators need to bring—T&EOs, references, and support if necessary. Evaluators also backbrief the commander prior to execution to ensure everyone is synchronized.

The OPFOR leaders backbrief the commander on their plan. The commander may adjust the OPFOR plan based on the training objectives. OPFOR capabilities should be sufficient to ensure flexibility during the event. The OPFOR must correctly portray the threat and be prepared to execute threat TTP. The commander or designated representative certifies that the OPFOR's portrayal is correct. The OPFOR must have countertasks identified so that they will prompt the unit to train and perform the collective and individual tasks to the Army standard (as stated in the T&EO).

Train the Trainers

Qualified OC/Ts have training to facilitate the appropriate type of AAR for the event (informal or formal). They must have full knowledge of the scenario, friendly forces, and OPFOR plans, training environment, and training objectives. They must understand all safety and medical evacuation procedures. The commander certifies the OC/Ts through backbriefs on the training and training requirements.

Qualified and competent trainers are critical in delivering quality, effective training to the unit. Trainers demonstrate task proficiency before teaching a task to others.

Commanders and leaders ensure that trainers are prepared to conduct performance-oriented training to standard. They ensure adequate preparation time so th trainers—

- Understand the commander's guidance.
- Know the tasks, conditions, and standards to be performed.
- Have demonstrated the tasks to standard.
- Review references, such as ADP 7-0, ADRP 7-0, FM 7-0, ATN, T&EOs, CAT CAR, Soldier's manuals, field manuals, and technical manuals as needed.
- Gather and prepare training support items as required.
- Conduct a reconnaissance of the training site prior to training.
- Prepare the training and materials needed.
- Integrate the risk assessment process.
- Schedule rehearsals for themselves and other trainers.
- Plan, prepare, and rehearse the conduct of AARs.

Certification

Certification is a measure of individual, crew, or team technical proficiency. Unit commanders are responsible for creating and managing unit certification programs Certification is not a normal part of day-to-day training. A higher headquarters decides to require certification after a deliberate process. Certification requirements f OC/Ts and individuals to supervise live-fire ranges and EXEVALs illustrate individu technical proficiencies that commanders may require to support training. Certificati is more often applied to processes and procedures that support training and opera tions, like conduct of live fire ranges.

Commanders may require certification to confirm a unit's collective training proficiency to perform a specific type of mission or task. Certification of an infantry squ tasked to conduct a specific stability or support task is an example of unit collective certification. Higher headquarters on a by-exception basis normally directs this confirmation requirement.

Note. Individual Soldier certifications are recorded in DTMS in the "Soldier Manag tab.

T-3: Conduct Rehearsals

At T-3, commanders conduct rehearsals. Prior to conducting a rehearsal, staffs conduct the final reconnaissance of the training site. Staffs completed the initial reconnaissance at T-8 (five weeks previously). Since that time, changes may have occurred. Sometimes these changes alter the plan slightly, such as changing the location of the assembly area or the route to the training area. The staff publishes new timings or graphics in a FRAGORD.

A rehearsal is a session in which a staff or unit practices expected actions to impro performance during execution (ADRP 5-0). Units conduct rehearsals before trainin events and early enough to conduct multiple rehearsals, if necessary. Rehearsals provide an invaluable means of ensuring actions during training are synchronized and executed to standard. Rehearsals also provide a mechanism for leaders and Soldiers to visualize what is supposed to happen and to correct deficiencies during subsequent rehearsals, if necessary. Rehearsals allow leaders to—

- Identify weak points in the plan.
- Teach effective training techniques.
- Coach trainers until they feel comfortable.
- Ensure safety and environmental considerations are met and updated.
- Determine if subordinate leaders are tactically and technically proficient.

Rehearsals

Rehearsals allow leaders and their Soldiers to practice executing key aspects of the concept of operations. These actions help Soldiers orient themselves to their environment and other units before executing the operation. Rehearsals help Soldiers to build a lasting mental picture of the sequence of key actions within the operation. Rehearsals are the commander's tool to ensure staffs and subordinates understand the commander's intent and the concept of operations. They allow commanders and staffs to identify shortcomings (errors or omissions) in the plan not previously recognized. Rehearsals also contribute to external and internal coordination as the staff identifies additional coordinating requirements.

Rehearsal Techniques

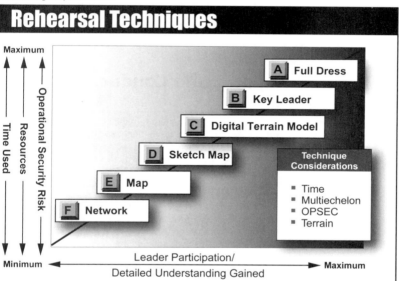

Ref: FM 6-0 (C2), Commander & Staff Organization and Operations, fig. 12-1, p. 12-3.

Effective and efficient units habitually rehearse during training. Commanders at every level routinely train and practice various rehearsal types and techniques. Local standard operating procedures (SOPs) identify appropriate rehearsal types, techniques, and standards for their execution. All leaders conduct periodic after action reviews to ensure their units conduct rehearsals to standard and correct substandard performances. After action reviews also enable leaders to incorporate lessons learned into existing plans and orders, or into subsequent rehearsals.

Refer to BSS6: The Battle Staff SMARTbook, 6th Ed. for further discussion. BSS6 covers the operations process (ADP 5-0); commander's activities; Army planning methodologies; the military decisionmaking process and troop leading procedures (FM 7-0 w/Chg 2); integrating processes (IPB, information collection, targeting, risk management, and knowledge management); plans and orders; mission command, C2 warfighting function tasks, command posts, liaison (ADP 6-0); rehearsals & after action reviews; and operational terms and military symbols (ADP 1-02).

Planning
Training

- Determine how the trainer will evaluate the Soldier's or unit's performance.
- Assess subordinate trainer competencies and provide feedback.
- Give subordinates confidence in their ability to train or operate.

FM 6-0 discusses rehearsals at length. Some leaders use the following checklist a a guide for conducting rehearsals:

- Rehearsal agenda.
- Conduct roll call.
- Participant orientation to terrain.
- Location of local civilians.
- Enemy situation brief.
- Friendly situation brief.
- Description of expected enemy actions.
- Discussion of friendly unit actions.
- Review of notes made by the recorder.

T-2: Finalize Support and Conduct Opposing Force Rehearsal

At T-2, commanders finalize support and conduct an OPFOR rehearsal. Staffs sub mit all administrative clearances and requests as necessary. These clearances ar requests can include convoy clearances, wash rack requests, and range requests include surface danger zone schematics.

Support Finalized

Commanders and planners complete a final review of all support requests for the event. They check and double check these to ensure that the support required an requested for the event in the T-weeks prior to T-2 will be present for T-Week. Thi includes a final check of all classes of supply, all ranges, training areas, TADSS, a all other required training support. This includes making personal contact between unit planners and facility and support managers. In many cases, training events fa because the unit did not make these crucial final support checks, which can resul training planned, but not conducted.

TADSS Certification Training

Units conduct TADSS certification training for trainers as scheduled during T-7.

OPFOR Rehearsal

The OPFOR conducts a rehearsal to ensure its plan facilitates the friendly force achieving its training objectives. This rehearsal includes the administrative move- ment and preparation for the event as well as the plan. The rehearsal enables sub ordinates to synchronize their plans with each other and enables leaders to addre possible decision points. The evaluators and OC/Ts attend the OPFOR rehearsal ensure they fully understand the execution of the event.

Draw Equipment and Supplies and Execute Subordinat Rehearsals and Checks

At T-1, if not previously done, the unit draws all required equipment and tests it to ensure it is operational, thereby providing time to work through problems before the event starts. Training support centers have exchange procedures for swappin unserviceable TADSS for serviceable items (if enough items are available). Units should plan sufficient time to exchange TADSS items, as necessary.

Training Site Preparation

Commanders conduct all final site preparation during T-1. If using a mission training complex to support training, commanders complete all preparations of the TADSS to be used.

Unit Rehearsal

Commanders conduct a unit rehearsal to ensure the plan is synchronized and enables the leaders to make decisions at the right time. The evaluators and OC/Ts attend the friendly force rehearsal to ensure they fully understand the execution of the event. The rehearsal can facilitate adjustments to the MSEL.

Communications Connectivity Test

Leaders conduct communications testing one week out from the event. This would include all unit communications devices, mission command systems, and TADSS connectivity, like the Multiple Integrated Laser Engagement System (known as MILES) equipment. Additionally, this includes any devices needed to support constructive or virtual training environments that drive the training event. Evaluator and OC/T communications checks are also conducted during this week.

-Week: Execute Training

At T-Week, commanders execute training. This execution entails conducting precombat checks, drawing supplies, conducting training, conducting informal AARs, leading hip-pocket training, and retraining tasks not trained to standard.

Precombat Checks

T-Week begins with precombat checks. Units conduct these detailed final checks immediately before and during the execution of training and operations. Units include these checks in unit SOPs. Normally, units conduct them as part of TLP.

See following page (p. 6-70) for further discussion.

Draw Supplies

Successful units draw and inventory supplies at the beginning of the training week. The installation distributes classes of supply within the plan to ensure the event is properly resourced. Leaders report any shortage of requested supplies immediately.

Conduct Training

The unit executes the plan developed and published earlier. While conducting training, the unit performs individual and collective tasks to the published standard as the plan evolves based on OPFOR action and reaction. Concurrently, the assessment plan is executed—OC/Ts observe and capture compliance with T&EO performance steps and measures—and staffs compile bottom-up feedback. As the plan develops, the unit tests its TTP; identifies new TTP; and develops or implements other TTP. The commander and all unit leaders are present and engaged and perform their tactical duties consistent with the plan.

Informal After Action Reviews (AARs)

Evaluators and leaders conduct informal AARs at all levels (from crew to battalion). They can be done for a unit or an individual. They may be scheduled or as needed during the training. Evaluators and leaders can record observations, insights, and lessons for future use to identify trends and prevent reoccurrences of bad practices.

Hip-Pocket Training

Hip-pocket training usually consists of individual tasks selected by the commander on which a unit can train when it experiences inactive periods during scheduled training. Hip-pocket training is another technique for managing sustainment training. The company commander selects tasks for this training so that the unit uses training time productively.

Precombat Checks (T-Week)

Ref: FM 7-0, Train to Win in a Complex World (Oct '16), pp. H-19 to H-20.

T-Week begins with precombat checks. Units conduct these detailed final checks immediately before and during the execution of training and operations. Units include these checks in unit SOPs. Normally, units conduct them as part of TLP. These precombat checks can be as simple or as complex as the training or operation dictates. Units start precombat checks—such as applying camouflage, setting radio frequencies, and distributing ammunition—in garrison and complete them in the assembly area or in the training location. Commanders allocate sufficient time for subordinate leaders to execute precombat checks and inspections to standard. Precombat checks can include the following:

- Staff briefed the OPORD briefed, and leaders and Soldiers know the expectations.
- Unit completed safety checks and briefings.
- Unit has all required TADSS on hand and operational. For example, unit has Multiple Integrated Laser Engagement System (known as MILES) equipment and zeroed it.
- Unit completed before-operations preventative maintenance checks and services on vehicles, weapons, communications, and other equipment.
- Unit inspected equipment. For example, unit inspected compasses, maps, and binoculars.
- Unit inspected and camouflaged Soldiers and equipment. For example, unit inspected identification cards and driver's licenses as well as camouflaged weapons.
- Unit checked Soldier packing lists and enforced any discrepancies.
- Unit verified medical support present and prepared.
- Unit completed communications checks.
- Unit verified ammunition (Class V) drawn, accounted for, prepared, and issued.
- Unit checked and confirmed vehicle load plans as well as secured the cargo.
- Unit verified rations (Class I) drawn and issued.
- Unit briefed and dispatched quartering party.
- OPFOR personnel deployed and ready to execute their OPORD.

Hip-pocket training provides leaders confidence in their ability to train, which results in a more efficient use of Soldiers' time. While the tasks selected for this type of training are usually individual tasks requiring sustainment training, leaders can inject new training (if time), training levels, and circumstances allow. Ideally, leaders train selected tasks in 15 to 30 minutes. Initial individual training or collective task training ordinarily requires more time and resources. Effective leaders use their initiative to ensure their individuals are well trained and their time is not wasted.

Retrain

Leaders allocate sufficient time to retrain tasks during or after training events. Not all tasks will be performed to standard on the first or even second attempt. Commanders do not allow an organization to end training believing that a substandard performance was acceptable. Therefore, leaders allocate and schedule time and other resources for unit retraining of key collective and individual tasks in their training plans. Retraining allows participants to implement corrective action. Ideally, units complete retraining at the earliest opportunity, if not immediately after they attempt the task. In some cases, a restart of an event may be necessary before moving to the next training event.

T+1: Recover, Conduct Final After Action Review, and Assess Training

In T+1 week, commanders recover, conduct final AARs, and assess training. Recovery is part of every training event. Leaders plan for recovery to ensure all the resources and personnel are available to return to full operation. Evaluators and leaders conduct a final AAR of the training event. The final step in a training event is to assess the training, specifically the collective and individual task proficiencies demonstrated or attained.

Recovery

Recovery is critical to every training event. Leaders use recovery to ensure the resources and personnel return to standard. The recovery process is training. Once recovery is complete, it signifies the end of the training event. Captured AAR comments reflect the effectiveness of the recovery and modification to the SOP.

See following page (p. 6-72) for further discussion.

Final After Action Review (AAR)

The final AAR takes place as soon as possible following the event. (Leaders conduct informal AARs as needed during the event.) This ensures that events are still fresh in the minds of all the participants, capturing the data as accurately as possible. OC/Ts, OPFORs personnel, and evaluators all provide their input to inform the commander's assessments. Using multiple recorders ensures a unit captures all lessons. Sound assessments of those lessons facilitate later success. A final AAR begins with the UTP. Leaders assess if event planning and preparation were sufficient and if the commander's training objectives were met. They also determine if administrative and tactical support were sufficient to conduct the training. OC/Ts, OPFORs, and evaluators record all the lessons learned and preserve them for retraining and future use.

MET Assessment

Commanders assess and evaluate training. The commander considers personal observations as well as observations, T&EOs, insights, and lessons from AARs and unit evaluations to inform both MET proficiency for the assigned mission and METL assessments for unit status reporting.

SOP Review

Leaders conduct an SOP review after the event to implement recommended changes gleaned from the observations, insights, and lessons. Quickly implementing the right changes allows the unit to begin improving performance sooner.

Recovery (T+1)

Ref: FM 7-0, Train to Win in a Complex World (Oct '16), p. H-21.

Recovery is critical to every training event. Leaders use recovery to ensure the resources and personnel return to standard. The recovery process is training. Once recovery is complete, it signifies the end of the training event. Captured AAR comments reflect the effectiveness of the recovery and modification to the SOP. Ideally, a unit performs the following sample recovery activities after a training event:

- Account for personnel health and welfare.
- Perform post-operations preventative maintenance checks and services.
- Ensure sensitive item accountability.
- Ensure accountability of organizational and individual equipment.
- Ensure that Class IV, Class V, TADSS, and other support items are maintained, accounted for, and turned in.
- Close out training areas and ranges.
- Conduct AARs.
- Allow time for the individual Soldiers to recover personal equipment and conduct personal hygiene.
- Conduct final inspections.

Recovery and Post Operations Checks

Post operations checks are those tasks a unit accomplishes at the conclusion of training. An effective unit SOP contains these checks. The checks vary depending on the type of training. For example, an FTX requires more extensive post operations checks than garrison-type training. Sample post operations checks include the following:

- Soldier accountability.
- Sensitive item accountability (such as weapons or communications security).
- Report closure of unit to higher headquarters.
- Ammunition and equipment turn-in (such as TADSS).
- Maintenance of vehicles, weapons, and communications including the following:
  - Equipment cleaned.
  - Thorough preventative maintenance checks and services after-operations checks.
  - Required services performed.
- Training assessments:
  - Leaders record results of training in leader books.
  - AARs completed.
  - After action report initiated, if appropriate.
- Soldier recovery.
- Chain of command inspections of Soldiers and equipment.

IV. Training Briefings (TB and QTB/YTB)

Ref: FM 7-0, Train to Win in a Complex World (Oct '16), appendix G and p. 3-10.

Commanders brief the plan to the next higher commander. This briefing formalizes the plan and the resources required to support it. The training briefing focuses exclusively on unit training and leader development planning; it does not cover other administrative matters. The training briefing is concise and focused. The training briefing is a contract between commanders. The unit commander agrees to train as described in the plan, and the higher commander approves the plan and agrees to provide resources to execute it. If the subordinate unit is deploying under another headquarters, the gaining commander or a representative participates in the briefing. The installation staff also participates in the briefing, since they manage the training support resources on the installation.

There are two types of training briefs (TBs). These are the TB and the QTB (Regular Army) or YTB (Reserve Component).

Training Briefs (TBs)

As described earlier, brigade and battalion commanders brief their UTP at the TB. The general format of a TB follows eleven basic slides:

- Brigade commander's training focus
- Operational environment
- Battalion training focus
- Battalion's commander training guidance
- Concept of operations: decisive operations
- Concept of operations: shaping operations #1 (individual training)
- Concept of operations: shaping operations #2 (leader development)
- Assessment plans
- Key resources required to train
- Training risks
- Training challenges

To begin a TB, a brigade commander discusses the brigade training focus and the training environment to which the brigade will train. All TB slides contain a title and bullet points. The figures in this section illustrate the details a user needs to add. Battalion commanders or command sergeants major follow the format of slides illustrated in figures G-3 through G-11 to complete the TB for their units. Commanders tailor the slides to meet their training requirements.

See p. 6-76 for sample training briefing (TB) slides.

Quarterly /Yearly Training Briefing

QTBs (for Regular Army) and YTBs (for Reserve Component) are periodic UTP updates to the commander two echelons above. These briefings support the TB that is briefed prior to the start of training.

See following pages (pp. 6-74 to 6-75) for sample QTB/YTB slides.

Planning
Training

Quarterly/Yearly Training Briefing (QTB/YTB)

Ref: FM 7-0, Train to Win in a Complex World (Oct '16), pp. G-4 to G-8.

The QTB (for Regular Army) and the YTB (for Reserve Component) are periodic conferences on training between battalion commanders and division commanders. These TBs directly support the UTP. QTBs and YTBs are integral to the mid-range planning for training.

This discussion illustrates briefing slides for presenting QTBs and YTBs. The exact format and content will vary from command to command based on the commander's guidance and preference. Users can download slides for TBs slides from ATN. Staffs post the brigade and battalion UTP calendars in the meeting room for commanders to use as a reference throughout the briefing.

These TBs focus on reporting the overall progress of the UTP, identifying issues related to execution of the UTP, and ensuring the UTP as published is on track. The briefing gives battalion commanders a venue to discuss training previously conducted, training being conducted, and training planned for the future. These briefings can also be the venue for proposing and approving potential changes to the UTP as necessary. If changes are necessary, the base UTP OPORD requires a FRAGORD once the higher commander approves the modification.

Similar to the TB, the brigade commander provides the brigade training overview, and battalion commanders and command sergeants major brief the current status of UTP progress. Battalion commanders in separate brigades and regiments present the QTB to corps major subordinate commanders. The YTB for Reserve Component units is normally presented to the next higher commander. The YTB is conducted prior to the start of the fiscal year in Reserve Component units. Separate Reserve Component battalion commanders and company commanders may also brief the next higher commander. Some Reserve Component units may not be able to conduct in-person briefings. Ideally installation training resource conferences should occur just prior to the QTBs or YTB to provide the most current and accurate information relating to the installation training resources and facility scheduling.

Sample QTB/YTB Slides

Brigade Commander Training Focus
- State the higher commander's training focus as stated in the unit training plan.
- Include who, what, when, where, and why. The 'what' includes the METs the higher unit will train on during the planning horizon.

MET   mission-essential task

Figure G-12. Sample slide for brigade training focus

Operational Environment
- Write a concise statement describing an operational environment the unit will train for (*train as you fight*).
- Break the statement down by operational variables—political, military, economic, social, information, infrastructure, physical environment, and time.

Figure G-13. Sample slide for training environment

Battalion Training Focus
- State the unit's training focus from the UTP.
- Answer who, what, when, where, and why. The 'what' includes the METs the unit will train on during the planning horizon to support the higher unit. If no mission is assigned, this should be the prioritized METL the unit will train.

MET   mission-essential task
METL   mission-essential task list
UTP   unit training plan

Figure G-14. Sample slide for battalion training focus

Battalion MET Assessments
- List the unit METL (and METL for assigned missions if applicable). Include subordinate unit METs assessments.
- Indicate the current assessments of the METs selected to train. This helps frame the training strategy to improve and sustain proficiencies.

MET   mission-essential task
METL   mission-essential task list

Figure G-15. Sample slide for battalion assessments

Last Quarter Training Highlights

- Review last quarter major multiechelon training events in accordance with the unit training plan. Review the associated training objectives and whether those objective were met or not met (and why).
- Discuss any training events planned but not conducted (and why).
- Discuss major training resources scheduled or ordered and not used (and why).
- Discuss plans to retrain and retry training objectives not met.

Figure G-16. Sample slide for last quarter training highlights

Current Quarter Training Highlights

- Review current quarter major multiechelon training events. Review the associated training objectives.
- Discuss any training events planned but not conducted (and why).
- Discuss major training resources scheduled or ordered and not used (and why).
- Discuss plans to retrain and retry training objectives not met.

Figure G-17. Sample slide for current quarter training highlights

Future Quarter Training Highlights

- Review plans for the future quarter (two quarters out) major multiechelon training events. Review the associated training objectives.
- Address other future training issues.

Figure G-18. Sample slide for future quarter training highlights

Training Resource Synchronization Conferences

- Discuss the unit's attendance at the last installation-level conference.
- Discuss the training resources (facilities and land) requested, not scheduled, and why.
- Discuss the unit's attendance at future installation training resource conferences (two quarters out).

Note: If possible, a representative of the installation DPTMS should attend the quarterly or yearly training briefing.
DPTMS   Directorate of Plans, Training, Mobilization and Security

Figure G-19. Sample slide for training resource synchronization conference

Soldier Training Assessment

- CSM and 1SG review individual Soldier training planned and conducted during the past, current, and future quarters.
- Discuss individual training planned, not conducted and why.
- Discuss the plan to retrain and retry individual tasks.
- Discuss the focus of opportunity (hip pocket) training tasks.

1SG   first sergeant
CSM   command sergeant major

Figure G-20. Sample slide for Soldier training assessment

Status of Schools

- Discuss the status of OES, WOES, NCOES, and troop schools' attendance for—
  - Current attendees.
  - Attendees projected two quarters out.
- Discuss personnel scheduled for training, but not attending and why.
- Discuss additional Soldier training needs of the unit.

NCOES   noncommissioned officer education system
OES   officer education system
WOES   warrant officer education system

Figure G-21. Sample slide for school statuses

Ammunition Status/Allocation

Show (by annual STRAC allocation/by DODIC and nomenclature):

Unit   Allocated   % Expended   Issues

DODIC   Department of Defense identification code
STRAC   standards in training commission

Figure G-22. Sample slide for ammunition status and allocation

Gunnery Scheduled

- Break out schedule in by-unit small arms, crew-served units, and by-gunnery units of gunnery and ranges scheduled and resourced two quarters out.
- Include basic rifle marksmanship and use of range simulations used in preparation for live-fire ranges and events.

Figure G-23. Sample slide for scheduled in gunnery

ITE Utilization

- Discuss unit utilization of ITE resources out to two quarters. Include constructive, virtual, and TADSS resources planned and coordinated.
- Discuss how these resources are planned and used in support of attaining training proficiency in METs selected to train.

Note: If possible, a representative of the installation DPTMS should attend the quarterly or yearly training briefing.
DPTMS   Directorate of Plans, Training, Mobilization and Security
ITE   integrated training environment
MET   mission-essential task
TADSS   training aids, devices, simulators, and simulations

Figure G-24. Sample for use of integrated training environment

Commander's Training Issues

- Discuss major training distracters last and current quarter.
- Discuss any unprogrammed taskings from higher headquarters that impacted approved, scheduled, and locked-in training.
- Discuss training issues the unit requires assistance to resolve.

Figure G-25. Sample slide for commander's training issues

Training Briefing (TB): Sample Slides

Ref: FM 7-0, Train to Win in a Complex World (Oct '16), pp. G-1 to G-4.

Brigade Commander's Training Focus

- State the brigade commander's training focus answering who, what, when, where, and why. The 'what' includes the METs the higher unit will focus training during the planning horizon.
- Include the training readiness rating (T-1 through T-4 in accordance with unit status reporting) the brigade will attain and sustain.

MET mission-essential task
T- training week

Figure G-1. Sample slide for brigade training focus

Operational Environment

- Write a concise statement describing an operational environment the unit will train for (*train as you fight*).
- Break the statement down by operational variables—political, military, economic, social, information, infrastructure, physical environment, and time.

Figure G-2. Sample slide for training environment

Battalion Training Focus

- State the unit's training focus resulting from mission analysis and the backbrief to the higher commander.
- Answer who, what, when, where, and why. The 'what' includes the METs the unit will focus training on during the planning horizon to support the higher unit's training focus.

MET mission-essential task

Figure G-3. Sample slide for battalion training focus

Battalion Commander's Training Guidance

- Write a concise (bulleted) statement of the commander's visualized end state for training.
- Include the current training proficiency assessments for each of the METs selected to train. Also include any additional training guidance given to subordinate units.

MET mission-essential task

Figure G-4. Sample slide for training guidance

Concept of Operations: Decisive Operations

- Using the training strategy, state how the unit will train from the training start date to the end of the planning horizon.
- Refer to the long-range training calendar. Indicate the major training events and training objectives that the unit proposes to train (crawl-walk-run).
- Discuss dates of the EXEVAL and CTC rotations, planning, and execution status (as appropriate).
- Include the time management cycle.
- Discuss how the command will leverage the integrated training environment.

CTC combat training center   EXEVAL external evaluation

Figure G-5. First sample slide for concept of operations

Concept of Operations:
Shaping Operations #1 (individual training)

- Discuss individual training that supports the METs selected to train. The unit CSM is the primary briefer.
- CSM briefs the current and projected status of—
  - The unit's individual through section training.
  - Tasks that are nested with the unit's METs selected to train.

CSM command sergeant major
MET mission-essential task

Figure G-6. Second sample slide for concept of operations

Concept of Operations:
Shaping Operations #2 (leader development)

- Include the focus of leader development and the supporting training events during the planning horizon. Include subjects and details of the commander's leader development plans.
- Discuss how specific training events contribute to leader development.
- Discuss the leader assessment plan.

Figure G-7. Third sample slide for concept of operations

Assessment Plans

- Discuss how the unit plans to assess progressively and how it will develop training readiness as it executes the plan.
- Include—
  - How OC/Ts are trained and certified.
  - EXEVAL support requirements.
  - Resource support requirements for evaluations.

EXEVAL external evaluation
OC/T observer-controller/trainer

Figure G-8. Sample slide for assessment plans

Key Resources Required to Train

- State any major or unique resources required to meet training requirements.
- Include resources and facilities that are key to the unit achieving training readiness. Also include resources or facilities difficult to schedule or not readily available on the installation.

Figure G-9. Sample slide for key resources

Training Risk

State any training risk that the commander has identified that puts the plan at risk. This is **not a safety risk.** The risk exists because—
- The key resources required to train are not available.
- There is insufficient time to train to the readiness level required.

Figure G-10. Sample training risks

Training Challenges

State any additional challenges to the plan that will impact attaining training readiness.

Figure G-11. Sample training challenges

Conducting Training Events & Exercises

Ref: FM 7-0, Train to Win in a Complex World (Oct '16), chap 3 and ADP 7-0, Training (Jul '19), chap 4.

Conducting training events encompasses all activities related to planning for, preparing for, executing, and assessing the training events that comprise the UTP. Commanders plan and coordinate training events in detail well before execution to synchronize METs and training objectives and to resource each event properly. Commanders use training meetings as the primary forum to ensure that coordination and planning for training events are on track.

Conducting Training

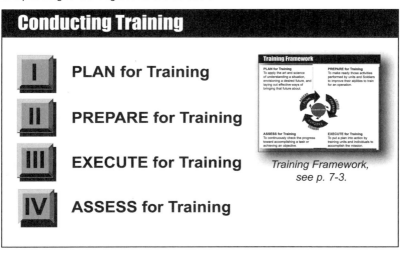

I PLAN for Training

II PREPARE for Training

III EXECUTE for Training

IV ASSESS for Training

Training Framework, see p. 7-3.

All successful training requires resources coordination, rehearsals, and precombat checks before training. Effective training requires time locked in on the UTP calendar for units and individuals to retrain tasks as training occurs. If the unit fails to meet the training objectives for a specific training event, the unit allocates time to ensure that it can retrain the tasks before the event is concluded. A unit must be proficient in a failed task before it advances to more complex collective tasks.

For discussion of PLAN for Training, see pp. 7-9 to 7-12.

For discussion of PREPARE Training, see pp. 7-13 to 7-16.

For discussion of EXECUTE Training, see pp. 7-17 to 7-18.

For discussion of ASSESS for Training, see pp. 8-1 to 8-6.

Where to Start

The UTP identifies the multiechelon training events crucial to attaining task proficiency. It is the starting point for leaders to begin to assign planning responsibility and begin the process of determining and coordinating resources. It focuses on the multiechelon training events that train the METs such as a staff training exercise (known as STAFFEX), command post exercise, live fire exercise (known as LFX), or FTX. These training events require substantial resources, coordination, and facilities.

Once multiechelon training events are accounted for and included in the UTP cale dar, the unit adds other events like unit-conducted classes, mandatory training, an those training events supported by internal unit-provided resources and coordinati for unit-wide visibility and action.

See pp. 7-19 to 7-32 for discussion of lane training exercises and pp. 7-33 to 7-37 for discussion of other types of training exercises.

Once leaders disseminate the UTP OPORD to subordinates, execution of the train ing plan begins. Leaders adapt to changes, as necessary. Thorough preparation to conduct training is essential. Assessment of unit and individual performance is a continual process. While units execute one event, they plan and prepare another. Plan, prepare, execute, and assess are not performed sequentially, but overlap in a series of dynamic and interrelated processes throughout the life cycle of the UTP u til the unit attains the commander's visualized end state for training. Training meetings facilitate this integrated process by assessing the collective tasks trained durir UTP execution, as well as coordinating resources and planning for future events.

Leaders must plan, prepare, execute, and assess each training event that supports the UTP. Training meetings and recovery after training are key activities that occur a each training event is conducted. These activities ensure that units execute the UTF and it meets the commander's desired objectives for unit training and leader develo ment.

Training execution occurs at all echelons, from a unified action training exercise to a first-line leader conducting individual training. Ideally, leaders execute training using the crawl-walk-run approach—as appropriate and tailored to the individual's, team's, or unit's needs and capabilities—to build confidence over time and emphasize fundamentals and standards. Effective training execution, regardless of the specific collective, leader, and individual tasks being executed, requires adequate preparation, effective presentation and practice, and thorough evaluation. After training is executed, leaders ensure individuals recover from training and review successes and challenges to apply observations, insights, and lessons to future training and operations.

1. Training Framework

Ref: FM 7-0, Train to Win in a Complex World (Oct '16), p. 3-1.

Unit leaders use the basic **Army operations process** as the training framework for conducting each training event that comprises the UTP.

Planning for training events does not significantly differ from planning for an operation. A commander's presence sends a message to Soldiers that training is crucial to unit success. It allows the commander to observe and assess the conduct of training, training effectiveness, resource utilization, leaders in action, the state of readiness, and individual morale. It also serves to strengthen mutual trust—trust between the leader and subordinates—that is integral to the chain of command.

Preparing for operations (and training) under the philosophy of mission command requires trust up and down the chain of command and between individuals and units.

Execution of training occurs with the resources available. Without the right resources available at the right time, meaningful and effective training will not occur and units will lose valuable, irreplaceable training time.

The **assessment** of tasks and leader proficiency is a constant process as units plan and train. Evaluations of task performance and bottom-up feedback are key because they provide the commander the information necessary to make accurate and timely MET assessments.

Training Framework

PLAN for Training
To apply the art and science of understanding a situation, envisioning a desired future, and laying out effective ways of bringing that future about.

PREPARE for Training
To make ready those activities performed by units and Soldiers to improve their abilities to train for an operation.

ASSESS for Training
To continuously check the progress toward accomplishing a task or achieving an objective.

EXECUTE for Training
To put a plan into action by training units and individuals to accomplish the mission.

For discussion of PLAN for Training, see pp. 7-9 to 7-12.

For discussion of PREPARE Training, see pp. 7-13 to 7-16.

For discussion of EXECUTE Training, see pp. 7-17 to 7-18.

For discussion of ASSESS for Training, see pp. 8-1 to 8-6.

Conducting Training

II. Realistic Training

Ref: FM 7-0, Train to Win in a Complex World (Oct '16), app. A.

Realistic training is a deliberate practice of conducting individual and collective tasks to e[n]able tactical and technical proficiency. This proficiency supports mission accomplishmen[t] in a training environment that approximates an operational environment in both sufficient complexity and substance. Realistic training incorporates the human, cultural, and politica[l] aspects of armed conflict to reflect the feeling of persistent danger in complex training environments. Realistic training also develops cohesive teams of Army professionals wh[o] can improve and thrive in ambiguous, complex, and challenging situations. Effective reali[s]tic training focuses on improving team and individual performances and decision making.

To win in a complex world, leaders work to enhance training realism in every training event. Leaders ensure that units and Soldiers train to attain more than technical and tacti[ti]cal proficiency. Realism involves robustly representing the complexities of variables in a[n] operational environment as well as their posed physical, mental, and ethical challenges.

Ultimately, realistic, well-planned, and executed training aims to produce Soldiers, leaders, and units with the right capabilities to win in a complex world. Realistic training develops and hones these capabilities. First, the training builds unit proficiencies in tasks. Second, a unit that sustains proficiency in tasks often operates in complex and stressful training environments successfully. When training concludes, the leaders and Soldiers in a unit are confident and able. They perform tasks to standard under dynamic and complex conditions with skill and determination. To sustain that task proficiency, units continue to provide training environments that are well planned, well resourced, and led by trained officers and NCOs.

Characteristics of Realistic Training

The characteristics of quality training become evident once training is planned, prepared for, and in the process of execution. The best training events enable units and individuals to attain training objectives, positively improve individual and collective task proficiency, and build Soldier confidence. Soldiers and leaders know when quality training is conducted; they fully embrace realistic training that challenges them. They also know when training is poorly planned, prepared for, and executed.

All Leaders are Present and Engaged

Quality training is commander-driven, but all unit leaders have a direct responsibility to train their organization. Leaders must be present, visible, engaged, and fulfilling their role at training. If it is their training event, then they command it. At a subordinate's event, they assess it. At a higher organization's event, they support it. Commanders and leaders actively display the behaviors that they require of their subordinates. While commanders are the unit's primary trainer, subordinate leaders are responsible for the proficiency of their respective organizations and subordinates.

Unit Effectively Leverages Training Resources

Good trainers and leaders know and use all available training resources. These resources include training doctrine, proponent publications, Army training support system resources, ITE enablers, and the ATMS. The ATMS consists of the ATN, the CATS, and the DTMS. To train effectively with limited time and resources, trainers leverage every available resource to maximize training proficiencies.

Leader Development is a Priority

Leader development occurs in all three training domains: institutional, operational, and self-development (see AR 350-1). In the operational training domain, leader development is more progressive and battle focused. As the unit trains, a leader's honest mistakes can be made without prejudice. Training is also the venue for leaders to try ain. Leaders who fail at the first attempting a task can retrain the task as necessary. Sometimes leaders develop other methods and techniques that may prove more effective. Once a leader displays task proficiency, the trainer increases the difficulty level. The increased difficulty induces a positive learning environment and builds the leader's confidence to master tasks under changing and more challenging conditions. Senior leaders actively plan and monitor subordinate leaders' progressive development. They underwrite honest mistakes and provide timely coaching and mentoring during the entire training process.

Leader Protects Training from Distracters

Once commanders lock in the training, approve the UTP calendar, and publish the training schedule, the training must not change. Senior commanders provide the necessary resources to train—including time—and protect subordinate units from unprogrammed taskings or other training distractions. Commanders establish and enforce a command climate that creates stability and predictability throughout the organization by protecting approved training. There is nothing more disruptive to unit training readiness than training planned, but not conducted because of unscheduled requirements.

Units and Soldiers Train with Those They Operate

Effective collective training is best conducted with higher, lower, and all supporting and supported elements available. Multiechelon and combined arms training consists of collective training performed simultaneously by all engaged echelons. This method of training optimizes the use of time, resources, and personnel while supporting a more realistic training environment. For example, to train to "Conduct a Combined Arms Breach of an Obstacle," an infantry unit requires artillery, engineer, and other functional support.

Training Replicates an Operational Environment

A training environment replicates an operational environment as much as possible. There is no better means of preparing Soldiers and units than making the training environment as realistic as possible. Units and Soldiers thrive on complex, dynamic, challenging, and realistic training that is well planned and well led. That training requires commanders to diligently ensure that resources to make training realistic and challenging are available when needed and to know how to leverage LVC training environments. Since units complete most training time at home station, commanders strive to make that training environment as realistic as possible. Realistic training creates units that are operationally adaptable and can quickly adjust to changing conditions.

After Action Reviews are Integral

AARs are well planned, resourced, and facilitated throughout the entire training process. These reviews do not just occur at the conclusion of a training event. Informal AARs also occur as training unfolds and when required. The best training ensures that leaders identify faulty execution early enough in an event to be corrected on the spot. No units or Soldiers should depart a training event without the confidence that they can execute tasks to the published standard.

Training Challenges Intellectually and Physically

Training is intellectual and physical in nature. Training challenges Soldiers intellectually because it requires them to demonstrate an extensive amount of unique expertise to conduct military operations. It challenges Soldiers physically as they use strength, endurance, and physical skills to apply force to defeat an opponent. Combat operations are tough, stressful, and unforgiving. Commanders create the right conditions, difficulty, and intensity for every training event. This tailoring includes unexpected changes in conditions that require subordinates to apply initiative and adaptability.

Realistic training must mentally challenge Soldiers and leaders to keep them engaged and motivated. Challenging training develops character, competence, commitment, and

Continued on next page

Continued on next page

Conducting Training

Continued from previous page

self-confidence in the individual while building mutual trust and cohesion in the unit as Soldiers share sense of accomplishment. Training accomplishments have the added benefit of strengthening personal morale and enhances unit ésprit de corps. It inspires excellence by fostering initiative, enthusiasm, and an eagerness to learn.

Training is Performance Oriented

Training is performance oriented. Performance-oriented training is hands-on and experiential; units and Soldiers train the task under conditions and to the standard specified. Units and Soldiers learn best through repetition, using a hands-on approach. As conditions in operational environments can and do change so do conditions in a training environment. Once a unit or Soldiers achieve task proficiency, training then includes variations of conditions. Soldiers train better, faster, and to a higher degree of proficiency when they know the task, conditions, and standards.

Training is Tailored to Drive Initiative and Adaptability

Training conditions that include unexpected changes require subordinates to apply initiative and adaptability. Effective training experiences, coupled with organized and timely candid feedback, build leaders' and subordinates' competence and trust. Leaders build unit, staff, and Soldier trust when they consistently demonstrate competence under unpredictable, changing, and stressful conditions. Together, character, competence, and commitment build the necessary trust that enables Soldiers and leaders to be agile, adaptive, and innovative.

Training Provides Continually Changing Conditions

Once proficiency is achieved under the task's published conditions, leaders continually change the conditions. They change the tactical scenario, higher and subordinate unit participation, the physical environment, and time of day. Such varied conditions provide the unit or Soldier the opportunity to perform the tasks under increasingly complex and challenging situations. Changes in leadership can also produce more adaptive performance, just as in real operations. When leaders cannot perform their role, subordinates must step in and lead. By continually changing the conditions, the unit becomes more confident in its ability to perform the task under increasingly more stressful situations.

Units Train One Level Down and Evaluate Two Levels Down

Commanders directly oversee the training of a subordinate unit one level down as they plan, prepare for, execute, and assess their training events. When they oversee these units, commanders also actively evaluate units two levels down. This level of command oversight helps ensure that subordinate units adhere to training plans and the battle focus of the higher unit and to demonstrate task proficiencies.

Units and Soldiers Train Repetitively

Practice makes perfect. The more units or Soldiers train a task to standard, the more proficient the units or Soldiers become. To master a task, units or Soldiers perform the task consistently and instinctively under various conditions. This is true from individual Soldier tasks to the more complex unit collective tasks. Units and Soldiers that train on tasks repeatedly and under increasingly more difficult conditions grow more comfortable and confident in their ability to perform the task. Leaders strive to train units and Soldiers to exceed the minimum standard, especially when units and Soldiers will perform the tasks in real world conditions that are complex and ambiguous.

Continued from previous page

See figures A-1 and A-2 (facing page) for sample training event planning scenarios.

MAJ Jordan, an experienced infantian combat veteran and newly assigned S-3 for the 1-22nd Infantry Battalion, is planning a battalion-level, home-station training event for the MET, "Conduct an Attack." The training event focuses on several collective tasks, battle drills, and individual tasks including—

- Plan an attack at battalion level.
- Conduct an assault at company level.
- Conduct an assault at platoon level.
- Evacuate casualties.
- Treat casualties.
- Execute fire support.
- Synchronize close air support.

In preparing for the training event, MAJ Jordan faces some challenges to make the training as realistic and demanding as possible. First, he determines how to represent joint forces, civilians on the battlefield, and a complex urban environment to the appropriate fidelity. Second, he checks if the battalion or higher headquarters has the ability to provide an OPFOR with overmatch in selected niche capabilities without significant external support. Third, he determines how the battalion will integrate fire support and close air support with appropriate simulated effects.

MAJ Jordan also recognizes the need to add more realism to casualty identification, assessment, and care under simulated battlefield conditions. In short, he needs to determine training events that address these challenges to better replicate—with the highest level of fidelity, complexity, and rigor that exist—an actual operational environment to meet training standards. Additionally, MAJ Jordan considers how to adequately engage, motivate, and challenge leaders and Soldiers during this training event, especially those with combat experience. He determines if the supporting infrastructure adequately delivers and can sustain the training enablers and products required for realistic training. MAJ Jordan ascertains methods to enhance current training capabilities to replicate the physical and intellectual hardships Soldiers faced in recent combat better. He then specifies the necessary tools and processes needed for more effective and efficient unit training in this realistic training.

Ref: FM 7-0 (Oct '16), fig. A-1. Realistic training vignette.

...utims overlooking Mega City, is just fleeing to Mega City and occupying structures. Objective 2 requires C Co. and D Co. to destroy or push enemy forces deeper into the mountain range. Fire support and close air support are available via C Co. fire support team with joint terminal attack controller (known as JTAC) attached.

The battalion S-3, a combat veteran, has identified key shortfalls to train for tactical and technical proficiencies in these tasks under conditions that more accurately represent the stressors and complexities of an operational environment:

1) Replicated joint, interagency, and multinational assets, an urban area with civilian population, and other aspects of an operational environment.
2) A hybrid OPFOR with overmatch in selected niche capabilities to include cyber and space.
3) Realistic wraparound to account for mission command requirements up two echelons (division) and adjacent units.
4) Tactical aircraft with appropriate ordnance, given limited availability of those assets.
5) Realistic tactical combat casualty identification, assessment, and care.

AA	avenue of approach	IN	infantry
BN	battalion	OBJ	objective
Co.	company	OPFOR	opposing force

Ref: FM 7-0 (Oct '16), fig. A-2. Graphic for realistic training vignette.

III. Presentation of Training

Trainers execute training using three basic methods of presentation.

Methods of Presentation

 A Demonstration

 B Conference

 C Lecture

These methods may be used in any combination to present training. The trainer's selection of a specific method depends on the complexity of the task(s) and proficiency of the soldiers (or unit) being trained.

A. Demonstration

Demonstration is the preferred method of presentation used at company level and below. Demonstrations accelerate the learning process. The impact of a brief visual demonstration showing the correct method of execution of a given task to standard cannot be overstated. Seeing a task performed correctly provides greater understanding than any amount of explanation. Demonstrations stimulate soldier interest by providing realism that other techniques do not offer. Demonstrations-

- Save time by showing soldiers the correct way to perform a task
- Use the leader as the primary trainer whenever possible
- Present information in a manner that properly motivates
- Conclude when soldiers understand the task

Trainers conduct demonstrations with very simple, basic tools such as map boards, dry-erase boards, and sand tables, or with more advanced tools such as simulations and simulators. The sand tables and terrain models can be used to conduct rock drills to demonstrate tasks before and after executing them on the ground during squad and platoon training. Sand tables and terrain models can also be used during STX and LFX rehearsals and AARs.

B. Conference

Conference provides soldiers the opportunity to discuss the information presented. The trainer initiates and guides the discussion. Conferences are most effective when soldiers are familiar with the subject, when there is more than one correct technique or solution, and when time is not critical. Conferences normally do not require hands-on performance. An example of a conference is an AAR.

C. Lecture

Lecture presents information with little discussion other than a question and answer period at the end of the training. Lectures are used when time is limited, when soldiers know little about the subject, and when the lecture is preparing them for demonstration and practice.

Lectures are appropriate only if there is a large group to be trained. An example of a lecture is a pre-deployment briefing. Lectures are the least preferred method of training.

I. PLAN
for Training

Ref: FM 7-0, Train to Win in a Complex World (Oct '16), pp. 3-2 to 3-5.

Following the operations process framework, the leader assigned as the primary planner for the training event reviews the initial training objectives for the event from the UTP. Following this review, the planner completes a mission analysis and confers with the commander for additional training guidance. Based on this discussion, the planner refines training objectives with additional details based on the guidance from the commander. (See the Event Details page found at the CATS Web site for major resources to assist the planner in mission analysis.) The planner uses T&EOs to identify other supporting collective and individual tasks that support higher collective tasks. Once planners identify these tasks, they determine all prerequisite tasks on which the unit must train prior to executing the event. CATSs help identify training gates for the event being planned.

I. PLAN for Training

PLAN for Training
To apply the art and science of understanding a situation, envisioning a desired future, and laying out effective ways of bringing that future about.

PREPARE for Training
To make ready those activities performed by units and Soldiers to improve their abilities to train for an operation.

ASSESS for Training
To continuously check the progress toward accomplishing a task or achieving an objective.

EXECUTE for Training
To put a plan into action by training units and individuals to accomplish the mission.

Ref: FM 7-0 (Oct '16), fig. 3-1. Plan phase of the operations process.

Planners evaluate an operational environment to consider how to replicate it in the training environment. The higher commander's CTG identifies a potential environment to replicate in the training environment, including role players, type of visibility, types of terrain, and enemy forces. Using the objective task evaluation criteria matrix in the T&EO, planners identify the complexity of the training environment based on the commander's desired end state for task proficiency at the end of the training event.

See discussion of the objective task evaluation criteria matrix in the T&EO on pp. 8-7 to 8-10.

II. 8-Step Training Model

Ref: FM 7-0, Train to Win in a Complex World (Oct '16), pp. 3-3 to 3-5.

At the company and platoon levels, training models are developed and used as a simpl
and effective planning and execution tool for small-unit, individual training events. Train
ing models do not provide a sufficient level of detail from which to develop a UTP, to ful
develop training events, or to coordinate training events. Instead, they serve as a usefu
tool for subordinate leaders to ensure major activities and steps are accomplished. Trai
ing models help manage training events that are not complex in planning or execution.
Units modify training models in the number of steps and procedures based on experien
and the efficiencies gained by their use. One training model is the 8-step training model
(below). The 8-step training model provides a flexible and reliable vehicle for creating
continuity for planning and managing simple training events.

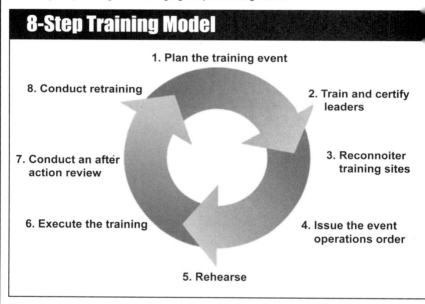

8-Step Training Model

1. Plan the training event
2. Train and certify leaders
3. Reconnoiter training sites
4. Issue the event operations order
5. Rehearse
6. Execute the training
7. Conduct an after action review
8. Conduct retraining

Ref: FM 7-0 (Oct '16), fig. 3-2. The 8-step training model.

Step 1 – Plan the Training Event
During step 1, leaders develop specific, obtainable, and measurable training objectives
for the upcoming event based on guidance from the commander. Leaders allocate and
ensure that there is adequate time scheduled for the event and it is indicated on the
unit's training schedule. They create scenarios and instructions to support the training
objectives. Leaders identify required resources, including necessary training areas and
possible trainers. They identify hazards and eliminate or mitigate associated risks. Lastly,
leaders develop training support and assessment plans, thereby establishing the ground-
work for high-quality training.

Step 2 – Train and Certify Leaders
Step 2 involves training and certifying leaders. Leaders consist of officers, NCOs, civilians, and Soldiers. Qualified leaders train and certify other leaders. Qualified personnel
are knowledgeable of the training subject matter and have performed the task themselves

standard. The train-the-trainer concept ensures that those responsible for training can provide proper instruction and certification to the unit. This step also includes training and certifying OPFOR leaders and training role players for the training environment.

Step 3 – Reconnoiter the Training Site

Leaders reconnoiter proposed training areas and facilities. Leaders verify that the location can adequately support the proposed training and enable the unit to accomplish training objectives. During step 3, leaders check that all resources, training areas, and training support plans are properly coordinated and prepared for execution. They make contact with support site personnel and review scheduling and coordination issues. If necessary, leaders modify the training event plan during step 3 to accommodate training site requirements and maximize training opportunities. Effective units do not perform training when training is not planned, coordinated, and supported properly with adequate resources.

Step 4 – Issue the Event Operation Order

Commanders and leaders ensure subordinates have all available information to perform the training. Through the OPORD, the commander clearly identifies the tasks to be trained, training objectives, and a clear mission statement. The commander also defines the scope of the training, how it will be conducted, and the tasks to train. A successful training event relies on all leaders understanding the expected outcome of the training, focused on the commander's training objectives.

Step 5 – Rehearse

Rehearsals are critical to the execution of any plan whether for operations or training. All those involved in the training event conduct rehearsals to ensure understanding, synchronization, and preparation of tactical actions. Leaders supervise rehearsals to ensure that those responsible for the training are prepared to conduct efficient, organized, and effective performance-oriented training. This step includes conducting the rehearsals necessary for OPFOR leaders and personnel.

Step 6 – Execute the Training

Commanders ensure the training event occurs as planned and on schedule. A training event requires maximum participation, minimum training distracters, and leaders checking and supervising where necessary. Trainers train Soldiers and ensure standards are met. To the greatest extent possible, commanders avoid planning training and not conducting it; they conduct every training planned. Commanders also minimize training distracters that interfere with training.

Step 7 – Conduct an After Action Review

During and after training, commanders review the tasks trained, assess the unit's training level in respect to the objectives, and obtain lessons learned to improve the training and unit's tactics, techniques, and procedures (TTP). Commanders record these assessments in DTMS for future use in other training events or to include these in unit SOPs.

Step 8 – Conduct Retraining

Units never depart a training event with tasks not trained to standard and training objectives not met. Units retrain tasks as necessary until they achieve the standard before they conclude the training event. Too often, units neglect this step because of limited time, limited resources, or other pressing requirements. However, step 8 is often the most critical step. Training instills competency and confidence in units, leaders, and Soldiers and enables the unit to develop task proficiency. Commanders honestly and objectively assess their units and ensure the unit meets task standards.

Conducting Training

When no training environment is identified, the commander can create a training environment by using the decisive action training environment (known as DATE) available on the ATN Web site. This training environment is a composite model of the real-world environment. It provides a useful training planning tool to replicate a operational environment for training when one is not specified.

The creation of optimal training conditions results from several factors. Planners identify required resources early in the planning for a training event. Those same planners share knowledge of resource activities and their locations on the installation. Planners focus on creating a training environment that replicates an operation environment to the highest possible fidelity. Sometimes, planners combine LVC training environments to approximate an operational environment. (See AR 350-2 for th details on an operational environment and OPFORs resources.)

During the planning phase, the planner verifies the training venue (as live, virtual, constructive) and locks in required resources. Ideally, the planners schedule these critical resources once the commander approves the COA to train. They reconnoiter the training site to ensure the unit can achieve the training objectives within the venue. Planners visualize the training event by drawing an event sketch and detailing how the unit will execute the training. They write a list of actions meet training objectives. They consider the time available to train versus the number of possible iterations to attain proficiency. This visualization serves as the concept for executing the training event. Once planners develop a sketch and visualized concept from sta to end and the commander approves it, then additional resourcing for the event can begin.

Planners identify and request resources early and track their availability throughout the planning and preparation phases. Effective planners use the CATS, T&EOs, and unit historical records as a starting point to identify resources. Historical record typically document resources the unit needed and when it needed them. Successful planners know what resources they used previously for like training events. The event planner ensures the event resources—including any newly identified resourc es—are available. The DTMS has a checklist tool that allows users to set up and track the status of training resources associated within events.

An event administrative OPORD is required to execute the training and includes all necessary coordination. It explains the concept, resourcing, and responsibilities to execute the training event. Additionally, the plan identifies both tactical orders and OPFOR orders to drive the training and stimulate task execution

III. T-Week Concept

The T-Week concept provides a logical, backward planning approach for developing training events. It provides detailed, chronological, and specific considerations for the planning and coordination necessary for each training event. The T-Week concept helps ensure that commanders consider and complete all significant actions necessary to execute training in a timely manner. Leaders use the concept as a guide for developing training events for the short-range planning horizon.

The T-Week concept ensures that units or individuals complete all critical actions before and after the training event. Leaders have to start early enough in the planning cycle to ensure the unit has all the resources to train when training begins. Unless the staff properly plans and prepares before training events, the unit may fail to attain the MET proficiencies that the commander envisioned during training execution. Additionally, commanders and leaders must thoroughly understand the home station's available training resources and facilities. See appendix H for an extensive discussion of the T-Week concept.

See pp. 6-49 to 6-72 for discussion of the T-Week concept.

II. PREPARE
for Training

Ref: FM 7-0, Train to Win in a Complex World (Oct '16), pp. 3-5 to 3-6.

Preparing for training involves those activities performed prior to training to improve the unit's abilities to train effectively. Preparing for training starts with ensuring trainers are subject matter experts in the tasks and the events trained. Trainers demonstrate task proficiency before teaching a task to others. Training and certifying leaders are critical in delivering quality, effective training to the unit. They ensure adequate preparation time and resources are available to conduct training. Preparation includes final coordination for training resources scheduled and programmed earlier in the plan phase. This preparation ensures that training resources are available when training begins.

II. PREPARE for Training

PLAN for Training
To apply the art and science of understanding a situation, envisioning a desired future, and laying out effective ways of bringing that future about.

PREPARE for Training
To make ready those activities performed by units and Soldiers to improve their abilities to train for an operation.

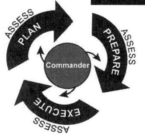

ASSESS for Training
To continuously check the progress toward accomplishing a task or achieving an objective.

EXECUTE for Training
To put a plan into action by training units and individuals to accomplish the mission.

Ref: FM 7-0 (Oct '16), fig. 3-3. Prepare phase of the operations process.

Every training event is an opportunity for leader training. Each event gives senior leaders the opportunity to coach and mentor subordinates Senior leaders actively develop subordinate leaders during preparations and develop specific leader training objectives for each training event.

Preparing for training also includes preexecution checks. Preexecution checks are the informal coordination measures conducted prior to conducting training events and must not be confused with precombat checks. Often, preexecution checks are tied to administrative resourcing or tasks that were identified within the event administrative OPORD. Leaders continuously track and conduct preexecution checks.

I. Preparing for Training

Ref: Adapted from ADRP 7-0, Training Units & Developing Leaders (Aug '12), pp. 3-9 to 3

Training Objectives

A training objective is a statement that describes the desired outcome of a training activity in the unit. A training objective consists of the task, conditions, and standard. Units focus their training execution on achieving the standards for these objectives during training events. Units achieve a training objective when they meet the standards. The time it takes to achieve the objective is not the deciding factor. Leaders allow enough time during training execution to retrain tasks if training units did not meet the standard. If necessary, units continue training beyond the scheduled time until the unit meets the standards. Retraining should be tailored to fix the shortcomings. If training units achieve the objectives before the scheduled end of the event, then leaders consider ending the training early or training on tasks that require additional training.

Training Supervision

The Army commander with administrative control of a unit oversees a unit's training until the unit is assigned or attached to a gaining unit. Once assignment or attachment occurs the gaining commander is responsible for not only the unit's training and leader development, but also for informing the providing commander about the unit's readiness.

Training supervision is a collaborative process. For a deploying ARFORGEN unit, the providing commander involves the gaining commander in the training process. The providing and gaining commanders share information, resources, and guidance to ensure the unit trains on the right tasks under the right conditions to accomplish the mission. This mutual involvement begins with the assignment of a mission to the unit and ends when the unit returns from deployment to enter the reset force pool of ARFORGEN.

The commander providing a subordinate unit to another commander for an operation is ultimately responsible for the unit's training. This responsibility includes approval of METLs and the unit training plan, provisioning of training resources, and assessments of training events. The gaining commander recommends tasks to train for the assigned mission and can help assess the training proficiency of the unit. The gaining commander shares information on the area of operations (which may have an impact on training), provides unit standard operating procedures, and visits key training events—especially during culminating training events.

Training Models

Training models can provide a framework for planning and managing training events. Training models, such as the eight-step training model, are only guides and not lock-step processes. They can be useful, but they are, effectively, just modifications of either the MDMP or TLP.

Support Requirements

Providing required resources for unit training and leader development is a shared responsibility between the unit's higher headquarters and the installation. The higher headquarters prioritizes units for training support and provides such resources for exercises. These resources include higher control, evaluators, and equipment and Soldier augmentation. The installation supports all units stationed on the installation through the garrison staff by providing facilities, ranges, maneuver space, ammunition, logistics support, and other training support services.

Commanders leverage the capabilities offered by mission command training complexes and employ an integrated training environment (known as ITE). Commanders use a combination of live, virtual, constructive and gaming training enablers to create a realistic training environment, optimize training time, and mitigate live resource shortfalls.

aining the Trainer

iners include leaders, evaluators, observer-controller-trainers, opposing force person-
, and role players. Commanders identify these individuals early enough to ensure
y are trained and rehearsed before training begins. These personnel not only improve
quality of the event, but these roles offer developmental opportunities since they can
serve how other units and leaders operate. Commanders ensure that these personnel
not only tactically and technically competent on the unit's tasks, but also that these
rsonnel understand how their role supports the unit's training.

reexecution Checks

nilar to pre-combat checks, pre-execution checks ensure that equipment is ready and
rviceable, trainers are prepared, training support resources are coordinated and avail-
le, and leaders have conducted initial risk management checks. The training plan must
ocate time for pre-execution checks.

bordinate leaders identify and select the collective, leader, and individual tasks neces-
ry to support the identified training objectives. They do this based on as bottom-up
edback from internal training meetings. Commanders develop tentative plans, including
quirements for preparatory training, multi-echelon training, concurrent training, and
ining resources. Often these plans take the form of verbal guidance issued during
ining meetings. When necessary, commanders prepare a written event training plan.
I training plans include time and other resources necessary for retraining.

aders use the DTMS to assist in tracking preexecution checks throughout the prepara-
n process.

ee pp. 6-48 and 6-56 for a list of possible preexecution checks.

Rehearsals

ehearsals help leaders and subordinates understand the conduct of events and their
sponsibilities. Rehearsals help the organization synchronize training with times, places,
gistics, and training support. A rehearsal of a concept drill helps leaders visualize an
vent as it unfolds as well as likely branches and sequels if leaders must adjust the train-
g. Commanders and other leaders also use rehearsals to:

- Ensure leaders and trainers understand training objectives
- Identify shortcomings and deficiencies in the training plan
- Instill confidence in the training plan
- Suggest effective training techniques to subordinates
- Identify and correct potential safety issues
- Understand how trainers intend to evaluate the performance of individuals and organizations and whether they understand how to conduct effective after action reviews
- Assess trainer competencies to conduct the training

Training Schedules

The OPORD developed for each training event provides enough guidance on preparation, execution, and assessment to leave room for the exercise of initiative. Once the
OPORD is published, units develop their training schedules. The schedule normally covers at least one week of training; however, commanders determine how far in advance
subordinate commanders must publish their training schedules. Commanders determine the approval authority for changes to the training schedule. Information in training
schedules normally includes, but is not limited to, the training audience, the time and
place to conduct the training, the individual responsible for the training, the uniform, and
the equipment.

Some informal coordination measures might include checking that—
- The OPFOR has been equipped and trained.
- Leaders are certified to conduct range operations.
- All identified classes of supply and materials were requested in accordance with the administrative OPORD and have arrived by the request suspense.

Preparing for training includes having units rehearse anticipated actions during the training event. Rehearsals provide a means of ensuring units synchronize and execute actions to standard during training. The OPFOR also rehearses its plan before executing the training event. The OPFOR rehearsal ensures this force understands its plan and can effectively stimulate quality training. Additionally, units rehearse large training exercises to synchronize timing and actions associated with the tactical situation. Rehearsals are essential for an effective and realistic training experience.

Prior to training, leaders and planners prepare and develop an assessment plan. This plan captures unit performance as it is executed and enables leaders and trainers the opportunity to evaluate the unit as action unfolds. This plan also includes OC/Ts walking training areas to ensure that as the unit executes tasks, OC/Ts observe task execution.

When preparing for training, planners ensure final preparations are complete. The commander approves all required resources when training schedules are published and six weeks before the unit executes the training. The commander protects approved and scheduled training from taskings and distracters. If taskings and distracters put training at risk, the commander engages the higher commander to mitigate necessary. As the event nears, planners ensure delivery of resources to the training site. Leaders check that TADSS are functional and that Soldiers know how to install and use them. Planners ensure the training site is set up in accordance with the administrative OPORD. Finally, they make final checks before the training event begins.

II. Dissemination of the UTP OPORD

Once leaders disseminate the UTP OPORD to subordinates, execution of the training plan begins. Leaders adapt to changes, as necessary. Thorough preparation to conduct training is essential. Assessment of unit and individual performance is a continual process. While units execute one event, they plan and prepare another. Plan, prepare, execute, and assess are not performed sequentially, but overlap in a series of dynamic and interrelated processes throughout the life cycle of the UTP until the unit attains the commander's visualized end state for training. Training meetings facilitate this integrated process by assessing the collective tasks trained during UTP execution, as well as coordinating resources and planning for future events.

Because the UTP is executed as a series of interrelated training events, each event builds upon the training proficiencies attainted from the previous events, ultimately leading the unit to the commander's visualized training proficiency. Event outcomes are usually a direct reflection of the amount and quality of the preparation that preceded it.

III. EXECUTE
for Training

Ref: FM 7-0, Train to Win in a Complex World (Oct '16), pp. 3-6 to 3-7 and ADP 7-0, Training (Jul '19), p. 4-10.

Units execute training when they put a plan into action to meet the training proficiencies and training objectives specified by the commander. Commanders establish measurable and attainable training objectives that develop and demonstrate collective task proficiencies. Well planned and communicated training guidance, well-developed plans, and maximized opportunities and resources enable units to execute quality training.

III. EXECUTE for Training

PLAN for Training
To apply the art and science of understanding a situation, envisioning a desired future, and laying out effective ways of bringing that future about.

PREPARE for Training
To make ready those activities performed by units and Soldiers to improve their abilities to train for an operation.

ASSESS for Training
To continuously check the progress toward accomplishing a task or achieving an objective.

EXECUTE for Training
To put a plan into action by training units and individuals to accomplish the mission.

Ref: FM 7-0 (Oct '16), fig. 3-4. Execute phase of the operations process.

During execution, leaders and OC/Ts perform evaluations using Training and Evaluation Outlines (T&EOs) to record a unit's performance as training is executed. Leaders conduct on-site, informal AARs during training, where training occurs to correct deficiencies in observed task execution. Trainers objectively measure unit training against published Army standards (found in the T&EOs). When standards are not met, the unit retrains tasks to meet the standard.

See pp. 7-4 to 7-7 for discussion of realistic training and pp. 7-19 to 7-32 for a description of lane training. See pp. 8-7 to 8-14 for discussion training and evaluation outlines (T&EOs) and pp. 8-15 to 8-24 for after action reviews.

Leaders must plan, prepare, execute, and assess each training event that supports UTP. Training meetings and recovery after training are key activities that occur as e training event is conducted. These activities ensure that units execute the UTP and meets the commander's desired objectives for unit training and leader development

II. Training Meetings

Training meetings provide an integrating function to allow the commander, staff, subordinate commanders, and other leaders to manage current and future training events that support the UTP. Training meetings provide commanders with continuous bottom-up feedback on requirements, task proficiency, task performance, and the quality of the training conducted.

Training meetings are the single most important meeting for managing training in brigades, battalions, and companies. Normally, platoons, companies, and battalio meet weekly. At company and platoon level, training meetings focus on the specif of assessing previous training events, training preparation, pre-execution checks, and execution. Companies must become proficient in individual skills and small-u collective tasks to support battalion and brigade collective task proficiency. At battalion level and above, training meetings primarily cover training management—es pecially resourcing issues—as well as staff training proficiencies. Meeting frequen is a function of command preference, but occurs often enough to ensure subordin units have what they require to execute training.

See pp.6-37 to 6-48 for discussion of training meetings.

III. Recovery After Training

Recovery after training is part of training. A training event has not ended until recove is complete. Recovery ends when the organization is again prepared to conduct colle tive training and operations.

Recovery includes—

- Inspecting and maintaining equipment and personnel.
- Accounting for personnel, equipment, training support items, and ammunition
- Gaining insights on how to make the next exercise or event better.

Conducting
Training

IV. Lane Training (STXs/LTXs)

Ref: FM 7-0, Train to Win in a Complex World (Oct '16), appendix E.

Leaders use situational training exercises (STXs) and lane training exercises (LTXs) to assess unit collective training. An STX is a mission-related, limited exercise. This short, scenario-driven exercise trains a group of related tasks or battle drills through practice. An STX usually contains multiple collective tasks linked to form a realistic scenario of a military operation, sometimes incorporating free play. STXs are used for training and evaluation, especially sustainment of task proficiency. STXs are developed by Army branch proponent schools reflected in the unit CATS or developed by a unit as required.

Leaders use lane training and LTXs to conduct training at the small-unit level. A lane is a standardized training exercise used to train on one or more collective tasks or the designated area or facility for the exercise. Lane training is a process—planning, execution, and assessment—for training company-size and smaller units on individual tasks, collective tasks, and battle drills that support a unit's METs. Although lane training is a technique for training company-size and smaller units (including platoons, sections, squads, crews, and teams), the emphasis is on the size unit, not the unit echelon. Commanders can use lane training to train small groups, elements, or staffs of any organization.

A lane training exercise is a standardized and structured exercise or simulation used to train on one or more collective tasks that includes a designated area, terrain, or facility. It usually focuses on one primary task. An LTX consists of the assembly area, rehearsal, lane execution, AAR, and retraining activities that culminate the lane training process. An LTX is an STX conducted using lane training principles and techniques. Trainers should consider the following when developing LTXs:

- An LTX is usually a mini-STX; however, it focuses on fewer collective tasks to enhance training efficiency.
- It has no free play.
- Its primary purpose is training, especially the development of task proficiency.
- LTXs are developed by units.
- A unit may train on several LTXs (several primary tasks) within a few days at one major training area.

An LTX is conducted in an LTX area. An LTX area is a training area selected and designed to train on one primary task. An LTX area is where the five LTX activities take place. The five LTX activities include assembly, rehearsal, lane execution, AAR, and retraining.

An LTX will include one or more lanes. A lane is a standardized and structured training exercise or simulation used to train on one or more collective tasks. A lane is designed to create the situation or conditions required for execution. When an LTX includes more than one lane, each lane can be used to train the same primary task. Ideally, units use different lanes for rehearsals, lane execution, and retraining on the same primary task.

Lane training is a systematic, performance-oriented training process. The rigor of the lane training process enables units to attain proficiency quickly and efficiently in tactical and technical tasks. It enables training to be effectively structured, administered, supported, and assessed by limiting the number of tasks, time, terrain, facilities, or other resources. Lane training provides a systematic and controlled approach to selected task proficiency.

I. Components of Lane Training

As a focused and controlled training event, lane training includes components ar personnel to ensure success. At a minimum, lane training includes the following components:

- The unit to be trained.
- Support structure conducting the training.
- OC/T teams.
- OPFOR teams, if appropriate.

A training exercise control cell may be created to manage lane training for one or more LTXs or units. (This cell is for training purposes only; it is not an operational cell.) The exercise control cell is supervised by an exercise director. It may be co posed of operations, communications, administration, and logistics cells.

The unit two echelons higher than the unit on the lane usually manages lane trair ing. For example, a brigade normally manages company lanes, a battalion norma manages platoon lanes, and a company normally manages squad and or section lanes.

Key Personnel

Table E-2 lists key personnel involved in managing lane training. Other personnel involved in lane training (and generating management or coordination requiremen include—

- Exercise planners.
- Unit Soldiers.
- OPFOR Soldiers.
- Maneuver support or sustainment unit customers (for example, personnel fro other units receiving services from a maneuver support or sustainment unit undergoing lane training).
- Role players.
- Higher headquarters' commanders, staffs, or representatives.
- Personnel from other units providing support.

Personnel	Description and Responsibilities
Exercise director	The individual responsible for managing all LTXs. This duty position is sometimes called chief controller or senior OC/T team chief.
Senior OC/T	The individual responsible for managing a specific LTX or LTX area. There is one senior OC/T for each LTX.
Other OC/Ts	Other personnel responsible for assisting senior OC/Ts or the exercise director. There may be an OC/T for each leader in a unit and each key event of each lane.
OPFOR leaders	Leaders of the element responsible for performing lane countertasks.
LTX resource managers	Personnel responsible for administration of logistic support for each LTX.
Unit leaders	Leaders responsible for the unit's training and for directing the unit during training.
Chain of command	Leaders responsible for supporting the planning, preparation, execution, and assessment of the unit's training.
LTX lane training exercise OC/T observer-controller/trainer OPFOR opposing force	

Ref: FM 7-0 (Oct '16), table E-2. Key personnel in managing lane training.

1. Lane Training Uses

Ref: FM 7-0, Train to Win in a Complex World (Oct '16), p. E-2.

The purpose of lane training is to build or sustain proficiency in Soldier and leader individual tasks, collective tasks, and battle drills. Lane training enables leaders to—

- Conduct initial, developmental, sustainment, refresher, and enhancement training and assessment for tactical and technical tasks.
- Train similar units—simultaneously or sequentially—using mission-related scenarios.
- Test, standardize, and train TTP.
- Develop and refine unit SOPs that support unit METs.
- Efficiently control training objectives (including tasks, conditions, standards, and training proficiencies) during training.
- Support initial training and retraining.
- Vary training conditions to the training level of the unit (which may be at the initial, refresher, or sustainment level).
- Integrate (both vertically and horizontally) specific task training, battle drills, and exercises from different functional areas (including maneuver, maneuver support, and sustainment) into unit training programs.
- Achieve proficiency on multiechelon, multi-unit, combined, joint, multinational, or interagency procedures and on other difficult, infrequent, or teamwork-based tasks.
- Achieve maximum results when training Soldiers and units while efficiently leveraging limited resources (including land, facilities, personnel, and equipment).
- Prepare for both formal/informal assessments, internal evaluations, and EXEVALs.
- Conduct competitions.

In certain instances, lane training may be the most efficient and effective means to train small units to attain and sustain selected task proficiencies. Lane training techniques may be indicated as a training method—

- When training assessments indicate there may be changes or performance deficiencies in team, squad, section, platoon, or company collective tasks. Potential situations or indicators include changes in—
  - Doctrine.
  - Organization.
  - Materiel.
  - Personnel.
  - Training.
  - Leader development.
  - Task performance.
- When units need to prepare for assigned missions or specific operational environments.
- When leaders units need to prepare Soldiers and units for major training events, including annual training, gunnery exercises, combat training center rotations, and EXEVALs.
- When sustainment training is needed.
- When task proficiency is perishable or easily atrophied.
- When there is a need to evaluate performance on collective and supporting individual tasks further.
- When there is a need for integrated multiechelon or multifunctional training.
- When training requires significant planning, management, or resource support.
- When the use of other training techniques proves more expensive or impractical.
- When directed by higher headquarters.

Conducting Training

III. Lane Training Characteristics

Ref: FM 7-0, Train to Win in a Complex World (Oct '16), pp. E-3 to E-4.

Lane training is a process for training company-size and smaller units on collective ta
that support a unit's capability or mission. The process consists of planning, execution
and assessment phases. In the planning phase, lane training emphasizes pre-exercis

- Certification of trainers and leaders.
- Validation of training plans and materials.
- Rehearsals.

Characteristics	Description
Small-unit focus	A focus by units of platoon size or below (including staffs and small groups) on training a unit of company size or below.
Disciplined scenario	A disciplined scenario concentrating on mission-focused tasks and providing structured stimuli to prompt friendly force behavior.
Battle-focus	A focus on a limited number of collective tasks for each lane training exercise to improve effectiveness.
Validated tasks	Doctrinally and technically correct tasks and training objectives that have been validated against current doctrine and Army standards.
Controlled tasks and events	Highly controlled tasks, countertasks, and events that are structured to provide specific stimuli and elicit specific responses from the unit being trained.
Trained OC/Ts	OC/Ts trained and verified on specific OC/T and LTX tasks.
Trained OPFOR	Forces trained and verified on specific OPFOR countertasks required in the LTX in appropriate force ratios.
Support from outside the unit trained	Support (including OC/Ts, OPFOR, and resources) provided from sources other than the unit being trained.
LTX	A training exercise using lane training principles and techniques.
LTX   lane training exercise   OC/T   observer-controller/trainer   OPFOR   opposing force

Ref: FM 7-0 (Oct '16), table E-1. Characteristics of lane training.

The execution phase (the LTX) focuses on specific collective tasks. Historically, lane training has usually been associated with tasks requiring movement over terrain (for ex ample, conduct a movement to contact or conduct an attack); however, movement is no required. Lane training is appropriate for most small-unit maneuver, maneuver support, and sustainment collective tasks requiring teamwork and practice, whether conducted in fixed facilities or in a field environment.

Lane training is performance-oriented training. Since performance-oriented training requires training to the task performance standard, an inherent element is performance evaluation. This evaluation focuses on verification (or certification) that Soldiers, leaders and units can perform tasks under specified conditions and standards. Effective lane training requires replication of missions and operational environments. Although lane training can be conducted in a live, virtual, or constructive training environment, it is normally conducted in a live environment (conducted in the field or duty site environment). However, the use of virtual or constructive environments to prepare for or to conduct lan training can dramatically enhance the effectiveness of lane training in live environments.

To ensure standardization, units develop LTXs to teach the doctrinally preferred way to perform specific missions or tasks. Initially, LTXs focus on a task or a few tasks at one time and exclude related tasks that may distract Soldiers from learning. However, once a unit is proficient in the tasks trained, more tasks may be included in more comprehensive LTXs to increase realism.

An LTX can consist of multiple lanes training the same task, but with different and varying conditions. LTXs are more flexible than drills, and units can tailor LTXs to meet a unit's METs or assigned mission requirements.

Lane training has characteristics that make it significantly different from other forms of training. Unit leaders consider these characteristics before planning and executing LTXs.

ders need an understanding of the tasks to be trained so they can develop a quality
. Leaders prepare themselves and their units. They coordinate training supplies and
ipment well in advance of the LTX. Detailed and meticulous planning is critical in mak-
an LTX that meets the training objectives.

ders conduct several activities prior to conducting an LTX. Trainers institute a pre-LTX
ing program to develop and verify the unit leaders' task proficiency. In this case, a
LTX training program means before the exercise or prior to arrival of the unit at the
area. Next, leaders institute a pre-LTX unit training and verification period after the
der training period. During this period, the unit's subordinate elements and personnel
elop proficiency (through training and rehearsal) on prerequisite Soldier, leader, and
ective tasks and battle drills.

r leaders and units develop proficiency on prerequisite tasks, they are ready to conduct
rehearsals. OC/Ts, OPFOR elements, leaders, and units all conduct rehearsals prior to
exercise. Leaders and units conduct rehearsals in the LTX area (in the assembly area or
earsal area) just prior to lane execution. Rehearsals enable trainers to perform a pre-LTX
dation, which is a tentative validation of training plans and materials prior to the exercise.

or to conducting an LTX, trainers coordinate for post-LTX activities, including AARs,
luations, retraining, and validation. For example, OC/Ts and unit leaders conduct
Rs immediately following lane execution to provide feedback to units. AARs are
ilitated by OC/Ts, are supported by the unit's leaders and OPFOR, and involve all
t participants. Post-LTX, senior unit leaders conduct a task performance evaluation.
is evaluation determines whether units performed tasks to standard or not. The senior
/T coordinates with the leader of the unit being trained. After an LTX, some units may
uire retraining. A retraining opportunity is an opportunity after the AAR to conduct re-
ining until a unit achieves standards. After retraining, the unit should have an opportu-
y to attempt the same tasks on a different lane, possibly with additional tasks, different
nditions, or different leaders. Additionally, OC/Ts and unit leaders perform a validation
training and training materials after each iteration of the LTX.

Begin Lane Training Event

Conduct rehearsal

Lane or event execution

After action review

Task GO or NO-GO?

Retrain task

NO-GO

GO

Begin next lane training event

The general flow of a lane follows a logical sequence of activities that includes rehearsals, task execution, AARs, evaluations, and the opportunity to retrain tasks not executed to standard. The lane can and should be repeated until the selected tasks are performed to the published standard.

Figure E-1 shows an example of the lane training process, including the sequence of activities that occur as the lane is executed.

Ref: FM 7-0 (Oct '16), fig. E-1. General sequence of activities during a lane training event.

Conducting Training

IV. Lane Training Process

Lane training is implemented using a systematic general process. This process includes planning, execution, and assessment phases. The activities described in table E-3 comprise the three lane training phases.

Lane Training Phase	Activities Included
Planning (pre-LTX)	Actions involving unit assessment, training assessment, analysis, design, development, scheduling, resource acquisition, support coordination, pre-training, and preparation for training.
Execution (LTX)	Actions involving preparation, presentation, and performance of collective tasks to standard.
Assessment (post-LTX)	AARs and follow-up actions (such as update unit SOPs). Although frequently considered to be a post-exercise phase, assessment consists primarily of AARs conducted during or immediately after LTX lane execution.
AAR after action review	LTX lane training exercise SOP standard operating procedures

FM 7-0 (Oct '16), table E-3. Lane training activities.

Although lane training activities generally occur sequentially in the general process, lane training activities in the detailed process activities can occur simultaneously for different phases. For example, in figure E-2, "Perform AAR procedures" actually consists of the same procedures as the assessment phase's activity "Perform AAR preparation procedures" and "Conduct an AAR." Also, in the assessment phase, "Perform AAR planning procedures" takes place during the planning phase. Figure E-2 illustrates how the lane training process is composed of the three subordinate processes of planning, execution, and assessment.

Lane Training Process

Planning Phase
- Conduct long-range planning
- Conduct mid-range planning
- Conduct short-range planning

Execution Phase
- Perform assembly procedures
- Perform rehearsal procedures
- Perform lane execution procedures
- Perform AAR procedures
- Perform retraining procedures

Assessment Phase
- Perform AAR planning procedures
- Perform AAR preparation procedures
- Conduct an AAR
- Perform follow-up procedures

Ref: FM 7-0 (Oct '16), fig. E-2. Detailed lane training process.

V. Lane Training Categories

Ref: FM 7-0, Train to Win in a Complex World (Oct '16), pp. E-7 to E-8.

Lane Training Exercise Categories

 Stand-Alone

 Integrated

 Mission Support

A. Stand-Alone

A stand-alone LTX is a single-function exercise requiring only one functional branch (for example, chemical) to accomplish a collective task. A stand-alone FTX is—

- Frequently executed at the lowest level (platoon, section, squad, or team) by units needing to develop proficiency.
- Able to provide OC/Ts the maximum flexibility and control over stopping the lane, resuming the lane, conducting AARs, and repeating the lane.
- Designed so several lanes may repeat identical tasks (sometimes with different conditions).
- More flexible than integrated or mission support FTX because it has fewer constraints.

B. Integrated

An integrated LTX is a multifunctional exercise requiring the integrated employment of two or more branches (for example, an infantry-armor company team) to accomplish a collective task. An integrated FTX is—

- Normally executed by units that exhibit high degrees of proficiency at the platoon or section level.
- Able to allow multiple units to interact, often interdependently, that are fully dedicated to training on the lane while participating under a master scenario.
- Difficult to restart as a single unit because that unit is a role player for another unit executing its task.
- More structured, complex, and time-phased than a stand-alone FTX, so OC/Ts have less flexibility and control.

C. Mission Support

A mission support LTX is an exercise in which the unit undergoes lane training while performing a mission on behalf of, or associated with, other units. An example includes a petroleum, oils, and lubricants (POL) platoon performing a refueling mission. A mission support LTX—

- Is difficult for OC/Ts to stop and restart because the unit may be performing a real mission in support of other units.
- Limits the OC/T's control, requires more evaluation, is more complicated, limits controlled stimuli, and has less repeatability than a stand-alone or integrated FTX.

Conducting Training

VI. Lane Training Exercise Activities

There are five basic activities that occur in the conduct of a LTX. These activities are executed sequentially and consist of assembly, rehearsal, execution, AAR, a retraining. Rehearsals, execution, and retraining activities may occur on differen lanes within the LTX area.

Assembly
Activities involving unit in-briefing, leader preparation, and troop leading procedu (including issuance of the unit's OPORD). These activities are normally conducte the assembly area (AA).

Rehearsal
Activities involving practices of unit task to be performed on the lane (or to execu the OPORD), normally conducted at a crawl or walk spped. These practices may take place in rehearsal areas, AAs, or on lanes.

Execution
Activities required to perform specific collective tasks on the lane (or to execute th OPORD), normally at run speed. These activities may take place over time.

After Action Review (AAR)
Activities required to provide:

- A structured, interactive, group-oriented review and evaluation of the unit's ta performance on the execution lane.
- Suggestions on how to improve future performance. These activities normall take place in an AAR area or on a lane.

Retraining
Activities required to enable the unit to perform lane taks to the desired standards. These activities normally take place in the retraining area, rehearsal area, or lane.

The execution of a lane follows a general pattern.

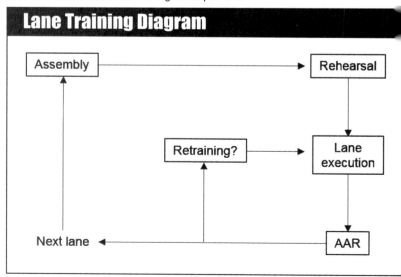

Ref: FM 7-0 (Oct '16), fig. E-4. Diagram of lane training and FM 7-0 (Oct '16), fig. E-3. Lane training execution process.

VII. Lane Training Methodology (Crawl-Walk-Run)

Ref: FM 7-0, Train to Win in a Complex World (Oct '16), pp. E-8 to E-9.

Lane training is based on a crawl-walk-run methodology. This methodology has three phases: crawl, walk, and run. These phases are described in table E-4.

Phase	Description
Crawl (explain and demonstrate)	The leader describes the task step-by-step, indicating what each individual does.
Walk (practice)	The leader directs the unit to execute the task at a slow, step-by-step pace.
Run (perform)	The leader requires the unit to perform the task at full speed, as if in an operation, under realistic conditions.

Normally, the entire crawl-walk-run process occurs within a short time frame of only a few hours or days. This is determined by the tasks selected to train and the number of Soldiers to train. However, for lane training, the crawl-walk-run process can occur over several weeks, months, or years (especially for units within the Reserve Component). Lane training normally follows the crawl-walk-run methodology described below:

A. Crawl

During the crawl phase, each Soldier receives instructions from unit leaders on the common and specific individual tasks supporting the collective tasks that will be conducted during the LTX. Leaders review training objectives to demonstrate and discuss tasks, conditions, standards, and training proficiencies. This includes a review of supporting individual tasks for the collective tasks, battle drills, and T&EOs to train prior to and during the LTX. Leaders demonstrate a way to perform each task.

Junior leaders train their units on common and duty-specific individual tasks. After meeting the standards for all required individual tasks, junior leaders explain the units' collective tasks and drills. Individual and prerequisite collective training should be completed at a home station location prior to deploying for the training area to participate in the LTX.

B. Walk

During the walk phase, leaders conduct individual tasks and drills. Leaders train on each collective task until each unit meets the published standard. This phase is usually conducted without combat effects or the OPFOR. When possible, units complete supporting individual and collective training at a home station location so these tasks can be immediately performed at a run speed during the LTX to support the primary collective tasks to be trained. At the LTX area (in an assembly area or rehearsal area)—

- Unit leaders rehearse the primary collective tasks.
- Leaders & Soldiers rehearse supporting individual and collective tasks and drills.

C. Run

During the run phase, the unit actually performs the LTX. On a lane, the unit conducts training at combat speed under tactical conditions. Training multipliers such as TADSS, OPFOR, or live munitions may be used to enhance training. The LTX may integrate maneuver, maneuver support, and sustainment activities.

OC/Ts conduct (or facilitate) scheduled AARs at the end of the run phase. Although OC/Ts normally avoid stopping lane execution, OC/Ts may halt any phase of training to conduct an AAR at logical breaks in the training, whenever standards are not being met, or to address safety and environmental issues. If training standards are not achieved, the unit retrains until the standards are achieved.

VIII. Lane Training Exercise Scenarios

Ref: FM 7-0, Train to Win in a Complex World (Oct '16), pp. E-11 to E-14.

The following figures depict examples of generic scenarios for LTX lanes. A lane has c primary collective task (or lane title) for a specific type of unit and one or more support collective tasks or task performance steps structured as events.

Note: An AAR is scheduled at the end of an LTX lane. Normally, an AAR is scheduled at the end of events for major collective tasks but not scheduled after events for task performance steps.

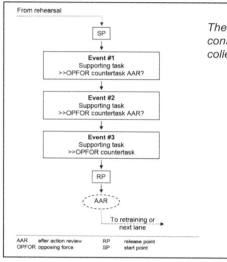

The LTX example lane in figure E-5 consists of three events for supporting collective tasks.

Figure E-5. Example generic lane scenario.

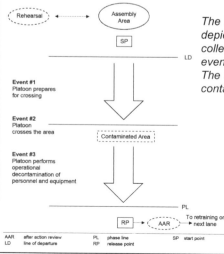

The LTX example diagram in figure E-6 depicts an example of a scenario for on collective task with three task steps as events. The unit depicted is a platoon. The unit's task is to cross a radiologica contaminated area.

Figure E-6. Example scenario for one collective task with three task steps.

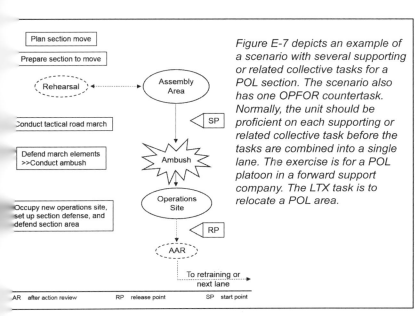

Figure E-7 depicts an example of a scenario with several supporting or related collective tasks for a POL section. The scenario also has one OPFOR countertask. Normally, the unit should be proficient on each supporting or related collective task before the tasks are combined into a single lane. The exercise is for a POL platoon in a forward support company. The LTX task is to relocate a POL area.

AR   after action review   RP   release point   SP   start point

Figure E-7. Example scenario with several supporting or related collective tasks.

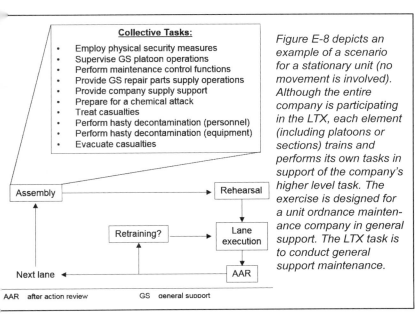

Figure E-8 depicts an example of a scenario for a stationary unit (no movement is involved). Although the entire company is participating in the LTX, each element (including platoons or sections) trains and performs its own tasks in support of the company's higher level task. The exercise is designed for a unit ordnance mainten- ance company in general support. The LTX task is to conduct general support maintenance.

AAR   after action review   GS   general support

Figure E-8. Scenario for a stationary unit.

Conducting
Training

IX. Support Requirements

Ref: FM 7-0, Train to Win in a Complex World (Oct '16), pp. E-14 to E-17.

Effective lane training requires support. FTX support requirements include (but are not limited to) the following items:

- Time.
- Personnel (lane planners, OC/Ts, OPFOR, customers, and role players).
- Doctrine and training publications and other training information.
- Training areas (maneuver areas, bivouac areas, ranges, and facilities).
- Materiel (vehicles, weapons, communications equipment, TADSS, tools, and special equipment).
- Supplies (ammunition, food, fuel, and POL).
- Funds.
- Operational tempo allocation.
- Other resources.

Time

Sufficient time is required to conduct adequate planning, execution, and assessment. Variables affecting the time required include the following:

- Planning requirements.
- Number of METs, other collective tasks, and supporting tasks to be trained.
- Difficulty and complexity of tasks.
- Number of lanes to be conducted.
- Number of units to be trained.
- Size and echelon of the units trained.
- Task proficiency of units trained.
- Distances involved between unit's garrison location and the training area, bivouac areas and LTXs in training area, and lane start points and release points.
- Safety and environmental issues.
- Available resources.
- Component of unit (Regular Army or Reserve Component). Reserve Component units have significantly fewer available work days per month than Regular Army units.
- Quality of lane training. Quality depends on effective leadership, planning, and resource support.

The lane training planning process is affected significantly by whether the unit is Regular Army or Reserve Component. Due to time constraints, planning for the Reserve Component must begin earlier than planning for the Regular Army.

The time required to conduct an LTX may range from a few hours to several days, primarily depending upon the layout of the LTX area, nature of LTX tasks, and number of tasks trained on a lane.

Although the time required to conduct an AAR can range from 30 minutes to 2 hours, the time required for planning and preparation is much longer. The time required to perform follow-up procedures depends upon the number and nature of issues identified during lane execution and subsequent AARs.

Personnel

Lane training, especially for company or platoon-size lanes, can be manpower intensive for any size unit due to the large numbers of personnel involved in managing the planning, execution, and assessment of the lane training process. See paragraph E-23 for details on personnel.

ormation

ning information is also an important resource. Sources of training information ude CATSs, battle drill manuals, Soldier training publications, Army doctrine publica-s, Army doctrine reference publications, field manuals, Army techniques publications, ning circulars, technical manuals, regulations, and SOPs. CATSs are a key source for rmation concerning tasks and resource requirements.

eral automated systems contain training information that can be used to support lane ning. Among them are the components of the ATMS. This system provides access to t and collective training information. Automated systems can also be used to develop ning COAs, plans, T&EOs, resource statuses and allocations, UTP calendars, training edules, briefings, and assessments.

mulations and Simulators

e effectiveness of lane training can be enhanced by using simulations and simulators ring lane training planning and execution. Trainers ensure that lane preparation and ecution are supported by appropriate training multipliers such as TADSS. Simulators, nulations, and other TADSS are training multipliers.

ercise planners and leaders should integrate simulations, simulators, and other DSS into their lane training process. The use of TADSS can enhance the replication of operational environment and increase training effectiveness.

ternal and External Support

e unit on an LTX should not provide its own support. This action prevents full participa-n in the LTX by all the unit's members. The lane training process and LTXs are catego-ed based on the primary source of resource support as either internally supported or ternally supported.

ternally Supported. Internally supported training is training for which resource support provided from within the unit responsible for managing training. Internally supported ne training is normally used when—

- Only one unit is undergoing lane training. In this situation, support functions frequently can be accomplished adequately by the next higher unit.

- Several units are undergoing training on one or more LTXs. In this situation, the supporting headquarters (two echelons above the training unit) identifies and obtains resources from units within the command.

xternally Supported. Externally supported training is training for which resource upport is provided from outside the unit responsible for managing training. Externally upported lane training is normally required when several units undergo training on ne or more LTXs and resource support cannot be provided from within the command esponsible for managing the training. In this situation, the supporting (or managing) eadquarters identifies desired resource requirements and obtains resources from out-ide the command. Efficient trainers use multiple lanes that require much more planning, cheduling, coordinating, and resourcing than single lanes require.

Resource Sources

Resource support for lane training may be available from a variety of sources, such as—
- Adjacent units.
- Higher headquarters.
- Installations.
- Centers of excellence or training proponents.
- Readiness groups, regional training teams, resident training detachments, and the Ground Forces Readiness Enhancement Program.
- Regular Army regional training brigades for OC/Ts.
- United States Army Reserve exercise divisions (for OC/Ts for example).
- Regional training sites.

Conducting Training

An LTX is used to train one collective task or a group of related tasks. The name c the LTX is the title of the primary collective task to be trained.

Exercise planners have flexibility in designing the structure of LTX lanes. The lane training structure can vary depending upon the tasks trained, the number of lanes and LTXs conducted, the number of units to be trained, and the size of the LTX are Usually more than one LTX area is set up at a training area. This creates additiona possibilities for LTX structures and improved efficiency, especially when several ur are trained and necessary transportation is available.

A lane is usually illustrated using a graphic scenario or lane diagram. This diagram represents a series of events on the lane (often in the execution area).

The LTX events list includes supporting tasks or task steps associated with the collective task being trained. All unit events are conducted and assessed in the sequence they are normally performed during operations and in relationship to hov they support the unit mission.

The event list may also indicate OPFOR events required for the lane. These event may include tasks or countertasks. OPFOR events are prefixed by a ">>." Key unit and OPFOR events performed on the lane are indicated in the graphic scenario or lane diagram.

AARs are planned to follow completion of lane execution but also may follow key supporting tasks or events occurring during lane execution. AAR events may also b indicated in a graphic scenario or lane diagram.

The following graphic control measures are frequently used for a lane involving unit movement:

- Assembly area.
- Start point.
- Line of departure.
- Phase lines.
- Boundaries (represented by lines with unit information).
- Objective.
- Release point.

V. Training Exercises

Ref: Adapted from previous references (FM 7-1 and FM 25-101, app. C).

Training Exercises

1 Map Exercise (MAPEX)

2 Tactical Exercise Without Troops (TEWT)

3 Fire Coordination Exercise (FCX)

4 Command Post Exercise (CPX)

5 Situational Training Exercise (STX)

6 Command Field Exercise (CFX)

7 Logistical Coordination Exercise (LCX)

8 Field Training Exercise (FTX)

9 Live Fire Exercise (LFX)

Commanders select a particular training exercise or combination of exercises based on specific training objectives and on available resources. When selecting exercises, commanders must consider several key questions:

- Who will be trained (soldiers, leaders, or units)?
- What are the training objectives?
- Which, if any, of the training exercises are most suitable to accomplish each objective?
- What are the available resources (time, training areas, equipment, money)?
- Which of the training exercises or combination will help meet the training objectives within the available training resources?

1. Map Exercise (MAPEX)

The MAPEX portrays military maps and overlays. It requires situations on a minimum number of support personnel and may be conducted in garrison or in the fie When conducted in garrison, it is low-cost in terms of training dollars and facilities is an excellent training tool for a resource-constrained unit. Communications equip ment may be used. A MAPEX helps the commander train his staff and leaders in planning, coordinating, and executing operations tasks on map boards, chalkboar training mock-ups, and sand tables. It is an excellent training tool before conducti other more costly exercises. A MAPEX trains the following:

- Functioning as an effective team
- Exchanging information
- Preparing estimates
- Giving appraisals
- Making recommendations and decisions
- Preparing plans
- Issuing orders
- Coordinating execution of orders

A MAPEX can be conducted internally at platoon, company, and battalion level or externally with a brigade or division MAPEX.

2. Tactical Exercise Without Troops (TEWT)

The TEWT is conducted on actual terrain with unit leaders and staffs, without soldiers. A TEWT allows the battalion TF or company commander to train his staff anc subordinate leaders. It also allows him to analyze, plan, and present how he would conduct an operation on the actual terrain.

TEWTs are normally conducted internally. Because only the battle staff and selecte support personnel are involved, the TEWT is an inexpensive way to familiarize lead ers with the area of operations. A TEWT can be used:

- To analyze terrain
- To employ units according to terrain analysis
- To emplace weapons systems to best support the unit's mission
- To prepare and validate plans
- To plan CS and CSS operations

3. Fire Coordination Exercise (FCX)

The FCX is used to train the combined arms team chain of command and related fir control elements to rapidly synchronize fires on the battlefield.

The exercise can use reduced-scale targets and ranges to depict combat situations. The chain of command must respond in the form of maneuver and fire coordination techniques and procedures. Commanders use FCXs:

- To develop the chain of command into a team
- To synchronize fires within the combined arms team
- To train the chain of command prior to a live fire exercise
- To exercise the communications net
- To assist in integrating new weapons system
- To portray a rapidly changing situation for the chain of command to react to

FCXs are normally used to train platoon- through battalion-level. The entire task force chain of command can be trained.

4. Command Post Exercise (CPX)

The CPX may be conducted in garrison or in the field. It requires the establishment of the command post. When compared with the MAPEX or TEWT, it represents a greater commitment of soldiers' time and resources. A CPX an expanded MAPEX for staff and all commanders to lead and control tactical operations by using tactical communications systems. Of ten the CPX is driven by a simulation or is part a larger exercise. Normal battlefield distances between CPs may be reduced. A CPX trains commanders and staff—

- To build teamwork and cohesion
- To exchange information by proper reporting IAW tactical SOPs
- To prepare estimates, plans, and orders
- To establish and employ tactical communications
- To displace headquarters and command posts
- To integrate synchronized warfighting functions

Battalions and companies may participate in a CPX as part of a larger force (brigade, division, and corps); they also may conduct internal CPXs.

5. Logistical Coordination Exercise (LCX)

LCXs allow leaders to become proficient at conducting unit sustainment operations such as supply, transportation, medical, personnel replacement, maintenance, and graves registration. LCXs provide a valuable, hands-on opportunity to deal with combat-related challenges of these activities. Most important, leaders can develop the SOPs so essential to their effective accomplishment. An LCX—

- Clarifies key elements of the battalion or TF logistics apparatus
- Exercises the flow of logistical information
- Incorporates a tactical war game that produces a wide variety of logistical requirements
- Allows plenty of opportunity for instruction and critique
- Exercises the communications network

As the primary leaders and soldiers train for the exercise, the interplay of CSS activities can be fully examined. Unit SOPs can be developed, modified, and verified. As proficiency in logistical operations is attained, LCX can be tied to other task force exercises to complete the integration of CSS with other combat operations.

6. Situational Training Exercise (STX)

Situational training exercises (STXs) are mission-related, limited exercises designed to train one collective task, or a group of related tasks and drills, through practice. STXs teach the doctrinally-preferred method for carrying out a task. STXs usually include drills, leader tasks, and individual soldier tasks. To ensure standardization, institutional schools and units develop STXs to teach the doctrinally-preferred way to perform specific missions and tasks. STXs may be modified based on the unit's METL, or expanded to meet special mission requirements.

STX training is especially helpful for training specific METL tasks. It is a useful technique primarily for training company team level and smaller units on a series of selected soldier, leader, and collective tasks using specific terrain. The concept provides an effective way to standardize TTPs and develop and rehearse tactical standing operating procedures (TACSOPs). STXs are a perfect opportunity to use crawl-walk-run training. Commanders narrow the focus and select specific collective tasks for the training. STX training may be resource-intensive, so commanders must maximize the benefit.

Conducting Training

STX training under varying conditions gives the unit a distinct advantage when executing combat operations. STX training at night and during adverse weather provides a training opportunity to execute critical tasks and drills under naturally occurring light and weather conditions, and enhances training realism. Reverse cycle training should be planned to take advantage of every opportunity to replicate a 24-hour operational environment.

STX training is structured to expose leaders and soldiers to unexpected situations, favorable and unfavorable. Tasks must be executed confidently and competently during the fog of battle. Tough, realistic training challenges leaders and soldiers to overcome the hardships and uncertainties of combat. Challenging training inspires excellence by fostering initiative, enthusiasm, confidence, and the ability to operate in all elements of the operational spectrum. Even if a unit accomplishes the assigned task to standard, the unit may retrain the exercise with more difficult conditions.

7. Command Field Exercise (CFX)

The CFX lies on a scale between the CPX and FTX. Available resources determine where the CFX fits on the scale. The CFX can also be a backup for the FTX if maneuver damage, weather, or other factors prohibit the planned FTX. The CFX is an FTX with reduced unit and vehicle density, but with full C2, CS, and CSS elements. For example, the platoon leader in his vehicle represents the entire platoon.

CFXs are excellent vehicles for training leaders and staff with full command, control, communications, and logistical systems. They are less expensive and exercise inter-system linkages and real distances. They sharpen unit skills in such areas as-

- Intelligence
- Fire support
- Slice integration
- CSS
- Rear area operations
- Command, control, and communications

A CFX can train as much, or as little, of the task force as necessary, depending on the commander's assessment and training objectives.

8. Field Training Exercise (FTX)

FTXs are conducted under simulated combat conditions in the field. FTXs fully integrate the total force in a realistic combat environment. They involve combat arms, CS, and CSS units. FTXs encompass such training as battle drills, crew drills, and STXs to reinforce soldier and collective training integration. They are used to train the commander, staff, subordinate units, and slice elements—

- To move and maneuver units realistically
- To employ organic weapons systems effectively
- To build teamwork and cohesion
- To plan and coordinate supporting fires
- To plan and coordinate logistical activities to support tactical operations

9. Live Fire Exercise (LFX)

Live fire exercises (LFXs) closely replicate battlefield conditions and provide significant advantages. LFXs-

- Develop confidence and esprit-de-corps.
- Provide soldiers with a realistic experience of the danger, confusion, and speed of combat operations.
- Require demonstrated proficiency at lower echelons before LFXs are conducted at higher echelons.

ASSESS
for Training

Ref: FM 7-0, Train to Win in a Complex World (Oct '16), pp. 3-7 to 3-14 and ADP 7-0, Training (Jul '19), pp. 4-10 to 4-11.

Leaders assess training by continuously checking progress toward task achievement or training objectives. Training events provide the venue for commanders and leaders to evaluate and measure the effectiveness of the collective tasks selected to train. The training objectives— determined and published by the commander for each training event—communicate the task, condition, standard, and expected training proficiencies for the collective tasks selected.

IV. ASSESS for Training

PLAN for Training
To apply the art and science of understanding a situation, envisioning a desired future, and laying out effective ways of bringing that future about.

PREPARE for Training
To make ready those activities performed by units and Soldiers to improve their abilities to train for an operation.

ASSESS for Training
To continuously check the progress toward accomplishing a task or achieving an objective.

EXECUTE for Training
To put a plan into action by training units and individuals to accomplish the mission.

Ref: FM 7-0 (Oct '16), fig. 3-5. Assess phase of the operations process.

Leaders use the assessment plan developed during preparation to evaluate unit performance. During execution, leaders use T&EOs to record a unit's performance every time it attempts a collective task. Evaluators—using the objective task evaluation criteria matrix on the T&EO—objectively record the proficiencies noted as the unit completes tasks. At the training meeting following the training event, evaluations are aggregated bottom-up, so the commander can assess whether the unit met the training objectives. The training meeting occurs the week following the start of training (T+1 per the T-Week concept). Using the training proficiency ratings, the commander completes the assessments and subsequently records them into DTMS. Training meetings conducted routinely by echelon are critical to the assessment process.

See p. 5-11 for discussion of training proficiency ratings.

Assessing Training

Assessment Considerations

Ref: FM 7-0, Train to Win in a Complex World (Oct '16), pp. 3-10 to 3-14.

When assessing training, commanders consider:

- Their own observations and those of subordinate leaders and other individuals
- Feedback from after action reviews
- Results of unit evaluations

An assessment is determination of the progress toward accomplishing a task, creating a condition, or achieving an objective (JP 3-0). Commanders determine training readiness using evaluations and assessments. Evaluations are based on the performance of tasks measured against an established standard under set conditions. Evaluations are recorded using T&EOs for collective and individual tasks. Users access T&EOs on ATN CATS, DTMS, and the CAR. These Web sites are the Army's only sources that provide the prescribed training tasks, conditions, and standards for all Army individual and collective tasks.

See p. 5-11 for discussion of training proficiency ratings.

Objective Considerations

To enable unit leaders and commanders to evaluate proficiency of collective tasks objectively, they use established task proficiency criteria and standards. Task proficiency criteria and standards differentiate the level of training a unit has achieved using the proficiency ratings. See the discussion beginning in paragraph 1-5 for Army task rating proficiency standards.

Evaluations of task performance steps—documented within a task performance measure of the task T&EO—are objective evaluation ratings assigned directly to demonstrated task proficiency. Evaluators observe performance of the tasks measures and grade the performance steps either as GO or as NO-GO.

Evaluators use the objective task evaluation criteria matrix found on every collective T&EO to help evaluate performance of collective tasks (see figure 3-7). By considering certain execution criteria—like the training environment and day or night conditions—the evaluator or unit commander can record a more accurate and objective evaluation of task performance. An accurate and objective evaluation yields a more objective assessment of task performance. See appendix B for details on objective task evaluation criteria matrixes and specific T&EO completion instructions. Evaluators for the Organizational Inspection Program also complete checklists. See appendix I for potential questions.

Subjective Considerations

While the T&EO and task proficiency standards provide objective criteria for determining task proficiency, assessments allow leaders to take into account the subjective nature of training. Leaders' assessments combine their professional observations with other information to develop an overall assessment of the unit's ability to accomplish its mission. Final authority of a unit's assessment lies solely with the commander. Commanders and leaders might consider the following information in their assessments:

- Assessment and feedback from higher.
- AARs.
- Subordinate leader and Soldier feedback.
- Evaluator and OC/T comments.
- Personal experience and observations.

Plan and Prepare				Execute						Assess
Operational Environment			Training Environment (L/V/C)	% Leaders present at training/authorized	% Present at training/authorized	External evaluation	Performance measures	Critical performance measures	Leader performance measures	Task assessment
SQD and PLT	CO and BN	BDE and above								
Dynamic (single threat)	Dynamic and complex (4 + OE variables and hybrid threat)	Dynamic and complex (all OE variables and hybrid threat)	Proponent establishes training environment standards — Night	≥85%	≥80%	Yes	≥90% GO	All	≥90%	T
				75-84%		Yes	80-90% GO	All	80-89%	T-
Static (single threat)	Dynamic (single threat)	Dynamic and complex (all OE variables and single threat)		65-74%	75-79%		65-79% GO		80-89%	P
				60-64%	60-74%	No	51-64% GO		<80%	P-
	Static (single threat)	Dynamic & complex (< all OE variables and single threat)	Proponent establishes training environment standards — Day	<60%	<60%	No	<51% GO	<All	<80%	U

BDE	brigade	OE	operational environment
BN	battalion	P	practiced
C	constructive	P-	marginally practiced
CO	company	PLT	platoon
L	live	SQD	squad

T	fully trained
T-	trained
U	untrained
V	virtual

Note: The percentages used in this figure are for illustration only. See the collective task's published training and evaluation outline for the applicable percentages.

Ref: FM 7-0 (Oct '16), fig. 3-7. Objective task evaluation criteria.

Assessments provide a final graded determination on an individual's, a leader's, or a unit's ability to perform a task to the published standard.

At the individual level, leaders observe Soldier task performance. They record the results of this performance using individual task T&EOs. Leaders also use the results of these assessments to counsel Soldiers to sustain or improve task performance.

In the assessment of leaders, commanders consider subordinate leaders' proficiency. An effective commander deliberately observes and assesses subordinate leaders. The commander pays particular attention to assessing the character, competence, and commitment of subordinate leaders.

At the unit level, leaders analyze and correlate observations and evaluations of observed unit performance. The resulting assessment is based on an aggregate of these many inputs. From company level and higher, these unit assessments form the basis of recording unit training readiness, which contributes to a unit status reporting.

Evaluations

Ref: FM 7-0, Train to Win in a Complex World (Oct '16), pp. 3-12 to 3-13.

Evaluations can be executed using internal assets or by an external agency. Normally commanders evaluate tasks during the execution phase of training events, but they also evaluate tasks during the planning and preparing phases of events. Leaders use evaluations as an opportunity to coach and mentor subordinates. Evaluations may be informal, formal, internal, external, or any combination of these.

Formal and Informal Evaluations

Informal

Internal
An evaluation by unit leadership whenever training is conducted. For example, a squad leader checks vehicle for PMCS.

External
An evaluation conducted by leaders during visits to training of subordinate units. For example, the CSM spot checks Soldiers' range cards.

Formal

Internal
An evaluation of squad and below proficiency. For example, squad leaders evaluate the squad individual and collective tasks.

External
An evaluation of unit proficiency. For example, battalion evaluates platoon training events.

Ref: FM 7-0 (Oct '16), fig. 3-8. Formal and informal evaluations.

When evaluating individual and small-unit training events, evaluators normally include every Soldier and leader involved in the training of the tasks. For large-scale training events, evaluators sample a number of individuals and subordinate organizations to determine proficiency in individual and collective tasks.

During and after formal evaluations, evaluators prepare their findings and recommendations in reports. Evaluators provide reports to the evaluated unit commander and higher commanders as required by the headquarters directing the evaluation. Evaluation documentation can range from an annotated individual training record or Training and Evaluation Outline (T&EO) for an internal training evaluation to a comprehensive report on Reserve Component units during annual training.

The completed T&EOs—including written comments, AAR comments, and coaching and mentoring comments—provide leaders and Soldiers with immediate and documented feedback on their performance. Commanders use evaluator input as a significant source of input for each MET or collective task when scoring training proficiency. However, the objective task evaluation criteria matrix is the primary input in determining the overall task proficiency assessment.

ormal Evaluation

rmal evaluations are conducted by leaders either internal, or external to the unit.
ey occur as training, or unit activities are executed. They are conducted on the spot
d require little to no supporting resources. They provide a quick and informal means of
viding immediate feedback to individual Soldiers or small units on their performance
sustain or improve that performance.

rmal Evaluation

rmal evaluations are conducted by leaders either internal or external to the unit. Eval-
tions can be scheduled or conducted without notice to evaluate training proficiency
to evaluate specific unit activities. Formal evaluations typically require supporting re-
urces to conduct. Resources range from facilities to conduct in/out briefings to facilities
conduct AARs to video devices to record task execution. Formal evaluations enable
cording and providing feedback to units on their proficiency and performance. Evalua-
s provide the results to sustain or improve the performance to the unit commander.

ternal Evaluation

ernal evaluations are conducted by unit leaders when training or when a unit conducts
tivities. They evaluate the unit's ability to perform specific tasks or activities. They can
either informal or formal in nature. The results of formal internal evaluations are pro-
ded to the unit commander. The commander then determines whether to either sustain
improve performance.

xternal Evaluation (EXEVAL)

EXEVALs are unit proficiency evaluations. They are formal in nature and conducted ex-
rnal to the unit. The EXEVAL provides commanders with an objective way to evaluate
eir unit METs or selected collective task proficiencies. All units in the Army undergo an
XEVAL to validate fully trained (T) or trained (T-) task proficiency ratings.

n EXEVAL includes the following key requirements:

- The higher commander two levels up approves and resources it (for example, a brigade approves and resources a company-level EXEVAL).
- The commander resources it to achieve a minimum of T or T-task proficiency rating.
- The higher commander (one or two levels up) trains and certifies external OC/Ts. The senior OC/T can be from an adjacent unit within the higher command of the unit evaluated.
- The higher commander trains and evaluates METs and battle tasks (to include battle drills).
- T&EOs are the objective basis of the evaluation.
- The higher commander two levels up supervises the final AAR.
- The formal commander (one level up) discusses with the unit commander the expected proficiency levels for METs and battle tasks (to include battle drills) and overall level of proficiency for readiness reporting units (see AR 220-1).

mmediately following an EXEVAL, the unit commander and the next higher commander
formally discuss the unit's proficiency on METs or collective tasks as well as on the unit's
overall training readiness assessment based on the EXEVAL.

The end state for the EXEVAL commanders' dialogue is for the two commanders to
agree on the units training proficiency and overall training readiness.

Commanders assess and evaluate all aspects of training—planning, preparation, execution, and ultimate task proficiency. Only the unit commander can assess the readiness of a MET. Assessment refers to the leader's judgment of the organization's ability to perform its METLs and, ultimately, its ability to accomplish its mission. Evaluation refers to the process used to measure the demonstrated ability of individuals and units to accomplish specified training objectives and achieve task proficiency. Leaders continuously monitor the unit's METL proficiency and the progress of the UTP.

Training Effectiveness

Commanders assess each training event by focusing on the extent to which the unit achieved the commander's intent, training objectives, and progress towards unit collective task proficiency. The training meeting is the best forum to aggregate evaluations of tasks by subordinates and the commander into the METL assessment.

Commanders assess METs as T—trained, P—needs practice or U—untrained. The commander records these assessments in the DTMS and uses these assessments to determine the organization's training ratings for readiness reporting. Training assessments also address such areas as training support, force integration, logistics, and personnel availability. Given these assessments, commanders adjust their future training plans.

See p. 5-11 for discussion of training proficiency ratings.

After Action Reviews (AARs)

After action reviews provide opportunities for units to develop critical thinking in leaders. An after action review is a guided analysis of an organization's performance conducted at appropriate times during and at the conclusion of a training event or operation with the objective of improving future performance. It includes a facilitator, event participants, and other observers. Organizations conduct after action reviews (AARs) to identify unit strengths to be sustained and weaknesses that need to improve. They apply observations, insights, and lessons to future training and operations to improve not only task proficiency, but also the quality of the training event. AARs are best conducted throughout an exercise at appropriate times, rather than just at the end of the exercise, to allow Soldiers and their leaders to take immediate, in-stride corrective actions. AARs are not critiques. They are part of an open learning environment where facilitators, participants, and observers freely discuss successes and honest mistakes. AARs help units and individuals understand what went right and why, what went wrong and why, and what to do better in future training and operations. Units share lessons learned with other units using various methods.

See section on AARs, pp. 8-15 to 8-24.

Training and Evaluation Outlines (T&EOs)

All training must be evaluated. Otherwise, the training time is wasted. Task standards reside in the training and evaluation outlines for each collective task. A training and evaluation outline is a summary document that provides information on collective training objectives, related individual training objectives, resource requirements, and applicable evaluation procedures for a type of organization. This document provides the task title, task description, the recommended conditions to use in training, the standard to be met and the task steps and performance measures to attain a 'GO/NO-GO' for each step. Trainers access training and evaluation outlines from ATN, through CATS and the DTMS. The training and evaluation outline provides the means to help leaders evaluate task execution and subjectively assess the unit's ability to perform the task.

I. Training & Evaluation Outlines (T&EOs)

Ref: FM 7-0, Train to Win in a Complex World (Oct '16), appendix B.

The T&EO is the Army's source for individual and collective task training standards. The T&EO consists of the major procedures (steps or actions) a unit or individual must accomplish to perform a task to standard. A collective task also describes the performance required of a unit under the conditions of the training environment. The training and evaluation outline is a summary document that provides information on individual or collective task training objectives, resource requirements, and evaluation procedures. T&EOs are developed, approved, and published by the responsible proponents.

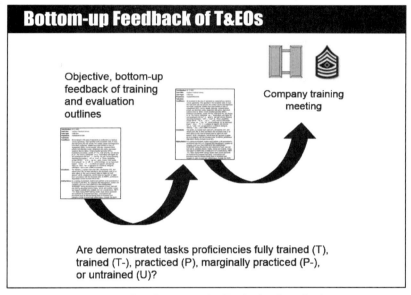

Bottom-up Feedback of T&EOs

Objective, bottom-up feedback of training and evaluation outlines

Company training meeting

Are demonstrated tasks proficiencies fully trained (T), trained (T-), practiced (P), marginally practiced (P-), or untrained (U)?

Ref: FM 7-0 (Oct '16), fig. B-1. Bottom-up feedback of task evaluations.

During training events, leaders strive to achieve the Army standard for tasks trained. During training events, leaders and evaluators use T&EOs to measure observed task proficiency. Completed T&EOs form the backbone of bottom-up feedback that company commanders and first sergeants review at the weekly training meeting (see figure B-1). The T&EOs provide the commander the necessary objective evaluations to assess unit training proficiency and ultimately to assess training readiness.

Repositories

The Army has several official repositories that contain T&EOs, to include:

- Army Training Network (ATN)
- Digital Training Management System (DTMS)
- Combined Arms Training Strategy (CATS)
- Central Army Registry (CAR)

Users access the DTMS, CATS, and CAR via the ATN. Users accessing T&EOs through the ATN do not require additional privileges to view and print the T&EOs.

Elements of the T&EO

Ref: FM 7-0, Train to Win in a Complex World (Oct '16), pp. B-2 to B-4.

Collective task T&EOs have the same basic elements in their outline. This appendix focuses on those elements that are crucial to conducting the evaluation and recording observed task performance. These elements include—

- Task number.
- Task title.
- Distribution restriction.
- Destruction notice.
- Foreign disclosure.
- Supporting references.
- Condition.
- Standard.
- Live fire.
- Notes.
- Performance steps.
- Performance measures.
- Task performance and evaluation summary block.
- Prerequisite collective tasks.
- Supporting collective tasks.

Figure B-2 illustrates a sample first page of a T&EO.

Training and Evaluation Outline Report

Task Number: 07-2-5135   28 March 2016

Task Title: Operate a Company Command Post – Company

Distribution Restriction: Distribution authorized to U.S. Government agencies only.

Destruction Notice: Destroy by any method that will prevent disclosure of contents or reconstruction of the document.

Foreign Disclosure: FD1 - This training product has been reviewed by the training developers in coordination with the MCoE G-2 foreign disclosure officer. This training product can be used to instruct international military students from all approved countries without restrictions.

Supporting Reference(s):

Step Number	Reference ID	Reference Name	Required	Primary
	ATP 3-90.1	Armor and Mechanized Infantry Company Team	Yes	Yes
	FM 3-21.10	The Infantry Rifle Company	Yes	No
	FM 6-0	Commander and Staff Organization and Operations	Yes	No
	ADRP 1-02	Terms and Military Symbols	Yes	No

Condition: The company is conducting operations in a live training environment as part of a battalion or larger force, and is required to operate a company command post (CP). The company is conducting operations at night in a dynamic and complex operational environment (OE) against a hybrid threat. All necessary personnel and equipment are available. The company has communications with higher, adjacent, and subordinate elements. The company has guidance on the rules of engagement (ROE).

Dynamic Operational Environment: Three or more operational and two or more mission variables change during the execution of the assessed task.

Complex Operational Environment: Changes to four or more operational variables impact the chosen friendly COA/mission.

Hybrid threat: Diverse and dynamic combination of regular forces, irregular forces, and/or criminal elements all unified to achieve mutually benefiting effects. Some iterations of this task should be performed in MOPP 4.

Standard: The company operates the CP in accordance with (IAW) FM 3-90.1, the order, and/or higher commander's guidance. The CP provides a centralized point for information gathering and dissemination

---

Ref: FM 7-0 (Oct '16), fig. B-2. Sample training and evaluation outline.

...k Number. A task number is a unique identifier specifying an individual or collective ...t. The individual task number system differs from that for collective tasks. For collec-...tasks, the task number consists of three groups of numbers separated by hyphens. ...e first two numbers indicate the school or proponent code (table B-1). The second ...nber of the task number indicates the echelon for which the collective task applies. ...he example of 07-2-5135, a 2 applies to a company (troop, battery, or detachment) ...el. See table B-2 for echelon codes. The school or proponent assigns the last set ...our digits of the task number. These four digits are unique to the particular task and ...nelon. In the example of 07-2-5135, the 5135 is the given example.

...k Title. The task title includes both the task evaluated and the echelon to which it ...plies. If a task applies to multiple unit types at the same echelon, the title only lists the ...nelon (like company). In the example in figure B-2, the task number 07-2-5135 identi-...s the infantry task: Operate a Company Command Post – Company.

...tribution Restriction. The distribution restriction identifies any restrictions to distri-...tion. The restriction is specified by the proponent.

...struction Notice. The destruction notice identifies special destruction guidance. Usu-...y the destruction notice correlates with a certain distribution restriction. The proponent ...cludes any destruction instructions here.

...reign Disclosure. The foreign disclosure identifies any restrictions imposed when ...aring the T&EO with foreign sources. The proponent provides any foreign disclosure ...structions here.

...pporting References. The supporting references element identifies the supporting ...ferences for each performance step. The table for the supporting references lists the ...ep number, reference identification, reference name, required, and primary reference ...urce.

...ondition. A task condition statement provides the general information required to allow ...ultiple units to perform a task to standard based on common doctrine. The condition ...atement identifies the situation and training environment in which the unit should be ...ole to perform the task to standard. See the sample text in figure B-2.

...tandard. The task standard statement provides the criteria for determining the mini-...um acceptable proficiency of task performance under operating conditions. Users ...eference the objective task evaluation criteria matrix (see figure B-3) for minimum ac-...eptable standards. The school or proponent specifies and modifies the matrix based on ...e requirements of the task, unit type, and echelon.

...ive Fire. The proponent will indicate any requirements or specifications for live fire as-...ociated with the task.

...afety Risk. This is the risk level for any identified hazards that may be associated with ...he conduct of the task. ATP 5-19 identifies these risk levels as extremely high (EH), ...igh (H), medium (M), and low (L).

...ue. A cue is a task condition that indicates why the unit performs the task. A cue also ...larifies the aiding and limiting factors that set the stage for the conduct of the task.

...anger, Warning, And Caution Notices. Users determine if the training warrants dan-...er, warning, or caution notices. Users rate the risk and complete the appropriate box. ...ee also ATP 5-19 for risk assessments.

Remarks. This element provides space for the school or proponent to add additional ...larifying details as necessary.

Notes. The notes element clarifies the objective task evaluation criteria matrix standards. The school or proponent identifies leader tasks (conducted by a leader or leaders) with an ...asterisk (*). The school or proponent identifies critical steps or child steps with a plus sign ...(+). Proponents specify the GO and NO¬GO criteria for both leader and critical steps.

Objective Task Evaluation Criteria Matrix

Ref: FM 7-0, Train to Win in a Complex World (Oct '16), pp. B-4 to B-5.

The objective task evaluation criteria matrix as seen in figure B-3 enables unit leaders t[o] evaluate unit task proficiency more accurately and more objectively. When the comman[d]er assesses unit task proficiency, and the unit has not performed the task at echelon (as an entire unit), the commander can then consider proficiency of subordinate units on the task. In this case, the commander's assessment of task proficiency should be no higher than the lowest task proficiency assessment of any subordinate unit. After commanders consider T&EOs and other sources of bottom-up feedback, commanders can subjective[ly] upgrade or downgrade an assessment of a unit's MET proficiency.

Plan and Prepare						Execute				Assess
Operational Environment			Training Environment (LV/C)	% Leaders present at training/authorized	% Present at training/ authorized	External evaluation	Performance measures	Critical performance measures	Leader performance measures	Task assessment
SQD and PLT	CO and BN	BDE and above								
Dynamic (single threat)	Dynamic and complex (4 + OE variables and hybrid threat)	Dynamic and complex (all OE variables and hybrid threat)	Night	≥85%	≥80%	Yes	≥90% GO	All	≥90%	T
				75-84%			80-90% GO		80-89%	T-
Static (single threat)	Dynamic (single threat)	Dynamic and complex (all OE variables and single threat)		65-74%	75-79%		65-79% GO			P
				60-64%	60-74%	No	51-64% GO			P-
	Static (single threat)	Dynamic & complex (< all OE variables and single threat)	Day	<60%	<60%		<51% GO	<All	<80%	U

◄——— **Task Dependent** ———► ◄——— **Task Independent** ———►

Proponent establishes training environment standards

BDE	brigade	OE	operational environment	T	fully trained
BN	battalion	P	practiced	T-	trained
C	constructive	P-	marginally practiced	U	untrained
CO	company	PLT	platoon	V	virtual
L	live	SQD	squad		

Note: The percentages used in this figure are for illustration only. See the collective task's published training and evaluation outline for the applicable percentages.

Ref: FM 7-0 (Oct '16), fig. B-3. Objective task evaluation criteria matrix.

erms of Reference

ponents use several terms of reference for the objective task evaluation criteria
trix.

perational Environment

e proponent describes the variables of an operational environment in the condition
agraph of the T&EO. The school or proponent builds a near-peer competitor into the
ning scenario. It uses the following terms: static, dynamic, complex, single threat,
rid threat.

aining Environment

e proponent sets training environment conditions. The three training environments
nsist of live training, virtual training, and constructive training.

ercent of Leaders Present

e unit records the percent of unit key leaders present at the training event. The objec-
e task evaluation criteria matrix compares the number present against the numbers
entified in the TOE, modified TOE, or TDA that authorized unit strength.

ercent Present for Training

e unit records the percent of the unit's members present at the training event. The ob-
ctive task evaluation criteria matrix compares the number present against the numbers
entified in the TOE, modified TOE, or TDA that authorized unit strength.

xternal Evaluation

EXEVAL is an evaluation planned, coordinated, and executed by an organization out-
de the unit two levels up. The evaluating unit can be one level up or another like-type
it or echelon. All readiness reporting units in the Army undergo an EXEVAL to achieve
d validate fully trained (T) or trained (T-) task proficiency standards.

erformance Measures

he proponent defines the performance measures for each task. The proponent identi-
es the performance measures in the applicable T&EO for the task.

ritical Performance Measures

he proponent defines critical performance measures for each task. The unit gets these
easures in the applicable T&EO for the task.

eader Performance Measures

he proponent defines the leader performance measures for each task. The proponent
entifies the performance measures in the applicable T&EO for the task.

Task Assessment

The overall task assessment is determined by the highest assessment level of the lowest
ated category. Once the evaluator has tallied up the GO and NO-GO performance steps
and measures, the evaluator circles those measures on the objective task evaluation
criteria matrix (see figure B-3). Present with other criteria that is aggregated across the
matrix, the evaluator makes an objective task assessment using the highest level assessment of the lowest rated category.

n figure B-3, all items except Leader performance measures were rated as fully trained
(T). Since the evaluator scored the performance measure as 80-89%, the Task assessment is scored as a trained (T-).

See p. 5-11 for discussion of training proficiency ratings.

Performance Steps

Performance steps are the major actions a unit must accomplish to perform a collective task to standard. Performance steps provide a sequential, step-by-step description of the discrete actions that compose a task. The steps are broken into plan steps, prepare steps, and execute steps. In each of these groups, the steps are numbered and in sequential order. A unit must perform each step. Some steps have no sub steps, and other steps have multiple sub steps. For instance in figure B-4, performance step #6 is "+The company commander issues an OPORD. Ensures that subordinates, attachments (as applicable), and staff section representatives(s) are present for the OPORD issuance." The performance step falls under the plan portion (not shown). In this example, step #6 has no sub steps but is a critical step (shown with the plus sign). Under the prepare step, step #8 reads "*Company leaders prepare for command post operations in coordination with the higher headquarters." This step has several sub steps and is conducted by a leader (shown with the asterisk). Each numbered performance step becomes a performance measure.

6.   +The company commander issues an OPORD. Ensures that subordinates, attachments (as applicable), and staff section representative(s) are present for the OPORD issuance.

7.   *The company commander conducts confirmation briefs with subordinates, attachments (as applicable), and staff section representative(s) immediately after the OPORD is issued to ensure they understand the commander's intent, specific tasks, concept of the operation, and the relationship between their mission and the other units in the operation.

PREPARE

8.   *Company leaders prepare for command post operations in coordination with the higher headquarters.
  a.   Conducts pre-combat checks and inspections.
  b.   Conducts rehearsals that include addressing the following actions:
    (1)   CP setup and organization.
    (2)   Actions on enemy contact.
    (3)   Battle drills.
    (4)   Formations and movement techniques.
    (5)   Casualty evacuation (CASEVAC).
  c.   Cross trains personnel based on manning constraints as required.
  d.   Issues supplementary orders (FRAGORDs) as necessary to address changes to the plan identified during reconnaissance, staff, higher headquarters' guidance, and higher headquarters' combined arms rehearsal.

EXECUTE

9.   The company conducts tactical movement from the start point (SP) or line of departure (LD) to the vicinity of the planned CP location(s) in coordination with the higher headquarters and the mission scheme of maneuver.

10. *Company leaders, including the quartering party, conduct a leader's reconnaissance.
  a.   Pinpoints the primary and alternate CP locations.

Ref: FM 7-0 (Oct '16), fig. B-4. Sample extract from T&EO illustrating performance steps.

Performance Measures

Performance measures are actions that are objectively observable, qualitative, and quantitative. Critical steps (or leader steps) are notated with a plus sign or an asterisk respectively. Evaluators and leaders use performance measures to determine if a unit satisfactorily achieves a performance step or sub step. Evaluators rate a unit's performance as GO, NO-GO, or N/A (for not applicable) measure (see figure B-5). If the performance step of a task was performed to standard, a GO is assessed for the associated performance measure. If a particular performance step in the task was not performed to standard, a NO-GO is assessed. If the measure does not apply at a particular echelon or is not observed during training of a particular unit, the evaluator can designate this in the N/A column so as not to affect the GO or NO-GO status of the unit.

PERFORMANCE MEASURES	GO	NO-GO	N/A
1. The company gained and/or maintained situational understanding.	✓ X		
2. +The company commander received the mission requiring operation of a command post and began execution of troop leading procedures.	✓ X		
3. * The company commander issued the warning order (WARNORD).	✓ X		
4. *The company commander coordinated with higher headquarters.	X	✓	
5. +The company commander conducted mission analysis focusing on the directed mission, enemy forces and their capabilities, terrain and weather effects, troops available, time available to execute the operation, and civil considerations (METT-TC) and developed a tentative plan.	X	✓	
6. +The company commander issued an OPORD.	X	✓	
7. *The company commander conducted confirmation briefs with subordinate immediately after the OPORD was issued to ensure subordinates understood commander's intent, specific tasks, concept of the operation, and the relationship between their mission and other units in the operation.	✓ X		
8. * Company leaders prepared for command post operations.	✓ X		
9. The company conducted tactical movement from the start point (SP) departure (LD) to the vicinity of the planned CP location(s).	X	✓	
10. *Company leaders, including the quartering party, conducted a leader's reconnaissance.		✓ X	
11. *The company commander or designated representative positioned the CP.	✓ X		
12. +The company established security and conducted operations.	✓ X		
13. * The company commander decided based on higher headquarters' OPORD and guidance whether to displace the command post.	✓ X		
14. The company conducted SREPs IAW the higher headquarters order.	X	✓	

TASK PERFORMANCE / EVALUATION SUMMARY BLOCK							
ITERATION	1	2	3	4	5	M	TOTAL
TOTAL PERFORMANCE MEASURES EVALUATED	14	14					28
TOTAL PERFORMANCE MEASURES GO	8	13					21
TRAINING STATUS GO/NO-GO	NO-GO	GO					

ITERATION: 1 ② 3   4   5   M

COMMANDER/LEADER ASSESSMENT: T Ⓣ P   P-   U

FRAGORD	fragmentary order	HQ	headquarters
M	mission-oriented protective posture	OPORD	operations order
P	practiced	P-	marginally practiced
T	fully trained	T-	trained
U	untrained		

Ref: FM 7-0 (Oct '16), fig. B-5. Sample extract from T&EO illustrating performance measures.

Task Performance and Evaluation Summary Block

This block provides the evaluator a means of recording GO and NO-GO observed performances based on the iterations conducted (times the task was attempted). In the T&EO, the task performance and evaluation block provides a table of spaces that evaluators use to total the number performance measures evaluated, total the number of performance measures that scored a GO, and total the number of units with a GO or NO-GO training status. In figure B-5, the unit evaluated conducted 2 iterations of this particular task. The evaluator recorded a total of 28 performance measures observed, 21 of these recorded as GO. Only the recorded performance for the final iteration is carried over to the objective task evaluation criteria matrix (see figure B-3). In this example, the performance recorded in the final iteration was 12 of 14 measures recorded as a GO. The resulting percentage of 85% is circled in the corresponding percentage block of the performance measures column of the objective task evaluation criteria matrix.

Iteration

This block provides a space for the evaluator to record the number of iterations (task attempts) the unit being observed performs. The 'M' column records an iteration performed while the unit was in mission-oriented protective posture (MOPP).

Commander/Leader Assessment

Since the final iteration performed is recorded in the objective task evaluation criteria matrix, the commander/leader records the corresponding performance rating here

- **Mission(s) Supported.** The proponent indicates any specific missions with which this task may be associated.
- **Mission-Oriented Protective Posture 4.** This block indicates if the task must be performed under a specific MOPP.
- **Mission-Oriented Protective Posture 4 Statement.** If the task is to be performed specifically in MOPP 4, the proponent identifies any additional performance requirements or limitations for task execution.
- **Night Vision Goggles.** This block indicates if this task must be performed under conditions of limited visibility and if night vision goggles (known as NVGs) are required in the execution of the task.
- **Night Vision Goggles Statement.** The proponent specifies any additional instructions or limitations in the use of night vision goggles that are used in the performance of the task.

Prerequisite Collective Tasks

Prerequisite collective tasks are tasks that have a first-order effect on setting the conditions for the task. Prerequisite collective tasks apply to the majority of the population trained. For several tasks on the T&EO, evaluators record each step number, each task number, the title of the task, the proponent of the task, and the status of the unit evaluated. The step number is the performance step and its associated title. The task number is the number that leads the T&EO. The task title is the title of the task number.

Opposing Force Tasks

OPFOR tasks list any OPFOR tasks required in support of the task trained.

Supporting Collective Tasks

A supporting collective task is a task that supports another collective task.

Supporting Individual Tasks

Supporting individual tasks are tasks performed to enable the successful performance of the supported collective task. The individual must perform the individual task so the unit can accomplish the collective task. Proficiency must occur at the individual task level before it can occur at the collective task level.

Supporting Drill Tasks

Supporting drill tasks are any drill tasks associated with the task trained. Supporting drills enable the successful performance of the supported collective task.

Supported Universal Joint Task List Tasks

If the task is linked to or associated with a universal joint task list (known as UJTL) task, note the task here.

Training Aids, Devices, Simulators, and Simulations

TADSS includes a list of any TADSS that units may use in support of the task trained.

Equipment and Materiel

Equipment and materiel lists the resources relevant to the task trained. For collective tasks, users limit the inclusion of equipment and materiel items to those relevant to the target population trained.

Environment

The proponent states specific environmental protection requirements for the task.

Safety

The proponent states any additional safety risk requirements associated with the task in accordance with ATP 5-19. These are in addition to the safety risk level.

II. After Action Review (AAR) for Training

Ref: FM 7-0, Train to Win in a Complex World (Oct '16), app. D.

An after action review is a guided analysis of an organization's performance, conducted at appropriate times during and at the conclusion of a training event or operation with the objective of improving future performance. It includes a facilitator, event participants, and other observers. The AAR provides valuable feedback essential to correcting training deficiencies. Feedback must be direct, immediate, and standards-based.

After Action Review Steps

 1 PLAN the AAR

 2 PREPARE the AAR

 3 CONDUCT the AAR

 4 ASSESS the AAR

The AAR is a professional discussion that requires the active participation of those being trained. AARs enable units or Soldiers to discover for themselves what happened and then develop a plan for improving performance. These reviews provide candid insights into strengths and weaknesses from various perspectives and feedback, and focus directly on the commander's guidance, training objectives, and standards. Leaders know and enforce standards for collective and individual tasks. Task standards are performance measures found in the respective T&EOs.

Leaders avoid creating the environment of a critique during AARs. A critique only gives one viewpoint and frequently provides little opportunity for discussion of events by participants. The climate of the critique, focusing only on what is wrong, prevents candid and open discussions of training events and stifles learning and team building. Since Soldiers and leaders participating in an AAR actively self-discover what happened and why, they learn and remember more than they would from a critique alone. Unlike a critique, an AAR:

- Focuses directly on training objectives.
- Emphasizes meeting the Army standard on collective and individual tasks rather than judging success or failure.
- Uses leading questions to encourage participants to self-discover important lessons from the training event.
- Allows a large number of Soldiers and leaders (including OPFORs) to participate so that more of the training can be recalled and more lessons learned can be shared.
- Assigns responsibility for a timeline to improve performance improvement measures.

Leaders make on-the-spot corrections when training Soldiers and units. These corrections occur when leaders understand the commander's guidance as well as the tasks to be trained to improve Soldier, leader, and unit performance. Units that conduct AARs and empower subordinates to make on-the-spot corrections are more effective.

Effective AARs reflect the commander and the commander's active role in unit training. AARs foster an environment of trust, collaboration, initiative, and cohesion necessary among Soldiers and leaders in decentralized operations.

Types of After Action Reviews

There are two types of AARs, formal and informal. A formal AAR is resource-intensive and involves planning for and preparing the AAR site, supporting training aids, and supporting personnel. Informal AARs require less planning and preparation. A AAR—formal or informal—also analyzes any moral-ethical decisions that the unit made during the execution of a task. Both AARs involve all Soldiers and focus on what was planned, what happened, what worked, and how to improve performance and increase complexity within the commander's guidance.

Formal

Leaders plan formal AARs at the same time they finalize their training plan (six to eight weeks before execution). Formal AARs require more planning and preparation than informal AARs. They require site reconnaissance and selection, coordination, training aids (such as terrain models or map blow-ups), and selection, set up, and maintenance of the AAR site.

During formal AARs, the AAR facilitator—unit leader or OC/T—identifies and facilitates a discussion of specific events based on training objectives, performance measures, the commander's guidance, and a plan to achieve it. The facilitator provides an overview of the training events plan (what was supposed to happen) and facilitates a discussion of actually what happened during execution, identifying strengths, weaknesses, and issues. Participants then identify what retraining needs to be conducted and how to conduct the tasks differently to achieve the desired outcomes. The facilitator concludes the AAR by reviewing key points, reviewing issues summarizing observed strengths and weaknesses, and restating the participants' identification of how to improve performance to meet the commander's guidance.

Informal

Leaders conduct the informal AAR after previously identified events or as on-the-spot coaching while reviewing unit and Soldier performance during training. Due to time constraints and other limitations, conducting informal AARs at appropriate time as the training event progresses allows for on-the-spot corrections that enable immediate improved performance. Informal AARs—with immediate correction and retraining—also enable overall improved unit performance as the unit concludes its training event or scenario. Informal AARs provide immediate feedback to Soldiers, leaders, and units during training. Ideas and solutions gathered during informal AARs can be put to use as the unit continues its training.

Informal AARs require fewer training aids than formal AARs. For example, after destroying an enemy observation post during a movement to contact, the squad leader conducts an informal AAR to make corrections and reinforce strengths. Using nothing more than pinecones to represent squad members, the squad leader and squad members discuss the contact from start to finish. The squad quickly—

- Identifies what was supposed to happen.
- Establishes what happened from all levels.
- Evaluates performance against the Army standard (as stated in the task's T&EO).
- Identifies strengths and weaknesses.
- Identifies opportunities to improve performance within the commander's guidance when training continues.

genda for a Training AAR

ef: FM 7-0, Train to Win in a Complex World (Oct '16), p. D-3.

\Rs conducted during training follow the same agenda as AARs conducted during
)erations:

- Review what was supposed to happen.
- Establish what happened.
- Determine what was right or wrong with what happened.
- Determine how to perform the task differently next time.

training AAR begins with a review of what was supposed to happen. A facilitator
ometimes called an evaluator), along with participants, reviews what was supposed
❯ happen. This review is based on the commander's guidance, training objectives, and
ısks to train. An OPORD or the training schedule typically contains information that
tates what was supposed to happen. This information is repeated in the training plan.
he facilitator also reviews the UTP, training objectives, applicable individual training
cords, and T&EOs. Ideally, the leader of the evaluated unit conducts the AAR with
ssistance from an evaluator or OC/T.

he training AAR continues as the evaluator establishes what happened. The facilitator
nd participants determine what actually occurred during the training event, phase, or
peration. The leader attempts to gather as many views or perspectives—such as from
┐e OPFOR, squad leader, team leader, or rifleman—as feasible. These views help to
stablish a common understanding of the operation or event. Leaders then understand
he complexity of an event and work to solve complex, ill-defined problems quickly. An
ffective AAR requires an accurate account of events. The evaluator and participants
letermine what actually happened during performance of the task. The discussion that
ollows is only as good as the accuracy of the events. For force-on-force training, OP-
OR members assist in describing the flow of the training event and both the evaluated
ınit and OPFOR discuss training outcomes from their respective points of view.

After establishing the events, the AAR covers what was right or wrong with what happened. Participants identify the strong and weak points of their performances based on
the commander's guidance and performance measures. The facilitator guides discussions to ensure maximum input that is operationally sound and relevant to the training
event. Effectively guided discussions reach conclusions that are doctrinally sound,
consistent with Army standards, and relevant to the unit mission. Participants and
evaluators assess and candidly discuss what happened in terms of whether actions
and decisions were ethical, effective, and efficient.

A training AAR concludes as the participants determine how the unit should complete
the task differently next time. The facilitator guides the unit in self-determining how
it might perform the task more effectively in the future. The unit identifies problems
and provides solutions as well as identifies who is responsible for making the recommended changes. Additionally, the facilitator guides the discussion to determine a more
effective way to train the tasks to achieve the commander's guidance. The evaluator
or OC/T assists the chain of command undergoing the training to lead the group in
determining exactly how participants will perform differently the next time the unit attempts the task. Ideally, this assistance motivates units and Soldiers to conduct future
sustainment training to standard.

Assessing
Training

Step 1. PLAN the After Action Review

Ref: FM 7-0, Train to Win in a Complex World (Oct '16), pp. D-3 to D-5.

Effective AARs, formal or informal, require leaders to plan, prepare for, execute, and assess. AAR planning is part of each training event. Successful training leaders understand the unit's mission and the commander's guidance for the training event. During planning, commanders identify opportunities to conduct AARs, assign OC/T responsibilities and lock in allocated time and resources to conduct AARs. As leaders conduct training, subordinate leaders assess unit and leader proficiency on collective and individual tasks, conduct on-the-spot coaching, and lead informal AARs. These tasks require that leaders understand the commander's guidance, concept of operations, and tasks to be trained during a training event.

The amount and level of detail needed during the planning and preparation processes depend on the type of AAR to be conducted and available resources. The AAR process has four steps:

- Plan.
- Prepare.
- Execute.
- Assess.

STEP 1: PLAN the After Action Review

The AAR plan provides the foundation for successful AARs. Commanders provide their guidance to develop an AAR plan for each training event. Subordinates then determine how to achieve the commander's guidance. The guidance applies to formal and informal AARs and identifies—

- Who will conduct the AAR.
- Who will provide information.
- Aspects of the operation an AAR evaluates.
- Who will attend the AAR.
- When and where the AAR occurs.

Leaders or OC/Ts use the AAR plan to identify critical places and events to observe to provide the unit a timely and valid assessment. Critical places can include unit maintenance collection points, passage points, and unit aid stations. The AAR plan identifies responsible persons who (either internal or external to the unit) facilitate the AAR for a particular event. The leader or OC/T is the individual tasked to observe training, provide control for the training, and lead the AAR.

Selecting and Training Observer-Controllers/Trainers

When planning an AAR, commanders select leaders and OC/Ts—

- Who demonstrate proficiency in the tasks to be trained.
- With knowledge of the duties they are to observe.
- With knowledge of current doctrine and TTP.

When using external OC/Ts, ideally they are at least equal in rank to the leader of the unit they will assess. If commanders must choose between experience and an understanding of current TTP or rank, they should go with experience. A staff sergeant with experience as a tank platoon sergeant is a better platoon OC/T than a sergeant first class who has no platoon sergeant experience. Commanders are responsible for training and certifying OC/Ts to include providing training on how to conduct an AAR. Ideally, inexperienced OC/Ts should observe properly conducted AARs before acting as an OC/T.

~iewing the Training and Evaluation Outline

1 planning the AAR, units review applicable T&EOs for understanding performance
sures and steps for all individual and collective tasks. T&EOs state the Army perfor-
:e standards for these tasks. Units and Soldiers access T&EOs through the ATN at
://atn.army.mil via the DTMS and the CATS. The commander specifies the guidance
e event along with the objectives and tasks to be trained. The commander also
s the training environment for the training event and the focus of the tasks trained.
ers review the T&EOs that lists the conditions and standards for the respective
idual or collective tasks. Leaders use the individual training records and T&EOs to
sure unit and Soldier performance.

lers and OC/Ts review the tasks to be trained as specified in the commander's guid-
: for an upcoming event. The T&EO states performance measures and the order
ifies the commander's guidance. The respective T&EOs are not only provided to
aining OC/T team members but also to the Soldiers in the unit. All members of the
review these documents to gain a complete and mutual understanding of the critical
es and phases to assess task performance.

hedule Stopping Points

n planning the AAR, commanders schedule the time and place to conduct it as an inte-
part of training events. Commanders plan for AARs during and at the end of each critical
se or major training event. For example, a leader may plan a stopping point after issuing
)PORD, upon the unit's arrival at a new position, or after consolidation on an objective.

nmanders plan for 30 to 45 minutes for platoon-level AARs, 1 hour for company-level
Rs, and about 2 hours for battalion-level and above AARs. Training to standard takes
rity over training to time. Soldiers receive better feedback on their performance and
ember the lessons longer as result of a quality AAR.

termining Attendance

AAR plan specifies who attends each AAR. At each echelon, an AAR has a primary
of participants. At squad and platoon levels, everyone attends and participates. At
npany or higher levels, it may not be practical to have everyone attend because of
tinuing operations or training. At company or higher levels, unit and OPFOR com-
nders, unit leaders, and other key players may be the only participants. Leaders or
/Ts may recommend additional participants attend based on specific observations.

noosing Training Aids

: AAR plan specifies training aids. Effective training aids directly support the discussion
he training and promote learning. The local training support center catalogs available
ning aids. Home station training support center support and training aids are available
nin the Army training support system.

ider the right conditions, dry-erase boards, video equipment, digital maps, terrain models,
l enlarged maps support AAR discussion. For example, if reconnaissance reveals no sites
vide a view of the exercise area, the AAR facilitator can use a terrain table or digital map.

nen choosing training aids in the AAR plan, leaders consider terrain visibility, group
e, suitability to task, and availability of electrical power. Leaders need only use a train-
] aid if it makes the AAR better.

eviewing the After Action Review Plan

ie AAR plan is only a guide. Commanders issue their guidance, and subordinates de-
mine how to achieve that guidance. Commanders, leaders, and OC/Ts regularly review
e AAR plan during training meetings to ensure the training meeting stays on topic and
e plan meets the unit's training needs. Commanders, leaders, and OC/Ts can adjust the
an as necessary, but changes take preparation and planning time away from subordi-
te leaders or OC/Ts. The AAR plan aims to allow OC/Ts and leaders as much time as
ssible to prepare for the AAR.

Step 2. PREPARE the After Action Review

Ref: FM 7-0, Train to Win in a Complex World (Oct '16), pp. D-5 to D-8.

Preparation is the key to the effective execution of any plan. Preparing for an AAR be before the training and continues until the actual event.

Review Guidance and Supporting Documentation

The commander's guidance and training objectives are the basis for observations an focus of the AAR. When preparing for an AAR, leaders and OC/Ts review the comma er's guidance, OPORD, training objectives, and T&EOs. These reviews occur before training and immediately before the AAR. Leaders and OC/Ts review current doctrine technical information, and applicable unit SOPs to ensure they have the tools to obse unit and individual performance properly. Leaders and OC/Ts read and understand al WARNORDs, OPORDs, and FRAGORDs that the unit issues before and during train to understand what is supposed to happen. The detailed knowledge that OC/Ts displa during these reviews adds credibility to their assessments.

Identify Important Training Events

Based on the commander's guidance, leaders or OC/Ts identify which training events MET or as identified by the commander—are critical. Leaders or OC/Ts also identify tl training events are positioned in the right place at the right time to observe the unit's actions. Critical events can include—

- Training events that demonstrate MET proficiency.
- The issuance of OPORDs and FRAGORDs.
- The issuance of the MDMP or TLP.
- Contact with OPFORs.
- Resupply and reconstitution operations.
- Passage of lines.

Identify After Action Review Facilitators

AAR facilitators are either internal or external evaluators. Internal leaders participate ir the training and are part of the organization whereas external evaluators—typically OC Ts—do not participate in the training. Both evaluators have the requirement to make and consolidate insights, observations, and lessons to facilitate the discussion of what happened. OC/Ts accurately record what they see and hear to prevent loss of valuable information and feedback. These records include events, actions, and observations by time sequence. OC/Ts can use any recording system—such as notebooks, mobile devices, prepared forms, or index cards—as long as it is reliable and sufficiently detaile (identifying times, places, and names). A recording system notates the date-time group each observation so evaluators can easily integrate their observations with observatior of other OC/Ts. This collection of observations provides a comprehensive and detailed overview of what happened. When OC/Ts have more time, they review the notes and fi in any details not written down earlier.

Leaders actively participate in the event and facilitate the AAR. They listen to professio discussions, feedback, and the participants in the AAR. The observations of participant during the event enable leaders to understand the execution of the tasks as well as the impact of the training environment. When participants share their observations, Soldiers and leaders develop mutual trust as they gain a common understanding of the unit's strengths and weaknesses.

One of the most difficult OC/T tasks involves determining when and where to observe training. The best location is where the OC/T can observe the performance of critical tasks and the overall flow of unit actions. The OC/T does not always need to stay close

e unit leader. The OC/T's position avoids distracting training participants. OC/Ts also
compromising the unit's location or guidance by being obvious. They are profes-
al, courteous, and as unobtrusive as possible at all times. They look and act like a member of the unit. For example, OC/Ts use individual and vehicle camouflage, move-
techniques, or cover and concealment.

ect After Action Review Sites

s occur at or near the training exercise site. During formal AARs, leaders identify and
ect designated AAR sites and prepare a site diagram showing the placement of train-
ids and other equipment. Designated AAR sites allow pre-positioning of training aids
rapid assembly of key personnel, minimizing wasted time.

ders often conduct informal AARs at or near the training site. The primary difference
formal AARs is that informal AARs use minimal training aids that facilitators often
on the ground (such as rocks or twigs). Based on the commander's guidance, lead-
determine the time and location of the AAR site when they prepare for the AAR.

effective AAR site allows Soldiers to see the terrain where the exercise or training took
e. If this is not possible, the trainer finds a location that allows them to see the terrain
re the most critical or significant actions occurred. Time and resources determine the type
complexity of the terrain model, enlarged map, sketch, or copy of the unit's graphics.

llect Observations

ders and senior OC/Ts need a complete picture of what happened during the training
onduct an effective AAR. Leaders and OC/Ts implement the Army problem solving
cess to establish the base logic for gathering information and observations.

ing an informal AAR, the leader or facilitator can rely upon the input from the unit
ng the AAR or gather observations from subordinates and OPFOR (if applicable).

ing a formal AAR, the senior OC/T receives input from subordinates, supporting units,
adjacent units. This combined input provides the senior OC/T with a comprehensive
ew of the observed unit and its impact on the higher unit's mission. The senior OC/T
receives input from OPFOR leaders, players, and OC/Ts. The OPFOR perspective is
ical in identifying why a unit was or was not successful.

ganize the After Action Review

/Ts gather all the observation information and organize notes in a chronological se-
ence to understand the flow of events. The leader or OC/T selects and sequences key
ents of the operation in their relevance to the commander's guidance, training objec-
es, tasks to train, and key discussion or teaching points.

aders and OC/Ts then organize the AAR using one of three techniques: chronological
der of events, warfighting functions, or key events, themes, or issues. The chronologi-
l order of events technique is logical, structured, and easy to understand. It follows the
w of training from start to finish. By covering actions in the order they took place, Sol-
ers and leaders can better recall what happened. The warfighting functions technique
uctures the AAR using the warfighting functions. The AAR focuses on the warfighting
nctions and their associated systems (people, organizations, information, and pro-
sses) and links to the commander's guidance and training objectives. Participants can
entify strengths and weaknesses across all phases and can recommend solutions. This
chnique is useful in training staff sections. The last technique focuses on key events,
emes, or issues. This technique focuses on critical training events, which directly sup-
ort training objectives. This technique is effective when time is limited.

ehearse

acilitators and OC/Ts rehearse delivery of the AAR during preparation. This rehearsal
cludes considering the possible questions or issues that participants may broach. Effec-
e rehearsals include all the training resources that will be used in the actual AAR.

Assessing
Training

Step 3. EXECUTE the After Action Review

Ref: FM 7-0, Train to Win in a Complex World (Oct '16), pp. D-8 to D-10.

The AAR begins when the training exercise stops, AAR preparation is complete, and players are at the designated AAR site. The leader or OC/T reviews the purpose and quence of the AAR to ensure everyone understands why an AAR is conducted. It is n time to conduct the AAR. The purpose of the AAR is for participants to discover stren and weaknesses, propose solutions, and adopt a COA to correct problems.

After Action Review Scenario

The battalion commander has certified SFC Banks as an observer-controller for Company B's EXEVAL next month. In preparation for his duties, he gathered all the T&EOs and publications to reference. The T&EOs support the overall evaluation plan and specifically the collective tasks he is to evaluate.

During the unit EXEVAL, SFC Banks observes 1st platoon, Company B executing the task, React to Direct Fire Contact, #07-3-D9501. Following the platoon's execution of the task, he conducts an informal AAR with the platoon and OPFOR personnel.

SFC Banks facilitates the AAR by asking SSG Richmond of 1st platoon to describe what was supposed to happen. SSG Richmond describes the mission and scheme of maneuver the platoon was directed to execute from the company operation order.

After SSG Richmond relayed what the platoon was supposed to do, SFC Banks asked PFC Smith to describe from his point of view what actually occurred. This generated some discussion in the platoon of what they believed went right and what went poorly. SFC Banks interjected at times, prompting platoon members to discuss how they could have executed the task to the published standard per the T&EO. Following this discussion, SFC Banks discussed his overall assessment of the platoon for this task. He also discussed how the platoon performed—with a go or a no go—for each performance step and measure as well as critical and leader steps. SFC Banks assessed the platoon as a P- based on his task evaluation and criteria met within the objective task evaluation criteria matrix as described in the T&EO.

After 15 minutes, SFC Banks is satisfied that the platoon better understands how to execute the tasks to achieve the standard. He releases the platoon to retrain the task for another iteration.

Provide an Introduction and Rules

In an introduction, the leader or OC/T requests the following:

- Everyone participates if they have an insight, observation, or question that will he the unit identify and correct deficiencies or sustain strengths. The AAR is a dynam candid, and professional discussion of training that focuses on unit performance measured against the task standards (as expressed in the T&EO).

- Participants avoid using the AAR as a critique. No one—regardless of rank, positic or strength of personality—has all the information or answers. AARs maximize trai ing benefits by allowing Soldiers to learn from each other.

- The AAR focuses on identifying weaknesses to improve and strengths to sustain.

Soldier participation directly correlates to the atmosphere created during the introduction and command climate. The AAR leader makes a concerted effort to draw in Soldiers wh seem reluctant to participate. The following techniques can help the leader or OC/T:

- Reinforce the fact that it is permissible to disagree respectfully.

- Focus on learning and encourage people to give honest opinions.

- Use open-ended and leading questions to guide the discussion of Soldier, leader, and unit performance.

- Enter the discussion only when necessary.

te the After Action Review Agenda

eader or OC/T states the AAR agenda. The leader or OC/T reviews the commander's
ng objectives and restates the tasks being reviewed, including the conditions and
dards for the tasks. Using tools—such as maps, operational graphics, terrain boards,
s, and rocks—the commander or leader restates the mission, guidance, and concept of
ations. The leader or OC/T may guide the discussion to ensure everyone understands
lan and the commander's guidance. Another technique is to have subordinate leaders
te the mission and discuss the commander's guidance and concept of operations.

ormal AAR, the OPFOR commander explains the OPFOR plan and actions. The
OR commander uses the same training aids as the friendly force commander, so that
articipants understand the correlation between the plans.

mmarize Events (What Actually Happened)

leader or facilitator guides the review using a logical sequence of events to describe
discuss what happened. The facilitator—leader or OC/T—and participants deter-
e to the extent possible what actually happened during the training event, phase, or
ration. The leader gathers as many views or perspectives (such as from the OPFOR,
ad leader, team leader, and rifleman) as possible. These varied perspectives help the
itator to establish a common understanding. Leaders then understand the complexity
n event and work to solve complex, ill-defined problems. They discuss the unit's risk
nagement integration and the Soldiers application of control measures to mitigate the
s. This is critical in helping Soldiers understand risk, act decisively, and accept prudent
in the future.

facilitator does not ask yes or no questions but encourages participation and guides
cussion by using open-ended, leading questions. An open-ended question allows the
son answering to reply based on what was significant to the Soldier. Open-ended
stions are also much less likely to put Soldiers on the defensive; these questions are
re effective in finding out what happened.

the discussion expands and more Soldiers add their perspectives, a clearer picture of
at really happened emerges. The leader or OC/T does not tell the Soldiers or lead-
what was good or bad. The leader or OC/T ensures that participants reveal specific
ues, both positive and negative. Skillful guidance of the discussion ensures the AAR
es not gloss over mistakes or unit weaknesses.

entify What Needs To Be Improved Or Sustained

e unit discusses both its successes and failures in the context of the training mission, ob-
tives, and performance measures. Participants consider whether the resulting decisions
d actions were ethical, effective, and efficient. To sustain success, the unit needs to know
at it performs well. Also, participants concentrate on identifying what went wrong and not
the person responsible. If necessary, it is better to identify the duty position rather than
e person. For example, they refer to "the platoon leader" rather than to "2LT Wilson."

etermine How the Task Should Be Done Differently

e facilitator—leader or OC/T—helps the unit determine a more effective method for the
it to perform the task in the future. The unit identifies conditions to modify to increase
mplexity. A more complex training environment challenges leaders and subordinates
they can better identify opportunities to take prudent risk within the commander's
idance. Additionally, the facilitator guides the discussion to determine a more effective
ethod the unit can implement to train the tasks to achieve the commander's guidance.

rovide Closing Comments

uring the summary, the facilitator reviews and summarizes key points identified during
e discussion. The AAR ends on a constructive note and links conclusions to future train-
g. The facilitator then leaves the immediate area to allow the unit or subordinate leaders
d Soldiers time to discuss the training in private.

Assessing Training

Step 4. ASSESS the After Action Review

Ref: FM 7-0, Train to Win in a Complex World (Oct '16), p. D-10.

AARs are the link between task performance and execution to standard. They provide commanders a critical assessment tool to plan Soldier, leader, and unit training. Through the professional and candid discussion of events, Soldiers can compare the performance against the standard and identify specific ways to improve proficiency.

The benefits of AARs come from applying results in developing future training. Successful leaders use the information to assess unit performance and to plan future training. Leaders apply the information to correct deficiencies and sustain task proficiency.

Retrain

Units and Soldiers retrain tasks to meet the standard. A lack of resources may prevent retraining on some tasks during the same exercise. Without the necessary resources, leaders reschedule the mission or training. Leaders ensure that a lack of proficiency in supporting collective and individual tasks found during the AAR are scheduled and retrained. Effective leaders do not delay retraining. If the leader delays retraining, then Soldiers and the unit must understand that they did not perform the task to standard and that retraining will occur later.

Revise Standard Operating Procedures (SOPs)

AARs may reveal problems with unit SOPs. If so, unit leaders revise the SOPs and ensure units implement the changes during future training.

AAR Fundamentals

Ref: FM 6-0 (C2), Commander and Staff Organization and Operations (Apr '16).

- Conducted during or immediately after each event
- Focus is on commander's intent, training objectives and standards
- Focus is also on Soldier, leader, and unit performance
- Involves all participants in the discussion
- Uses open-ended questions
- Encourages initiative and innovation in finding more effective ways to achieve standards and meet training objectives and commander's intent
- Determines strengths and weaknesses
- Links performance to subsequent training

Refer to BSS6: The Battle Staff SMARTbook, 6th Ed. for further discussion. BSS6 covers the operations process (ADP 5-0); commander's activities; Army planning methodologies; the military decisionmaking process and troop leading procedures (FM 7-0 w/Chg 2); integrating processes (IPB, information collection, targeting, risk management, and knowledge management); plans and orders; mission command, C2 warfighting function tasks, command posts, liaison (ADP 6-0); rehearsals & after action reviews; and operational terms and military symbols (ADP 1-02).

III. (OIP) Organizational Inspection Program

Ref: FM 7-0, Train to Win in a Complex World (Oct '16), appendix I.

Unit training is a subset of the unit's overall Organizational Inspection Program (known as OIP). This section provides a training management inspector with the basic overarching program and then focuses on the specifics for training management. Refer to AR 1-201 for details on inspections.

Guidance for Inspectors

All inspections have a major purpose: to provide feedback to commanders so they can make decisions that will improve the Army. Inspections focus on measuring compliance against established standards to ensure that the Army as a whole can function effectively in its combat role. The five principles of Army inspections support the five basic elements of an inspection. Those five elements are—

• Measure performance against a standard.
• Determine the magnitude of the problem.
• Seek the root cause of the problem.
• Determine a solution.
• Assign responsibility to the appropriate individuals or agencies.

Checklist Structure

Section I provides an inspector with a checklist for identifying training management processes in the unit. The presence of these processes imply that the unit has an understanding of the doctrine and contains the parts essential for planning, preparing, executing, and assessing unit training.

Section II focuses on evaluating the indicators of an effective training management program. It provides indicators of specific inspection items that allow for a more detailed assessment. The second section may require multiple observations of training planning, preparation, and execution to provide an accurate review of the unit's training program effectiveness.

Section I –Brigade, Battalion, and Company Inspection Checklist

This series of questions measures the unit's training. These questions enable an inspector to determine if the foundations of effective unit training exist. The series of questions is not an indicator of unit training effectiveness. The key to any training program is the commander's personal involvement. As the unit's primary trainer, the commander has direct involvement in the planning, preparation, execution, and assessment of training proficiencies and ensures compliance with the commander's vision and guidance for training. Ideally, a unit conducts annual formal inspections with semiannual internal informal inspections.

As a staff completes the checklist, it aims to answer each question in the affirmative (YES). If the staff cannot answer in the affirmative, it adds notes or comments to the checklist. Often those items require retraining.

Task

As staffs check each item in the checklist, they note if the unit sustains or improves the task and add a comment to elaborate.

Unit Training Plan

The UTP ensures units plan and prepare for training. Inspectors ask the following questions pertaining to the UTP:

- Is the higher headquarters UTP available and posted in DTMS?
- Is the inspected unit's UTP published? Is it posted to DTMS?
- Does the UTP contain the higher headquarters mission?
- Does the UTP contain the higher headquarters METL?
- Does the UTP contain the higher headquarters commander's training guidance?
- Does the UTP contain the unit mission?
- Does the UTP contain the commander's guidance?
- Does the UTP contain a concept of operations that includes—
  - A collective training plan?
  - An individual training plan in support of the collective training plan?
  - A leader development plan?
- Does the UTP contain a time management cycle?
- Does the UTP contain tasks to subordinate units?
- Does the UTP contain an assessment plan?
- Does the UTP contain the training environment?
- Does the UTP contain resources required?
- Does the UTP contain risks and mitigation for key tasks not trained?
- Does the UTP contain the UTP calendar?

Commanders' Dialogues

Commanders' dialogues ensure commanders communicate with each other. Inspector ask the following questions pertaining to commanders' dialogue:

- Did commanders' conduct dialogues?
- Did the higher commander approve the unit's METs selected to train (key output of mission analysis)?
- Is the output of the mission analysis recorded?

Mission-Essential Task List

The METL ensures units have a list of tasks to attain. Inspectors ask the following questions pertaining to the METL:

- Is the unit METL available?
- Is the unit METL posted to the DTMS and to the CATS?
- For battalion and company, does the unit METL reflect the unit's as-designed capabilities as described by the TOE or TDA?
- Is the unit METL reportable on the unit status report?

Training Objectives

Training objectives are an essential part of the commander's training vision. Overall collective task objectives help sequence training events from simple to increasingly more complex tasks. The progressive nature of the training helps build upon previously mastered skills. Inspectors ask the following questions pertaining to training objectives:

- Are training objectives published for each major training event?
- Do the training objectives support training the unit METs for each event?
- Are objectives for the leader, collective leader, collective tasks, and individual tasks identified for each major training event?

Training Schedules

Training schedules are necessary to inform Soldiers and leaders and to focus support, project resource requirements, and allow companies optimum time to prepare for training events. Inspectors ask the following questions pertaining to training schedules:

Are the company training schedules complete, approved, and signed by the battalion commander?

Are company training schedules changed frequently?

Are changes to the training schedules approved by the brigade commander?

aining Meetings

ining meetings ensure units complete training preparation, resource coordination, d provide opportunities for training plan corrections and modifications. Units use se meetings to keep the training plan on track and to prepare successfully for training ents. Inspectors ask the following questions pertaining to training meetings:

Are brigade, battalion, and company training meetings held?

Do the right personnel attend?

Is there a standard training meeting agenda?

igital Training Management System

e DTMS ensures units engage in digital training. Inspectors ask the following questions rtaining to the DTMS:

Does the unit use the DTMS?

Is there a certified DTMS master trainer on hand? Is this individual appointed on orders by the commander (to include one alternate)?

Is there a log of unit personnel with their privilege levels available and approved by the commander?

- Does each battalion have a DTMS operator?
- Is the DTMS used to manage company-level individual training records?
- Are incoming and outgoing personnel entered and removed from the DTMS as necessary?
- Has the unit published a DTMS SOP?

ssessment and Evaluation

nit assessment plans help validate the current assessment of the unit METs and the TP. Inspectors ask the following questions pertaining to assessment and evaluations:

- Does each major training event include an assessment plan?
- Are unit OC/Ts trained and certified by the unit commander?
- Does the unit conduct AARs during and at the conclusion of training events?
- Are AAR results available?
- Does the unit follow the AAR process as outlined in this publication (see appendix D)?
- Are AAR results provided to the commander and used for assessing MET task proficiencies?
- Are the latest training evaluations or inspection reports available?
- Does the unit use individual training records and T&EOs for collective, leader, and individual tasks?
- Are T&EOs used for bottom-up feedback that informs the commander's assessment of METs?

Training Briefing

The TB ensures higher commanders have visibility of UTPs. Inspectors ask the following questions pertaining to TBs:

- Are TBs conducted?
- Are the TBs tied to the higher commander's approval of the UTP?
- Are the TB's results recorded?
- Are installation staff, supporting unit, and gaining commanders present as appropriate?

Assessing Training

Training Resource Management

Inspectors check resources concerning training ammunition. They ask the following questions:

- Are annual ammunition forecasts available?
- Does the unit have a plan to use annual forecasted ammunition?
- Is DA Form 581 (Request for Issue and Turn-In of Ammunition) on hand and does support the applicable training event?
- Are projected shortfalls addressed during the commanders' dialogue and TB?
- Are Class V handlers certified by the commander?

Inspectors check resources concerning vehicle mileage. They ask the following questions:

- Is there a restriction on vehicle mileage?
- Does the UTP account for mileage caps?
- Does the unit use the CATS to help project unit mileage?

Live, Virtual, and Constructive

LVC training environments provide varied training environments for units. Inspectors ask the following questions pertaining to LVC training environments:

- Are the right LVC training environments assets considered and used to meet training objectives when necessary?
- Has the unit incorporated LVC assets into the training plan?

Training Aids, Devices, Simulators, and Simulations

TADSS ensures units train with varied items. Inspectors ask the following questions pertaining to TADSS:

- Does the unit incorporate the use of TADSS to support training events?
- Does the unit identify and adequately plan for TADSS that support collective and individual tasks?

Time Management

Time management ensures units manage their time. Inspectors ask the following questions pertaining to time management:

- Has the unit established or does it follow a higher headquarters or installation time management cycle (such as Green-Amber-Red cycle)?
- Has the unit established or does it follow a higher headquarters or installation external task 'lock¬in' program that protects training time from unprogrammed requirements?

Leader Development

Leader development ensures units develop subordinate leaders. Inspectors ask the following questions pertaining to leader development:

- Has the commander established a unit leader development program?
- Is a leader certification program part of the leader development program?
- Are leader development training objectives and assessments integrated and identified in each major training event?

Rehearsals and Precombat Checks

Rehearsals and precombat checks ensure units practice training events. Inspectors ask the following questions pertaining to rehearsals and precombat checks:

- Does the unit schedule and execute rehearsals prior to each major training event?
- Do all applicable leaders and trainers attend the rehearsals?
- Does the unit conduct precombat checks and inspections prior to training execution?

Retraining

Retraining ensures units train to standard. Inspectors ask the following question: Does the unit schedule time to retrain tasks not meeting standards?

ction II —Evaluation

e inspector interviews leaders throughout the unit to evaluate the effectiveness of ning management execution. The inspector moves beyond simply measuring the sence of the required elements of the program (Section I) and begins to determine the gnitude of the problem, seeks the root cause of the problem, begins to determine a ution, and discovers where to recommend responsibility to the appropriate individuals agencies.

completing the earlier questions first, the inspector gains knowledge of any potential engths and shortfalls in unit training. By completing the earlier questions first, the pector has knowledge of any strengths and shortfalls in the required elements of the ining management program.

ommander and Leader Responsibilities

e inspector uses questions and considerations to determine if the commanders and bordinate leaders are meeting their responsibilities according to unit training. The ques- ns are not all-inclusive but can help the inspector gain a basic understanding and lead fuller conversation to determine the effectiveness of the program or root cause of any sues. For commanders at every echelon, the following questions apply:

- Do commanders use the principles of mission command to give subordinates latitude in determining how best to train their units to achieve commanders' visualized end state for training?
- Do commanders provide subordinates training objectives for each training event or suspense's for proficiency levels in their METs? Describe the processes.
- Do commanders provide subordinates the training time and resources they require? How? (Do they use the commanders' dialogue during development of the UTP? Do commanders allocate sufficient time for subordinates to train? When and how do com- manders become involved in resourcing subordinate commanders and leaders?).
- Do commanders ensure subordinate leaders have the necessary skills and knowledge to manage unit training so that leaders and units can achieve desired levels of training readiness? How? Do commanders train subordinate leaders to use the unit training system? How?
- Do commanders ensure they were providing quality training to subordinates? Do com- manders define quality training? How?

he next two paragraphs apply to commanders and leaders at every echelon (select everal at each echelon to determine if the programs in place are used throughout the ommand or if there are any systemic problems at certain levels).

low did commanders—

- Personally observe, participate in, and evaluate the quality and consistency of training at all echelons?
- Receive training feedback directly from subordinate leaders and Soldiers?
- Identify, resolve if possible, and bring to the chain of command's attention issues in training planning, leadership, management, support, resourcing, and other key func- tions?
- Check the adequacy of external training support and report inconsistencies to the chain of command?
- Maintain awareness of safety issues and make on-the-spot corrections?

The inspector uses some questions to gain an informed perspective of the commander and leader's understanding of their roles and responsibilities throughout the unit. Inspec- tors can add questions to explore any systemic problems or to develop recommendations to fix any issues found. Inspectors select several at each echelon to determine if the pro- grams in place are used throughout the command or if there are any systemic problems at certain levels. The following questions apply to NCOs at every echelon:

- Do NCOs influence or plan training for individual Soldiers, crews, small teams? How?

- Do NCOs conduct standards-based, performance-oriented training? How?
- Do NCOs use T&EOs?
- Do NCOs or the commander or platoon leader establish training objectives for the events NCOs controlled?
- Does an NCO identified individual, small-unit collective tasks and drills that suppo the unit METL? Identify individual.
- Does individual Soldier task training relate to the collective tasks the unit trains an these relate to the unit's METL? How?
- Are NCOs involved in planning, preparing, and executing training, conducting AAF and providing bottom-up feedback? How?
- Do NCOs maintain awareness of hazards and associated control measures durin individual, crew, and small-team training? How?

A. Planning Training

When planning for training, instructors follow certain instructions. First, they review the OPORD or FRAGORD for the last several training events. Second, they compare the training objectives for the training events to the training objectives identified in the UTF The inspector determines if the unit uses the operations process to develop its UTP, if resulting plan nests with higher, and if adjusting the plan increases the difficulty as the unit masters or adjusts skills to overcome any training short falls.

When planning training, commanders and S-3s at each echelon answer the following questions:

- Do commanders and S-3s develop the UTP? What planning method do they use?
- Do commanders and S-3s use a different method to plan training events?
- Do commanders and S-3s conduct planning sessions? Who is involved in planning sessions?
- Do commanders and S-3s adjust the UTP or training events? How, when, and whe did commanders and S-3s make these adjustments?
- Do commanders & S-3s manage the planning & preparation for training events? Ho

The inspector drills down (by echelon) with questions. Inspectors use the questions to determine root causes, solutions, and where to recommend responsibility for fixes.

Brigade-level inspectors review the current UTP OPORD asking the following question

- Do the training objectives complement higher headquarters' training objectives for multiechelon events?
- Do the training objectives reflect mastery of previously identified training objectives'
- Do the event and UTP training objectives match?
- Is an evaluation plan articulated?
- Are prior evaluations available for planning?
- Does the higher unit's UTP calendar have unaccounted time available? How much?

Brigade-level inspectors ask the brigade executive officer, brigade command sergeant major, principal staff officers, staff NCOs, and drivers the following questions:

- Do executive officer, command sergeant major, principal staff officers, staff NCOs, and drivers provide input to the training plan?
- Are executive officer, command sergeant major, principal staff officers, staff NCOs, and drivers aware of the training objectives for the training events?
- Are the training objectives building upon previously mastered skill sets?
- Are executive officer, command sergeant major, principal staff officers, staff NCOs, and drivers using previous assessments for event planning?
- Is the staff section assessments maintained? Where?
- Are the procedures for processing and tracking training resource requests from the units acceptable? Confirm.

ttalion-level inspectors should review UTP OPORD and the UTP calendar. They review ? OPORDs or FRAGORDs for the last two training events. They also review the unit)Ps for battalion-level training meetings and identify the date and time for the last four ining meetings. Battalion-level inspectors ask the following questions:

Are the training meetings scheduled at least weekly?
* Is there a set agenda for the training meetings?
* Does the agenda allow for timely identification and procurement of resources?
* Are the training meeting focused on training or are other issues addressed as well?
* Are the results recorded?

attalion-level inspection asks the battalion executive officer, battalion command sergeant ajor, battalion staff officers, battalion staff NCOs, and battalion staff drivers these ques->ns:

• Do battalion executive officer, battalion command sergeant major, battalion staff officers, battalion staff NCOs, and battalion staff drivers provide input to the training plan?
• Are battalion executive officer, battalion command sergeant major, battalion staff officers, battalion staff NCOs, and battalion staff drivers involved in the MDMP for developing the UTP?
• Are the training objectives building upon previously mastered skill sets?
• Are battalion executive officer, battalion command sergeant major, battalion staff officers, battalion staff NCOs, and battalion staff drivers using previous assessments for event planning?
• Do the training meetings focus on training?
• Do the training meetings allow for adequate planning?
• Do battalion executive officer, battalion command sergeant major, battalion staff officers, battalion staff NCOs, and battalion staff drivers provide planning input during the training meeting?
• Are procedures for processing and tracking training resource requests from the units acceptable?
• Is training time allocated to subordinates acceptable? How much time is allocated?

:ompany-level inspectors review the company UTP, the last two weekly training sched-les, and OPORDs or FRAGORDs for the last two training events. These inspectors ask 1e following:

• Are the training meetings scheduled at least weekly?
• Is there a set agenda for the training meetings?
• Does the agenda allow for timely identification and procurement of resources?
• Are the training meetings focused on training or are other issues addressed?
• Are the results recorded?

:ompany-level inspectors ask the company commander, company executive officer, :ompany first sergeant, platoon leader, platoon sergeant, section leader, and crew chief :he following questions:

• Do company commander, company executive officer, company first sergeant, platoon leader, platoon sergeant, section leader, and crew chief provide input to the training event?
• Are company commander, company executive officer, company first sergeant, platoon leader, platoon sergeant, section leader, and crew chief involved in the TLP for developing the UTP?
• Are the training objectives building upon previously mastered skill sets?
• Are company commander, company executive officer, company first sergeant, platoon leader, platoon sergeant, section leader, and crew chief using previous assessments for event planning?

- Do the company training meetings focus on only on training?
- Do the company training meetings allow for adequate planning?
- Do company commander, company executive officer, company first sergeant, platoon leader, platoon sergeant, section leader, and crew chief provide planning input during the training meeting?
- Is training time provided adequate to plan training? How much time is allocated?

B. Preparing Training

Inspectors use this portion of the evaluation to determine the efficiency of the preparation activities of resourcing, rehearsing, and preexecution checks.

Inspectors ask commanders and S-3s at each echelon the following questions:

- Do commanders and S-3s have procedures for processing and tracking training resource requests? What are the procedures?
- Are there problematic resource requests? What are they?
- Are resources managed at echelon? What are they? How are they managed?
- Do commanders and S-3s begin preparation for training events? How?
- Do commanders and S-3s emphasize parts of preparation? What parts?
- Do commanders and S-3s plan your rehearsals? When
- How do you schedule rehearsals? When?
- Are commanders and S-3s' rehearsals evaluated? Who evaluates them?
- Do rehearsals help commanders and S-3s prepare for training? How?
- Do commanders and S-3s have procedures for conducting preexecution checks? What are they?
- Do commanders and S-3s plan for precombat checks? How?

Brigade and battalion-level inspectors ask the executive officer, command sergeant major, staff section officer, and staff section NCO the following questions:

- Do executive officer, command sergeant major, staff section officer, and staff section NCO assist units in training preparation? How?
- Do executive officer, command sergeant major, staff section officer, and staff section NCO give help to units in training preparation? How?

Battalion-level inspectors review the battalion training meeting agenda for specific training preparation topics. These inspectors ask the following questions:

- Are leader, trainer, and evaluator certification times discussed?
- Are rehearsal times discussed?
- Are preexecution times discussed?
- Do executive officer, command sergeant major, staff section officer, and staff section NCO track the progress of resource requests? How?

Company-level inspectors review the last four weekly training schedules. These inspectors ask the following questions:

- Are rehearsal times scheduled?
- Are preexecution inspection times scheduled?

Company-level inspectors ask the company commander, company executive officer, company first sergeant, platoon leader, platoon sergeant, section leader, and crew chief the following questions:

- Are preexecution checks standardized?
- Are trainers certified? Who certifies the trainers?
- Do company commander, company executive officer, company first sergeant, platoon leader, platoon sergeant, section leader, and crew chief from battalion and brigade receive preparation assistance? What preparation assistance is received?

Executing Training

pectors use this portion of the inspection to focus on training execution. Successful
ining execution results from good preparation and planning. Adaptive leaders help
ining execution through responsive assistance by maximizing training opportunities,
ative conditions, and accurate assessments.

gade and battalion-level inspections for training execution focus on facilitating the
ining and providing resources. Brigade and battalion commanders ensure that they are
multaneously training their respective staffs and providing the necessary guidance for
ining execution.

igade and battalion-level inspectors ask the executive officer, command sergeant major,
aff section officer, and staff section NCOs the following questions:

- Do executive officer, command sergeant major, staff section officer, and staff section NCOs have roles during subordinate unit training execution? What are they?
- Do executive officer, command sergeant major, staff section officer, and staff section NCOs evaluate their own ability to assist training execution?
- Do executive officer, command sergeant major, staff section officer, and staff section NCOs assist subordinate unit training execution? How?

ompany-level inspectors ask the commander, executive officer, first sergeant, platoon
ader, platoon sergeant, section leader, and crew chief the following questions:

- Do commander, executive officer, first sergeant, platoon leader, platoon sergeant, section leader, and crew chief make training challenging? How?
- Do commander, executive officer, first sergeant, platoon leader, platoon sergeant, section leader, and crew chief plan to capture and record training data during execution? How?
- Do commander, executive officer, first sergeant, platoon leader, platoon sergeant, section leader, and crew chief have a plan for retraining? During, after, or as separate events?
- Do commander, executive officer, first sergeant, platoon leader, platoon sergeant, section leader, and crew chief always achieve training objectives during allotted time for training events? If not, what do commander, executive officer, first sergeant, platoon leader, platoon sergeant, section leader, and crew chief do in response?
- Do commander, executive officer, first sergeant, platoon leader, platoon sergeant, section leader, and crew chief allot enough subordinate training time prior to collective and multiechelon events? How?
- Do commander, executive officer, first sergeant, platoon leader, platoon sergeant, section leader, and crew chief make sure adequate training areas are scheduled or used to train unit? How?
- Do commander, executive officer, first sergeant, platoon leader, platoon sergeant, section leader, and crew chief ensure that training is done to standard for the tasks to be trained? How?
- Are commander, executive officer, first sergeant, platoon leader, platoon sergeant, section leader, and crew chief able to get adequate resources routinely for unit training? What do they do when problems or shortfalls occur?
- Do commander, executive officer, first sergeant, platoon leader, platoon sergeant, section leader, and crew chief ensure leaders are present at the right place and time for training? How?
- Do commander, executive officer, first sergeant, platoon leader, platoon sergeant, section leader, and crew chief ensure the unit executes training safely? How?
- Do commander, executive officer, first sergeant, platoon leader, platoon sergeant, section leader, and crew chief make sure safety precautions do not limit training realism or reduce the impact? How?

- Do commander, executive officer, first sergeant, platoon leader, platoon sergeant, tion leader, and crew chief train the OPFOR properly and ensure the OPFOR pos as an adequate challenging threat? How?
- Do commander, executive officer, first sergeant, platoon leader, platoon sergeant, tion leader, and crew chief train, certify, and position OC/Ts to observe, control, an train the unit as necessary? How?
- Do commander, executive officer, first sergeant, platoon leader, platoon sergeant, tion leader, and crew chief integrate Army mission command systems into exercis How?

D. Assessing Training

Inspectors use this portion of the inspection to focus on the assessment of training. As sessment occurs throughout the training management process.

Brigade and battalion-level inspections focus on the assessment of their respective st sections and assessment of their roles in subordinate unit training. Inspectors review recorded assessments to assess their thoroughness.

Brigade and battalion-level staff inspectors ask the executive officer, command serger major, staff section officer, and staff section NCOs the following questions:

- Do executive officer, command sergeant major, staff section officer, and staff sectio NCOs plan for assessment of staff sections, section leaders, and individuals? How and when?
- Do executive officer, command sergeant major, staff section officer, and staff sectio NCOs record assessments? How?
- Do executive officer, command sergeant major, staff section officer, and staff sectio NCOs use AARs to improve task proficiency and training quality?

Battalion-level inspectors ask the executive officer, command sergeant major, staff sec tion leaders, and staff section NCOs the following questions:

- Do executive officer, command sergeant major, staff section leaders, and staff sect NCOs train, certify, rehearse, and otherwise prepare the observers? How?
- Does the commander assess the unit METL and determine MET proficiency? How'
- Does the unit have procedures to ensure MET assessments are recorded in the DTMS?
- Do the training assessments address such areas as training support, force integrati logistics, and personnel availability? How?
- Are there procedures that link training proficiency to resources and does the UTP g adjusted based on training proficiency measures?
- Does the commander ensure observers are qualified and familiar with applicable T&EOs used to evaluate task execution? How does the commander review an ob- server's subjective assessment on the unit's ability to perform a task?
- When an AAR identifies a unit training strength to be sustained or a weakness to improve, does that information get routed back into the planning and trained in the continuum of the operations process for training? How?
- Do leaders use criteria to select appropriate times during a training event to conduct an AAR with the objective of improving future performance?
- Are immediate in-stride corrections allowed?
- Does the commander guide MET proficiency training? How?
- Are AARs used to improve task proficiency and training quality? How?
- Are AARs conducted as part of an open learning environment where facilitators, par ticipants, and observers freely discuss successes and honest mistakes?
- Do executive officer, command sergeant major, staff section leaders, and staff sectio NCOs share lessons learned with other units?

SMARTbooks
INTELLECTUAL FUEL FOR THE MILITARY

ognized as a "**whole of government**" doctrinal reference standard by
ary, national security and government professionals around the world,
ARTbooks comprise a **comprehensive professional library** designed
all levels of Soldiers, Sailors, Airmen, Marines and Civilians in mind.

e SMARTbook reference series is used by **military, national security,
d government professionals** around the world at the organizational/
stitutional level; operational units and agencies across the full range of
erations and activities; military/government education and professional
velopment courses; combatant command and joint force headquarters;
d allied, coalition and multinational partner support and training.

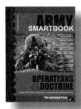

Purchase/Order

SMARTsavings on SMARTbooks! Save big when you order our tit** together in a SMARTset bundle. It's the most popular & least expensive ** to buy, and a great way to build your professional library. If you need a q** or have special requests, please contact us by one of the methods bel**

View, download FREE samples and purchase online**
www.TheLightningPress.co**

Order SECURE Online
Web: www.TheLightningPress.com
Email: SMARTbooks@TheLightningPress.com

24-hour Order & Customer Service Line
Place your order (or leave a voicemail)
at 1-800-997-8827

Phone Orders, Customer Service & Quot**
Live customer service and phone orders available**
Mon - Fri 0900-1800 EST at (863) 409-8084

Mail, Check & Money Order
2227 Arrowhead Blvd., Lakeland, FL 33813

Government/Unit/Bulk Sales

The Lightning Press is a **service-disabled, veteran-owned small business**, DOD-approv** vendor and federally registered—to include the** SAM, WAWF, FBO, and FEDPAY.

We accept and process both **Government Purchase Cards** (GCPC/GPC) and **Purchase** **Orders** (PO/PR&Cs).

Keep your SMARTbook up-to-date with the latest doctrine! In ** addition to revisions, we publish incremental "**SMARTupdates**" wh** feasible to update changes in doctrine or new publications. These ** SMARTupdates are printed/produced in a format that allow the rea** to insert the change pages into the original GBC-bound book by ** simply opening the comb-binding and replacing affected pages. Le** more and sign-up at: **www.thelightningpress.com/smartupdates**